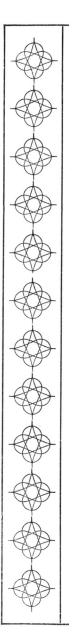

T H E N E W

M O D E R N

American

& British

P O E T R Y

EDITED WITH NOTES AND
CRITICAL INTRODUCTIONS
BY LOUIS UNTERMEYER

Mid-Century Edition

Harcourt Brace Jovanovich, Inc.

NEW YORK   CHICAGO   SAN FRANCISCO
ATLANTA   DALLAS

Permissions to reprint any of the poems in this volume must be obtained from the authors, agents, or publishers, holders of the copyright, as follows:

D. APPLETON-CENTURY COMPANY, INC. — for the selections from *Going-to-the-Sun* by Vachel Lindsay, copyright 1926, and *Merchants from Cathay* by William Rose Benét, copyright 1913.

BOBBS-MERRILL COMPANY — for the selections from *The Complete Works of James Whitcomb Riley,* copyright 1913, and reprinted by special permission of the publishers.

A. & C. BONI and THOMAS SELTZER — for the selections from *The Singing Crow* by Nathalia Crane, copyright 1926.

BRANDT & BRANDT — for " Renascence " from *Renascence,* published by Harper and Brothers, copyright 1917, 1924, by Edna St. Vincent Millay, " Elegy " from *Second April,* published by Harper and Brothers, copyright 1921, 1924, by Edna St. Vincent Millay, " Pity Me Not " from *The Harp-Weaver and Other Poems,* published by Harper and Brothers, copyright 1920, 1921, 1922, 1923, by Edna St. Vincent Millay, " The Anguish " and " On Hearing a Symphony of Beethoven " from *The Buck in the Snow,* published by Harper and Brothers, copyright 1928, by Edna St. Vincent Millay; " Bread and Music," " Miracles," " The Puppet Dreams " from *Selected Poems* by Conrad Aiken, published by Charles Scribner's Sons, copyright 1918, 1921, 1929, by Conrad Aiken, and " Morning Song from ' Senlin,' " from *Selected Poems* by Conrad Aiken, published by Charles Scribner's Sons, copyright 1925, by Horace Liveright, Inc.; " Portrait of a Boy " from *Young Adventure* by Stephen Vincent Benét, published by Yale University Press, copyright 1918, and " 1935 " from *Selected Works of Stephen Vincent Benét* published by Rinehart & Company, copyright, 1935, by Stephen Vincent Benét.

COWARD-MCCANN, INC. — for the selection from *Compass Rose* by Elizabeth Coatsworth, copyright 1929, by Coward-McCann, Inc.

THE DIAL PRESS — for the selections from *Love Poems,* copyright 1947, by George Barker.

DODD, MEAD & COMPANY — for the selections from *Lyrics of Love and Laughter,* by Paul Laurence Dunbar, copyright 1903, by Dodd, Mead & Company; *Poems* by G. K. Chesterton, copyright 1915; *The Collected Poems of Rupert Brooke,* copyright 1915; *Golden Fleece* by William Rose Benét, copyright 1927 by William Rose Benét, copyright 1933, 1935 by Dodd, Mead & Company.

DOUBLEDAY & COMPANY, INC. — for the selections from *Moons of Grandeur* by William Rose Benét, copyright 1920, *Man Possessed* by William Rose Benét, copyright 1927; *The Man with the Hoe* by Edwin Markham, and *Lincoln and Other Poems* by Edwin Markham, copyright 1899; *Trees and Other Poems* by Joyce Kilmer,

FOREWORD

This collection is a condensation of *Modern American Poetry* and *Modern British Poetry*. It conforms to the Mid-Century Editions of those two volumes, yet it also contains certain poems and biographical and critical matter not to be found in either of the larger books.

In order to introduce newer and more representative writers several of the poets included in the preceding editions have been omitted. Thus, appearing for the first time are William Carlos Williams, Theodore Spencer, Karl Shapiro, Elizabeth Bishop, Peter Viereck, and Randall Jarrell among the Americans; and Gerard Manley Hopkins, C. Day Lewis, Louis MacNeice, W. H. Auden, Stephen Spender, George Barker, Dylan Thomas, and Norman Nicholson among the British. These are chiefly writers who have become prominent during the Thirties and Forties and who in large part typify the contemporary directions in modern poetry. In the American section the dividing line has been moved back more than a century to include Walt Whitman, a poet whose influence is far greater now than it was during his lifetime. In the British section the boundary has now been fixed a few years later in order to begin with Thomas Hardy, who anticipated the direct speech and straightforward accents adopted by his successors.

Not only have new poets been added but also the major poets of our time have been more fully represented. Among other important poets, Walt Whitman, Robert Frost, Carl Sandburg, A. E. Housman, and W. B. Yeats are given increased space. Emily Dickinson, as an example, is represented by nine additional poems, and the whole of T. S. Eliot's " The Hollow Men " is now given. The editorial notes for the major poets have also been expanded, in keeping with an attempt throughout the book to amplify reading aids for the student.

The question of reading aids has been uppermost in the editorial preparation for these poems. The introductory essay, *Appreciation of Poetry*, is both a guide to poetry in general and, in particular, a key to the poems which follow. It is new to this edition. Moreover, both the notes on the individual poets and the footnotes have been directed toward clarifying obscure or difficult meanings in the poems. The paragraphs preceding the individual poets may be used to determine what effect, if any, climate and condition exert on the creator's expression: how much the gaunt and granite hills of New England manifest themselves in the soliloquies of E. A. Robinson and Robert Frost, how the energy of the Middle West booms and rattles through the high-pitched syllables of Vachel Lindsay, and how the prairie silences are given voice in the words of Carl Sandburg. These notes, with their brief critical as well as biographical and bibliographical data, have also been prepared on the theory that poet and person have a definite relation to each other, and that the enjoyment of the one is enhanced by an acquaintance with the other.

While emphasis has been placed upon the contribution of living writers, little stress has been laid on the subject of form. Free verse, so called because of its uneven lines and irregular rhythms, is no longer a matter for controversy; it is by no means so unorthodox as it once seemed. Moreover, the latest tendencies indicate a return to disciplined and strictly patterned verse. The modern poet is not committed to any particular form. He relishes experiment but he also appreciates tradition; he employs old devices and new departures with equal interest. He is, in short, what the word " poet " indicates: a man who is not only a craftsman but a " maker."

CONTENTS

MODERN American POETRY

EMILY DICKINSON (1830–1886)

JOHN HAY (1838–1905)

BRET HARTE (1839–1902)

CONTENTS

CONTENTS

CONTENTS

MODERN British POETRY

CONTENTS

C. DAY LEWIS (1904–   )

LOUIS MACNEICE (1907–   )

W. H. AUDEN (1907–   )

STEPHEN SPENDER (1909–   )

GEORGE BARKER (1913–   )

DYLAN THOMAS (1914–1953)

NORMAN NICHOLSON (1914–   )

INDEX OF AUTHORS AND TITLES

An Appreciation of Poetry

THE REASONS FOR POETRY

What are the reasons for poetry, and what are some of its uses? A poet who recently was awarded the Nobel Prize has given a memorable answer. "Poetry," writes T. S. Eliot, " may make us see the world afresh, or some new part of it. It may make us from time to time *a little more aware of the deeper, unnamed feelings to which we rarely penetrate.*"

It is these " deeper, unnamed feelings," common to us all, which the poet reveals. Discovering our hidden emotions, he becomes their interpreter. He gives our inarticulate sensations words — the right words — and thereby makes us articulate. He takes a small detail and shows us its overwhelming truth. Calling our attention to things we neglect or fail to recognize, he makes us understand not only their nature but our own.

Poetry, then, is not something odd; it is not a special " study," a thing set apart from ordinary individuals. On the contrary, it is a vital part of every man, the expression of his deepest emotions. It is not for the few. It is for everyone, *in* everyone. It might even be said that man inherited poetry from the universe. Before man was conscious of what was about him, even before he was evolved, the universe was full of rhythm. There was a rhythmic balance of light and darkness; day followed night with inevitable regularity. The sun sank, the moon climbed heaven, and all the stars revolved in rhythmical order. The tides rose and fell with a never-ending repetition. The seasons were set to a constant rhythm of four quarters; the earth turned in a rhythm of twenty-four hours and made a circle about the sun in a rhythm of three hundred and sixty-five days. When prehistoric man came upon the scene, he responded to the sway of a universal pendulum. All the rhythms of creation were repeated within him: the beat of his heart, the rise and fall of his breath, the alternation of his waking and sleeping. Mothers echoed the eternal rhythm whenever they rocked a baby to sleep or crooned a wordless lullaby. Savage priests danced around campfires, putting their prayers into poetic chants, making magic, and stamping their barbaric rhythms into rituals.

Rhythm is the base of poetry. It is the heartbeat and the pulse in the lifeblood of our language. Our daily speech is full of rhythm. When speech becomes uplifted or exalted the rhythm becomes more pronounced, and, as the rhythm is emphasized, the prosaic becomes poetic. Deeply emotional passages in the Bible, parts of certain novels like Melville's "Moby Dick," and Lincoln's Gettysburg Address are printed as prose, but they are so rhythmical that they are often classified as poetry. Poetry, therefore, may be said to be the rhythmical expression of man's highest thoughts and his deepest dreams.

THE PREJUDICE AGAINST POETRY

Although it is plain that poetry fulfills a great human need, it is also true that some people have a prejudice against poetry, especially modern poetry. They claim that it is obscure and difficult. They say that it is written on queer subjects by queer creatures, that poets are a lot of moon-struck dreamers, starry-eyed simpletons, and long-haired incompetents who are unconscious of the real world.

Prejudice and truth have little in common. It is worth looking at the truth about poetry if only to dispel the prejudice against it. There have been a few writers, painters, and composers who were strange and eccentric, just as there are strange and eccentric persons in every walk of life. But poetry has been written chiefly by men who were anything but weak or odd. The great poets have also been great persons. They did not try to escape from the workaday world and live isolated lives in some fanciful "ivory tower." Some of them were called upon to perform important missions, and practically all of them were vigorously engaged in the world's work. Chaucer, "the father of English poetry," was an ambassador, but he kept company with millers and peasants as well as knights and priests. Philip Sidney was a gallant soldier. Walter Raleigh was an explorer, a statesman, and a warrior. Shakespeare was an actor and manager of a theatrical troupe, besides being a small-town boy who became the world's greatest poet-playwright. John Milton, champion of the rights of the free man, acted as England's secretary of foreign affairs. The Elizabethan Ben Jonson was a bricklayer. Robert Herrick, author of exquisite lyrics, was a goldsmith. Robert Burns was a farmer.

These men meditated in the midst of action, as have poets in later days. John Keats is sometimes thought of as a fragile spirit; but, before he succumbed to tuberculosis, he was an athlete, a skilled cricket-player, a boxer, and an all-round good fighter. Emerson is pictured as a preaching philosopher, but he was a rugged citizen of the outdoors and still went swimming in Walden Pond at the age of seventy-eight. Whittier, another famous New England poet, started life as a chore-boy, cobbled shoes, and grew up to be one of the country's most courageous foes of slavery. Besides being the poet of democracy, Whitman was a carpenter, teacher, and active journalist. Tennyson wrote dainty lyrics, but he could bend horse-shoes and throw a crowbar farther than any man in his village. "The great poets," wrote T. W. H. Crosland, "are not only the sanest people in the world, but physically and temperamentally the toughest."

This is equally true of the poets of our own times. Far from being frail in body and precious in thought, John Masefield, poet laureate of England, spent his youth before the mast, sailed the seven seas and, during his stay in America, earned his living in a carpet factory in Yonkers. Edwin Arlington Robinson worked in the New York subway. Robert Frost was a bobbin-boy in the mills of Massachusetts before he became a farmer and teacher in Vermont and New Hampshire. Carl Sandburg drove a milk-wagon, was a harvesthand, dish-washer, truck-handler, handyman, and enlisted as a soldier during the Spanish-American War. Vachel Lindsay pitched hay and tramped across the country, spreading his "gospel of beauty" and trading rhymes for bread. Rupert Brooke and Joyce Kilmer were two of the many soldier-poets who died for their countries. Langston Hughes was a hotel busboy. Merrill Moore left doctoring in Boston to risk his life in China during World War II, and Karl Shapiro wrote much of his best poetry while serving on an island in the South Pacific.

These poets are close to us. They tell about ordinary things: an old wall, a few wildflowers, coal mines, skyscrapers, factories, trees, journeys, homesick blues. They celebrate simple people. One of the great poems of our times is Robert Frost's conversational " The Death of the Hired Man " (page

105); the most striking section in Carl Sandburg's *The People, Yes* is the part entitled "Yarns of the People" (page 122), which is a summary of proverbs, superstitions, country wisdom, tall tales, and folk-sayings. The poets make readers see ordinary things in a sharper focus and feel them with a greater understanding.

There is an unsuspected wealth of beauty in daily speech; we make our language more vivid by using swift poetic phrases. We aren't satisfied to say that a thing is merely "fast"; it achieves increased speed when we say it is "fast as lightning." To make it still more colorful we used a poetic device called *hyperbole* (which means exaggeration) by saying it is as fast "as *greased* lightning! " Contrariwise, an old horse isn't just "slow." It is (to use another comparison or *simile*) as "slow as molasses" or, to make it still slower, "as molasses *in January*." The power of simple poetic comparison is shown in such well-known phrases as "plain as a turnip," "sharp as a knife," "clever as a fox," "hungry as a bear," "scarce as hens' teeth," "cute as a kitten," "busy as a bee." We say these things without being aware that we are using the same devices of speech as the poet.

Even slang has its roots in poetry. Slang, sometimes called "the shorthand of the people," intensifies language when we speak of "crashing" a party, or "muscling" in. To be "burned up" is a more fiery as well as a more poetic way of saying "incensed." "I'll tell the world! " is certainly more dramatic than "divulge" or "publicize."

The common man's poetic instinct is strikingly illustrated by the popular names given to wildflowers. In every instance the country name is more charming, and more accurately descriptive, than the technical name. A certain plant is known to the botanist as *Arisaema triphyllum;* but the ordinary nature-lover recognizes it as a "Jack-in-the-Pulpit," a name which is imaginative and poetically humorous. Instead of the botanical *Digitalis*, we prefer the whimsical "Foxglove." We say "Monkshood" (which is what the flower looks like) instead of *Aconite*. We are being unconsciously poetic when we refer casually to such wayside weeds as "Dandelions" (originally "Dent de Lion" or "Lion's Tooth"), "Baby's Breath," "Butter-and-Eggs," "Deadly Nightshade," "Aster" (meaning "a star"), "Heal-All," "Solomon's Seal," "Jewelweed," "Thimbleweed," "Black-eyed Susan," etc. The common daisy is like a diminutive sun with its golden center and outspreading rays; it was called, like the sun, the "Eye of Day" or "Day's Eye," hence "daisy."

Like the character in Molière's play who was delighted to find that he had been talking prose all his life, we are continually using poetry for emphasis or for color, even when we are unconscious of it. We are all part-time poets whether we realize it or not.

THE DEFINITION OF POETRY

A good poem creates excitement; the beat of rhythm and the leap of rhyme keep the reader in a state of animation. In all ages men have been moved by lively songs and roused by dramatic poems. Long before poetry was actually written or printed, the ancient bards sang their tales, celebrating heroic battles and glorifying gallant deeds in verse. Poems which tell stories are popular because so often they reach down into the heart of the folk; like folk-tales, they originate among the people. The old tales in verse were made for crowds in market places; they were sung in taverns, and repeated on street corners. The ancient singers put the history of their time into galloping measures and ringing rhymes; they embroidered legends with highly colored figures and turned the news of the day into literature.

It is said that one obstacle to the appreciation of poetry is that the great many different kinds of poetry make it almost impossible to define it. Although poetry may be indefinable, it is unmistakable. Nevertheless it is natural to want an interpretation, if not a definition, which will explain the peculiar power and appeal of poetry.

The poets themselves have tried to describe some of the ways poetry differs from prose. "Prose," declared Samuel Taylor, "consists of words in their best order. Poetry consists of the *best* words in the best order." Matthew Arnold put the same idea somewhat differently: "Poetry is simply the most beautiful, the most impressive, *and* the most effective mode of saying things." "Poetry is the record of the best and happiest moments of the best minds," wrote Percy Bysshe Shelley; "a poem is the very image of life expressed in its eternal truth." Edgar Allan Poe considered poetry "the rhymical creation of beauty." Robert Frost says that a living poem is "a reaching out toward expression, an effort to find fulfilment. A complete poem is one where an emotion has

found its thought and the thought has found the words."
Recognizing that it is a combination of romantic beauty and
everyday realism Carl Sandburg writes: " Poetry is a synthesis
of hyacinths and biscuits."

It is obvious that interpretations differ; there is no final
all-inclusive definition of poetry. Technically, it might be
summarized this way: Poetry is a rhythmical pattern of
words expressing deeply felt emotion and/or experience
and/or imagination. The greater the combination of emotion,
experience, and imagination, the greater the poem.

THE ART OF POETRY

Every art has its techniques or " devices." To achieve his
effects, the painter must understand composition, perspective,
how to draw, and how to mix his paints. The composer must
know the principles of harmony and counterpoint. The architect must study engineering; he must be acquainted with such
things as columns, arches, " spans," and " stresses " so that his
structures will be not only beautiful but practical. The art of
poetry, like these other arts, needs skill as well as a desire to
create. To appreciate it fully, the reader must understand
some of the techniques or " devices " by which the poet
makes a poem. The principal " devices " of poetry are
rhythm and *rhyme; epithet* (the power of words); *comparison* (simile and metaphor); *onomatopoeia* (words as sounds);
inversion; alliteration and *repetition; foot, meter,* and *form.*

RHYTHM AND RHYME

Rhythm has already been discussed. The dictionary tells
us it is " a movement with uniform recurrence of a beat or
accent." In its crudest form rhythm has a beat with little or
no meaning. Savages repeat strongly marked syllables to
evoke a charm or magic spell; children use them in games
and counting-out rhymes. In poetry, rhythm, broadly speaking, is a recognizable pulse, or " recurrence," which gives a
distinct beat to a line and also gives it a shape.

Rhyme is not only a recurrence but a *matching* of sounds.
The pleasure of pairing words to make a kind of musical
echo is as old as mankind. The child of this generation may
be millions of years away from prehistoric man, but the lul-
labies and dancing games of today are not much different
from those of the cave-dweller. As in the old days, there is a

real connection between poetry and magic, between poetry and memory. Children begin with rhyme and rhythm; even before they can talk, boys and girls echo nursery rhymes and the jingles of Mother Goose. They learn their numbers painlessly by repeating such rhymes as:

> One, two,
> Buckle my shoe.
> Three, four,
> Shut the door.

They know the days of the month by memorizing:

> Thirty days hath September,
> April, June, and November. . . .

They even pick up bits of history by remembering such simple rhymes as:

> Columbus sailed the ocean blue
> In fourteen-hundred-ninety-two

But it is not only children who find things easier when they are said in rhyme and rhythm. Farmers and housewives prefer verse to prose for their wise sayings; the music of a rhyme helps them to remember. It points up their proverbs and gives a quick turn to the meaning:

> A sunshiny shower
> Won't last an hour.

———

> Rain before seven;
> Clear by eleven.

———

> March winds and April showers
> Bring forth May flowers.

———

> Wishes
> Won't wash dishes.

———

> Early to bed and early to rise
> Makes a man healthy, wealthy, and wise.

The devices of poetry are always being used — and abused — in daily life. Not only children and farmers but businessmen understand the value of verse and " apt alliteration's artful aid." Roadside signs, cards in buses, advertisements in newspapers, commercials on radio and television, prove that an idea fastens itself quickly in the mind when it is rhymed. Christmas cards, birthday wishes, condolences, and greetings are most effective when they are in verse. The fourteenth of February brings out the poet in everyone.

Even on the lowest plane, poetry is rarely " rhyme without reason." It sharpens the wit's cleverness and heightens the lover's dearest sentiments. Poetry ranges all the way from the childish "Roses are red, violets are blue" to Robert Burns's immortal song " My love is like a red, red rose." When we are deeply aroused, we express ourselves in some sort of poetry; our emotions spill over into a football cheer, a ballad, or a love lyric. A poem expresses our inner excitement, eases our pain, and glorifies our joy. Because of its strongly accented beat and its ability to convey intense feeling, poetry is the most powerful form of speech.

THE POWER OF WORDS: THE EPITHET

Poetry is a bringing together of many things: feelings, forms, phrases, figures of speech. It begins with an emotion — an emotion which, as Robert Frost said, develops into a thought, and the thought finds expression in words. " The poet's mind," wrote T. S. Eliot, is " a receptacle for seizing and storing up numberless feelings, phrases, images, which remain there until all the particles which can unite to form a new compound are present together." In the act of creation all the " particles " — emotion, memory, associations, a sense of rhythm — are fused, and the result is a new thing, a blending of all the parts, a union of the conscious and the unconscious: a poem. Words are the material with which the poet must frame his thoughts, and the greater the poet the more striking is his power of choosing and shaping words. Poetry is essentially a combination of the familiar and the surprising, and the most successful surprises are achieved by the use of carefully descriptive words or *epithets*.

An epithet is a word which makes the reader see the object described in a clearer or sharper light. It is both exact and imaginative. Distinctive epithets are found in the ancient Greek classic, *The Odyssey:* " *wine-dark* sea," " *wave-girdled* island," "*blindfolding* night." Our national flag is a "*star-spangled* banner." In "Thanatopsis" Bryant speaks of the ocean's "gray and *melancholy* waste." In "Home Thoughts from Abroad" Browning describes the "*gaudy*" melon flower and the "*wise*" thrush. Michael Lewis tells of an oncoming storm with its "*frantic*" wind, "*whipped*" clouds, and "*panicky*" trees. In A. E. Housman's poem, "Bredon Hill*" (see page 279), there is a much-quoted verse which runs:

Here of a Sunday morning
My love and I would lie,
And see the colored counties,
And hear the larks so high
About us in the sky.

A. E. Housman's brother, Laurence, has revealed how his famous brother found the exact and suggestive epithet "colored" to describe the scene. When he wrote the poem, Housman put down an ordinary adjective which did not satisfy him. Then, with the poem in his head, he went to bed and dreamed; in his dream he hit on the word "painted." This was better. But when he awoke he was still not satisfied. He thought of using "sunny," "pleasant," "checkered," "crowded," and "patterned." Finally, he came back to "painted" which suddenly prompted "colored." This was not only exact and imaginative, but the consonant "c" in "colored" gave a musically repeated sound (alliteration) when joined to "counties," and thus made the line more memorable.

Turn now to a much-discussed modern poem, Amy Lowell's "Meeting-House Hill" on page 92. You will notice several things about it that make it different from many other poems you know. For one thing, it is in "free verse" — that is, it has a free, or irregular, rhythm. For another thing, it has no rhymes. But its outstanding feature is its daring use of words. Observe the way sight and sound are combined, so that "the curve of a blue bay" is "shrill and sweet" — and, to accentuate the shrill sweetness, it is like "the sudden springing of a tune." Everything is intensified. An ordinary white church in a city square seems as beautiful as the Parthenon, loveliest of Greek temples. The poet is so thrilled by the scene that the unmoving structure is given motion. The spire "sweeps" the sky — and the movement is intensified by the comparison of the spire with a mast in motion, a mast of a ship in full sail straining before a stiff wind. The comparison carries the poem abroad. The bay beyond the railroad track turns into a harbor with an old-fashioned clipper-ship returning from China — and the past is united with the present. All of this is accomplished by the skillful selection and unusual arrangement of words.

Rupert Brooke is another modern poet who used words with charm yet with great precision. His " The Great Lover " (page 373) is an excellent example of the definition of poetry as " the best words in the best order "; it is full of epithets which are surprising but logical, exact and yet imaginative. Brooke delights the reader with such phrases as " *unthinking* silence," " *drowsy* Death," " we have *beaconed* the world's night," " *crying* flames," " *feathery* dust," " *friendly* bread," " the blue *bitter* smoke of wood," " *many-tasting* food," " the *cool kindliness* of sheets," " the keen *unpassioned* beauty of a great machine," " the *benison* [blessing] of hot water," " sweet water's *dimpling* laugh," " the *deep-panting* train," " the *cold graveness* of iron," " turn with *traitor* breath."

Robert Frost admits that poetry is impossible to define, but he adds: " If I were forced to attempt to define it, I would say that poetry is *words which have become deeds*." This active power of words was emphasized by Emily Dickinson in one of the briefest of her poems:

> A word is dead when said,
>   Some say.
> I say it just begins to live
>   That day.

SIMILE AND METAPHOR

Poetry is, first of all, a communication — a thought or message conveyed by the writer to the reader. It is not only an act of creation, but an act of sharing. It is therefore important to the reader that he understands how the poet uses words, how he puts fresh vigor and new meaning into words. The reader's understanding is immeasurably increased if he is familiar with the many techniques or devices of poetry, as explained on page xxx. Some of these are extremely simple; a few are rather elaborate.

The simplest and also the most effective poetic device is the use of comparison. It might almost be said that poetry is founded on two main means of comparing things: *simile* and *metaphor*. In an earlier paragraph it was shown that we heighten our ordinary speech by the continual use of such comparisons as " fresh as a daisy," " tough as leather," " comfortable as an old shoe," " it fits like the paper on the wall," " gay as a lark," " happy as the day is long," " pretty as a picture." These are all recognizable similes; they use the words " as " or " like."

A metaphor is another kind of comparison. It is actually a condensed simile, for it omits " as " or " like." A metaphor establishes a relationship at once; it leaves more to the imagination. It is a shortcut to the meaning; it sets two unlike things side by side and makes us see the likeness between them. When Robert Burns wrote " My love is *like* a red, red rose " he used a simile. When Robert Herrick wrote " You *are* a tulip " he used a metaphor. Emily Dickinson used comparison with great originality. She mixed similes and metaphors superbly in such poems as " A Book," " Indian Summer," and " A Cemetery."

One of the poems in her group (" A Book ") illustrates another device of poetry: association — a connection of ideas. The first two lines of " A Book " compare poetry to a ship; the next two to a horse. But Emily Dickinson thought that the words " ship " and " horse " were too commonplace. The ship became a " frigate," a beautiful full-sailed vessel of romance; and the everyday " horse," the plodding beast of the field and puller of wagons, became instead a " courser," a swift and spirited steed, an adventurous creature whose hoofs beat out a brisk rhythm, " prancing " — like a page of inspired poetry.

Thus, because of comparison and association, familiar objects become strange and glamorous. It might be said that a poet is a man who sees resemblances in all things.

WORDS AS SOUNDS: ONOMATOPOEIA

Such devices bring out the full flavor of words. Comparison and association are sometimes strengthened by syllables which imitate or reproduce the sounds they describe. When this occurs, it is called *onomatopoeia* (a Greek word meaning " name-making "), for the sounds literally *make* the meaning in such words as " buzz," " crash," " whirr," " clang," " hiss," " purr," " squeak," " mumble," " hush," " boom." Poe lets us hear the different kinds of sounds made by different types of bells in his famous poem "The Bells." His choice of the right word gives us the right sound when he speaks of "tinkling" sleigh bells; "clanging" fire bells; mellow "chiming" wedding bells; "tolling," "moaning," and "groaning" funeral bells.

Tennyson makes us feel the heaviness of a drowsy summer day by using a series of "m" sounds in the wonderfully weighted lines:

> The moan of doves in immemorial elms,
> And murmuring of innumerable bees.

Countless examples of association of ideas and imitation of sounds may be found in this volume. Two of the most striking and dramatic are Vachel Lindsay's "The Congo" on page 127, and G. K. Chesterton's "Lepanto" on page 328. No poems written in our time are richer in vivid colors, galloping rhythms, and constantly varying sound effects.

WORDS OUT OF ORDER: INVERSION

Another device of poetry is the changing of the usual order of words. This is called *inversion*, and is found mostly in the work of older classical poets. But it is sometimes used by modern writers for the sake of emphasis. Emily Dickinson was fond of arranging words outside of their familiar order. For example in "Chartless" (page 40) she writes "Yet know I how the heather looks" and "Yet certain am I of the spot." Instead of saying "Yet I know" and "Yet I am certain" she reverses the usual order and shifts the emphasis to the more important words. In these lines she calls attention to the swiftness of her knowledge and the power of her certainty.

Similarly in "Love in Jeopardy" (page 365) there is a peculiar but logical inversion. Humbert Wolfe wrote:

> Here by the rose-tree
> they planted once
> of Love in Jeopardy
> an Italian bronze.

Wolfe was describing an old statue and he wanted to suggest an old-fashioned effect. He got his "antique" effect partly by using queer rhymes like "once-bronze," and "zither-together," partly by twisting the ordinary manner of speaking. Had he written "Once upon a time they erected (or planted) a bronze figure named 'Love in Jeopardy' (or Danger) next to a rose-tree" it would have seemed commonplace, and the poet would have lost the quaintness of the picture as well as the arresting oddity of phrasing.

This is one reason why a writer chooses poetry rather than prose. By a trick of a word or the turn of a phrase, he arrests the attention of the reader, and makes him see old things in a new light. Even the very shape of a poem says "Stop! Look! and Listen!"

RHYME, ALLITERATION, AND REPETITION

Rhyme has been called a kind of musical punctuation. It is not only an aid to memory, as we have discovered in proverbs and nursery rhymes, but it is also a pleasure to the ear. Poetry should not only be read, it should be read aloud. To see it on the printed page is not enough; poetry should be heard as well as seen. "The Ballad of Father Gilligan" by William Butler Yeats (page 289) and "Gunga Din" by Rudyard Kipling (page 291) are both narrative. Totally different in theme, they have one thing in common: a simple but superb use of rhyme. The strong accent of the rhyming captivates the reader and lifts the story above its prose statement into poetry.

Rhyme is the matching of vowels and the coupling of vowel sounds. Like rhythm, it is a kind of *recurrence* — but rhyme has a recurrence of *sound* as well as *beat*. The following jingle has rhythm:

> One, two,
> Buckle my belt;
> Three, four,
> Snap the lock.

The rhythm of these lines becomes more musical — and much easier to remember — when rhyme is added. We then get the recurring vowel sound of:

> One, two,
> Buckle my shoe;
> Three, four,
> Shut the door.

A somewhat similar effect is achieved by the matching or repetition of consonants. This is called *alliteration,* or the repeating of the same letter (or sound) at the beginning of words following each other immediately or at short intervals. A famous example is to be found in the two lines by Tennyson on page xxxvi. The ancient poets often used alliteration instead of rhyme; in *Beowulf* there are three alliterations in every line. For example:

> Now **B**eowulf **b**ode in the **b**urg of the Scyldings,
> **L**eader be**l**oved, and **l**ong he ru**l**ed
> In **f**ame with all **f**olk since his **f**ather had gone . . .

Modern poets also avail themselves of alliteration, especially as a substitute for rhyme. Edwin Markham's " Lincoln, the Man of the People " (page 64) is in unrhymed blank verse, but there are many lines as alliterative as:

> She left the **H**eaven of **H**eroes and came down
> To **m**ake a **m**an to **m**eet the **m**ortal need. . . .
> A **m**an to **m**atch the **m**ountains and the sea. . . .
> The friendly **w**elcome of the **w**ayside **w**ell. . . .

Robert Frost's " The Death of the Hired Man " (page 105) begins:

> Mary sat musing on the lamp-flame at the table
> Waiting for Warren. When she heard his step. . . .

The eye immediately sees the alliteration in the " m's " in " Mary sat musing " and the " w's " in " Waiting for Warren. When. . . ." But it is the ear that picks up the half-buried " m " sounds in " lamp-flame " — sounds which act like faint and distant rhymes.

Like rhyme, alliteration is a great help to memory. It is so powerful a device that prose has borrowed it. It is the alliteration which makes us remember such phrases as: " sink or swim," " do or die," " fuss and feathers," " the more the merrier," " watchful waiting," " poor but proud," " hale and hearty," " green as grass," " live and learn," " money makes the mare go."

While alliteration is the recurrence of single letter-sounds, there is another kind of recurrence which is the echo or *repetition* of a word or phrase. This is found in many kinds of poetry, from nonsense rhymes to ballads. The repeated words or syllables add an extra beat and accentuate the rhythm. They are often heard in "choruses" or "refrains," as in Shakespeare's "With a hey and a ho and a hey nonino" or Rudyard Kipling's:

For it's Tommy this, an' Tommy that, an' "Chuck him out, the brute!"
But it's "Savior of 'is country" when the guns begin to shoot.

Excellent use of repetition occurs through the whole of Kipling's "Tommy" (page 297), "Danny Deever" (page 296), and Alfred Noyes's "The Barrel-Organ" (page 349), especially in such lines as:

Come down to Kew in lilac-time, in lilac-time, in lilac-time;
Come down to Kew in lilac-time (it isn't far from London!)
And you shall wander hand in hand with love in summer's wonderland;
Come down to Kew in lilac-time (it isn't far from London!)

THE FORM OF POETRY

THE FOOT

In putting words together the poet gives them a particular form or design. A poem, therefore, must be built before it can be felt by the reader or listener. The simplest unit in its design is the *foot*, a group of two or three syllables. Ancient poetry had more than twenty different types of *feet*, but most English verse consists of four kinds. In the order of popularity, they are as follows:

1. *The iambic foot.* This consists of a weak (or unstressed) syllable followed by a strongly accented one. It is sometimes called the "skipping" foot: ta-*dum* ta-*dum*. An iambic foot is illustrated by such words as *afraid, begin, hello, receive, because*. The following, by Robert Frost, is an iambic line of verse:

Whose woods / these are / I think / I know

2. *The trochaic foot.* This is the exact opposite of the iambic foot: it consists of a strongly accented syllable fol-

lowed by a weak (or unstressed) one. It is known as the "marching" foot: *dum*-ta, *dum*-ta. A trochaic foot is illustrated by such words as *weary, willow, twinkle, flowing, silent*. The following, by Longfellow, is an example of trochaic verse:

Thén the / líttle / Hía / wátha

3. *The dactylic foot.* This consists of three syllables: a strongly stressed syllable followed by two weak ones. It is a "waltzing" foot, and the rhythm is illustrated by such words as *fortunate, Saturday, daffodil, murmuring, rhapsody*. The following, by Thomas Hood, illustrates a dactylic line:

Táke her up / ténderly

4. *The anapestic foot.* This is another foot of three syllables. A "galloping" foot, it begins with two rapid unaccented syllables and ends on a strong down-beat. The anapest is illustrated by such words as *interrupt, contradict, engineer, masquerade, Galilee*. The following, from Browning's "How They Brought the Good News from Ghent to Aix," is an example of a speedy anapestic line:

Till at léngth / into Áix / Roland gál / loped and stóod.

THE METER

Feet are combined to make a line of poetry. The length, or measure, of a line is called the *meter*. The shortest line of poetry contains only one foot (*monometer*); one of the longest (*octameter*) consists of eight feet. Perhaps the best known is the five-foot line (*pentameter*), usually with an iambic beat and therefore called *iambic pentameter*. It is easily recognized in the plays of Shakespeare, the blank verse of Milton, and the unrhymed narratives of Robert Frost.

THE STANZA

Every poem has a pattern, and it is the line which determines the pattern. The foot is the unit of the line; the measured line is the unit of the verse, or stanza; the stanza is the unit that shapes the poem as a whole.

The shortest stanza is the *couplet*. As the name implies, it consists of two lines. Sometimes a couplet may form a complete poem, as, for example, this German proverb:

> Away with recipes in books!
> Hunger is the best of cooks!

The three-line stanza is sometimes called a *triplet*, sometimes a *tercet*. Many poems are written in this form, such as the Latin epigram:

> " Now I know everything! " so cries
> The foolish youth. But when he sighs
> " Ah, I know nothing," he is wise.

Other examples of tercets are Louis Untermeyer's " Long Feud " (page 152), Alfred Kreymborg's " The Ditty the City Sang " (page 135) and, except for the last stanza, John Masefield's " A Consecration " (page 334).

Sometimes the three-line stanza is so arranged that the first and third line of each tercet is rhymed, and the end-word of the second (unrhymed) line is carried over as the first and third rhymes of the stanza following. This stanza form is known as *terza rima* (literally " third rhyme "). It is the basis of Dante's *Divine Comedy* and Shelley's " Ode to the West Wind," which begins:

> O wild West Wind, thou breath of Autumn's being,
> Thou from whose unseen presence the leaves dead
> Are driven, like ghosts from an enchanter fleeing
>
> Yellow, and black, and pale, and hectic red,
> Pestilence-stricken multitudes! O thou
> Who chariotest to their dark wintry bed
>
> The wingéd seeds, where they lie cold and low,
> Each like a corpse within its grave, until
> Thine azure sister of the Spring shall blow
>
> Her clarion o'er the dreaming earth, and fill
> (Driving sweet buds like flocks to feed in air)
> With living hues and odors plain and hill. . . .

The four-line stanza, or *quatrain*, is the most common of all verse forms. In its simplest meter (the so-called ballad stanza) only the second and fourth lines are rhymed, as in most of Emily Dickinson's poems (pages 35–44) and Sara Teasdale's:

> I asked the heaven of stars
>   What I should give my love —
> It answered me with silence,
>   Silence above.

Usually, however, all the lines of the quatrain are rhymed; the first line is rhymed with the third, the second with the fourth. This book contains countless examples of this form of quatrain, notably Elinor Wylie's " Sea Lullaby " (page 144), Robert Frost's " Blue-Butterfly Day " (page 103), Edwin Arlington Robinson's " Miniver Cheevy " (page 74), Oscar Wilde's " Requiescat " (page 274), W. E. Henley's " Invictus " (page 270), and Richard Hovey's " Unmanifest Destiny " (page 71), which ends:

> I do not know beneath what sky
>   Nor on what seas shall be thy fate;
> I only know it shall be high,
>   I only know it shall be great.

Another form of the quatrain in which all the lines rhyme is composed of two couplets. It rhymes in pairs (a-a-b-b), as in Paul Laurence Dunbar's " A Coquette Conquered " (page 89), Elizabeth Coatsworth's " A Lady Comes to an Inn " (page 214), Robert Louis Stevenson's " Romance " (page 272), A. E. Housman's " The Carpenter's Son " (page 281), and Edwin Markham's " Outwitted ":

> He drew a circle that shut me out —
> Heretic, rebel, a thing to flout.
> But Love and I had the wit to win:
> We drew a circle that took him in!

Another interesting quatrain form, also with all lines rhyming, is known as " enclosed rhyme " (a-b-b-a); the first and last lines seem to bracket, or enclose, the inner pair of rhymes. Recent examples are Robert Frost's " The Pasture " (page 100), William Butler Yeats's " When You Are Old " (page 287), and W. H. Davies's " Days Too Short " (page 310), which begins:

> When primroses are out in Spring,
>   And small blue violets come between;
>   When merry birds sing on boughs green,
> And rills, as soon as born, must sing. . . .

There are still other variations of the quatrain form, the best of which is the so-called " Omar stanza " because it was popularized by Edward FitzGerald in his *Rubáiyát of Omar Khayyám*. Three of the four lines are rhymed, but not the third (a-a-x-a). For example:

> The moving finger writes; and, having writ,
> Moves on: nor all your piety nor wit
>   Shall lure it back to cancel half a line,
> Nor all your tears wash out a word of it.

Less familiar are stanzas of five lines (*cinquain* or *quintet*), six lines (*sestet*), seven lines (illustrated by the *rhyme royal* of William Morris and John Masefield), eight lines (*octave*), and nine lines. The last, used frequently by Keats and Byron, is at its best in the *Spenserian stanza*, so called because Spenser employed it so smoothly in " The Faerie Queen." Longer stanzas are rare; but one of them, the sonnet, has been immensely popular ever since it originated in Italy more than seven centuries ago.

THE SONNET

The sonnet is a fourteen-line poem which consists of two parts: an eight-line stanza (*octave*) followed by a six-line stanza (*sestet*). Sometimes the two parts are separated; sometimes they are united without a break. But the two parts always join to form a poem of unusual depth and dignity.

Different rhyme-schemes have led scholars to give different names to various forms of the sonnet: the Petrarchan sonnet (named after the Italian poet Petrarch), the Shakespearian sonnet, the Miltonic sonnet, and others. But, no matter how the rhymes are distributed, the fourteen lines are built to present a single idea or emotion with great strength. The Shakespearian sonnet is easily recognized, for it ends with a couplet. Many of Shakespeare's concluding couplets are sharply condensed poems in themselves. For example:

> But if the while I think on thee, dear friend,
> All losses are restored, and sorrows end.
>
> ———
>
> For sweetest things turn sourest by their deeds;
> Lilies that fester smell far worse than weeds.

If this be error and upon me proved,
I never writ, nor no man ever loved.

———

Yet do thy worst, old Time. Despite thy **wrong**,
My love shall in my verse live ever young.

———

So shalt thou feed on Death, that feeds on men;
And Death once dead, there's no more dying then.

The following two poems are two of the most famous in English literature; both are love poems and both are sonnets. They should be examined for their differences as well as their similarities.

Shall I compare thee to a summer's day?	a
Thou art more lovely and more temperate:	b
Rough winds do shake the darling buds of May,	a
And summer's lease hath all too short a date:	b
Sometime too hot the eye of heaven shines,	c
And often is his gold complexion dimmed;	d
And every fair from fair sometime declines,	c
By chance or nature's changing course untrimmed;	d
But thy eternal summer shall not fade,	e
Nor lose possession of that fair thou ow'st,	f
Nor shall death brag thou wander'st in his shade,	e
When in eternal lines to time thou grow'st:	f
So long as men can breathe, or eyes can see,	g
So long lives this, and this gives life to thee.	g

———

How do I love thee? Let me count the ways.	a
I love thee to the depth and breadth and height	b
My soul can reach, when feeling out of sight	b
For the ends of Being and ideal Grace.	a
I love thee to the level of every day's	a
Most quiet need, by sun and candle-light.	b
I love thee freely, as men strive for Right;	b
I love thee purely, as men turn from Praise.	a
I love thee with the passion put to use	c
In my old griefs, and with my childhood's faith.	d
I love thee with a love I seemed to lose	c
With my lost saint — I love thee with the breath,	d
Smiles, tears, of all my life! — and, if God choose,	c
I shall but love thee better after death.	d

The first, by William Shakespeare, is a Shakespearian sonnet. The rhyme-scheme is simple: three quatrains followed by a couplet. The octave and the sestet are separated; there is a distinct change of thought between the first eight lines and the succeeding six lines. The second, by Elizabeth Barrett Browning, is a Petrarchan sonnet. Instead of being simple, like the Shakespearian sonnet, the rhyme-scheme of the Petrarchan is elaborate. The octave is restricted to two rhymes instead of (as in the Shakespearian) four; the sestet has two rhymes instead of three; and all the rhymes are interwoven. The thought is also woven closely together throughout; there is no break in idea between the octave and the sestet.

It might be interesting to examine the sonnets in this volume for their differences and similarities. Modern poets use the sonnet almost as frequently as their predecessors; some of them keep strictly to the classic form, others vary it with considerable freedom. Among the most notable are Lizette Woodworth Reese's " Tears " (page 66) and " Spicewood " (page 66), E. A. Robinson's " Cliff Klingenhagen " (page 79) and " Calvary " (page 80), Walter de la Mare's " Peace " (page 326), Elinor Wylie's " Puritan Sonnet " (page 145) and " August " (page 146), Ezra Pound's " A Virginal " (page 148), Robinson Jeffers' " Compensation " (page 176), Edna St. Vincent Millay's " Pity Me Not " (page 206), Countee Cullen's " From the Dark Tower " (page 231), Merrill Moore's " American " sonnets (pages 234–235), Siegfried Sassoon's " Dreamers " (page 368), Rupert Brooke's " The Soldier " (page 375), Charles Hamilton Sorley's " Two Sonnets " (page 388), and C. Day Lewis's " When They Have Lost " (page 396).

THE KINDS OF POETRY

In ancient times poetry was sung rather than spoken. The Greeks chanted the stately choruses as they moved rhythmically to the lines of the great dramas of Sophocles and Euripides. The Vikings took their singers on their most dangerous explorations; the Norse gleemen celebrated the sea-fights and land conquests in lusty songs. The French troubadours brought their ballads from the market place to the castle. In the time of Queen Elizabeth verse was constantly sung; many of the English poets were also musicians and composers.

Today, however, poetry is rarely sung; most of it is not

even spoken. It exists chiefly on the printed page — and, for the most part, it is read silently. This is a pity, for poetry is written not so much for the eye as for the ear. The combination of rhyme and rhythm, of vowels and consonants, of melody and percussion is not effective until it is heard. The voice is needed to bring the poem to life. The poets, therefore, have paid particular attention to the sound of words; they have been careful in their selection of words which not only carry ideas and emotions but also create music.

It is this music which we re-create when we read a poem aloud. The balanced rhythms and the ringing rhymes make stories more exciting than when they are told in prose. Ballad-singers of the past held audiences breathless with half-sung, half-spoken narratives of wild adventures, daring outlaws, passionate deeds, savage love and hate. We know the dramatic stories of such heroes as Robin Hood and Sir Patrick Spens through the ballads written about them.

THE STORY POEM

Modern poets know that the effectiveness of a story is increased by the gathering momentum of rhythm, by the bells of rhyme, by the sharpening of sounds, of echo, and repetition. If we were to tell the story of " Danny Deever " in prose, we would present two soldiers talking over a crime that has just happened. A fellow-soldier, Danny Deever, quarreled with his comrade and shot him while he slept. One of the speakers, nicknamed " Files-on-Parade " (a term which shows he is an ordinary private) is timid and sympathetic; the other, the " Color-Sergeant," who has charge of the flags, is older, more experienced and " hard-boiled." The two soldiers watch the regiment form ceremonially (" in 'ollow square ") while the disgraced Danny Deever is stripped of his insignia — " they've taken of his buttons off an' cut his stripes away." Then, after the slow roll of the drums, the band strikes up a lively air (" the quickstep ") and the hanging is over.

Now read " Danny Deever " (page 296) as told by the poet, Rudyard Kipling. The story is immediately keyed up. The accent of the verse sharpens the narrative and gives it a sudden sense of tension. The dramatic note is increased by the device of repetition, by the short questions and grim answers, by the insistent beat of rhythm. The suspense is heightened as the color-sergeant's tough humor, and the clipped phrases give us the story little by little. It becomes plain that the story has been told more vividly and more swiftly because of the condensation, the clearly measured speech, the " economy of words " which so fundamentally makes poetry differ from prose. Thus two different characters — two different types of humanity — have been revealed against a tragic background.

The same power of condensation and economy, the same strong rhythms and forceful phrasing, distinguish Kipling's other poems, notably " Gunga Din " (page 291), " The Return," (page 294), " Tommy " (page 297), and " Recessional " (page 300). It is interesting to determine which poem says the most in the least space, which is the most powerful, and which character is the most unforgettable.

With these effects in mind, other story poems in this volume might be examined to good purpose. Expressive details can be found throughout the volume, especially in William Rose Benét's " Jesse James " (page 159), which the author has subtitled " A Design in Red and Yellow for a Nickel Library." This poem is a remarkable contrast to the same poet's " Merchants from Cathay " (page 156), John Hay's " Jim Bludso " (page 45), Bret Harte's " Jim " (page 48), Elizabeth Coatsworth's " A Lady Comes to an Inn " (page 214), Walter de la Mare's " The Listeners " (page 323), Siegfried Sassoon's " The Rear-Guard " (page 369), W. W. Gibson's " The Stone " (page 340), and Roy Helton's " Old Christmas Morning " (page 180).

The first thing about these poems that must strike the reader is their great variety of subjects. Some of the stories are simple, some elaborate; some are realistic and some are fanciful. John Hay's " Jim Bludso," for example, is highly dramatic, even melodramatic, while Bret Harte's " Jim " is broadly humorous; yet both are character narratives, stories of the American frontier. " Jesse James " is another story poem based on a native American subject; the story is told in the manner of a folk-ballad (simple rhymes, repetition, and choruses), but it is developed with the bold exaggeration of tall tales and it ends in sheer fantasy. On the other hand Walter de la Mare's " The Listeners " is definitely a fantastic poem: its atmosphere is mystery. There is a " plot," but we have to supply the details. Are the listeners behind the door real people or ghosts — or merely creatures of the imagination? Is the whole poem symbolic? The rider who came and " kept his word " is a brave and challenging spirit. Does he, perhaps, represent Man (" the lonely Traveler ") facing the darkness, riding against the great Unknown? There are no right or wrong answers to such questions. The poet wants to stimulate our imagination — he prompts the questions but does not reply to them. The meaning is left open; the poem is, in fact, so rich with meanings that the answer is whatever the reader wants it to be.

Similarly, we must fill out the rest of the suggested story in Elizabeth Coatsworth's " A Lady Comes to an Inn." What would a lovely lady be doing in such an odd place accompanied by such queer companions? All the details arouse our curiosity and provoke our questions. Why was her breast tattooed? And what was the meaning of the design? What was the business of the three men? Can you supply the " story behind the story "?

" The Rear-Guard " actually happened to Siegfried Sassoon. His experiences as a soldier help to give the poem its complete realism. What are the details which afford the reader a feeling of horror and a sense of weariness? Does the climax come as a shock? Is it plain that the scene is an underground trench? How does the speaker " unload hell behind him step by step "?

" Richard Cory " (page 78) is another example of a story heightened by poetry. Had this story been told in prose, it would have been rather commonplace. But the short lines and the abrupt rhymes give the story an extra feature, a sharpness that could not be achieved by prose. The short biography is intensified by the terse rhythm, and the ending comes with a particular surprise as a result of the stanza form.

W. W. Gibson's " The Stone " is a story which is fully told by the speaker. It gets its effect, partly from the story itself, but chiefly from the deliberate way in which it is told: by the repetitions, the insistently repeated words, the hammering rhymes, the slow summing up of details. The tension is increased as we sense the outcome; we are half-prepared for the ending and yet startled by it.

Roy Helton's " Old Christmas Morning " is a ghost story, a fantastic tale founded on reality. Told like an old ballad, it is enacted against a modern background. The time is now; the place is the Kentucky hills. Its central theme is a bloody feud, and the grim drama is played out in an atmosphere of pervading terror. As a newspaper item this would be little more than another account of a killing. But it becomes a remarkable tale when it is transformed into poetry. The atmosphere changes as the brusque dialog reveals the facts; it mounts from casual talk between two mountain women to cold horror. Although the period and setting are today, the tone is ancient; the spirit is that of faraway, of a legend from some other country, even from another world.

Other similarities and differences may be found by comparing the story poems in this book with those of an older time. They may be contrasted with "Edward, Edward," "Lord Randall," "Johnnie Armstrong," and other early English and Scottish ballads of unknown origin, as well as with such favorites as Longfellow's "Paul Revere's Ride," Tennyson's "The Charge of the Light Brigade," Hood's "The Bridge of Sighs."

THE MONOLOG

A monolog is a speech or a story or a poem uttered by one person — it can even be a one-sided conversation. In poetry, it is a tale or meditation told in the first person singular. Sometimes the poet is the speaker, sometimes it is a character in the poem that speaks. The monolog, therefore, is a soliloquy: thinking out loud.

Often the monolog recounts the story of an action, a stirring deed, or a noteworthy event. It is then known as a "dramatic monolog." Many older as well as modern poems are in this form. Robert Browning's "Incident of the French Camp" is such a poem. One of Napoleon's aides tells an incident which occurred during an attack on a town vital to the Emperor's success. The speaker sets the stage, builds a situation, and creates a mood in a few lines. What is more, he creates two living people: Napoleon and the young boy who, wounded to death, brings the news of victory.

A quieter dramatic monolog is presented in Robert Frost's "The Death of the Hired Man" (page 105). Here the poet is the speaker although much of the poem is in dialog. He tells the story and he reveals the lives of three people: a country man, his wife, and the old hired man. The hired man never speaks, yet he is the central figure; the poet shows him more fully than either of the other two characters. Little side-lights — like the contrasting definitions of "home" — make us see the two speakers with great understanding. Although nothing happens until the very end of the poem, the homely talk sustains the pitch of deep feeling and the atmosphere of suspense.

W. W. Gibson's " The Stone," mentioned on page xlviii, is another tense and vividly dramatic monolog.

A monolog need not be long. It can be a brief meditation, a flashing thought. Meditative monologs, as well as dramatic, may be found in this book, especially in the pages devoted to Robert Frost, Edwin Arlington Robinson, Vachel Lindsay, Thomas Hardy, William Butler Yeats, Rudyard Kipling, and Walter de la Mare. These monologs make their effect because they center about a person and bring him to life in the living words of the poet.

THE LYRIC

The lyric is the form of verse which is nearest to music. It is derived from the Greek word *lyrikos,* for the lyric originally was a song accompanied by the lyre, an ancient stringed instrument. Today the lyre is rarely heard, and the lyric makes its own music.

The lyric has many changes of pitch and pace, but it has one constant characteristic. It is short. Unlike the narrative, it expresses a mood instead of telling a story; therefore it is highly concentrated, usually personal, and almost always emotional. The great German poet, Heinrich Heine, wrote that " lyrical poetry is much the same in every age, as the songs of the nightingales in every springtime." The first rule of the lyric is that it must sing. The second rule is that its song must be clear and swift.

This combination of swiftness and singing clarity, of motion and emotion, is beautifully illustrated by Yeats's " The Lake Isle of Innisfree " (page 286), one of the loveliest and most quoted of modern lyrics. It is obvious at once that the emotion is homesickness. The poet, surrounded by the roar of the city, longs for the peace and comfort of the country, even for an unearthly quiet, literally " out of this world." That is the immediate idea or " meaning " of the poem. But what makes the lyric so different from this commonplace summary, what makes it so rich and memorable, is the haunting music which expresses the mood. The very name " Innisfree " is music. We do not have to know where it is or anything about it to understand its power of enchantment. The poem shows us its beauty, and the quiet of the place is suggested by the softly moving lines; it is emphasized by the single epithet, " the *bee-loud* glade." Serenity flows from the poem as the lines make us feel peace to be something more than an abstract idea; peace comes with healing: " dropping slow, dropping from the veils of morning." Nothing here can disturb the heart. Midnight brings no fear; it is a starry " glimmer." Noon bathes the day in " a purple glow." Evening brings the late birds home. Even the waves are hushed; we hear their soothing murmur in the soft alliteration of " l's " and " w's " in " lake water lapping with low sounds by the shore." Magic has been created by the union of personal feeling and musical form.

This volume is full of singing words. The haunting combination of melody and meaning, of love and grief and memory, of joy in Nature as well as the understanding of human nature, is heard in the lyrics of Emily Dickinson (page 35), Lizette W. Reese (page 66), Sara Teasdale (page 139), Elinor Wylie (page 142), Conrad Aiken (page 194), Edna St. Vincent Millay (page 200), A. E. Housman (page 278), William Butler Yeats (page 286), W. H. Davies (page 309), Ralph Hodgson (page 317), and Walter de la Mare (page 322), among others.

THE EPIGRAM

The epigram is the most condensed and concentrated form of poetry. Webster defines it as " A short poem treating concisely, pointedly, often satirically, a single thought or event, usually ending with a witticism." The poet of " The Rime of the Ancient Mariner," Samuel Taylor Coleridge, defined it even more concisely:

> What is an epigram? A dwarfish whole;
> Its body brevity, and wit its soul.

The epigram may be said to be a miniature lyric, a sharpened arrow of verse. It may be grave or gay or clever, but its real point is — its point. Besides its incisiveness, it must be perfect in form and finish. One can no more imagine a clumsy epigram than a long one. Every word counts, every syllable must be carefully balanced, every rhyme sharply matched. Since the epigram consists of only a few phrases, there can be no fumbling, no uncertainty of aim, no superfluous ideas. The epigram is all essence.

An American columnist who died some years ago, Keith

Preston, was a master of the epigram. Here are two of his favorites:

> No humorist laughs at his own wheeze:
> A snuff-box has no right to sneeze.
>
> ----
>
> The alienist is not a joke;
> He finds you cracked and leaves you broke.

Another expert in the form, Hilaire Belloc, was at his best when he added irony to his rhymes; it was said that he dipped his pen in vitriol instead of ink. Belloc's satirical " Epitaph on the Politician " is on page 313; here are three more of his quick-witted epigrams:

> Of old when folk lay sick and sorely tried,
> The doctors gave them physic, and they died.
> But here's a happier age; for now we know
> Both how to make men sick and keep them so.
>
> ----
>
> The Devil, having nothing else to do,
> Went off to tempt My Lady Poltagrue.
> My Lady, tempted by a private whim,
> To his extreme annoyance, tempted him.
>
> ----
>
> When I am dead, I hope it may be said:
> " His sins were scarlet, but his books were read."

Many of Emily Dickinson's poems are actually epigrams. So are Edwin Markham's " Outwitted " (page 62), " The Avengers " (page 63), and " Preparedness " (page 63), Nathalia Crane's " Destiny " (page 240), and " The Colors " (page 241).

Other examples show the characteristics of the epigram: speed, point, and perfection of form. Like the flight of the arrow to which it has been compared, the epigram pierces almost as soon as it leaves the pen. A breath, a short flight, and the bolt strikes home.

UNDERSTANDING A POEM

A poem is created when the poet composes it; it is re-created each time it is read with understanding. Before we can appreciate a poem, we must know how to read it. And as we read

it, we must be aware of certain values. It will not be difficult
if we remember five things about poetry.

1. *Poetry is concentrated thought.* A poem says much in little; therefore, we should try to anticipate that concentration.
We must focus our attention on the thought, not hurry past
the idea.

2. *Poetry is a kind of word-music.* A poem has a tune of its
own. In reading aloud we should be careful not to spoil the
music by using a high-pitched tone or a sing-song voice. Follow the beat naturally; give it full value, but do not force it.

3. *Poetry expresses all the senses.* A poem communicates
thoughts by the poet's choice of words; therefore, to extract
full meaning from the words we should listen with all our
faculties. We should listen for the characteristic and changing
sounds as well as for the descriptive and unusual words. We
should look for the arresting phrase and the illuminating
image. We should feel the power of fresh epithets and old
allusions. We should smell the perfume and taste the flavor
carried by the words themselves.

4. *Poetry answers our demand for rhythm.* A poem beats
time simply and strongly; therefore, we need only respond to
it with our own natural rhythm. Whether or not we are
poets, we are all rhythmical by nature; we breathe, walk, run,
sing, cheer, dance, even work in rhythm. The poet patterns
this rhythm, and the reader enjoys the beat of the lines because they satisfy a deep-seated rhythmic impulse.

5. *Poetry is observation plus imagination.* The poet has written under the spell of emotional and intellectual excitement.
He has been seized by some mood or the force of some incident, and there has been conceived in him this living thing,
this order out of chaos: a poem. The reader should react im-
aginatively to this intense creation. He should share as much
of the emotion as possible. He will then understand not only
the *meaning* of the poem, but its suggestions and implications.

With these five observations about poetry in mind, turn to
Edna St. Vincent Millay's "Renascence" (page 200), one of
the most imaginative and widely read of modern poems. The
poem begins with easy grace yet with concentrated power.
Casually, in the tones of ordinary speech, in the simplest possible rhythm, the poet establishes the scene and its background. The reader sees the details of the Maine coast in the
opening lines:

> All I could see from where I stood
> Was three long mountains and a wood;
> I turned and looked another way,
> And saw three islands in a bay.

The poem's beat and tone are thus established; the lines proceed as innocently as a child's counting-out rhyme. The rhythm is so definite, the speech so direct, that an intimate contact between the reader and the poet is immediately achieved.

> So with my eyes I traced the line
> Of the horizon, thin and fine,
> Straight around till I was come
> Back to where I'd started from;
> And all I saw from where I stood
> Was three long mountains and a wood.

Thus the very simplicity, the " tone of speech," has vividly reflected not only the landscape seen by the poet, but the mood evoked by it. As one reads further the contact grows closer; the reader yields more and more to the spell of the words. Familiar details take on larger significance. The actual scene is so surcharged with emotion that it becomes *more* than real and is lifted to the plane of the spiritual.

> I saw and heard, and knew at last
> The How and Why of all things, past,
> And present, and forevermore.
> The universe, cleft to the core,
> Lay open to my probing sense. . . .

Lying upon the grass, the young poet is in such close touch with the sky, the mountains, and Infinity, that what started to be a rhymed record of a scene becomes a vision of immensities. The small and the large are one; the poet becomes part of the earth itself, suffers all its pangs, is pierced by every twisting root. The very epithets — " *envious* thrust," " *brooded* wrong," " *heavy* night " — emphasize the emotion.

> . . . Mine was the weight
> Of every brooded wrong, the hate
> That stood behind each envious thrust;
> Mine every greed, mine every lust.

She sees a man starving in Capri — and starves with him. She sees two ships strike together in a great fog-bank, hears a thousand screams smite the heavens — " and every scream tore through my throat." As the poem proceeds, we realize she is sharing not only the anguish of earth but all its growths and joys. As though she herself were deep in the ground, she feels each penetrating drop of rain, every searching sunbeam. She prays to be restored to finite existence, to the little things of everyday. And suddenly she feels:

> The grass, a-tip-toe at my ear . . .
> I felt the rain's cool finger-tips
> Brushed tenderly across my lips . . .
> And all at once the heavy night
> Fell from my eyes and I could see —

She has found an answer to the overpowering immensities. From now on she is vibrantly identified with all that lives and struggles and grows about her.

> O God, I cried, no dark disguise
> Can e'er hereafter hide from me
> Thy radiant identity!
> Thou canst not move across the grass
> But my quick eyes will see Thee pass,
> Nor speak, however silently,
> But my hushed voice will answer Thee . . .
> God, I can push the grass apart
> And lay my finger on Thy heart!

So the poem draws to its close, mounting ever higher with a quiet but convincing certainty. And the reader mounts with it. The poet's identification of all of life has been shared, apprehended, completed. *And it is the reader who has made the final completion.* By means so simple and yet so subtle that he is hardly aware of it, the reader has ceased being merely a reader and has become the chief actor in the poem — has become, during the taking-on of this intense emotional experience, the poet herself.

Another poem in which the different effects and poetic devices increase the reader's enjoyment is G. K. Chesterton's "Lepanto" (page 328). This is the famous Mediterranean naval battle which took place on October 7, 1571, when the

Allied Christian powers broke the domination of the Turks. The conflict has additional historical importance because it was the last great encounter between fleets of galleys and also because it was the last of the Crusades. The poem ends with a brief glimpse of Cervantes, author of *Don Quixote*, who fought in the battle and smiled (" but not as Sultans smile ") at the outcome. The contrasts in sight and sound are immediately established as the poem begins:

> White founts falling in the Courts of the sun

The gathering of the aroused Christians is indicated in the subdued but pronounced alliteration of:

> Dim drums throbbing, in the hills half heard

It increases with the stronger alliterative accents of:

> Strong gongs groaning as the guns boom far,
> Stiff flags straining in the night-blasts cold,
> In the gloom black-purple, in the glint old-gold

Finally the music breaks out in full force with:

> Torchlight crimson on the copper kettle-drums,
> Then the tuckets, then the trumpets, then the cannon, and he
>   comes.

Chesterton's shrewd choice of words adds sharpness to the meaning as well as the music. Elizabeth is " the *cold* queen of England " because she refused to take part in the expedition; the daring Don John of Austria is " the *crownless* prince " risen from " a *doubtful* seat " because he was the illegitimate brother of King Philip of Spain; the Christian captives are " *sick* and *sunless* " " like a race in *sunken* cities " because they are slaves, chained to their oars in the dark holds of the Turkish ships. Other descriptive terms and resounding phrases indicate the progress of the poem — the ominous and quiet laughter, the continually mounting excitement, the full blast of battle, the final victory.

Further appreciation may be attained by comparing such a poem, in which sound effects are of primary importance, with Vachel Lindsay's " The Congo " (page 127), John Masefield's

"Rounding the Horn" (page 336), and Harold Monro's "Every Thing" (page 346). In each, the words project the idea and the emotion with a force and clarity which any sympathetic reader can understand. Such understanding will increase with each reading and enlarge one's receptiveness to the enjoyment of poetry.

THE SHARING OF POETRY

Poetry is not, as some suppose, the poet talking to himself exclusively or using a special language to impress a few other poets. It is an act of sharing. The poet hopes to interest all of us; he uses certain devices and forms of poetry in order to make the communication more intense and more memorable to the reader. If we comprehend the poet's intent and grasp his meaning, the sharing of his ideas and emotions makes the poet's world our world.

Essentially the poet's world *is* our world — a world enlarged by the imagination and enriched with beauty. It is there for us to enjoy by the simple process of reading — reading creatively. In one of his rare and profoundly serious moments, the author of *Life With Father*, Clarence Day, Jr., wrote this wonderfully condensed essay about reading: "The world of books is the most remarkable creation of man. Nothing else that he builds ever lasts. Monuments fall, nations perish, civilizations grow old and die out; and, after an era of darkness, new races build others. But in the world of books are volumes that have seen this happen again and again, and yet live on, still young, still as fresh as the day they were written, still telling men's hearts of the hearts of men centuries dead."

In the vast world of books it is poetry, more than any other kind of writing, which lives on "still young, still as fresh as the day it was written " — still packed with the power of life, "telling men's hearts of the hearts of men centuries dead." There is no more powerful and no nobler form of speech.

Modern American Poetry

PREFACE

The sources of modern American poetry are many. It may be rewarding to explore the backgrounds and survey the outstanding forces and figures which marked its beginnings and the course of its development.

END OF THE CIVIL WAR

The Civil War inspired volumes of military, religious, and patriotic verse without adding more than four or five memorable pieces to the anthologies of today. Its end marked the end of an epoch, political, social, and literary. The arts declined; the famous New England group began to disintegrate; the poets like Emerson, Lowell, and Bryant had outsung themselves. " They had been borne into an era in which they had no part," writes Fred Lewis Pattee (*A History of American Literature Since 1870*), " and they contented themselves with reechoings of the old music." For them poetry ceased to be a reflection of actuality, an extension of experience.

Suddenly the break came. America developed a national consciousness; the West discovered itself, and the East discovered the West. Grudgingly at first, the aristocratic leaders made way for a new expression; crude, jangling, vigorously democratic. All the preceding writers — poets like Emerson, Lowell, Longfellow, Holmes — were products of the New England colleges, typically " Boston gentlemen of the early Renaissance." To them the new men must have seemed like a regiment recruited from the ranks of vulgarity. Walt Whitman, Mark Twain, Bret Harte, John Hay, Joaquin Miller, James Whitcomb Riley — these were men who had graduated from the farm, the frontier, the mine, the pilot-house, the printer's shop. For a while, the movement seemed of little consequence; the sharp impact of Whitman and the Westerners was averted. But it was gathering force.

WALT WHITMAN

Whitman, who was to influence future generations profoundly in Europe as well as in America, had already appeared. The third edition of *Leaves of Grass*, had been printed in 1860. Almost immediately after, the publisher failed and the book passed out of public notice. In 1865 a petty official discovered that Whitman was the author of the " notorious " *Leaves of Grass*, and, in spite of Whitman's sacrifice in nursing hundreds of wounded soldiers, in spite of his many past services and his present poverty, the offending poet was dismissed from his clerkship in the Department of the Interior at Washington, D. C. Other reverses followed rapidly. But Whitman, broken in health, lived to see not only a seventh edition of his work published in 1881, but a complete collection printed in his seventy-third year (1892) in which the twelve poems of the experimental first edition had grown to nearly four hundred.

The influence of Whitman can scarcely be overestimated. It has touched every shore of letters, quickened every current of contemporary art. Whitman has been praised as a prophet, as a pioneer, as a rebel, as a fiery humanist in America, in England, and throughout Europe.

It was not only in the matter of form that Whitman became a poetic emancipator. He led the way toward a wider aspect of democracy; he took his readers out of dim and musty libraries into the coarse sunlight and the common air. He was, as Burroughs wrote, preëminently the poet of vista; his work had the power " to open doors and windows, to let down bars rather than to put them up, to dissolve forms, to escape narrow boundaries, to plant the reader on a hill rather than in a corner." Whitman could do this because, first of all, he believed implicitly in life — in its physical as well as its spiritual manifestations; he sought to grasp existence as a whole, not rejecting the things that, to other minds, had seemed trivial or tawdry. The cosmic and the commonplace were synonymous to him; he declared he was part of elemental, primitive things and constantly identified himself with them. His long poem " Song of Myself " is a magnificent example of his revelation of the wonder of everyday, especially in the lines beginning on page 22.

I believe a leaf of grass is no less than the journeywork of the stars.

It is his large naturalism, an affection for all that is homely and of the soil, that sets Whitman apart as our first distinctively American poet. This blend of familiarity and grandeur animates all his work. It swings with tremendous vigor through " Crossing Brooklyn Ferry "; it sharpens the sturdy rhythms (and occasional rhymes) of the " Song of the Broad-Ax "; it beats sonorously through " Drum-Taps "; it whispers immortally through the " Memories of President Lincoln " (particularly that magnificent elegy " When Lilacs Last in the Dooryard Bloom'd "); it quickens the " Song of the Open Road " with what Tennyson called " the glory of going on," and lifts with a Biblical solemnity " Out of the Cradle Endlessly Rocking."

The final estimate of Whitman's work is yet to be written. Whitman's universality — and his inconsistencies — have defeated his commentators. To the craftsmen, Whitman's chief contribution was his form; they placed their emphasis on his flexible sonority, his orchestral color, his piling up of details into a symphonic structure. To the philosophers, he was the first of modern prophets: a mystic with a startling understanding of democracy. To the psychologist, he was the most revealing of autobiographers; " whoever touches this book, touches a man," he wrote. To the lay reader, he was a protagonist of " the divine average." Celebrating himself, he celebrated humanity.

But it is Whitman's spirit, not his technique nor his subject-matter, which assures him permanence. It is the broad and resistless affirmation which quickens everything he wrote and which so profoundly affected the spirit (if not the letter) of subsequent writing. It is the translation of the commonplace into the glorious, the recognition of neglected beauty, the wonder in the egg of a wren and a running blackberry, the miracles to be seen in the bones of a man's hand, a mouse, and a grain of sand.

Perhaps it is as a prophet of an enlarging America that Whitman will be longest remembered. It was he who devoted most of his life to the insistent demand that America should produce its own legends, its own culture, independent and proud. Whitman did not ignore the priceless heritage of the old world, but he placed his reliance on the new. The ancient myths, the old gods, are dead, he declared again and again. " Turn to the present and face the problems of today," he cried to all those who believed in the spirit of the country.

Turn from lands retrospective recording proofs of the past,
From the singers that sing the trailing glories of the past,
From the chants of the feudal world, the triumphs of kings, slav-
    ery, caste.
Turn to *this* world, the triumphs reserved and to come — give up
    that backward world.
Leave to the singers of hitherto, give them the trailing past. . . .
Then turn, and be not alarmed — turn your undying face,
To where the future, greater than all the past,
Is swiftly, surely, preparing for you.

EMILY DICKINSON

Contemporary with Whitman, though, as far as the records show, utterly unaware of him, that strange phenomenon,
Emily Dickinson, lived and wrote her curious poetry. Only
four of her poems were published during her lifetime; she
cared nothing for a public, less for publicity. It was not until
forty years after her death that she was recognized as one of
the most original of American poets and, in some ways, the
most remarkable woman poet since Sappho. Her centenary,
occurring in 1930, was signaled by salvos of appreciation.

Like her contemporary, the great English poet Christina
Rossetti, Emily Dickinson led a life marked by " the great ab-
negation " — Christina because she could not face marriage,
Emily because, it is assumed, the man she loved was married
and she could face misery without him better than social tragedy with him.

Rumor to the contrary, there was nothing nun-like about
Emily Dickinson. If the episodes of her childhood were not
sufficient to prove it, the poetry is. The freedom of her spirit
manifests itself in the audacity of her images, the wild leap
of her epithets, the candor which extends from irreverent mischief to divine challenge. Sometimes indirect and full of remote allusions, sometimes so concentrated as to be cryptic,
hers is a poetry of continual surprise.

Could anyone have failed to recognize this revelation at the
outset? One supposes a few tense quatrains, a dozen arresting
syllables must have been sufficient to reveal the definiteness of
her genius. The " authorities " disdained or forgot her. As late
as 1914 *The New International Encyclopaedia* dismissed her
life and work in ten lines, concluding " In thought her intro-
spective lyrics are striking but are deficient in form." *The
Encyclopædia Britannica* seemed even less aware of her exist-

ence until 1926; the thirteenth edition contained only a mention, a cross-reference by way of comparison; her name did not appear in the Index. Yet her *Poems* (*First Series*) had appeared as early as 1890, and two subsequent collections had been published before 1896. In these volumes — as well as in *The Single Hound* (1915) and *Further Poems* (1929) — Emily Dickinson anticipated not only her avowed disciples but a score of poets unaware of her influence.

Thus Emily Dickinson became a puzzle. Biographers supplied fresh confusions and misleading clues in a mistaken zeal for detection. As in life, the poet escaped them all. Much of her problem remains in the realm of the mysterious. She imitated no other poet; her very " roughnesses " were individual. Time and again she skipped the expected rhyme, twisted the easy phrase, and put her indubitable mark on every line she wrote. Unlike any other poetry, her work is unique; her influence, negligible at first, is now incalculable.

THE AWAKENING OF THE WEST

By 1870 the public had been surfeited with sugared conceits and fine-spun delicacies of mid-nineteenth century verse. For a decade Whitman had exposed the overrefinements of the period, but comparatively few had listened. Yet an instinctive distaste for affectations had been growing, and when the West began to express itself in the raw accents of Mark Twain and Bret Harte, people turned to them with enthusiasm and relief. Mark Twain revealed the Mississippi and the vast mid-West; Bret Harte, who was writing a new kind of American fiction, ushered in the wild humor and poetry of California. To the loose swagger of the West, Joaquin Miller added a theatrical touch. His lines boomed with the pomposity of a brass band; floods, fires, hurricanes, extravagantly blazing sunsets, the thunder of a herd of buffaloes — all were unrestrainedly piled up to high heaven. Yet Miller's poetry occasionally captured the grandeur of his surroundings, the spread of the Sierras, the seething energy of the Western world.

RENASCENCE

The last of the nineteenth century was socially a period of increasing restlessness. It was a time of reaction against the past, but with little confidence in the present and undefined fear of the future. In poetry, the mood was one of escape. Bohemianism became a vogue; one of the favorite books, *Songs from Vagabondia*, by Bliss Carman and Richard Hovey started a series of wanderlusty volumes. The songs were jolly and lightly insurgent; they were enthusiastic about the open road, unfettered abandon, gypsy blood, a laughing challenge to fate, a chip on the shoulder, and a stein on the table.

Early in 1899, the name of Edwin Markham flashed across the land when, out of San Francisco, came " The Man with the Hoe." This poem, which was once called " the battle-cry of the next thousand years," caught up the passion for social justice in poetry. Markham intensified the unrest that was in the air. In the figure of one man with a hoe, he drew a picture of men in the mines, men in the sweat-shop, men working without joy, without hope. To social consciousness he added social conscience. In a ringing, rhetorical blank verse, Markham distilled the ferment of the period.

Suddenly a fresh and forthright poetry burst upon the country with unexpected vigor and variety. October, 1912 saw the first issue of *Poetry: A Magazine of Verse*, a monthly that was to introduce the work of hitherto unknown poets, schools, and " movements." The magazine came at the very moment of the breaking of the storm. Flashes and rumblings had already been troubling the literary heavens; a few months later came the deluge. Strange names made poetic news: Edwin Arlington Robinson, Robert Frost, Amy Lowell, Edgar Lee Masters, Vachel Lindsay, Carl Sandburg, Ezra Pound, T. S. Eliot, and others. By 1918 the " new poetry " was ranked as " America's first national art." People who never before had read verse, found they could not only read but relish it. They discovered that for the enjoyment of poetry it was no longer necessary to have a dictionary of rare words and classical references; they were not required to be acquainted with Latin legendry and the minor love-affairs of the Greek divinities. The new work spoke to them in their own language. It was not only closer to their soil but nearer to their souls.

EDWIN ARLINGTON ROBINSON

One reason why the new poetry achieved so sudden a success was its freedom from the traditionally stilted " poetic diction." Revolting strongly against the assumption that poetry must have a special vocabulary of its own, the poets of the new era spoke in the oldest and most stirring tongue; they used a language that was the language of the people. In the tones of ordinary speech they rediscovered the strength, the dignity, and beauty of the commonplace.

Edwin Arlington Robinson had already been employing the sharp epithet, the direct tone and clarifying utterance which was to become part of the present technique. As early as 1897, in *The Children of the Night*, Robinson anticipated the brief characterizations and etched outlines of Masters' *Spoon River Anthology;* he stressed the psychological element with artistry and sureness of touch. His sympathetic studies of men whose lives were, from a worldly standpoint, failures were a sharp reaction to the current high valuation on financial achievments, ruthless efficiency, and success at any cost. Ahead of his period, Robinson had to wait until 1916, when a public prepared for him by the awakened interest in native poetry discovered *The Man Against the Sky*. After that, his audience increased steadily. The Pulitzer Prize for Poetry was thrice awarded to him, and there was no longer any doubt as to the importance of his contribution to American literature. Death in 1935 found him at the peak of his fame.

EDGAR LEE MASTERS

Masters' most famous book ranks as a landmark. In it, Masters made a composite of the small towns of the mid-West with a background unmistakably local but with implications that are universal. Beneath its tales and dramas, its condensation of grocery-store gossip, *Spoon River Anthology* was a great part of America in microcosm; it prepared the way for Sinclair Lewis' *Main Street* and the critical fiction of small-town life.

The success of the volume was sensational. In a few months, it went into edition after edition. Perhaps most readers passed over the larger issues (Masters' revelation of the sordid cheats and hypocrisies) intent on seeing their neighbors pitilessly exposed. Yet had Masters dwelt only on the drab disillusion of the village, had he (as he was constantly in danger of doing) overemphasized the morbid episodes, he would have left only a spectacular and poorly balanced work. But the book ascends to a definite exaltation and ends on a plane of half-victorious idealism. Native to its roots, it is stark, unflinching, unforgettable.

ROBERT FROST

The same year that brought forth *Spoon River Anthology* saw the American edition of Frost's *North of Boston*. It was evident at once that the true recorder of New England and a great American poet had arrived. Frost was as native as the lonely farmhouses, the dusty blueberries, the isolated people, the dried-up brooks and mountain intervals that he described. Loving, above everything else, the beauty of the fact, he shared, with Robinson and Masters, the determination to tell not merely the actual but the factual truth. But Frost, a less disillusioned though a more saddened poet, wore his realism with a difference. Where Robinson was definite, Frost diverged, going roundabout and, in his speculative wandering, covering a wider territory of thought. Where Masters was violent and hotly scornful, Frost was reticent and quietly sympathetic. Where Masters wrote *about* his characters, Frost was *of* his people.

North of Boston was well described by the poet's own subtitle: " a book of people." In it one not only sees a countryside of people living out the intricate pattern of their lives, one catches them thinking out loud; one can hear the very tones of their voices. Here we have speech so arranged and translated that the speaker is heard on the printed page; any reader will be led by the kind and color of these words into reproducing the changing accents in which they are supposed to be uttered. It is this insistence that " all poetry is the reproduction of the tones of actual speech " which gives these poems, as well as the later lyrics, a quickly communicated emotional appeal. It endows them with the deepest power of which words are capable — the power to transmit significant sounds. These sounds, let in from the vernacular, are full of a robust, creative energy.

Frost was by no means the dark naturalist that some of his critics suspected. Behind the mask of " grimness " which many critics fastened upon him, there is a continual elfin pucker; a whimsical smile, a half-disclosed raillery glints beneath his most somber monologs. The later *New Hampshire* (1923) and *West-Running Brook* (1928) proved his " other side "; Frost's lyrics are no less personal for being philosophical. His greatness is not only due to his self-limited choice of material; Frost's concrete facts are symbols of spir-'tual values. Through his very reticence as well as through his revelations one hears much more than the voice of New England, one hears universal values.

CARL SANDBURG

The great mid-West, that vast region of steel mills and slaughter-houses, of cornfields and prairies, of crowded cities and open skies, spoke through Carl Sandburg. In Sandburg, industrial America found its voice: *Chicago Poems* (1916), *Cornhuskers* (1918), *Smoke and Steel* (1920), and *Good Morning, America* (1928) vibrate with the immense purring of dynamos, the rhythms of threshing arms, the gossip and laughter of construction gangs, the gigantic and tireless energy of the machine. Frankly indebted to Whitman, Sandburg's poems are less sweeping but more varied.

Like Frost, Sandburg was true to *things*. But Frost was content with the inexhaustible fact and its spiritual implications; he never hoped to drain it all. Sandburg also fed on the fact, but it did not satisfy him. He had strange hungers; he hunted eagerly for the question behind, the answer beyond. The actual scene, to him, was a point of vivid and abrupt departure. Reality, far from being the earth on which he dwelt, was, for Sandburg, the ground he touched before rising; realism acted merely as a springboard from which this poet dove into fantasy.

When *Chicago Poems* first appeared, it was received with disfavor. Sandburg was accused of verbal anarchy, of a failure to distinguish prose matter from poetic material, of uncouthness, vulgarity, assaults on the English language, and a score of other crimes. In the face of those who still see only a coarseness and distorted realism in Sandburg, it cannot be said too often that he is brutal only when dealing with brutal things; that his " vulgarity " springs from love of life as a whole, not from affection for a drab part of it; that his bitterest invectives are the result of a disgust of shams. The strength of his hatred is exceeded by the challenge of his love.

THE IMAGISTS AND AMY LOWELL

Sandburg established himself as the most daring user of American words — words ranging from the racy metaphors of the soil to the slang of the street. But long before this, the possibilities of a new vocabulary were being tested. As early as 1865, Whitman was saying, "We must have new words, new potentialities of speech — an American range of self-expression. . . . The new times, the new people need a tongue according, yes, and what is more, they will have such a tongue — will not be satisfied until it is evolved." It is curious that one of the most effective agents to fulfill Whitman's prophecy was that little band of preoccupied specialists, the Imagists.

Ezra Pound was the first to gather the insurgents into a definite group. During 1913, he wrote and collected a number of poems illustrating the Imagist point of view, conceiving Imagism as a discriminating term like "lyricism." The poems were by English as well as American poets, and Pound had them printed in a volume: *Des Imagistes* (1914). A little later Pound withdrew from the clan. The original group began to disintegrate, and Amy Lowell, then in England, brought some of the younger members together in three yearly anthologies (*Some Imagist Poets*) which appeared in 1915, 1916, and 1917. There were, in Miss Lowell's new grouping, three Englishmen (D. H. Lawrence, Richard Aldington, F. S. Flint), three Americans (H. D., John Gould Fletcher, Amy Lowell), and their creed, summed up in six statements, was as follows:

1. To use the language of common speech, but to employ always the *exact* word, not the merely decorative word.

2. To create new rhythms — as the expression of new moods. We do not insist upon "free-verse" as the only method of writing poetry. . . . We do believe that the individuality of a poet may often be better expressed in free verse than in conventional forms.

3. To allow absolute freedom in the choice of subject.

4. To present an image (hence the name: "Imagist"). We are not a school of painters, but we believe that poetry should render particulars exactly and not deal in vague generalities, however magnificent and sonorous.

5. To produce poetry that is hard and clear, never blurred or indefinite.

6. Finally, most of us believe that concentration is the very essence of poetry.

It does not seem possible that these six principles (which the Imagists often neglected in their poetry) could have provoked the storm of argument, fury, and downright vilification that broke as soon as the militant Miss Lowell began to champion them. Many conservative critics rushed wildly to combat these "heresies"! They forgot that, in trying to protect the future from such lawlessness as "using the exact word," from "freedom in the choice of subject," from the importance of "concentration," they were actually attacking the highest traditions of the past.

The quarrel succeeded in doing more good than did the work of the Imagists themselves. It was not long before they ceased to be identified as part of a "movement." The task of the Imagists was done. Its members began to develop by themselves. They had helped to swell the tide of romantic but unsentimental poetry — a tide of which their contribution was a breaker that carried its impact far inshore.

FOLK–RHYTHMS AND LINDSAY

In a country that has not been mellowed by antiquity, that has not possessed songs for its peasantry or traditions for its singers, one cannot yet look for a wealth of folk-stuff. In the United States folk-poetry followed the path of the pioneer. At first these homely songs were mere adaptations and localized versions of English ballads and border minstrelsy. But a more definitely native spirit found expression in various sections of these States. In the West (during the Seventies) Bret Harte and John Hay celebrated, in their own accents, the rough miners, ranchers, steamboat pilots, the supposed descendants of the emigrants from Pike County, Missouri. In the Middle West the desire for local color and music led to the popularity of James Whitcomb Riley's Hoosier ballads and the spirited jingles of Eugene Field. In the South the inspiration of the Negro spirituals and ante-bellum songs was utilized to good effect by Joel Chandler Harris, Paul Laurence Dunbar, and the contemporary Negro poets. John A. Lomax and his son Alan published several volumes of cowboy songs — most of them anonymous — full of tang, wild fancy, and robust humor. Mary Austin, Natalie Curtis Burlin, and Lew Sarett are chief among those who attempted to bring the spirit of Indian tunes and chants into our poetry. A huge assemblage of words and music from small towns, railroad stations, backwoods, and prairies (to say nothing of barber-shops) was collected by Carl Sandburg and published in 1927 under the accurate title *The American Songbag*. But, of all contemporaries who approximated the spirit of folk-poetry, none made more striking or more indubitably American contributions than Vachel Lindsay of Springfield, Illinois.

Lindsay was essentially a people's poet. He did not hesitate to express himself in terms of the lowest common denominator; his fingers seemed alternately on his pen and on the public pulse. Lindsay was tremendously influenced by the colorful suggestions, the fantastic superstitions, the revivalistic gusto, and, above all, by the intoxicating, syncopated music that characterized the Negro in America. In " The Congo," " John Brown," and " Simon Legree," the words roll with the solemnity of an exhortation, dance with a grotesque fervor, or snap, crackle, and leap with all the humorous rhythms of a piece of intricate jazz. Lindsay caught the burly color and boisterous music of camp-meetings, minstrel shows, revival jubilees. He was an itinerant evangelist preaching the Gospel through a saxophone.

Lindsay did more. He carried his democratic determinations further than any of his *confrères*. Dreaming of a great communal art, he insisted that all villages should be centers of beauty, all citizens should be artists. At heart a missionary even more than a minstrel, Lindsay often lost himself in his own doctrines. He cheapened himself and caricatured his own gift by pandering to the vaudeville instinct, putting a noisy " punch " into everything, regardless of taste, artistry, or a sense of proportion. He was most impressive when purely fantastic or when a great theme is combined with artistic restraint (as in " The Eagle That Is Forgotten ") to create a preaching that does not cease to be poetry.

ELIOT AND HIS INFLUENCE

Two strongly opposed tendencies were noticeable immediately after 1916. The one was a growing use of the colloquial speech popularized by Sandburg, Lindsay, and Masters and heightened by Frost; the other was a striking departure from both the conversational tone and the traditional " poetic " language to which such poets as E. A. Robinson and Edna St. Vincent Millay remained loyal. The break in idiom was brought about by T. S. Eliot, who brought it from France. Eliot used the technique of the Symbolist school with such skill that he soon had a host of imitators on both sides of the Atlantic. Some were unable, some unwilling to follow Eliot's inner difficulties and despairs, but all were fascinated by his technical devices. The formula was, roughly, this: To reveal man in his complex relation to the universe the poet must show him not only concerned with the immensities but with the trivialities of daily life, with a sense of the past continually interrupting the present, and with swiftly contradictory moods. This was, obviously, a difficult if not impossible program to achieve in any one poem or even a set of poems.

Eliot attempted to show the ruin of present-day culture by making a disrupted poetry from the wreckage of the literature of the past. His technique was equally contradictory and often confusing: a rapid leaping from image to image with a minimum of "explanatory" metaphors; a liberal use of discords, juxtaposing tense images and prosy statements; the continual play of free association, in which one idea prompted a chain of others, sometimes gaining a new series of overtones, sometimes sacrificing all continuity.

Following Eliot, the ultra-modern poet built a world of his own, a world of private allusions, personal allegories, and themes far removed from those of the ordinary world. The results were bewildering and often baffling; the poems were like sets of ornate, decorative, and mostly unintelligible hieroglyphics. But many of them were not without their admirers and disciples.

THE NEW LYRICISTS

The lyric note was bound to be affected by the opposing tendencies in the modern idiom. It, too, fluctuated to express the shift from convention to revolt, from decision to doubt. John Crowe Ransom, at first influenced by Frost and Eliot, perfected his own tone, half tart, half tender. Conrad Aiken developed a peculiarly wavering music capable of haunting effects, both in the early lyrics and the later somber preludes. Stephen Vincent Benét and William Rose Benét, brothers in blood and balladry, plundered modernity and antiquity for their fancies; the former, taking the Civil War for a background in *John Brown's Body*, constructed a many-voiced lyric of epic proportions. Archibald MacLeish combined the old music with a new meaning, and Robinson Jeffers brought a fresh vigor, even violence, to the long, unrhymed line. The short lyrics of Robert Frost grew consistently in strength and suggestiveness.

The work of the women ranged from the outspoken to the involved. Two distinct influences governed many of them: Emily Dickinson and Lizette Woodworth Reese. The epigrammatic condensations of the former affected an entire generation with increasing force. The firm speech and sparse imagery of the latter won many away from the cloying old-fashioned love-songs. Edna St. Vincent Millay, in her later sonnets no less than in the early " Renascence," deepened an already impassioned note, increasing the admiration as well as the size of her audience. Sara Teasdale intensified a simple but flexible melodic line. Jean Starr Untermeyer lifted the ordinary round of woman's everyday into novelty and, not seldom, into ecstasy. The overtones of the late Elizabethans are in the accents of Louise Bogan, Léonie Adams, and Elinor Wylie, among others. Elinor Wylie acknowledged the relationship implicitly; the title of her first volume (*Nets to Catch the Wind*) was taken from a poem by Webster, the title of her last (*Angels and Earthly Creatures*) from a sermon by Donne.

EFFECTS OF THE DEPRESSION

The financial crash of October, 1929, and the ensuing depression were not immediately reflected in the poetry of the period. But by 1933 it was evident that a crisis had occurred in literature as well as in finance and government. The poets turned, tentatively enough, to a consideration of economic and social problems; some of them deserted poetry altogether. It is noteworthy that whereas the five years from 1913 to 1918 produced a dozen or more poets of national importance, not more than two or three new poets of any significance appeared between 1930 and 1940.

Poetry seemed to suffer a partial paralysis, unable to express the depressed times except by negation. Yet, no matter what the conditions, man cannot remain inarticulate for long, and there were signs that the younger poets were grappling with the situation. Archibald MacLeish stimulated his contemporaries with a new questioning note; not content to regard contemporary American life alone in its present troubles, he turned to our earliest history in search of some understanding of the American dream. Other poets attempted to express the universal bewilderment, doubtfully, even desperately. It was a difficult task. Values were distorted, standards questioned, the traditional responses were deadened. But the basic feelings of poets, disturbed and temporarily stunned, could not remain paralyzed.

WORLD WAR II—AND AFTER

The generation that grew up between two World Wars was nursed on anxiety. Youth was torn between a nostalgia for a comforting past and an apprehension — half fear, half hope — of a new order which was not defined and which was barely beginning to declare itself. There were the combined threats of another and greater war, prolonged social struggles, and impending chaos. The emotional climate of the country was scarcely conducive to stability. The mood ranged from uneasy optimism to shrugging apathy, from false complacency to grim disillusion.

Pearl Harbor and America's entry into the war transformed psychological anxieties into terrible realities. The temper of the 1940s was dangerous; the condition was, in every sense, critical. Writers expressed their attitudes to war in various ways. Only a few versifiers, or poets who had abandoned poetry for journalistic patrioteering, rejoiced in the war and attempted to glorify it. The most convincing contributors to *War and the Poet* (1945), edited by Richard Eberhart and Selden Rodman, and *The War Poets* (1945), edited by Oscar Williams, recognized that war was not only devastating but debasing, not only merciless but mad. " War," wrote Mark Van Doren, " could be beautiful to Homer and Shakespeare because it could be tragic. It has ceased to be that. . . . Now it is all catastrophe, with nothing to guide our measurement of its meaning. It is epidemic calamity." Such a conclusion was continually reaffirmed; it was repeated in the anger and sympathy of Karl Shapiro, the mingled pity and outrage of Randall Jarrell, the passionate condemnations of Peter Viereck.

Post-war tendencies in the arts were not always consistent and were often contradictory. Poetry, however, was somewhat more sharply directed. The trend was increasingly toward greater intensity of feeling as well as greater honesty.

SUMMARY: THE WIDER PANORAMA

The modern poets answered the demands put upon them by a rapidly changing civilization. They reflected the energy of the age, its contradictory appetite for realism and fantasy, its skepticism and its submerged faith. They sounded a range hitherto barely suggested in America, creating a panoramic poetry. Differing widely from most of their English fellow-craftsmen, they were far less hampered by the burdens of tradition or the necessity of casting them off. Geographically, the range was wide. As the country enlarged, the poets grew with it, springing up in most unlikely places, ready to celebrate urban miracles of stone and steel no less than the traditional landscapes and scenes. They found their material in a world of honest reality. They learned to distinguish beauty from prettiness, and to look for truth even in forbidding places. They proved that their art was not only a craft but a medium of important communication.

This volume attempts to show the rich mixture of tradition and experiment, the play between convention and revolt, which is so typical of our times. It is not claimed that every poem in this collection is a great poem. It is maintained, however, that the selection from each poet combines the force of the imagination with the feel of truth which is the essence and power of poetry.

WALT WHITMAN

Walt Whitman was born May 31, 1819, in West Hills, near Huntington, Long Island ("fish-shaped Paumanok"). When he was still a child, his father left the farm which had been in the family for generations, and the Whitmans moved to Brooklyn. There, after a fitful schooling, young Whitman became a printer's apprentice. For twenty years he earned his living as printer, reporter, editorial writer, occasional critic and wandering journalist. He even wrote a crude temperance tract disguised as a novel. Whitman was, however, anything but the "unlettered and uncultured primitive" whom his detractors (and some of his well-meaning apologists) have pictured. He had not merely read but absorbed Shakespeare, Homer, the Bible — and the elemental surge of these can be heard in his early prose poems and in the first edition of *Leaves of Grass*.

The first edition of *Leaves of Grass* (1855) made its appearance as a poorly printed pamphlet of twelve poems brought out anonymously and bearing, instead of a signature, a portrait of the author with one hand in his pocket, one on his hip, open shirt, and a slouch hat rakishly tilted. One of the first copies of the pamphlet was sent to Ralph Waldo Emerson, which — considering Whitman's indebtedness to Emerson in spirit if not in form — was no more than proper. With something of the master's gratification on being hailed by an unknown but fervent disciple, Emerson immediately wrote, "I give you joy of your free and brave thought. . . . I find the courage of treatment which so delights us, and which large perception only can inspire. I greet you at the beginning of a great career."

A few other American writers realized that a new force had been flung up in the Western world; in England, Swinburne and Rossetti were roused by the "buffalo strength" of this strange voice. But criticism, for the most part, was adverse, and the favorites of the reading public continued to be the established group in and around Boston. Whitman, undeterred by jeers, feeling his foothold "tenon'd and mortis'd in granite," labored upon his magnum opus, changed titles, added entire sections, revealed, for all but careless readers, his natural artistry. By 1861 *Leaves of Grass* was in its third edition.

During the Civil War, Whitman served as nurse and wound-dresser and, in 1865, he was given a position in the Department of the Interior. Here a certain secretary, James Harlan, having read *Leaves of Grass*, conferred immortality upon himself by dismissing Whitman because of his "pernicious writing." In 1866 Whitman's *Drum-Taps* appeared, a volume that not only reflected his war experiences but contained two of the most stirring elegies ever written, notably "When Lilacs Last in the Dooryard Bloom'd," in which Lincoln is mourned and immortally eulogized. Less provocative than his first "barbaric yawps," such later works as *Goodbye My Fancy* (1891) are no less rich in observation and eloquence. Whitman died in Camden, New Jersey, March 26, 1892.

A complete understanding of Whitman is difficult, especially since so much of his work is self-contradictory. It has mass and magnitude, yet it is also curiously private and personal. There are large convictions here, and small affectations. The American speech is stressed — "a new, native language" — yet there are many queer interruptions of hybrid and almost ridiculous phraseology.

The contradictions remain to trouble the appraiser; Whitman's final significance has not yet been summarized. But no one can fail to recognize the greatness of his contribution. His wide and windy optimism is an emotional if not an intellectual influence. His wholeheartedness, his large yea-saying, his sense of released power, the separate illuminating pictures and prophecies — all these have an irresistible appeal. They enlarge horizons; they expand the air.

Whitman's poetry will persist because it transcends the man and his times. The poet was not exaggerating when he claimed that his monumental book "contained multitudes." For all his inconsistencies he achieved permanence; employing words, he harnessed elements.

Whitman is most himself in the longer, panoramic poems — and one of those would far exceed the allotment of space here. The selections which follow are no more than a taste of the poet's magnitude.

I Hear America Singing

I hear America singing, the varied carols I hear,
Those of mechanics, each one singing his as it should be blithe
    and strong,
The carpenter singing his as he measures his plank or beam,
The mason singing his as he makes ready for work, or leaves
    off work,
The boatman singing what belongs to him in his boat, the
    deckhand singing on the steamboat deck,
The shoemaker singing as he sits on his bench, the hatter singing as he stands,
The wood-cutter's song, the plowboy's on his way in the
    morning, or at noon intermission or at sundown,
The delicious singing of the mother, or of the young wife at
    work, or of the girl sewing or washing,
Each singing what belongs to him or her and to none else,

The day what belongs to the day — at night the party of
  young fellows, robust, friendly,
Singing with open mouths their strong melodious songs.

from Song of Myself

1

I celebrate myself, and sing myself,
And what I assume you shall assume,
For every atom belonging to me as good belongs to you.
I loafe and invite my soul,
I lean and loafe at my ease observing a spear of summer
  grass. . . .

6

A child said *What is the grass?* fetching it to me with full
  hands;
How could I answer the child? I do not know what it is any
  more than he.

I guess it must be the flag of my disposition, out of hopeful
  green stuff woven.

Or I guess it is the handkerchief of the Lord,
A scented gift and remembrancer designedly dropt,
Bearing the owner's name someway in the corners, that we
  may see and remark, and say *Whose?* . . .

And now it seems to me the beautiful, uncut hair of graves.

Tenderly will I use you, curling grass.
It may be you transpire from the breasts of young men;
It may be if I had known them I would have loved them;
It may be you are from old people, and from women, and
  from offspring taken soon out of their mothers' laps.
And here you are the mothers' laps.

This grass is very dark to be from the white heads of old
  mothers,
Darker than the colorless beards of old men,
Dark to come from under the faint red roofs of mouths.
O I perceive after all so many uttering tongues,

And I perceive they do not come from the roofs of mouths
for nothing.
I wish I could translate the hints about the dead young men
and women,
And the hints about old men and mothers, and the offspring
taken soon out of their laps.

What do you think has become of the young and old men?
And what do you think has become of the women and children?

They are alive and well somewhere;
The smallest sprout shows there is really no death. . . .
All goes onward and outward — nothing collapses.

18

With music strong I come, with my cornets and my drums,
I play not marches for accepted victors only, I play marches
for conquer'd and slain persons.

Have you heard that it was good to gain the day?
I also say it is good to fall, battles are lost in the same spirit
in which they are won.

Vivas to those who have fail'd!
And to those whose war-vessels sank in the sea!
And to those themselves who sank in the sea!
And to all generals that lost engagements, and all overcome
heroes!
And the numberless unknown heroes equal to the greatest
heroes known!

20

In all people I see myself, none more and not one a barley-
corn less,
And the good or bad I say of myself I say of them.
I know I am solid and sound,
To me the converging objects of the universe perpetually
flow,
All are written to me, and I must get what the writing means.

I know I am deathless,
I know this orbit of mine cannot be swept by a carpenter's
compass,

I know I shall not pass like a child's curlacue cut with a burnt
    stick at night.

I know I am august,
I do not trouble my spirit to vindicate itself or be understood,
I see that the elementary laws never apologize.

I exist as I am, that is enough,
If no other in the world be aware I sit content,
And if each and all be aware I sit content.

One world is aware and by far the largest to me, and that is
    myself,
And whether I come to my own today or in ten thousand or
    ten million years,
I can cheerfully take it now, or with equal cheerfulness I can
    wait.
My foothold is tenon'd and mortis'd [1] in granite,
I laugh at what you call dissolution,
And I know the amplitude of time.

21

I am he that walks with the tender and growing night,
I call to the earth and sea half-held by the night.

Press close bare-bosom'd night — press close magnetic nour-
    ishing night!
Night of south winds — night of the large few stars!
Still nodding night — mad naked summer night.

Smile O voluptuous cool-breath'd earth!
Earth of the slumbering and liquid trees!
Earth of departed sunset — earth of the mountains misty-
    topt!
Earth of the vitreous pour of the full moon just tinged with
    blue!
Earth of shine and dark mottling the tide of the river!
Earth of the limpid gray of clouds brighter and clearer for
    my sake!
Far-swooping elbow'd earth — rich apple-blossom'd earth!
Smile, for your lover comes.

[1] As a carpenter's son, Whitman enjoyed using such a carpenter's phrase as "tenon'd and mortis'd." It means firmly joined, solidly fixed.

31

I believe a leaf of grass is no less than the journeywork of the
    stars,
And the pismire [1] is equally perfect, and a grain of sand, and
    the egg of the wren,
And the tree-toad is a chef-d'œuvre [2] for the highest,
And the running blackberry would adorn the parlors of
    heaven,
And the narrowest hinge in my hand puts to scorn all ma-
    chinery,
And the cow crunching with depress'd head surpasses any
    statue,
And a mouse is miracle enough to stagger sextillions of in-
    fidels.

32

I think I could turn and live with animals, they are so placid
    and self-contain'd,
I stand and look at them long and long.
They do not sweat and whine about their condition,
They do not lie awake in the dark and weep for their sins,
They do not make me sick discussing their duty to God,
Not one is dissatisfied, not one is demented with the mania of
    owning things,
Not one is respectable or unhappy over the whole earth.

44

Immense have been the preparations for me,
Faithful and friendly the arms that have help'd me.

Cycles ferried my cradle, rowing and rowing like cheerful
    boatmen.
For room to me stars kept aside in their own rings. . . .
All forces have been steadily employ'd to complete and de-
    light me;
Now on this spot I stand with my robust soul.

48

Why should I wish to see God better than this day?
I see something of God each hour of the twenty-four, and
    each moment then,

---

[1] The ant.   [2] A masterpiece.

In the faces of men and women I see God, and in my own
    face in the glass,
I find letters from God dropt in the street, and every one is
    sign'd by God's name,
And I leave them where they are, for I know that wheresoe'er
    I go,
Others will punctually come for ever and ever.

51

Do I contradict myself?
Very well then I contradict myself,
(I am large, I contain multitudes).

52

The spotted hawk swoops by and accuses me, he complains of
    my gab and my loitering.

I too am not a bit tamed, I too am untranslatable,
I sound my barbaric yawp over the roofs of the world.

The last scud of day holds back for me,
It flings my likeness after the rest and true as any on the
    shadow'd wilds,
It coaxes me to the vapor and the dusk. . . .

I bequeath myself to the dirt to grow from the grass I love;
If you want me again look for me under your boot-soles.

You will hardly know whom I am or what I mean,
But I shall be good health to you nevertheless,
And filter and fibre your blood.

Failing to fetch me at first keep encouraged,
Missing me one place search another,
I stop somewhere waiting for you.

from Crossing Brooklyn Ferry

It avails not, time nor place — distance avails not, . . .
I am with you, you men and women of a generation, or ever
    so many generations hence,
Just as you feel when you look on the river and sky, so I felt,

Just as any of you is one of a living crowd, I was one of a
crowd,
Just as you are refresh'd by the gladness of the river and the
bright flow, I was refresh'd,
Just as you stand and lean on the rail, yet hurry with the swift
current, I stood yet was hurried,
Just as you look on the numberless masts of ships and the
thick-stemm'd pipes of steamboats, I look'd.

Song of the Open Road
(*A Fragment*)

Afoot and light-hearted I take to the open road,
Healthy, free, the world before me,
The long brown path before me leading wherever I choose.

Henceforth I ask not good-fortune, I myself am good-fortune,
Henceforth I whimper no more, postpone no more, need
nothing,
Done with indoor complaints, libraries, querulous criticisms,
Strong and content I travel the open road.

Reconciliation

Word over all, beautiful as the sky,
Beautiful that war and all its deeds of carnage must in time be
utterly lost,
That the hands of the sisters Death and Night incessantly
softly wash again, and ever again, this soil'd world;
For my enemy is dead, a man divine as myself is dead,
I look where he lies white-faced and still in the coffin — I draw
near,
Bend down and touch lightly with my lips the white face in
the coffin.

When I Heard the Learn'd Astronomer

When I heard the learn'd astronomer,
When the proofs, the figures, were ranged in columns before
me,

When I was shown the charts and diagrams, to add, divide,
    and measure them,
When I sitting heard the astronomer where he lectured with
    much applause in the lecture-room,
How soon unaccountable I became tired and sick,
Till rising and gliding out I wander'd off by myself,
In the mystical moist night-air, and from time to time,
Look'd up in perfect silence at the stars.

Miracles

Why, who makes much of a miracle?
As to me I know of nothing else but miracles,
Whether I walk the streets of Manhattan,
Or dart my sight over the roofs of houses toward the sky,
Or wade with naked feet along the beach just in the edge of
    the water,
Or stand under trees in the woods,
Or talk by day with any one I love,
Or sit at table at dinner with the rest,
Or look at strangers opposite me riding in the car,
Or watch honey-bees busy around the hive of a summer fore-
    noon,
Or animals feeding in the fields,
Or the wonderfulness of the sundown, or of stars shining so
    quiet and bright,
Or the exquisite delicate thin curve of the new moon in
    spring;
These with the rest, one and all, are to me miracles,
The whole referring, yet each distinct and in its place.
To me every hour of the light and dark is a miracle,
Every cubic inch of space is a miracle,
Every square yard of the surface of the earth is spread with
    the same,
Every foot of the interior swarms with the same.

To me the sea is a continual miracle,
The fishes that swim — the rocks — the motion of the waves —
    the ships with men in them,
What stranger miracles are there?

The Last Invocation

At the last, tenderly,

From the walls of the powerful fortress'd house,
From the clasp of the knitted locks, from the keep of the well-
   closed doors,
Let me be wafted.
Let me glide noiselessly forth;
With the key of softness unlock the locks — with a whisper,
Set open the doors O soul.

Tenderly — be not impatient,
(Strong is your hold O mortal flesh,
Strong is your hold O love.)

from When Lilacs Last in the Dooryard Bloom'd [1]

1

When lilacs last in the dooryard bloom'd,
And the great star early droop'd in the western sky in the
   night,
I mourn'd, and yet shall mourn with ever-returning spring.

Ever-returning spring, trinity sure to me you bring,
Lilac blooming perennial and drooping star in the west,
And thought of him I love.

2

O powerful western fallen star!
O shades of night — O moody, tearful night!
O great star disappear'd — O the black murk that hides the
   star!
O cruel hands that hold me powerless — O helpless soul of
   me!
O harsh surrounding cloud that will not free my soul.

[1] This poem, one of the noblest elegies in the English language,
and " O Captain! My Captain! " which follows, are part of a group
which Whitman entitled " Memories of President Lincoln."

3

In the dooryard fronting an old farm-house near the white-
   wash'd palings,
Stands the lilac-bush tall-growing with heart-shaped leaves of
   rich green,
With many a pointed blossom rising delicate, with the perfume strong I love,
With every leaf a miracle — and from this bush in the dooryard,
With delicate-color'd blossoms and heart-shaped leaves of
   rich green,
A sprig with its flower I break.

4

In the swamp in secluded recesses,
A shy and hidden bird is warbling a song.

Solitary the thrush,
The hermit withdrawn to himself, avoiding the settlements,
Sings by himself a song.

Song of the bleeding throat,
Death's outlet song of life, (for well dear brother I know,
If thou wast not granted to sing thou would'st surely die.)

5

Over the breast of the spring, the land, amid cities,
Amid lanes and through old woods, where lately the violets
   peep'd from the ground, spotting the gray débris,
Amid the grass in the fields each side of the lanes, passing the
   endless grass,
Passing the yellow-spear'd wheat, every grain from its shroud
   in the dark-brown fields uprisen,
Passing the apple-tree blows of white and pink in the orchards,
Carrying a corpse to where it shall rest in the grave,
Night and day journeys a coffin.

6

Coffin that passes through lanes and streets,
Through day and night with the great cloud darkening the
   land,

With the pomp of the inloop'd flags with the cities draped in
    black,
With the show of the States themselves as of crape-veil'd
    women standing,
With processions long and winding and the flambeaus of the
    night,
With the countless torches lit, with the silent sea of faces and
    the unbared heads,
With the waiting depot, the arriving coffin, and the somber
    faces,
With dirges through the night, with the thousand voices ris-
    ing strong and solemn,
With all the mournful voices of the dirges pour'd around the
    coffin,
The dim-lit churches and the shuddering organs — where amid
    these you journey,
With the tolling tolling bells' perpetual clang,
Here, coffin that slowly passes,
I give you my sprig of lilac.

O Captain! My Captain!

O Captain! my Captain, our fearful trip is done,
The ship has weather'd every rack, the prize we sought is
    won,
The port is near, the bells I hear, the people all exulting,
While follow eyes the steady keel, the vessel grim and daring;
        But O heart! heart! heart!
            O the bleeding drops of red,
                Where on the deck my Captain lies,
                Fallen cold and dead.

O Captain! my Captain! rise up and hear the bells;
Rise up — for you the flag is flung — for you the bugle trills,
For you bouquets and ribbon'd wreaths — for you the shores
    a-crowding,
For you they call, the swaying mass, their eager faces turning;
        Here Captain! dear father!
            The arm beneath your head!
                It is some dream that on the deck,
                You've fallen cold and dead.

My Captain does not answer, his lips are pale and still,
My father does not feel my arm, he has no pulse nor will,
The ship is anchor'd safe and sound, its voyage closed and
    done,
From fearful trip the victor ship comes in with object won;
        Exult O shores, and ring O bells!
            But I with mournful tread,
                Walk the deck my Captain lies,
                    Fallen cold and dead.

Dirge for Two Veterans

        The last sunbeam
Lightly falls from the finished Sabbath,
On the pavement here, and there beyond it is looking,
        Down a new-made double grave,

        Lo, the moon ascending,
Up from the east the silvery round moon,
Beautiful over the house-tops ghastly, phantom moon,
        Immense and silent moon.

        I see a sad procession,
And I hear the sound of coming full-key'd bugles,
All the channels of the city streets they're flooding,
        As with voices and with tears.

        I hear the great drums pounding,
And the small drums steady whirring,
And every blow of the great convulsive drums,
        Strikes me through and through.

        For the son is brought with the father,
(On the foremost ranks of the fierce assault they fell,
Two veterans son and father dropt together,
        And the double grave awaits them).

        Now nearer blow the bugles,
And the drums strike more convulsive,
And the daylight o'er the pavement quite has faded,
        And the strong dead-march enwraps me.

In the eastern sky up-buoying,
The sorrowful vast phantom moves illumin'd,
('Tis some mother's large transparent face,
     In heaven brighter growing).

O strong dead-march, you please me!
O moon immense with your silvery face, you soothe me!
O my soldiers twain! O my veterans passing to burial!
     What I have I also give you.

The moon gives you light,
And the bugles and the drums give you music,
And my heart, O my soldiers, my veterans,
     My heart gives you love.

Come Up from the Fields, Father

Come up from the fields, father, here's a letter from our Pete.
And come to the front door, mother, here's a letter from thy
     dear son.

Lo, 'tis autumn,
Lo, where the trees, deeper green, yellower and redder,
Cool and sweeten Ohio's villages with leaves fluttering in the
     moderate wind,
Where apples ripe in the orchards hang and grapes on the
     trellis'd vines,
(Smell you the smell of the grapes on the vines?
Smell you the buckwheat where the bees were lately buzz-
     ing?)
Above all, lo, the sky so calm, so transparent after the rain and
     with wondrous clouds,
Below too, all calm, all vital and beautiful, and the farm pros-
     pers well.

Down in the fields all prospers well,
But now from the fields come father, come at the daughter's
     call,
And come to the entry mother, to the front door come right
     away.
Fast as she can she hurries, something ominous, her steps trem-
     bling,
She does not tarry to smooth her hair nor adjust her cap.

Open the envelope quickly,
O this is not our son's writing, yet his name is sign'd,
O a strange hand writes for our dear son, O stricken mother's
  soul!

All swims before her eyes, flashes with black, she catches the
  main words only,
Sentences broken, *gunshot wound in the breast, cavalry skir-
  mish, taken to hospital,*
At present low, but will soon be better.

Ah now the single figure to me,
Amid all teeming and wealthy Ohio with all its cities and
  farms,
Sickly white in the face and dull in the head, very faint,
By the jamb of a door leans.

Grieve not so, dear mother, (the just-grown daughter speaks
  through her sobs,
The little sisters huddle around speechless and dismay'd,)
See dearest mother, the letter says Pete will soon be better.

Alas poor boy, he will never be better, (nor may-be needs to
  be better that brave and simple soul,)
While they stand at home at the door he is dead already,
The only son is dead.

But the mother needs to be better,
She with thin form presently drest in black,
By day her meals untouch'd, then at night fitfully sleeping,
  often waking,
In the midnight waking, weeping, longing with one deep
  longing,
O that she might withdraw unnoticed, silent from life escape
  and withdraw,
To follow, to seek, to be with her dear dead son.

On the Beach at Night

On the beach at night,
Stands a child with her father,
Watching the east, the autumn sky.

Up through the darkness,
While ravening clouds, the burial clouds, in black masses
    spreading,
Lower sullen and fast athwart and down the sky,
Amid a transparent clear belt of ether yet left in the east,
Ascends large and calm the lord-star Jupiter,
And nigh at hand, only a very little above,
Swim the delicate sisters the Pleiades.

From the beach the child holding the hand of her father,
Those burial clouds that lower victorious soon to devour all,
Watching, silently weeps.

Weep not, child,
Weep not, my darling,
With these kisses let me remove your tears,
The ravening clouds shall not long be victorious;
They shall not long possess the sky, they devour the stars only
    in apparition,
Jupiter shall emerge, be patient, watch again another night,
    the Pleiades shall emerge,
They are immortal, all those stars both silvery and golden
    shall shine out again,
The great stars and the little ones shall shine out again, they
    endure,
The vast immortal suns and the long-enduring pensive moons
    shall again shine.

Then dearest child mournest thou only for Jupiter?
Considerest thou alone the burial of the stars?

Something there is,
(With my lips soothing thee, adding I whisper,
I give thee the first suggestion, the problem and indirection,)
Something there is more immortal even than the stars,
(Many the burials, many the days and nights, passing away,)
Something that shall endure longer even than lustrous Jupiter,
Longer than sun or any revolving satellite,
Or the radiant sisters the Pleiades.[1]

[1] *Pleiades:* In Greek mythology, the seven daughters of Atlas
and a nymph. They were transformed into a group of stars — a
conspicuous cluster visible to the average eye.

A Noiseless Patient Spider

A noiseless patient spider,
I mark'd where on a little promontory it stood isolated.
Mark'd how to explore the vacant vast surrounding,
It launch'd forth filament, filament, filament, out of itself.
Ever unreeling them, ever tirelessly speeding them.

And you O my soul where you stand,
Surrounded, detached, in measureless oceans of space,
Ceaselessly musing, venturing, throwing, seeking the spheres
   to connect them.
Till the bridge you will need be form'd, till the ductile anchor
   hold,
Till the gossamer thread you fling catch somewhere, O my
   soul.

A Clear Midnight

This is thy hour, O Soul, thy free flight into the wordless,
Away from books, away from art, the day erased, the lesson
   done,
Thee fully forth emerging, silent, gazing, pondering the
   themes thou lovest best:
Night, sleep, death, and the stars.

EMILY DICKINSON

Emily (Elizabeth) Dickinson was born in Amherst, Massachusetts, December 10, 1830. She died in the house in which she was born. In her youth she was high-spirited and full of humor, but after the age of twenty-six she became a physical recluse and a kind of spiritual hermit; she rarely set foot beyond her doorstep. "She habitually concealed her mind, like her person, from all but a very few friends," wrote Thomas Wentworth Higginson, who may be said to have discovered her, "and it was with great difficulty that she was persuaded to print, during her lifetime, three or four poems." She disliked publicity so much that those four published poems had to be taken from her almost by stealth, and, though she wrote more than twelve hundred poems in secrecy, the first volume of her poetry did not appear until 1890, four years after her death.

Keeping herself strictly to herself, she became a mystery, a legend even in her own lifetime. Undisturbed by the outside world, she continued to ignore all people except her immediate family and a few intimate friends. She devoted herself to the household, to her baking, her preserving, and her poetry. In 1885 she was suddenly taken ill; she died of Bright's disease in her fifty-sixth year, May 15, 1886.

Her fame grew gradually; only a small circle of readers appreciated the peculiar keenness and concision of her thought. But she was never without enthusiastic admirers. *Poems* (1890) was followed by *Poems: Second Series* (1890) and *Poems: Third Series* (1896), the contents being collected and edited by her two friends, Thomas Wentworth Higginson and Mabel Loomis Todd. Several years later, a further generous volume was assembled by her niece, Martha Dickinson Bianchi, entitled *The Single Hound* (1914).

Although the revival of interest in poetry drew attention to the individuality of Emily Dickinson's expression, her readers remained few. Many were cool and critical. An occasional article appeared, showing her "lack of control" or, beneath a cover of condescension, ridiculing her "hit-or-miss grammar, sterile rhythms, and appalling rhymes." Suddenly, without warning, she leaped into international prominence. Almost forty years after her death, her name was everywhere. The year 1924 saw the publication of Martha Dickinson Bianchi's important volume, *The Life and Letters of Emily Dickinson*, the first collected *Complete Poems of Emily Dickinson*, and the first English compilation, *Selected Poems of Emily Dickinson*, edited with a splendid prefatory essay by Conrad Aiken.

The enthusiasm attending the triple appearance was unbounded. Martin Armstrong, the English poet, said in a review, " Mr. Aiken calls Emily Dickinson's poetry ' perhaps the finest by a woman in the English language,' I quarrel only with his ' perhaps.' " Nor were the other comments less definite. " A feminine Blake," " an epigrammatic Walt Whitman," " a New England mystic," were a few of the characterizations fastened upon her. Other appraisals sought to " interpret " her verses in the light of the " mystery " of her life. It is no secret that Emily Dickinson fell in love with a man already married, that she renounced her love, and withdrew from the world. But " the Amherst nun " would have repudiated the analysts as vigorously as she, whose verses and letters brim with mischievous fancy, would have laughed at the grandiose epithets.

In 1929 a collection of " undiscovered " or " withheld " poems, *Further Poems of Emily Dickinson*, was edited by Martha Dickinson Bianchi and Alfred Leete Hampson. There were one hundred and seventy-six hitherto unpublished pieces, and their clear beauty as well as mysterious appearance caused something of a furor. The excitement increased in 1930, the centenary of Emily Dickinson's birth, when three biographers differed with each other. A new volume, *Unpublished Poems by Emily Dickinson*, appeared toward the end of 1935. Another collection entitled *Bolts of Melody* (1945) contained more than 650 poems, many of which were published for the first time and could be numbered among the poet's most characteristic work. Various biographies attempted to reveal the secret of her life and the key to her poetry. The most imaginative of these was Genevieve Taggard's *The Life and Mind of Emily Dickinson* (1930); the most thorough and plausible was *This Was a Poet* (1938) by George Frisbie Whicher.

Emily Dickinson wrote chiefly of four things: Nature, Love, Life, and Death. Much of her work is like inspired improvisations. Some of it is erratic, obviously unfinished, thrown off in the heat of creation; some of it is obscure. But in most of the poems the leaps of thought are so daring, the epithets so fanciful and yet so exact, the imagination so startling and original that the lines are little short of revelation. One gasps at the way this poet packs huge ideas into tense quatrains. Hers is a kind of super-observation which arrests us in such magical and startling phrases as: a dog's "belated feet, like intermittent plush," a hummingbird whose flight is "a route of evanescence, a resonance of emerald," an engine "neighing," a mushroom whose whole career "is shorter than a snake's delay," leaves that "unhooked" themselves from trees, lightnings that "skipped" like mice, the wind "tapping like a tired man."

Her letters, like her poems, have an unpredictable way of turning about their subject. They combine the impish with the mystical; they announce tremendous things in an offhand tone of voice. Few definitions of poetry give us the *feeling* of poetry as sharply as her informal: "If I read a book and it makes my whole body so cold no fire can ever warm me, I know it is poetry. If I feel physically as if the top of my head were taken off, I know this is poetry. These are the only ways I know it."

I'm Nobody! Who Are You?

I'm nobody! Who are you?
Are you nobody, too?
Then there's a pair of us — don't tell!
They'd banish us, you know.

How dreary to be somebody!
How public, like a frog.
To tell your name the livelong day
To an admiring bog!

Hope Is the Thing with Feathers

Hope is the thing with feathers
That perches in the soul,
And sings the tune without the words,
And never stops at all,

And sweetest in the gale is heard;
And sore must be the storm
That could abash the little bird
That kept so many warm.

I've heard it in the chillest land,
And on the strangest sea;
Yet, never, in extremity,
It asked a crumb of me.

Success Is Counted Sweetest

Success is counted sweetest
By those who ne'er succeed.
To comprehend a nectar
Requires sorest need.

Not one of all the purple host
Who took the flag to-day
Can tell the definition,
So clear, of victory,

As he, defeated, dying,
On whose forbidden ear
The distant strains of triumph
Break, agonized and clear.

I Took My Power in My Hand

I took my power in my hand
And went against the world;
'T was not so much as David had,
But I was twice as bold.

I aimed my pebble, but myself
Was all the one that fell.
Was it Goliath was too large,
Or only I too small?

The Return

Though I get home how late, how late!
So I get home, 't will compensate.
Better will be the ecstasy
That they have done expecting me,
When, night descending, dumb and dark,
They hear my unexpected knock.
Transporting must the moment be,
Brewed from decades of agony!

To think just how the fire will burn,
Just how long-cheated eyes will turn
To wonder what myself will say,
And what itself will say to me,
Beguiles the centuries of way!

Escape

I never hear the word " escape "
Without a quicker blood,
A sudden expectation,
A flying attitude.

I never hear of prisons broad
By soldiers battered down,
But I tug childish at my bars —
Only to fail again!

The Bee

Like trains of cars on tracks of plush
I hear the level bee:
A jar across the flowers goes,
Their velvet masonry

Withstands until the sweet assault
Their chivalry consumes,
While he, victorious, tilts away
To vanquish other blooms.

His feet are shod with gauze,
His helmet is of gold;
His breast, a single onyx
With chrysoprase,[1] inlaid.

His labor is a chant,
His idleness a tune;
Oh, for a bee's experience
Of clovers and of noon!

The Mountain

The mountain sat upon the plain
In his eternal chair,
His observation omnifold,
His inquest everywhere.

The seasons prayed around his knees,
Like children round a sire:
Grandfather of the days is he,
Of dawn the ancestor.

The Humming-Bird

A route of evanescence
With a revolving wheel;
A resonance of emerald,
A rush of cochineal;[2]

And every blossom on the bush
Adjusts its tumbled head —
The mail from Tunis, probably,
An easy morning's ride!

[1] *chrysoprase:* a light green stone.   [2] *cochineal:* a red dye.

The Wind

The wind tapped like a tired man,
And like a host, " Come in,"
I boldly answered; entered then
My residence within

A rapid, footless guest,
To offer whom a chair
Were as impossible as hand
A sofa to the air.

No bones had he to bind him,
His speech was like the push
Of numerous humming-birds at once
From a superior bush.

His countenance a billow,
His fingers, if he pass,
Let go a music, as of tunes
Blown tremulous in glass.

He visited, still flitting;
Then, like a timid man,
Again he tapped — 't was flurriedly —
And I became alone.

The Stone

How happy is the little stone
That rambles in the road alone,
And doesn't care about careers,
And exigencies never fears;
Whose coat of elemental brown
A passing universe put on;
And independent as the sun,
Associates or glows alone,
Fulfilling absolute decree
In casual simplicity.

A Book

There is no frigate like a book
   To take us lands away,
Nor any courser like a page
   Of prancing poetry.
This traverse may the poorest take
   Without oppress of toil;
How frugal is the chariot
   That bears a human soul!

Chartless

I never saw a moor,
I never saw the sea;
Yet know I how the heather looks,
And what a wave must be.

I never spoke with God,
Nor visited in Heaven;
Yet certain am I of the spot
As if the chart were given.

Indian Summer

These are the days when birds come back,
A very few, a bird or two,
To take a backward look.

These are the days when skies put on
The old, old sophistries of June, —
A blue and gold mistake.

Oh, fraud that cannot cheat the bee,
Almost thy plausibility
Induces my belief,

Till ranks of seeds their witness bear,
And softly through the altered air
Hurries a timid leaf!

Oh, sacrament of summer days,
Oh, last communion in the haze,
Permit a child to join,

Thy sacred emblems to partake.
Thy consecrated bread to break.
Taste thine immortal wine!

Suspense

Elysium [1] is as far as to
The very nearest room,
If in that room a friend await
Felicity or doom.

What fortitude the soul contains,
That it can so endure
The accent of a coming foot,
The opening of a door.

Inebriate of Air

I taste a liquor never brewed,
From tankards scooped in pearl;
Not all the vats upon the Rhine
Yield such an alcohol!

Inebriate of air am I,
And debauchee of dew,
Reeling, through endless summer days,
From inns of molten blue.

When landlords turn the drunken bee
Out of the foxglove's door,
When butterflies renounce their drams,
I shall but drink the more!

Till seraphs swing their snowy hats,
And saints to windows run,
To see the little tippler
Leaning against the sun!

[1] *Elysium:* The imaginary dwelling place of happy souls. The
ancient poets claimed it was in the Isles of the Blessed.

Joy in Insecurity

Go not too near a house of rose,
The depredation of a breeze
Or inundation of a dew
Alarm its walls away;
Nor try to tie the butterfly;
Nor climb the bars of ecstasy.
In insecurity to lie
Is joy's insuring quality.

Beclouded

The sky is low, the clouds are mean,
A traveling flake of snow
Across a barn or through a rut
Debates if it will go.

A narrow wind complains all day
How some one treated him;
Nature, like us, is sometimes caught
Without her diadem.

Pedigree

The pedigree of honey
    Does not concern the bee;
A clover, any time, to him
    Is aristocracy.

Beauty and Truth

I died for beauty, but was scarce
Adjusted in the tomb,
When one who died for truth was lain
In an adjoining room.

He questioned softly why I failed?
" For beauty," I replied.
" And I for truth, — the two are one;
We brethren are," he said.

And so, as kinsmen met a night,
We talked between the rooms,
Until the moss had reached our lips
And covered up our names.

Mysteries

The murmur of a bee
A witchcraft yieldeth me.
If any ask me why,
'Twere easier to die
Than tell.

The red upon the hill
Taketh away my will;
If anybody sneer,
Take care, for God is here,
That's all.

The breaking of the day
Addeth to my degree;
If any ask me how,
Artist, who drew me so,
Must tell!

A Cemetery

This quiet Dust was Gentlemen and Ladies,
          And Lads and Girls;
Was laughter and ability and sighing,
          And frocks and curls.
This passive place a Summer's nimble mansion,
          Where Bloom and Bees
Fulfilled their Oriental Circuit,
          Then ceased like these.

Precious Words

He ate and drank the precious words.
His spirit grew robust;
He knew no more that he was poor,

Nor that his frame was dust.
He danced along the dingy days.
And this bequest of wings
Was but a book. What liberty
A loosened spirit brings!

Hunger

I had been hungry all the years;
My noon had come to dine;
I, trembling, drew the table near,
And touched the curious wine.

'Twas this on tables I had seen,
When turning, hungry, lone,
I looked in windows, for the wealth
I could not hope to own.

I did not know the ample bread;
'Twas so unlike the crumb
The birds and I had often shared
In nature's dining-room.

The plenty hurt me, 'twas so new —
Myself felt ill and odd,
As berry of a mountain bush
Transplanted to the road.

Nor was I hungry; so I found
That hunger was a way
Of persons outside windows,
The entering takes away.

JOHN HAY

John Hay was born at Salem, Indiana, October 8, 1838, was
graduated from Brown University in 1858, and was admitted to the
Illinois bar a few years later. He became private secretary to Lincoln, then major and assistant adjutant-general under General Gill-
more, then secretary of legation at Paris, *chargé d'affaires* at Vi-
enna and secretary of legation at Madrid.

JOHN HAY

45

His few vivid *Pike County Ballads* came as a happy accident.
When Hay returned from Spain in 1870, bringing with him his
Castilian Days, he had visions of becoming a traditional lyric poet.
But he found everyone reading Bret Harte's short stories and the
new expression of the rude West. He speculated upon the possi-
bility of doing something similar, translating the characters into
poetry. The result was the six racy ballads in a vein utterly different from everything Hay wrote before or after.

Hay was in politics all the latter part of his life, and one of the
most brilliant Secretaries of State. He died in 1905.

Jim Bludso

Wall, no! I can't tell whar he lives,
    Becase he don't live, you see;
Leastways, he's got out of the habit
    Of livin' like you and me.
Whar have you been for the last three year
    That you haven't heard folks tell
How Jimmy Bludso passed in his checks
    The night of the Prairie Belle?

He warn't no saint, — them engineers
    Is all pretty much alike, —
One wife in Natchez-under-the-Hill
    And another one here, in Pike;
A keerless man in his talk was Jim,
    And an awkward hand in a row,
But he never flunked, and he never lied, —
    I reckon he never knowed how.

And this was all the religion he had:
    To treat his engine well;
Never be passed on the river;
    To mind the pilot's bell;
And if ever the Prairie Belle took fire,
    A thousand times he swore,
He'd hold her nozzle agin the bank
    Till the last soul got ashore.

All boats has their day on the Mississip,
    And her day come at last, —
The Movastar was a better boat,

But the Belle she *wouldn't* be passed.
And so she came tearin' along that night —
  The oldest craft on the line —
With a nigger squat on her safety-valve,
  And her furnace crammed, rosin and pine.

The fire bust out as she clar'd the bar,
  And burnt a hole in the night,
And quick as a flash she turned and made
  For that willer-bank on the right.
Thar was runnin' and cussin', but Jim yelled out,
  Over all the infernal roar,
" I'll hold her nozzle agin the bank
  Till the last galoot's ashore."

Through the hot, black breath of the burnin' boat
  Jim Bludso's voice was heard,
And they all had trust in his cussedness,
  And knowed he would keep his word.
And, sure's you're born, they all got off
  Afore the smokestacks fell, —
And Bludso's ghost went up alone
  In the smoke of the Prairie Belle.

He warn't no saint, — but at Jedgment
  I'd run my chance with Jim,
'Longside of some pious gentlemen
  That wouldn't shook hands with him.
He seen his duty, a dead-sure thing. —
  And went for it thar and then;
And Christ ain't a-goin' to be too hard
  On a man that died for men.

BRET HARTE

(Francis) Bret Harte was born August 25, 1839, at Albany, New York. Late in 1853, his widowed mother went to California with a party of relatives, and when he was fifteen Bret Harte followed. There he became a journalist.

Harte's fame came suddenly. Late in the sixties, he had written a burlesque in rhyme ("Plain Language from Truthful James") about two Western gamblers trying to fleece a guileless Chinaman who claimed to know nothing about cards but who, it turned out, was scarcely as innocent as he appeared. Instead of passing unnoticed, the poem was quoted everywhere; it swept the West and captivated the East. When *The Luck of Roaring Camp* followed, Harte became not only a national but an international figure. *East and West Poems* appeared in 1871; in 1872 Harte published an enlarged *Poetical Works* including many earlier pieces. His scores of short stories represent Harte at his best; they are the work of a lesser and self-conscious Dickens.

In 1878 he went to Germany as consul. Two years later he was transferred to Scotland and, after five years there, went to London, where he remained the rest of his life. Harte's later period remains mysteriously shrouded. He never came back to America; he separated himself from all the most intimate associations of his early life, and died, suddenly, at Camberley, England, May 6, 1902.

The Aged Stranger
(*An incident of the war*)

" I was with Grant — " the stranger said;
    Said the farmer, " Say no more,
But rest thee here at my cottage porch,
    For thy feet are weary and sore."

" I was with Grant — " the stranger said;
    Said the farmer, " Nay, no more, —
I prithee sit at my frugal board,
    And eat of my humble store.

" How fares my boy, — my soldier boy,
    Of the old Ninth Army Corps?
I warrant he bore him gallantly
    In the smoke and the battle's roar! "

" I know him not," said the aged man,
    " And, as I remarked before,
I was with Grant — " " Nay, nay, I know,"
    Said the farmer, " say no more:

" He fell in battle, — I see, alas!
    Thou'dst smooth these tidings o'er, —
Nay, speak the truth, whatever it be,
    Though it rend my bosom's core.

" How fell he? — with his face to the foe,
  Upholding the flag he bore?
Oh, say not that my boy disgraced
  The uniform that he wore! "

" I cannot tell," said the aged man,
  " And should have remarked before
That I was with Grant — in Illinois —
  Some three years before the war."

Then the farmer spake him never a word,
  But beat with his fist full sore
That aged man, who had worked for Grant
  Some three years before the war!

" Jim "

Say there! P'r'aps
Some on you chaps
  Might know Jim Wild?
Well, — no offense:
Thar ain't no sense
  In gittin' riled!

Jim was my chum
  Up on the Bar:
That's why I come
  Down from up yar,
Lookin' for Jim.
Thank ye, sir! *You*
Ain't of that crew, —
  Blest if you are!

Money? Not much:
  That ain't my kind;
I ain't no such.
  Rum? I don't mind,
Seein' it's you.

Well, this yer Jim, —
Did you know him?
Jes' 'bout your size;

Same kind of eyes; —
Well, that is strange:
    Why, it's two year
    Since he came here,
Sick, for a change.

Well, here's to us:
        Eh?
The h—— you say!
        Dead?
That little cuss?

What makes you star',
You over thar?
Can't a man drop
's glass in yer shop
But you must r'ar?
    It wouldn't take
    D——d much to break
You and your bar.

        Dead!
Poor — little — Jim!
Why, thar was me,
Jones, and Bob Lee,
Harry and Ben, —
No-account men:
Then to take *him!*

Well, thar — Good-bye.
No more, sir — I —
        Eh?
What's that you say?
Why, dern it! — sho! —
No? Yes! By Joe!
        Sold!
Sold! Why, you limb,
You ornery,
    Derned, old,
Long-legged Jim.

Cincinnatus (Heine) Miller, or, to give him the name he adopted, Joaquin Miller, was born in 1841 of immigrant parents. As he himself writes, " My cradle was a covered wagon, pointed west. I was born in a covered wagon, I am told, at or about the time it crossed the line dividing Indiana from Ohio." The distance covered from the midwestern to the far western home was about 3000 miles, and it took almost eight months to make the journey.

At fifteen Miller lived with the Indians as one of them; in 1859 (at the age of eighteen) he attended a mission-school " college " in Eugene, Oregon; between 1860 and 1865 he was express-messenger, editor of a pacifist newspaper suppressed for opposing the Civil War, lawyer and, occasionally, a poet. He held a minor judgeship from 1866 to 1870.

His first book (*Specimens*) appeared in 1868, his second (*Joaquin et al.*, from which he took his name) in 1869. No response — not even from " the bards of San Francisco Bay " to whom he dedicated the latter volume. He was chagrined, discouraged, angry. He shook the dust of America from his feet; went to London; published a volume (*Pacific Poems*) at his own expense and — overnight — became a sensation! When he entered Victorian parlors in his velvet jacket, hip-boots, and flowing hair, childhood visions of the " wild and woolly Westerner " were realized; the very bombast of his work was glorified as " typically American."

In 1887 he returned to California, helping to found an experimental Greek academy for aspiring writers. He died there, after a determinedly picturesque life, in 1913.

from Byron

In men whom men condemn as ill
I find so much of goodness still,
In men whom men pronounce divine
I find so much of sin and blot,
I do not dare to draw a line
Between the two, where God has not.

Columbus

Behind him lay the gray Azores,
   Behind the Gates of Hercules;
Before him not the ghost of shores,
   Before him only shoreless seas.
The good mate said: " Now must we pray,

For lo! the very stars are gone.
Brave Admiral, speak, what shall I say? "
  " Why, say ' Sail on! sail on! and on! ' "

" My men grow mutinous day by day;
  My men grow ghastly wan and weak."
The stout mate thought of home; a spray
  Of salt wave washed his swarthy cheek.
" What shall I say, brave Admiral, say,
  If we sight naught but seas at dawn? "
" Why, you shall say at break of day,
  ' Sail on! sail on! sail on! and on! ' "

They sailed and sailed, as winds might blow,
  Until at last the blanched mate said,
" Why, now not even God would know
  Should I and all my men fall dead.
These very winds forget their way,
  For God from these dread seas is gone.
Now speak, brave Admiral, speak and say " —
  He said: " Sail on! sail on! and on! "

They sailed. They sailed. Then spake the mate:
  " This mad sea shows his teeth tonight.
He curls his lip, he lies in wait,
  With lifted teeth, as if to bite!
Brave Admiral, say but one good word:
  What shall we do when hope is gone? "
The words leapt like a leaping sword:
  " Sail on! sail on! sail on! and on! "

Then, pale and worn, he kept his deck,
  And peered through darkness. Ah, that night
Of all dark nights! And then a speck —
  A light! a light! a light! a light!
It grew, a starlit flag unfurled!
  It grew to be Time's burst of dawn.
He gained a world; he gave that world
  Its grandest lesson: " On! sail on! "

Edward Rowland Sill was born at Windsor, Connecticut, in 1841. In 1861 he was graduated from Yale and shortly thereafter his poor health compelled him West. After various unsuccessful experiments, he drifted into teaching, mostly in the English department of the University of California. *The Hermitage*, his first volume, was published in 1867. Two posthumous books are *Poems* (1887) and *Hermione and Other Poems* (1899).

Sill died, after bringing something of the Eastern culture to the West, in 1887. " Opportunity " has persisted not only because of its "message" but because of its vigorous expression.

Opportunity

This I beheld, or dreamed it in a dream: —
There spread a cloud of dust along a plain;
And underneath the cloud, or in it, raged
A furious battle, and men yelled, and swords
Shocked upon swords and shields. A prince's banner
Wavered, then staggered backward, hemmed by foes.
A craven hung along the battle's edge,
And thought, " Had I a sword of keener steel —
That blue blade that the king's son bears, — but this
Blunt thing — ! " he snapt and flung it from his hand,
And lowering crept away and left the field.
Then came the king's son, wounded, sore bestead,
And weaponless, and saw the broken sword,
Hilt-buried in the dry and trodden sand,
And ran and snatched it, and with battle-shout
Lifted afresh he hewed his enemy down,
And saved a great cause that heroic day.

SIDNEY LANIER

Sidney Lanier was born at Macon, Georgia, February 3, 1842. His was a family of musicians, and it is not surprising that his verse emphasizes — even overstresses — the influence of music on poetry. He attended Oglethorpe College, was graduated at the age of eighteen and, a year later, volunteered as a private in the Confederate army. After several months' imprisonment (he had been cap-

tured while acting as signal officer on a blockade-runner), Lanier
was released in February, 1865.

After a brief career as lawyer, Lanier became a flute-player in
the Peabody Symphony Orchestra in Baltimore. Here he wrote
his best poetry. In 1879 he was made lecturer in Johns Hopkins
University; it was for his courses there that he wrote a brilliant if
not conclusive study, *The Science of English Verse*. Besides his
highly rhythmical and almost hypnotic poetry, he wrote several
books for boys, the two most popular being *The Boys' Froissart*
(1878) and *The Boys' King Arthur* (1880). He died, a victim of
tuberculosis, in the mountains of North Carolina, September 7,
1881.

"The Marshes of Glynn" is generally accepted as Lanier's
most important poem. It has depth of feeling, impressive word-
pictures, and a musical undercurrent which sustains the lines. The
continually changing rhythms rise and fall with almost orchestral
richness. But the poem's greatest accomplishment is its emotional
progress. Beginning with a slow description of dusky woods, the
poem grows lighter and swifter, opens wide vistas, and ends on a
note of spiritual greatness.

The Marshes of Glynn

Glooms of the live-oaks, beautiful-braided and woven
With intricate shades of the vines that myriad-cloven
   Clamber the forks of the multiform boughs,—
      Emerald twilights,—
      Virginal shy lights,
Wrought of the leaves to allure to the whisper of vows,
When lovers pace timidly down through the green colon-
      nades
Of the dim sweet woods, of the dear dark woods,
   Of the heavenly woods and glades,
That run to the radiant marginal sand-beach within
      The wide sea-marshes of Glynn;—

Beautiful glooms, soft dusks in the noon-day fire,—
Wildwood privacies, closets of lone desire,
Chamber from chamber parted with wavering arras of
      leaves,—
Cells for the passionate pleasure of prayer to the soul that
      grieves,
Pure with a sense of the passing of saints through the wood,
Cool for the dutiful weighing of ill with good;—

O braided dusks of the oak and woven shades of the vine,
While the riotous noon-day sun of the June-day long did
    shine
Ye held me fast in your heart and I held you fast in mine;
But now when the noon is no more, and riot is rest,
And the sun is a-wait at the ponderous gate of the West,
And the slant yellow beam down the wood-aisle doth seem
Like a lane into heaven that leads from a dream, —
Ay, now, when my soul all day hath drunken the soul of the
    oak,
And my heart is at ease from men, and the wearisome sound
    of the stroke
    Of the scythe of time and the trowel of trade is low,
    And belief overmasters doubt, and I know that I know,
    And my spirit is grown to a lordly great compass within,
That the length and the breadth and the sweep of the marshes
    of Glynn
Will work me no fear like the fear they have wrought me of
    yore
When length was fatigue, and when breadth was but bitter-
    ness sore,
And when terror and shrinking and dreary unnamable pain
Drew over me out of the merciless miles of the plain, —

Oh, now, unafraid, I am fain to face
    The vast sweet visage of space.
To the edge of the wood I am drawn, I am drawn,
Where the gray beach glimmering runs, as a belt of the dawn,
    For a mete and a mark
        To the forest-dark: —
            So:
Affable live-oak, leaning low, —
Thus — with your favor — soft, with a reverent hand
(Not lightly touching your person, Lord of the land!),
Bending your beauty aside, with a step I stand
On the firm-packed sand,
        Free
By a world of marsh that borders a world of sea.

    Sinuous southward and sinuous northward the shimmering
        band
    Of the sand-beach fastens the fringe of the marsh to the
        folds of the land.

Inward and outward to northward and southward the beach-
    lines linger and curl
As a silver-wrought garment that clings to and follows the
    firm sweet limbs of a girl.
Vanishing, swerving, evermore curving again into sight,
Softly the sand-beach wavers away to a dim gray looping of
    light.
And what if behind me to westward the wall of the woods
    stands high?
The world lies east: how ample, the marsh and the sea and
    the sky!
A league and a league of marsh-grass, waist-high, broad in the
    blade,
Green, and all of a height, and unflecked with a light or a
    shade,
Stretch leisurely off, in a pleasant plain,
To the terminal blue of the main.

Oh, what is abroad in the marsh and the terminal sea?
    Somehow my soul seems suddenly free
From the weighing of fate and the sad discussion of sin,
By the length and the breadth and the sweep of the marshes
    of Glynn.

Ye marshes, how candid and simple and nothing-withholding
    and free
Ye publish yourselves to the sky and offer yourselves to the
    sea!
Tolerant plains, that suffer the sea and the rains and the sun,
Ye spread and span like the catholic man who hath mightily
    won
God out of knowledge and good out of infinite pain
And sight out of blindness and purity out of a stain.

As the marsh-hen secretly builds on the watery sod,
Behold I will build me a nest on the greatness of God:
I will fly in the greatness of God as the marsh-hen flies
In the freedom that fills all the space 'twixt the marsh and the
    skies:
By so many roots as the marsh-grass sends in the sod
I will heartily lay me a-hold on the greatness of God:
Oh, like to the greatness of God is the greatness within
The range of the marshes, the liberal marshes of Glynn.

And the sea lends large, as the marsh: lo, out of his plenty the
    sea
Pours fast: full soon the time of the flood-tide must be:
Look how the grace of the sea doth go
About and about through the intricate channels that flow
      Here and there,
         Everywhere,
Till his waters have flooded the uttermost creeks and the low-
    lying lanes,
And the marsh is meshed with a million veins,
That like as with rosy and silvery essences flow
In the rose-and-silver evening glow.

      Farewell, my lord Sun!
The creeks overflow: a thousand rivulets run
'Twixt the roots of the sod; the blades of the marsh-grass stir;
Passeth a hurrying sound of wings that westward whirr;
Passeth, and all is still; and the currents cease to run;
And the sea and the marsh are one.
How still the plains of the waters be!
The tide in his ecstasy.
The tide is at his highest height:
      And it is night.

And now from the Vast of the Lord will the waters of sleep
Roll in on the souls of men,
But who will reveal to our waking ken
The forms that swim and the shapes that creep
      Under the waters of sleep?
And I would I could know what swimmeth below when the
    tide comes in
On the length and breadth of the marvelous marshes of
    Glynn.

JAMES WHITCOMB RILEY

James Whitcomb Riley, possibly the most widely read native
poet of his day, was born October 7, 1849, in Greenfield, Indiana,
twenty miles from Indianapolis, where he spent his later years and
died July 22, 1916. Riley was not, as may be inferred from his bucolic poems, a struggling child of the soil. His father was a lawyer

in comfortable circumstances, and Riley was given a good education and prepared for the law. However, his temperament was restless; it made him try sign-painting, circus advertising, journalism.

In 1882, when he was on the staff of the Indianapolis *Journal,* he began the series of dialect poems which he claimed were by a rude and unlettered farmer, one "Benj. F. Johnson, of Boone, the Hoosier poet," and Riley printed long extracts from "Johnson's" ungrammatical and badly-spelled letters to prove his "find." A collection of these rustic verses appeared, in 1883, as *The Ole Swimmin' Hole,* and Riley leaped into widespread popularity. Other collections followed rapidly: *Afterwhiles* (1887), *Old-Fashioned Roses* (1888), *Rhymes of Childhood* (1890). All met an instant response; Riley endeared himself, by his homely idiom and his ingenuity, to a countryful of readers, adolescent and adult.

Riley's simplicity is not always as artless as it seems. Time and again, one can see him consciously trading on the emotions of his readers. He is the poet of sentiment rather than of convictions, of philosophies that never disturb, of sweet truisms rather than searching truths.

That work of his which may endure will survive because of the personal flavor that Riley often poured into it. Such poems as "When the Frost is on the Punkin" and "The Raggedy Man" are a part of American folk literature.

"When the Frost Is on the Punkin"

When the frost is on the punkin and the fodder's in the shock,
And you hear the kyouck and gobble of the struttin' turkey-
    cock,
And the clackin' of the guineys, and the cluckin' of the hens,
And the rooster's hallylooer as he tiptoes on the fence;
O, it's then the time a feller is a-feelin' at his best,
With the risin' sun to greet him from a night of peaceful rest,
As he leaves the house, bareheaded, and goes out to feed the
    stock,
When the frost is on the punkin and the fodder's in the shock.

They's something kindo' harty-like about the atmusfere
When the heat of summer's over and the coolin' fall is here —
Of course we miss the flowers, and the blossoms on the trees,
And the mumble of the hummin'-birds and buzzin' of the
    bees;
But the air's so appetizin'; and the landscape through the haze
Of a crisp and sunny morning of the airly autumn days

Is a pictur' that no painter has the colorin' to mock —
When the frost is on the punkin and the fodder's in the shock.

The husky, rusty russel of the tossels of the corn,
And the raspin' of the tangled leaves as golden as the morn;
The stubble in the furries — kind o' lonesome-like, but still
A-preachin' sermuns to us of the barns they growed to fill;
The strawstack in the medder, and the reaper in the shed;
The hosses in theyr stalls below — the clover overhead! —
O, it sets my heart a-clickin' like the tickin' of a clock
When the frost is on the punkin and the fodder's in the shock.

Then your apples all is gethered, and the ones a feller keeps
Is poured around the cellar-floor in red and yaller heaps;
And your cider-makin's over, and your wimmern-folks is
     through
With theyr mince and apple-butter, and theyr souse and sau-
     sage too! . . .
I don't know how to tell it — but ef such a thing could be
As the angels wantin' boardin', and they'd call around on
me —
I'd want to 'commodate 'em — all the whole-indurin' flock —
When the frost is on the punkin and the fodder's in the shock.

A Parting Guest

What delightful hosts are they —
    Life and Love!
Lingeringly I turn away,
    This late hour, yet glad enough
They have not withheld from me
    Their high hospitality.
So, with face lit with delight
    And all gratitude, I stay
    Yet to press their hands and say,
" Thanks. — So fine a time! Good night."

Born in St. Louis, Missouri, September 3, 1850, Eugene Field belongs to the literature of the West. Colorado and the Rocky Mountain region claimed him as their own and Field never repudiated the allegiance. Field's area of education embraced New England, Missouri, and what European territory he could cover in six months. At twenty-three he became a reporter on the St. Louis *Evening Journal*, and devoted the rest of his life to journalism.

Though Field may be overrated by some readers, there is little doubt that certain of his child lyrics, his ballads, and his brilliant burlesques will occupy a niche in American letters. Readers will find much to delight them in his happy, homely, and often sentimental verses. Field died in Chicago, Illinois, November 4, 1895.

Little Boy Blue

The little toy dog is covered with dust,
    But sturdy and stanch he stands;
The little toy soldier is red with rust,
    And his musket molds in his hands.
Time was when the little toy dog was new,
    And the soldier was passing fair;
And that was the time when our Little Boy Blue
    Kissed them and put them there.

" Now don't you go till I come," he said,
    " And don't you make any noise! "
So, toddling off to his trundle bed,
    He dreamt of the pretty toys;
And, as he was dreaming, an angel song
    Awakened our Little Boy Blue —
Oh! the years are many, the years are long,
    But the little toy friends are true!

Ay, faithful to Little Boy Blue they stand,
    Each in the same old place,
Awaiting the touch of a little hand,
    The smile of a little face;
And they wonder, as waiting the long years through
    In the dust of that little chair,
What has become of our Little Boy Blue,
    Since he kissed them and put them there.

Seein' Things

I ain't afraid uv snakes or toads, or bugs or worms or mice,
An' things 'at girls are skeered uv I think are awful nice!
I'm pretty brave I guess; an' yet I hate to go to bed,
For, when I'm tucked up warm an' snug an' when my prayers
    are said,
Mother tells me " Happy Dreams " an' takes away the light,
An' leaves me lyin' all alone an' seein' things at night!

Sometimes they're in the corner, sometimes they're by the
    door,
Sometimes they're all a-standin' in the middle uv the floor;
Sometimes they are a-sittin' down, sometimes they're walkin'
    round
So softly and so creepy-like they never make a sound!
Sometimes they are as black as ink, an' other times they're
    white —
But color ain't no difference when you see things at night!

Once, when I licked a feller 'at had just moved on our street,
An' father sent me up to bed without a bite to eat,
I woke up in the dark an' saw things standin' in a row,
A-lookin' at me cross-eyed an' p'intin' at me — so!
Oh, my! I wuz so skeered 'at time I never slep' a mite —
It's almost alluz when I'm bad I see things at night!

Lucky thing I ain't a girl or I'd be skeered to death!
Bein' I'm a boy, I duck my head an' hold my breath.
An' I am, oh so sorry I'm a naughty boy, an' then
I promise to be better an' I say my prayers again!
Gran'ma tells me that's the only way to make it right
When a feller has been wicked an' sees things at night!

An' so when other naughty boys would coax me into sin,
I try to skwush the Tempter's voice 'at urges me within;
An' when they's pie for supper, or cakes 'at's big an' nice,
I want to — but I do not pass my plate f'r them things twice!
No, ruther let Starvation wipe me slowly out o' sight
Then I should keep a-livin' on an' seein' things at night!

Edwin Markham was born in Oregon City, Oregon, April 23, 1852, the youngest son of pioneer parents. His father died before the boy reached his fifth year and in 1857 he was taken by his mother to a wild valley in the Suisun Hills in central California. Here he grew to young manhood; farming, broncho-riding, laboring on a cattle ranch, educating himself in the primitive country schools and supplementing his studies with whatever books he could procure.

In his forties a new force surged through him; a sense of outrage at the inequality of human struggle voiced itself in the sweeping and sonorous poem, "The Man with the Hoe." Inspired by Millet's painting, Markham made the bowed, broken French peasant a symbol of the poverty-stricken toiler in all lands — his was a protest not against labor but the drudgery, the soul-destroying exploitation of labor. The success of the poem upon its appearance in the San Francisco *Examiner* (January 15, 1899) was instantaneous and universal. Soon it appeared in every part of the globe; it was quoted and copied in every walk of life, in the literary world, the leisure world, the labor world. It was incorporated in Markham's first volume *The Man with the Hoe and Other Poems* (1899).

The same passion that fired Markham to champion the common worker equipped him to write fittingly of the Great Commoner in *Lincoln, and Other Poems* (1901). Markham's other volumes are less distinctive, although none is without his humanitarian spirit. Never reaching the greatest heights, there are accents of dignity in *The Shoes of Happiness* (1914), *The Gates of Paradise* (1920), and *New Poems: Eighty Songs at Eighty* (1932), published with a nice appropriateness on the poet's eightieth birthday. Many of the quatrains are memorable epigrams.

Markham came East in 1901, where he made his home on Staten Island, New York, until his death on March 7, 1940.

Brotherhood

The crest and crowning of all good,
Life's final star, is Brotherhood;
For it will bring again to Earth
Her long-lost Poesy and Mirth;
Will send new light on every face,
A kingly power upon the race.
And till it come, we men are slaves,
And travel downward to the dust of graves.
Come, clear the way, then, clear the way;

Blind creeds and kings have had their day;
Break the dead branches from the path;
Our hope is in the aftermath —
Our hope is in heroic men
Star-led to build the world again.
Make way for Brotherhood — make way for Man!

Outwitted

He drew a circle that shut me out —
Heretic, rebel, a thing to flout.
But Love and I had the wit to win:
We drew a circle that took him in!

The Man with the Hoe

(Written after seeing Millet's world-famous painting)

Bowed by the weight of centuries he leans
Upon his hoe and gazes on the ground,
The emptiness of ages in his face,
And on his back the burden of the world.
Who made him dead to rapture and despair,
A thing that grieves not and that never hopes,
Stolid and stunned, a brother to the ox?
Who loosened and let down this brutal jaw?
Whose was the hand that slanted back this brow?
Whose breath blew out the light within this brain?

Is this the Thing the Lord God made and gave
To have dominion over sea and land;
To trace the stars and search the heavens for power;
To feel the passion of Eternity?
Is this the dream He dreamed who shaped the suns
And marked their ways upon the ancient deep?
Down all the caverns of Hell to their last gulf
There is no shape more terrible than this —
More tongued with censure of the world's blind greed —
More filled with signs and portents for the soul —
More packed with danger to the universe.

What gulfs between him and the seraphim!
Slave of the wheel of labor, what to him

Are Plato and the swing of Pleiades?
What the long reaches of the peaks of song,
The rift of dawn, the reddening of the rose?
Through this dread shape the suffering ages look;
Time's tragedy is in that aching stoop;
Through this dread shape humanity betrayed,
Plundered, profaned, and disinherited,
Cries protest to the Judges of the World,
A protest that is also prophecy.

O masters, lords and rulers in all lands,
Is this the handiwork you give to God,
This monstrous thing distorted and soul-quenched?
How will you ever straighten up this shape;
Touch it again with immortality;
Give back the upward looking and the light;
Rebuild in it the music and the dream;
Make right the immemorial infamies,
Perfidious wrongs, immedicable woes?

O masters, lords and rulers in all lands,
How will the Future reckon with this man?
How answer his brute question in that hour
When whirlwinds of rebellion shake all shores?
How will it be with kingdoms and with kings —
With those who shaped him to the thing he is —
When this dumb terror shall rise to judge the world,
After the silence of the centuries?

The Avengers

The laws are the secret avengers,
    And they rule above all lands;
They come on wool-soft sandals,
    But they strike with iron hands.

Preparedness

For all your days prepare,
    And meet them ever alike:
When you are the anvil, bear —
    When you are the hammer, strike.

Lincoln, the Man of the People

When the Norn [1] Mother saw the Whirlwind Hour
Greatening and darkening as it hurried on,
She left the Heaven of Heroes and came down
To make a man to meet the mortal need.
She took the tried clay of the common road —
Clay warm yet with the genial heat of earth,
Dasht through it all a strain of prophecy;
Tempered the heap with thrill of human tears;
Then mixt a laughter with the serious stuff.
Into the shape she breathed a flame to light
That tender, tragic, ever-changing face;
Moving — all husht — behind the mortal veil.
Here was a man to hold against the world,
A man to match the mountains and the sea.

The color of the ground was in him, the red earth;
The smack and tang of elemental things:
The rectitude and patience of the cliff;
The good-will of the rain that loves all leaves;
The friendly welcome of the wayside well;
The courage of the bird that dares the sea;
The gladness of the wind that shakes the corn;
The pity of the snow that hides all scars;
The secrecy of streams that make their way
Under the mountain to the rifted rock;
The tolerance and equity of light
That gives as freely to the shrinking flower
As to the great oak flaring to the wind —
To the grave's low hill as to the Matterhorn [2]
That shoulders out the sky. Sprung from the West,
He drank the valorous youth of a new world.
The strength of virgin forests braced his mind,
The hush of spacious prairies stilled his soul.
His words were oaks in acorns; and his thoughts
Were roots that firmly gript the granite truth.

Up from log cabin to the Capitol,
One fire was on his spirit, one resolve —

[1] One of the Norse goddesses who determines the fates of men.
[2] *Matterhorn:* one of the highest mountains in the Alps.

To send the keen ax to the root of wrong,
Clearing a free way for the feet of God,
The eyes of conscience testing every stroke,
To make his deed the measure of a man.
He built the rail-pile as he built the State,
Pouring his splendid strength through every blow;
The grip that swung the ax in Illinois
Was on the pen that set a people free.

So came the Captain with the mighty heart;
And when the judgment thunders split the house,
Wrenching the rafters from their ancient rest,
He held the ridgepole up, and spiked again
The rafters of the Home. He held his place —
Held the long purpose like a growing tree —
Held on through blame and faltered not at praise.
And when he fell in whirlwind, he went down
As when a lordly cedar, green with boughs,
Goes down with a great shout upon the hills,
And leaves a lonesome place against the sky.

LIZETTE WOODWORTH REESE

Lizette Woodworth Reese was born January 9, 1856, near Baltimore, Maryland, where she lived until she died, December 17, 1935,
a few weeks before her eightieth birthday. She was educated chiefly
in private schools, and taught English in the Western High School
at Baltimore. In 1923 the alumni of the High School where she had
taught more than a score of years presented the school with a
bronze tablet inscribed with her sonnet " Tears," which had become one of the most famous of American poems.

A Handful of Lavender (1891), *A Quiet Road* (1896), and *A
Wayside Lute* (1909) establish an artistry which, for all its seemingly old-fashioned elegance, is as spontaneous as it is skillful.
Here are no verbal tricks, no false postures; here are the qualities
which are never dependent on literary fashion. From 1909 to 1920
there was a silence. Suddenly her work appeared again, keener
than ever. *Spicewood* was published in 1920, *Wild Cherry* in 1923.
Both volumes, as well as *Selected Poems* (1926), are full of the
same things which formerly held Miss Reese. Again and again she
writes of lilacs and blackberry rain, of judas-blossoms and daffo-

dils, of Spring ecstasy and lost love. But there is always something which makes the very repetitions take on a light which is fresh and clear and persuasive.

Tears

When I consider Life and its few years —
A wisp of fog betwixt us and the sun;
A call to battle, and the battle done
Ere the last echo dies within our ears;
A rose choked in the grass; an hour of fears;
The gusts that past a darkening shore do beat;
The burst of music down an unlistening street, —
I wonder at the idleness of tears.

Ye old, old dead, and ye of yesternight,
Chieftains, and bards, and keepers of the sheep,
By every cup of sorrow that you had,
Loose me from tears, and make me see aright
How each hath back what once he stayed to weep:
Homer his sight, David his little lad! [1]

Spicewood

The spicewood burns along the gray, spent sky,
In moist unchimneyed places, in a wind,
That whips it all before, and all behind,
Into one thick, rude flame, now low, now high.
It is the first, the homeliest thing of all —
At sight of it, that lad that by it fares,
Whistles afresh his foolish, town-caught airs —
A thing so honey-colored and so tall!

It is as though the young Year, ere he pass,
To the white riot of the cherry tree,
Would fain accustom us, or here, or there,

[1] *Homer:* the blind Greek poet, author of the *Iliad* and *Odyssey.* . . . *David:* King of Israel, who mourned the death of his son Absalom. " O my son Absalom! Would God I had died for thee, O Absalom, my son, my son! " *2 Samuel:* 18.

To his new sudden ways with bough and grass,
So starts with what is humble, plain to see,
And all familiar as a cup, a chair.

A Flower of Mullein [1]

I am too near, too clear a thing for you,
A flower of mullein in a crack of wall,
The villagers half see, or not at all;
Part of the weather, like the wind or dew.
You love to pluck the different, and find
Stuff for your joy in cloudy loveliness;
You love to fumble at a door, and guess
At some strange happening that may wait behind.

Yet life is full of tricks, and it is plain,
That men drift back to some worn field or roof,
To grip at comfort in a room, a stair;
To warm themselves at some flower down a lane:
You, too, may long, grown tired of the aloof,
For the sweet surety of the common air.

BLISS CARMAN

(William) Bliss Carman was born at Fredericton, New Brunswick, Canada, April 15, 1861, of a long line of United Empire Loyalists who withdrew from Connecticut at the time of the Revolutionary War. Carman was educated at the University of New Brunswick, Edinburgh, and Harvard. He took up residence in the United States about 1889 and lived there until his death in Connecticut in 1929.

In 1893 Carman issued his first book, *Low Tide on Grande Pré: A Book of Lyrics*. It was immediately successful, running quickly into a second edition. A vivid buoyancy made his worship of Nature frankly pagan as contrasted to the moralizing tributes of most of his predecessors. This freshness and irresponsible whimsy made Carman the natural collaborator for Richard Hovey, and when their first joint *Songs from Vagabondia* appeared in 1894, Carman's fame was established.

[1] *Mullein:* a common wayside weed.

Although the *Vagabondia* collections contain Carman's best poems, several of his other volumes (he published more than twenty) vibrate with a bounding pulse. A kind of radiance rises from *Ballads of Lost Haven* (1897), *From the Book of Myths* (1902), *Songs of the Sea Children* (1904), and *Wild Garden* (1929).

A Vagabond Song

There is something in the autumn that is native to my
    blood —
Touch of manner, hint of mood;
And my heart is like a rhyme,
With the yellow and the purple and the crimson keeping
    time.

The scarlet of the maples can shake me like a cry
Of bugles going by.
And my lonely spirit thrills
To see the frosty asters like a smoke upon the hills.

There is something in October sets the gypsy blood astir;
We must rise and follow her,
When from every hill of flame
She calls and calls each vagabond by name.

Hem and Haw

Hem and Haw were the sons of sin,
Created to shally and shirk;
Hem lay 'round and Haw looked on
While God did all the work.

Hem was a fogy, and Haw was a prig,
For both had the dull, dull mind;
And whenever they found a thing to do,
They yammered and went it blind.

Hem was the father of bigots and bores;
As the sands of the sea were they.
And Haw was the father of all the tribe
Who criticize today.

But God was an artist from the first,
And knew what he was about;
While over his shoulder sneered these two,
And advised him to rub it out.

They prophesied ruin ere man was made;
" Such folly must surely fail! "
And when he was done, " Do you think, my Lord,
He's better without a tail? "

And still in the honest working world,
With posture and hint and smirk,
These sons of the devil are standing by
While man does all the work.

They balk endeavor and baffle reform,
In the sacred name of law;
And over the quavering voice of Hem
Is the droning voice of Haw.

Daisies

Over the shoulders and slopes of the dune
I saw the white daisies go down to the sea,
A host in the sunshine, an army in June,
The people God sends us to set our hearts free.

The bobolinks rallied them up from the dell,
The orioles whistled them out of the wood;
And all of their singing was, " Earth, it is well! "
And all of their dancing was, " Life, thou art good! "

RICHARD HOVEY

Richard Hovey was born May 4, 1864, at Normal, Illinois, and
graduated from Dartmouth in 1885. After leaving college, he became, in rapid succession, a theologian, an actor, a journalist, a
lecturer, professor of literature at Barnard, a poet, and a dramatist.
His exuberance found its outlet in the series of lusty poems pub-

lished in collaboration with Bliss Carman — the three volumes of
Songs from Vagabondia (1894, 1896, 1900). Here he let himself go
completely. His lines fling themselves across the page; shout with
a wild irresponsibility; leap, laugh, carouse, and carry off the
reader in a gale of high spirits.

"At the Crossroads" is a vivid example of this gypsy-like spirit
which could sound deeper notes with equal strength. The famous
"Stein Song" is only an interlude in the midst of a far finer poem
that begins:

> I said in my heart, "I am sick of four walls and a ceiling.
> I have need of the sky.
> I have business with the grass.
> I will up and get me away where the hawk is wheeling,
> Lone and high,
> And the slow clouds go by. . . ."

Although the varied lyrics in *Songs from Vagabondia* are the
best-known examples of Hovey, a representative collection of his
riper work may be found in *Along the Trail* (1898). He died in
New York, February 24, 1900.

At the Crossroads

> You to the left and I to the right,
> For the ways of men must sever —
> And it well may be for a day and a night,
> And it well may be forever.
> But whether we meet or whether we part
> (For our ways are past our knowing),
> A pledge from the heart to its fellow heart
> On the ways we all are going!
> Here's luck!
> For we know not where we are going.
>
> Whether we win or whether we lose
> With the hands that life is dealing,
> It is not we nor the ways we choose
> But the fall of the cards that's sealing.
> There's a fate in love and a fate in fight,
> And the best of us all go under —
> And whether we're wrong or whether we're right,
> We win, sometimes, to our wonder.
> Here's luck!
> That we may not yet go under!

With a steady swing and an open brow
We have tramped the ways together,
But we're clasping hands at the crossroads now
In the Fiend's [1] own night for weather;
And whether we bleed or whether we smile
In the leagues that lie before us
The ways of life are many a mile
And the dark of Fate is o'er us.
Here's luck!
And a cheer for the dark before us!

You to the left and I to the right,
For the ways of men must sever,
And it well may be for a day and a night
And it well may be forever!
But whether we live or whether we die
(For the end is past our knowing),
Here's two frank hearts and the open sky,
Be a fair or an ill wind blowing!
Here's luck!
In the teeth of all winds blowing.

Unmanifest Destiny [2]

To what new fates, my country, far
    And unforeseen of foe or friend,
Beneath what unexpected star
    Compelled to what unchosen end.

Across the sea that knows no beach,
    The Admiral of Nations guides
Thy blind obedient keels to reach
    The harbor where thy future rides!

The guns that spoke at Lexington
    Knew not that God was planning then
The trumpet word of Jefferson
    To bugle forth the rights of men.

[1] The Fiend is Satan, man's chief enemy.

[2] The phrase "manifest destiny" came into ordinary usage during the Spanish-American War. It indicated America's paternal (or, as the opposing faction claimed, imperialistic) mission in governing the Filipinos, Cubans, and other peoples. Hovey was among those who denied any selfish motives to his country.

To them that wept and cursed Bull Run,
  What was it but despair and shame?
Who saw behind the cloud the sun?
  Who knew that God was in the flame?

Had not defeat upon defeat,
  Disaster on disaster come,
The slave's emancipated feet
  Had never marched behind the drum.

There is a Hand that bends our deeds
  To mightier issues than we planned;
Each son that triumphs, each that bleeds,
  My country, serves It's dark command.

I do not know beneath what sky
  Nor on what seas shall be thy fate;
I only know it shall be high,
  I only know it shall be great.

A Stein Song

Give a rouse, then, in the Maytime
  For a life that knows no fear!
Turn night-time into daytime
  With the sunlight of good cheer!
    For it's always fair weather
    When good fellows get together,
  With a stein on the table and a good song ringing clear.

When the wind comes up from Cuba,
  And the birds are on the wing,
And our hearts are patting juba [1]
  To the banjo of the spring,
    Then it's no wonder whether
    The boys will get together,
  With a stein on the table and a cheer for everything.

For we're all frank-and-twenty
  When the spring is in the air;
And we've faith and hope a-plenty,

[1] *Juba:* a wild, West Indian dance, thought to be of African origin.

And we've life and love to spare:
   And it's birds of a feather
   When we all get together,
With a stein on the table and a heart without a care.

For we know the world is glorious,
   And the goal a golden thing,
And that God is not censorious
   When his children have their fling;
      And life slips its tether
      When the boys get together,
With a stein on the table in the fellowship of spring.

EDWIN ARLINGTON ROBINSON

Edwin Arlington Robinson was born December 22, 1869, in the village of Head Tide, Maine. When he was still a child, the Robinson family moved to the nearby town of Gardiner, which figures in Robinson's poetry as "Tilbury Town." In 1891 he entered Harvard College, but left in 1893. A little collection of verse (*The Torrent and the Night Before*) was privately printed in 1896 and the following year marked the appearance of Robinson's first representative work, *The Children of the Night* (1897).

At thirty Robinson determined to make a living by writing and went to New York. Here he almost starved. He could find no work, and publishers refused to interest themselves in his poetry. At thirty-four he got a job in the subway as time-checker, living most of the day in darkness, literally in the lowest depths. By a lucky accident, President Theodore Roosevelt saw some of Robinson's verse, and offered the poet a clerical position in the Custom House. Robinson never knew precisely what his duties were, but he was saved. "Now," he wrote, "I will be able to own two pairs of shoes at one time!"

Meanwhile Robinson was still unknown to most readers. It was not until the publication of *The Man Against the Sky* (1916) that his unique power, his dry and tonic idiom, was generally acknowledged. Robinson's philosophy was that of a skeptic, a man desperately searching for the truth, but a true seeker. He was, however, first of all a portrait painter; nothing, with the exception of some of Frost's monologs, presents pictures which are at once so keen and so kindly. In etchings like "Miniver Cheevy," "Bewick Finzer," and "Richard Cory" — lines where Robinson's irony is inextricably mixed with tenderness — his art is at its height. Because of his own struggles Robinson was particularly sympathetic to those who were, in the eyes of the world, incompetents and failures. "The Master," one of the finest evocations of Lincoln, is, at the same time, a bitter commentary on the commercialism of the times and the "shopman's test of age and worth." In his reanimations of the Arthurian legends, *Merlin* (1917) and *Launcelot* (1920), which differ radically from the idyls of Tennyson, Robinson colored the tale with somber reflections of the collapse of old orders, the darkness of an age in ashes.

Avon's Harvest, which the author called "a dime novel in verse," appeared in 1921. In the same year his first *Collected Poems* received the Pulitzer Prize. *The Man Who Died Twice* (1924), which was awarded the Pulitzer Prize for that year, is a single long poem: a tale which is a cross between a grotesque recital and inspired metaphysics. *Dionysus in Doubt* (1925) contains, besides several characteristic extended poems, a dozen of Robinson's finest dramatic sonnets. *Tristram* (1927) vividly modernizes the immortal love story and moves with an emotional warmth that is unusual in Robinson. After 1928 Robinson wrote too rapidly. Each year for seven years he planned a long narrative poem, but his work declined in strength and substance. A new and comprehensive *Collected Poems,* running to almost 1500 pages, was published in 1937.

From 1911 until his death Robinson spent most of his time at the well-known haven for artists, the MacDowell Colony at Peterborough, New Hampshire, wintering in New York and Boston. Early in 1935 his illness, which he had concealed from his friends, made it necessary for him to be taken to the New York Hospital where he died April 6, 1935.

Critics and poets of all schools joined in praising Robinson. All admired him for his reticence and integrity, for the dignity with which he carried his fame and, as Robinson Jeffers wrote, "followed his own sense of direction, unbewildered and undiverted." His work as a whole challenged those who accused him of holding a negative attitude; it showed a stubborn philosophy, a dogged desire for a deeper faith, a greater light.

Miniver Cheevy

Miniver Cheevy, child of scorn,
　　Grew lean while he assailed the seasons;
He wept that he was ever born,
　　And he had reasons.

Miniver loved the days of old
　　When swords were bright and steeds were prancing;
The vision of a warrior bold
　　Would set him dancing.

Miniver sighed for what was not,
　　And dreamed, and rested from his labors;
He dreamed of Thebes [1] and Camelot,[2]
　　And Priam's [3] neighbors.

Miniver mourned the ripe renown
　　That made so many a name so fragrant;
He mourned Romance, now on the town,
　　And Art, a vagrant.

Miniver loved the Medici,[4]
　　Albeit he had never seen one;
He would have sinned incessantly
　　Could he have been one.

Miniver cursed the commonplace
　　And eyed a khaki suit with loathing;
He missed the medieval grace
　　Of iron clothing.

Miniver scorned the gold he sought,
　　But sore annoyed was he without it;
Miniver thought, and thought, and thought,
　　And thought about it.

Miniver Cheevy, born too late,
　　Scratched his head and kept on thinking;
Miniver coughed, and called it fate,
　　And kept on drinking.

The Master

*(Lincoln as seen, presumably, by one of his contemporaries shortly
after the Civil War)*

　　A flying word from here and there
　　Had sown the name at which we sneered,

　　　[1] *Thebes:* a ruined city of ancient Egypt.
　　　[2] *Camelot:* the legendary place where King Arthur had his
court.
　　　[3] *Priam:* the last king of Troy.
　　　[4] *Medici:* the fabulously powerful Florentine family of the 14th
to 16th centuries whose members were famous as rulers and art
patrons.

But soon the name was everywhere,
To be reviled and then revered:
A presence to be loved and feared,
We cannot hide it, or deny
That we, the gentlemen who jeered,
May be forgotten by and by.

He came when days were perilous
And hearts of men were sore beguiled;
And having made his note of us,
He pondered and was reconciled.
Was ever master yet so mild
As he, and so untamable?
We doubted, even when he smiled,
Not knowing what he knew so well.

He knew that undeceiving fate
Would shame us whom he served unsought:
He knew that he must wince and wait —
The jest of those for whom he fought;
He knew devoutly what he thought
Of us and of our ridicule;
He knew that we must all be taught
Like little children in a school.

We gave a glamour to the task
That he encountered and saw through,
But little of us did he ask,
And little did we ever do.
And what appears if we review
The season when we railed and chaffed?
It is the face of one who knew
That we were learning while we laughed.

The face that in our vision feels
Again the venom that we flung,
Transfigured to the world reveals
The vigilance to which we clung.
Shrewd, hallowed, harassed, and among
The mysteries that are untold,
The face we see was never young,
Nor could it ever have been old.

For he, to whom we have applied
Our shopman's test of age and worth,
Was elemental when he died,
As he was ancient at his birth:
The saddest among kings of earth,
Bowed with a galling crown, this man
Met rancor with a cryptic mirth,
Laconic — and Olympian.

The love, the grandeur, and the fame
Are bounded by the world alone;
The calm, the smoldering, and the flame
Of awful patience were his own:
With him they are forever flown
Past all our fond self-shadowings,
Wherewith we cumber the Unknown
As with inept Icarian [1] wings.

For we were not as other men:
'Twas ours to soar and his to see.
But we are coming down again,
And we shall come down pleasantly;
Nor shall we longer disagree
On what it is to be sublime,
But flourish in our perigee [2]
And have one Titan [3] at a time.

An Old Story

Strange that I did not know him then,
    That friend of mine!
I did not even show him then
    One friendly sign;

But cursed him for the ways he had
    To make me see
My envy of the praise he had
    For praising me.

[1] Icarus and his father Daedalus escaped from prison by using wings made of feathers. Icarus flew too near the sun; the wax of the wings melted and he plunged into the sea.

[2] *Perigee:* the lowest point.

[3] *Titan:* being of enormous size; a mythological giant.

I would have rid the earth of him
　　Once, in my pride! . . .
I never knew the worth of him
　　Until he died.

The Dark Hills

Dark hills at evening in the west,
Where sunset hovers like a sound
Of golden horns that sang to rest
Old bones of warriors under ground,
Far now from all the bannered ways
Where flash the legions of the sun,
You fade — as if the last of days
Were fading, and all wars were done.

Richard Cory

Whenever Richard Cory went down town,
　　We people on the pavement looked at him:
He was a gentleman from sole to crown,
　　Clean favored, and imperially slim.

And he was always quietly arrayed,
　　And he was always human when he talked;
But still he fluttered pulses when he said,
　　" Good morning," and he glittered when he walked.

And he was rich — yes, richer than a king,
　　And admirably schooled in every grace:
In fine, we thought that he was everything
　　To make us wish that we were in his place.

So on we worked, and waited for the light,
　　And went without the meat, and cursed the bread;
And Richard Cory, one calm summer night,
　　Went home and put a bullet through his head.

Cliff Klingenhagen

Cliff Klingenhagen had me in to dine
With him one day; and after soup and meat,
And all the other things there were to eat,
Cliff took two glasses and filled one with wine
And one with wormwood. Then, without a sign
For me to choose at all, he took the draught
Of bitterness himself, and lightly quaffed
It off, and said the other one was mine.

And when I asked him what the deuce he meant
By doing that, he only looked at me
And grinned, and said it was a way of his.
And though I know the fellow, I have spent
Long time a-wondering when I shall be
As happy as Cliff Klingenhagen is.

Bewick Finzer

Time was when his half million drew
    The breath of six per cent;
But soon the worm of what-was-not
    Fed hard on his content;
And something crumbled in his brain
    When his half million went.

Time passed, and filled along with his
    The place of many more;
Time came, and hardly one of us
    Had credence to restore,
From what appeared one day, the man
    Whom we had known before.

The broken voice, the withered neck,
    The coat worn out with care,
The cleanliness of indigence,
    The brilliance of despair,
The fond imponderable dreams
    Of affluence, — all were there.

Poor Finzer, with his dreams and schemes,
　Fares hard now in the race,
With heart and eye that have a task
　When he looks in the face
Of one who might so easily
　Have been in Finzer's place.

He comes unfailing for the loan
　We give and then forget;
He comes, and probably for years
　Will he be coming yet, —
Familiar as an old mistake,
　And futile as regret.

Calvary

Friendless and faint, with martyred steps and slow,
Faint for the flesh, but for the spirit free,
Stung by the mob that came to see the show,
The Master toiled along to Calvary;
We gibed him, as he went, with houndish glee,
Till his dimmed eyes for us did overflow;
We cursed his vengeless hands thrice wretchedly, —
And this was nineteen hundred years ago.

But after nineteen hundred years the shame
Still clings, and we have not made good the loss
That outraged faith has entered in his name.
Ah, when shall come love's courage to be strong!
Tell me, O Lord — tell me, O Lord, how long
Are we to keep Christ writhing on the cross!

The Clerks

I did not think that I should find them there
When I came back again; but there they stood,
As in the days they dreamed of when young blood
Was in their cheeks and women called them fair.
Be sure they met me with an ancient air —
And, yes, there was a shopworn brotherhood
About them; but the men were just as good
And just as human as they ever were.

And you that ache so much to be sublime,
And you that feed yourselves with your descent,
What comes of all your visions and your fears?
Poets and kings are but the clerks of Time,
Tiering the same dull webs of discontent,
Clipping the same sad alnage [1] of the years.

Credo

I cannot find my way: there is no star
In all the shrouded heavens anywhere;
And there is not a whisper in the air
Of any living voice but one so far
That I can hear it only as a bar
Of lost, imperial music, played when fair
And angel fingers wove, and unaware,
Dead leaves to garlands where no roses are.

No, there is not a glimmer, nor a call,
For one that welcomes, welcomes when he fears,
The black and awful chaos of the night;
But through it all — above, beyond it all —
I know the far-sent message of the years,
I feel the coming glory of the Light!

EDGAR LEE MASTERS

Edgar Lee Masters was born at Garnett, Kansas, August 23, 1869, of old Puritan and pioneering stock. When he was still a boy, the family moved to Illinois, where he studied law in his father's office at Lewiston. He then went to Chicago, where he became a successful and prominent attorney. Before going to Chicago, Masters had composed a great quantity of verse in traditional forms; by the time he was twenty-four he had written about four hundred poems betraying the obvious influence of Poe, Shelley, and Swinburne. His work, previous to the publication of *Spoon River Anthology*, was undistinguished. Masters died in 1950.

Taking as his model *The Greek Anthology*, which his friend

[1] *alnage:* a small measure of cloth.

William Marion Reedy had pressed upon him, Masters evolved *Spoon River Anthology* (1914), over two hundred epitaphs, in which the dead of a Middle Western town are supposed to have written the truth about their lives. Through these frank revelations, the village lives again, with all its intrigues, hypocrisies, feuds, martyrdoms, and occasional exaltations. The monotony of existence in a drab township, the defeat of ideals, the struggle toward higher goals — all are synthesized in these crowded pages. All moods and all manner of voices are here — even Masters's, who explains the reason for the form of his verses through "Petit, the Poet."

Songs and Satires (1916) is notable for several soliloquies and the eloquent "Silence." *Starved Rock* (1919), *Domesday Book* (1920), *Godbey* (1931), and *Invisible Landscapes* (1935) are, like all Masters's later books, queer mixtures of good, bad, and derivative verse. Masters continued to work with increasing speed and lessening self-restraint. Between 1935 and 1938 he wrote a lengthy autobiography (*Across Spoon River*), a novel, three controversial biographies (Whitman, Lindsay, Twain), and two new books of poems: *Poems of People* (1936) and *The New World* (1937). In these the intention was greater than the execution. As Robert Littell wrote, "What we remember is the expedition, and its desperately honest, saltless aftertaste, but we don't remember any of the individuals. There were no characters, and what we mistook for such were case histories in the clinic of life's hospital, with Mr. Masters as surgeon rather than artist."

Petit, the Poet

Seeds in a dry pod, tick, tick, tick,
Tick, tick, tick, like mites in a quarrel —
Faint iambics that the full breeze wakens —
But the pine tree makes a symphony thereof.
Triolets, villanelles, rondels, rondeaus,[1]
Ballades by the score with the same old thought:
The snows and the roses of yesterday are vanished;
And what is love but a rose that fades?
Life all around me here in the village:
Tragedy, comedy, valor and truth,
Courage, constancy, heroism, failure —
All in the loom, and, oh, what patterns!

[1] *Triolets, villanelles, rondels, rondeaus, ballades:* these are complicated forms of verse which were once widely used but are no longer popular.

Woodlands, meadows, streams and rivers —
Blind to all of it all my life long.
Triolets, villanelles, rondels, rondeaus,
Seeds in a dry pod, tick, tick, tick,
Tick, tick, tick, what little iambics,
While Homer and Whitman roared in the pines!

Lucinda Matlock

I went to the dances at Chandlerville,
And played snap-out at Winchester.
One time we changed partners,
Driving home in the moonlight of middle June,
And then I found Davis.
We were married and lived together for seventy years,
Enjoying, working, raising the twelve children,
Eight of whom we lost
Ere I had reached the age of sixty.
I spun, I wove, I kept the house, I nursed the sick,
I made the garden, and for holiday
Rambled over the fields where sang the larks,
And by Spoon River gathering many a shell,
And many a flower and medicinal weed —
Shouting to the wooded hills, singing to the green valleys.
At ninety-six I had lived enough, that is all,
And passed to a sweet repose.
What is this I hear of sorrow and weariness,
Anger, discontent and drooping hopes?
Degenerate sons and daughters,
Life is too strong for you —
It takes life to love Life.

Anne Rutledge

Out of me unworthy and unknown
The vibrations of deathless music;
"With malice toward none, with charity for all."
Out of me the forgiveness of millions toward millions,
And the beneficent face of a nation
Shining with justice and truth.
I am Anne Rutledge who sleep beneath these weeds,

Beloved in life of Abraham Lincoln,
Wedded to him, not through union,
But through separation.
Bloom forever, O Republic,
From the dust of my bosom!

STEPHEN CRANE

Stephen Crane, whose career was one of the most brilliant and short-lived in American letters, was born at Newark, New Jersey, November 1, 1871. After studying at Lafayette College, he entered journalism at sixteen and became a reporter and writer of newspaper sketches. When he died, at the age of thirty, he had produced ten printed volumes (one of which, the novel *The Red Badge of Courage,* is a classic); two more were announced for publication, and two others were appearing serially.

At various periods in Crane's brief career, he experimented in verse, seeking to find new effects in unrhymed lines. The results were embodied in two volumes of unusual poetry, *The Black Riders* (1895) and *War Is Kind* (1899); highly suggestive lines that anticipated the Imagists and the epigrammatic free verse that followed fifteen years later. It was not until 1930 that his *Collected Poems* appeared.

It is likely that his feverish energy of production aggravated the illness that caused Crane's death. He reached the Black Forest only to die at the journey's end, June 5, 1900.

I Saw a Man

I saw a man pursuing the horizon;
Round and round they sped.
I was disturbed at this;
I accosted the man.
" It is futile," I said,
" You can never " —

" You lie," he cried,
And ran on.

The Wayfarer

The wayfarer,
Perceiving the pathway to truth,
Was struck with astonishment.
It was thickly grown with weeds.
" Ha," he said,
" I see that no one has passed here
In a long time."
Later he saw that each weed
Was a singular knife.
" Well," he mumbled at last,
" Doubtless there are other roads."

The Heart

In the desert
I saw a creature, naked, bestial,
Who, squatting upon the ground,
Held his heart in his hands,
And ate of it.
I said, " Is it good, friend? "
" It is bitter — bitter," he answered;
" But I like it
Because it is bitter,
And because it is my heart."

The Blades of Grass

In Heaven,
Some little blades of grass
Stood before God.
" What did you do? "
Then all save one of the little blades
Began eagerly to relate
The merits of their lives.
This one stayed a small way behind,
Ashamed.
Presently, God said,
" And what did you do? "

The little blade answered, " Oh, my Lord,
Memory is bitter to me,
For, if I did good deeds,
I know not of them."
Then God, in all his splendor,
Arose from his throne.
" Oh, best little blade of grass! " he said.

T. A. DALY

Thomas Augustine Daly was born in Philadelphia, Pennsylvania, May 28, 1871. He attended Villanova College and Fordham University, leaving at the end of his sophomore year to become a newspaper man. He was on the staff of various Philadelphia journals, writing reviews, editorials, travel notes and running the columns in which his much-quoted verse originally appeared.

Canzoni (1906) and *Carmina* (1909) contain the best-known of Daly's varied dialect verse. Although he wrote in a dozen different idioms including "straight" English, his half-humorous, half-pathetic interpretations of Irish and Italian immigrants were his specialty. "Mia Carlotta" ranks with the best dialect of the period; "The Song of the Thrush" is a more personal communication.

Seldom descending to caricature. Daly exhibits the foibles of his characters without exploiting them; even the lightest passages in *McAroni Ballads* (1919) are done with delicacy and a not too sentimental appreciation. Less popular than Riley or Dunbar, Daly is more skillful and versatile than either; his range and quality are comparable to Field's. A representative *Selected Poems* (1936) was prefaced by Christopher Morley. Daly died in 1948.

The Song of the Thrush

Ah! the May was grand this mornin'!
Shure, how could I feel forlorn in
Such a land, where tree and flower tossed their kisses to the
breeze?
Could an Irish heart be quiet
While the Spring was runnin' riot,
An' the birds of free America were singin' in the trees?
In the songs that they were singin'
No familiar note was ringin',

But I strove to imitate them an' I whistled like a lad.
       Oh, my heart was warm to love them
       For the very newness of them —
For the ould songs that they helped me to forget — an' I was
       glad.

       So I mocked the feathered choir
       To my hungry heart's desire,
An' I gloried in the comradeship that made their joy my
       own.
       Till a new note sounded, stillin'
       All the rest. A thrush was trillin'!
Ah, the thrush I left behind me in the fields about Athlone!
       Where, upon the whitethorn swayin',
       He was minstrel of the Mayin',
In my days of love an' laughter that the years have laid at
       rest;
       Here again his notes were ringin'!
       But I'd lost the heart for singin' —
Ah, the song I could not answer was the one I knew the best.

Mia Carlotta

       Giuseppe, da barber, ees greata for " mash,"
       He gotta da bigga, da blacka mustache,
       Good clo'es an' good styla an' playnta good cash.

       W'enevra Giuseppe ees walk on da street,
       Da peopla dey talka, " how nobby! how neat!
       How softa da handa, how smalla da feet."

       He raisa hees hat an' he shaka hees curls,
       An' smila weeth teetha so shiny like pearls;
       O! many da heart of da seelly young girls
               He gotta —
           Yes, playnta he gotta —
               But notta
               Carlotta!

       Giuseppe, da barber, he maka da eye,
       An' lika da steam engine puffa an' sigh,
       For catcha Carlotta w'en she ees go by.

Carlotta she walka weeth nose in da air,
An' look through Giuseppe weeth far-away stare,
As eef she no see dere ees som'body dere.

Giuseppe, da barber, he gotta da cash,
He gotta da clo'es an' da bigga mustache,
He gotta da seelly young girls for da " mash,"
      But notta —
    You bat my life, notta —
      Carlotta!
      I gotta!

PAUL LAURENCE DUNBAR

Paul Laurence Dunbar was born in 1872, at Dayton, Ohio, the son of Negro slaves. Before and even after he wrote poetry, he was an elevator boy. He tried newspaper work, but he was unsuccessful. In 1899 he was given a position in the Library of Congress.

Dunbar's first collection, *Lyrics of Lowly Life* (1896), contains many of his most characteristic poems. In an introduction, in which mention was made of the octoroon Dumas and the great Russian poet Pushkin, who was a mulatto, William Dean Howells wrote, " So far as I can remember, Paul Dunbar was the only man of pure African blood and of American civilization to feel the Negro life æsthetically and express it lyrically." *Lyrics of the Hearthside* (1899) and *Lyrics of Love and Laughter* (1903) are two other volumes full of folk-stuff. And though the final *Lyrics of Sunshine and Shadow* (1905) is less original, being full of echoes, it contains a few of Dunbar's least-known but keenest interpretations.

Dunbar died in Dayton, Ohio, February 10, 1906.

The Turning of the Babies in the Bed

Woman's sho' a cur'ous critter, an' dey ain't no doubtin' dat.
She's a mess o' funny capahs f'om huh slippahs to huh hat.
Ef yo' tries to un'erstan' huh, an' yo' fails, des' up an' say:
" D' ain't a bit o' use to try to un'erstan' a woman's way."

I don' mean to be complainin', but I's jes' a-settin' down
Some o' my own obserwations, w'en I cas' my eye eroun'
Ef yo' ax me fu' to prove it, I ken do it mighty fine,
Fu' dey ain't no bettah 'zample den dis ve'y wife o' mine.

In de ve'y hea't o' midnight, w'en I's sleepin' good an' soun',
I kin hyeah a so't o' rustlin' an' somebody movin' 'roun'.
An' I say, "Lize, whut yo' doin'?" But she frown an' shek
    huh haid,
"Hesh yo' mouf, I's only tu'nin' of de chillun in de bed.

"Don' yo' know a chile gits restless, layin' all de night one
    way?
An' yo' got to kind o' 'range him sev'al times befo' de day?
So de little necks won't worry, an' de little backs won't
    break;
Don' yo' t'ink 'cause chillun's chillun dey haint got no pain
    an' ache."

So she shakes 'em, an' she twists 'em, an' she tu'ns 'em 'roun'
    erbout,
'Twell I don' see how de chillun evah keeps f'om hollahin'
    out.
Den she lif's 'em up head down'ards, so's dey won't git livah-
    grown,
But dey snoozes des' ez peaceful ez a liza'd on a stone.

W'en hit's mos' nigh time fu' wakin' on de dawn o' jedge-
    ment day,
Seems lak I kin hyeah ol' Gab'iel lay his trumpet down an'
    say,
"Who dat walkin' 'roun' so easy, down on earf ermong de
    dead?" —
'T will be Lizy up a-tu'nin' of de chillun in de bed.

A Coquette Conquered

Yes, my ha't's ez ha'd ez stone —
Go 'way, Sam, an' lemme 'lone.
No; I ain't gwine change my min';
Ain't gwine ma'y you — nuffin' de kin'.

Phiny loves you true an' deah?
Go ma'y Phiny; whut I keer?
Oh, you needn't mou'n an' cry —
I don't keer how soon you die.

Got a present! Whut yo' got?
Somef'n fu' de pan er pot!
Huh! Yo' sass do sholy beat —
Think I don't git 'nough to eat?

Whut's dat un'neaf yo' coat?
Looks des lak a little shoat.
'Taint no possum? Bless de Lamb!
Yes, it is, you rascal, Sam!

Gin it to me; whut you say?
Ain't you sma't now! Oh, go 'way!
Possum do look mighty nice;
But you ax too big a price.

Tell me, is you talkin' true,
Dat's de gal's whut ma'ies you?
Come back, Sam; now whah's you gwine?
Co'se you knows dat possum's mine!

AMY LOWELL

Amy Lowell was born in Brookline, Massachusetts, February 9, 1874, of a long line of noted publicists and poets, the first colonist (a Percival Lowell) arriving in Newburyport in 1637. The poet and critic James Russell Lowell was a cousin of her grandfather; Abbott Lawrence, her mother's father, was minister to England; and Abbott Lawrence Lowell, her brother, was president of Harvard University.

Her first volume, *A Dome of Many-colored Glass* (1912), was an unpromising book. The subjects were conventional; the tone was without a trace of personality. It was a queer prolog to the vivid *Sword Blades and Poppy Seed* (1914) and *Men, Women and Ghosts* (1916), which marked a totally new individuality. These two volumes contained, in addition to many poems written in the usual forms, a score of pictorial pieces illustrating Miss Lowell's identification with the Imagists, and the first appearance in English of "polyphonic prose."

Can Grande's Castle (1918), like the later *Legends* (1921), reveals Miss Lowell as the gifted narrator, the teller of bizarre and brilliant stories. The feverish agitation is less prominent in her quieter and more personal *Pictures of the Floating World* (1919). *Legends* (1921) contains eleven stories placed against seven different backgrounds. Among her posthumous work, *What's O'Clock?* (1925) is the most outstanding; it includes verses which establish a close kinship with her environment. *East Wind* (1926) and *Ballads for Sale* (1927) are other posthumous books, the first a set of New England tales, the second a miscellaneous collection.

Besides the original poetry, Miss Lowell undertook many studies in foreign literatures; she made the English versions of poems translated from the Chinese in *Fir-Flower Tablets* (1921). Two years after its publication she acknowledged the authorship of the anonymous *A Critical Fable* (1922), a modern sequel to James Russell Lowell's *A Fable for Critics*. Her monumental *John Keats*, an exhaustive biography and analysis of the poet in two volumes, appeared early in 1925.

For years Miss Lowell had been suffering from ill health. In April, 1925, her condition became worse; she was forced to cancel a projected lecture trip through England and to cease all work. She died on May 12, 1925. A comprehensive, if uncritical, biography, *Amy Lowell* (1935), was written by S. Foster Damon; it communicates something of the poet's creative excitement.

Solitaire [1]

When night drifts along the streets of the city,
And sifts down between the uneven roofs,
My mind begins to peek and peer.
It plays at ball in odd, blue Chinese gardens,
And shakes wrought dice-cups in Pagan temples
Amid the broken flutings of white pillars.
It dances with purple and yellow crocuses in its hair,
And its feet shine as they flutter over drenched grasses.
How light and laughing my mind is,
When all good folk have put out their bedroom candles,
And the city is still.

A Lady

You are beautiful and faded,
Like an old opera tune
Played upon a harpsichord;
Or like the sun-flooded silks

[1] *Solitaire:* a game which one person can play alone. It usually refers to games of cards, but here the poet suggests what happens in the mind of a solitary person — especially an imaginative writer who spent much of her time alone, writing late at night.

Of an eighteenth-century boudoir.
In your eyes
Smolder the fallen roses of outlived minutes,
And the perfume of your soul
Is vague and suffusing,
With the pungence of sealed spice-jars.
Your half-tones delight me,
And I grow mad with gazing
At your blent colors.

My vigor is a new-minted penny,
Which I cast at your feet.
Gather it up from the dust
That its sparkle may amuse you.

Meeting-House Hill

I must be mad, or very tired,
When the curve of a blue bay beyond a railroad track
Is shrill and sweet to me like the sudden springing of a tune,
And the sight of a white church above thin trees in a city
    square
Amazes my eyes as though it were the Parthenon.
Clear, reticent, superbly final,
With the pillars of its portico refined to a cautious elegance,
It dominates the weak trees,
And the shot of its spire
Is cool and candid,
Rising into an unresisting sky.
Strange meeting-house
Pausing a moment upon a squalid hill-top.
I watch the spire sweeping the sky,
I am dizzy with the movement of the sky;
I might be watching a mast
With its royals set full
Straining before a two-reef breeze.
I might be sighting a tea-clipper,
Tacking into the blue bay,
Just back from Canton
With her hold full of green and blue porcelain
And a Chinese coolie leaning over the rail
Gazing at the white spire
With dull, sea-spent eyes.

Wind and Silver

Greatly shining,
The Autumn moon floats in the thin sky;
And the fish-ponds shake their backs and flash their dragon
    scales
As she passes over them.

A Decade

When you came, you were like red wine and honey,
And the taste of you burnt my mouth with its sweetness.
Now you are like morning bread,
Smooth and pleasant.
I hardly taste you at all, for I know your savor;
But I am completely nourished.

Madonna of the Evening Flowers [1]

All day long I have been working,
Now I am tired.
I call: " Where are you? "
But there is only the oak tree rustling in the wind.
The house is very quiet,
The sun shines in on your books,
On your scissors and thimble just put down,
But you are not there.
Suddenly I am lonely:
Where are you?
I go about searching.

Then I see you,
Standing under a spire of pale blue larkspur,
With a basket of roses on your arm.
You are cool, like silver,
And you smile.

[1] *Madonna:* literally "My lady," but usually a designation of
the Virgin Mary. In this poem the lady admired by the poet takes
on a look of holiness against a background of " the blue steeples
of the larkspur " surrounded by the flowering Canterbury bells.

I think the Canterbury bells are playing little tunes,
You tell me that the peonies need spraying,
That the columbines have overrun all bounds,
That the pyrus japonica should be cut back and rounded.
You tell me these things.
But I look at you, heart of silver,
White heart-flame of polished silver,
Burning beneath the blue steeples of the larkspur,
And I long to kneel instantly at your feet,
While all about us peal the loud, sweet *Te Deums* [1] of the
     Canterbury bells.

Night Clouds

The white mares of the moon rush along the sky
Beating their golden hoofs upon the glass Heavens;
The white mares of the moon are all standing on their hind
     legs
Pawing at the green porcelain doors of the remote Heavens.
Fly, mares!
Strain your utmost,
Scatter the milky dust of stars,
Or the tiger sun will leap upon you and destroy you
With one lick of his vermilion tongue.

Patterns

I walk down the garden paths,
And all the daffodils
Are blowing, and the bright blue squills.
I walk down the patterned garden-paths
In my stiff brocaded gown.
With my powdered hair and jeweled fan,
I too am a rare
Pattern, as I wander down
The garden paths.

My dress is richly figured,
And the train

[1] The *Te Deum* is an ancient Latin hymn of praise to God

Makes a pink and silver stain
On the gravel, and the thrift
Of the borders.
Just a plate of current fashion,
Tripping by in high-heeled, ribboned shoes.
Not a softness anywhere about me,
Only whalebone and brocade.
And I sink on a seat in the shade
Of a lime tree. For my passion
Wars against the stiff brocade.
The daffodils and squills
Flutter in the breeze
As they please.
And I weep;
For the lime-tree is in blossom
And one small flower has dropped upon my bosom.

And the plashing of waterdrops
In the marble fountain
Comes down the garden-paths.
The dripping never stops.
Underneath my stiffened gown
Is the softness of a woman bathing in a marble basin,
A basin in the midst of hedges grown
So thick, she cannot see her lover hiding,
But she guesses he is near,
And the sliding of the water
Seems the stroking of a dear
Hand upon her.
What is Summer in a fine brocaded gown!
I should like to see it lying in a heap upon the ground.
All the pink and silver crumpled up on the ground.

I would be the pink and silver as I ran along the paths,
And he would stumble after,
Bewildered by my laughter.
I should see the sun flashing from his sword-hilt and the
    buckles on his shoes.
I would choose
To lead him in a maze along the patterned paths,
A bright and laughing maze for my heavy-booted lover.
Till he caught me in the shade,

And the buttons of his waistcoat bruised my body as he
　　clasped me,
Aching, melting, unafraid.
With the shadows of the leaves and the sundrops,
And the plopping of the waterdrops,
All about us in the open afternoon —
I am very like to swoon
With the weight of this brocade,
For the sun sifts through the shade.

Underneath the fallen blossom
In my bosom
Is a letter I have hid.
It was brought to me this morning by a rider from the Duke.
" Madam, we regret to inform you that Lord Hartwell
Died in action Thursday sen'night."
As I read it in the white, morning sunlight,
The letters squirmed like snakes.
" Any answer, Madam? " said my footman.
" No," I told him.
" See that the messenger takes some refreshment.
" No, no answer."
And I walked into the garden,
Up and down the patterned paths,
In my stiff, correct brocade.
The blue and yellow flowers stood up proudly in the sun,
Each one.
I stood upright too,
Held rigid to the pattern
By the stiffness of my gown;
Up and down I walked,
Up and down.

In a month he would have been my husband.
In a month, here, underneath this lime,
We would have broke the pattern;
He for me, and I for him,
He as Colonel, I as Lady,
On this shady seat.
He had a whim
That sunlight carried blessing.
And I answered, " It shall be as you have said."
Now he is dead.

In Summer and in Winter I shall walk
Up and down
The patterned garden-paths
In my stiff, brocaded gown.
The squills and daffodils
Will give place to pillared roses, and to asters, and to snow.
I shall go
Up and down
In my gown.
Gorgeously arrayed,
Boned and stayed.
And the softness of my body will be guarded from embrace
By each button, hook, and lace.
For the man who should loose me is dead,
Fighting with the Duke in Flanders,
In a pattern called a war.
Christ! What are patterns for?

ROBERT FROST

Robert (Lee) Frost was born in San Francisco, California, March 26, 1875. At the age of ten he came East to the towns and hills where, for eight generations, his forefathers had lived. After graduating from the high school at Lawrence, Massachusetts, in 1892, Frost entered Dartmouth College, where he remained only a few months. The routine of study was too much for him; he decided to earn his living, and became a bobbin boy in one of the mills at Lawrence. He had already begun to write poetry; a few of his verses had appeared in *The Independent*. But the strange, soil-flavored quality which even then distinguished his lines was not relished by the editors. For twenty years Frost continued to write his highly characteristic work in spite of the discouraging apathy, and for twenty years the poet remained unknown.

After another unsuccessful attempt to achieve culture *via* college (Harvard, 1897), Frost turned to labor. Some years before, at the age of seventeen, he had tramped through the Carolinas looking for work. Now he engaged in a variety of industries: for three years he taught school, made shoes, edited a weekly paper, and became a farmer at Derry, New Hampshire. During the next eleven years Frost struggled to wrest a living from the stubborn granite hills. The rocks refused to give him a living; the world continued oblivious of his existence. In the twenty years before 1913 his poetry had brought him two hundred dollars — an average of ten dollars a year! Frost sought a change of environment and, after a few years' teaching at Derry and Plymouth, New Hampshire, sold his farm and, with his wife and four children, sailed for England in September, 1912.

A few months later, *A Boy's Will* (1913), his first collection, was published, and Frost was recognized at once as an authentic voice of modern poetry. In the spring of the same year, *North of Boston* (1914), one of the most intensely American books ever printed, was published in England. This is, as he has called it, a " book of people." And it is more than that — it is a book of backgrounds as living and dramatic as the people they overshadow. Frost vivifies a stone wall, an empty cottage, an apple tree, a mountain, a forgotten wood-pile left

> To warm the frozen swamp as best it could
> With the slow, smokeless burning of decay.

North of Boston, like its successors, contains much of the finest poetry of our time. Rich in actualities, richer in spiritual values, the lines move with the double force of observation and implication. The poet's characters are close to their soil; they remain rooted in realism. But Frost is never a photographic realist. " There are," he once said, " two types of realist — the one who offers a good deal of dirt with his potato to show that it is a real one; and the one who is satisfied with the potato brushed clean. I'm inclined to be the second kind. . . . To me, the thing that art does for life is to strip it to form."

The delicate accents of speech find their most sympathetic recorder here. Frost's lines disclose the subtle shades of emphasis by presenting only a significant detail. " If I must be classified as a poet," Frost once said, with the suspicion of a twinkle, " I might be called a Synecdochist; for I prefer the synecdoche in poetry — that figure of speech in which we use a part for the whole." Frost's work, with its genius for understatement, cannily combines humor and philosophy.

In March, 1915, Frost came back to America. *North of Boston* had been published in the United States, and its author, who had left the country an unknown writer, returned to find himself famous. *Mountain Interval,* containing some of Frost's most beautiful poems, appeared in 1916. The idiom is the same as in the earlier volumes, but the convictions are stronger. The essential things are unchanged. The first poem in Frost's first book sums it up:

> They would not find me changed from him they knew —
> Only more sure of all I thought was true.

New Hampshire (1923), which was awarded the Pulitzer Prize for the best volume of poetry published in 1923, synthesizes Frost's qualities: it combines the stark unity of *North of Boston* and the diffused geniality of *Mountain Interval*. If one thing predominates it is a feeling of quiet classicism; the poet's voice is lowered, but not its strength. *Selected Poems* (revised in 1928 and 1935) and a rearranged *Collected Poems* (1930), which again won the Pulitzer Prize, confirmed the conclusions; the unpretentious bucolics had become contemporary classics.

It has been charged that Frost's work suffers from an exclusiveness, and even his most ardent admirers admit that his is not an inclusive passion like Whitman's. But Frost loves what he loves with a fierce attachment and a tenderness fixed beyond an easily transferred regard. His devotion to earth is, even more than Wordsworth's, rich in its fidelity; what his poetry may lack in range is compensated for by its depth.

This is more true than ever of *West-Running Brook* (1928) which is a reflection and restatement of all that has gone before. The lyrics are tender and semi-autobiographical. Beyond the fact ("the dearest dream that labor knows"), beyond the tone of voice, there is that unifying emotion which is Frost's peculiar quality and his uplifting spirit. *A Further Range* (1936) won Frost the Pulitzer Prize for the third time. It proved that Frost had no contemporary rival in America and, except for William Butler Yeats, none in England. In this volume the effects are broader, the play is more pronounced, the style is an inimitable blend of fact and fantasy. *A Witness Tree* (1942) won the Pulitzer Prize, giving Frost the award for the fourth time, proving once more that his work refused to date. *Come In*, a collection annotated by the editor and published when the poet was nearing seventy, was republished with additions as *The Pocket Book of Robert Frost's Poems* (1946). *Steeplebush* (1947), which appeared when the author was seventy-two, glints with curiously youthful play and mellow wisdom sharpened by mischievous wit. Two poetic plays (*A Masque of Reason*, 1945, and *A Masque of Mercy*, 1947) showed that the spirit of questioning youth and quizzical age could sometimes be joined. Still another edition of Frost's *Complete Collected Poems* appeared in 1949.

All these books displayed Frost's fondness for paradox, for combinations which seem like contradictions. "The style is not only the man, but the way the man takes himself," Frost wrote of Edwin Arlington Robinson. "If it is with outer seriousness, it must be with inner humor. If it is with outer humor, it must be with inner seriousness. Neither one without the other will do." The casual tone was deceptive; Frost's offhand manner, his fusion of somberness and teasing, beauty and banter, first persuades and finally convinces the reader. Readers are heartened by the poet's serenity, invigorated by his strength. This is a poetry which rewards us with unsuspected depths of feeling, an act of continual sharing which "begins in delight and ends in wisdom."

The Pasture

I'm going out to clean the pasture spring;
I'll only stop to rake the leaves away
(And wait to watch the water clear, I may):
I shan't be gone long. — You come too.

I'm going out to fetch the little calf
That's standing by the mother. It's so young,
It totters when she licks it with her tongue.
I shan't be gone long. — You come too.

Mowing

There was never a sound beside the wood but one,
And that was my long scythe whispering to the ground.
What was it it whispered? I knew not well myself;
Perhaps it was something about the heat of the sun,
Something, perhaps, about the lack of sound —
And that was why it whispered and did not speak.
It was no dream of the gift of idle hours,
Or easy gold at the hand of fay or elf:
Anything more than the truth would have seemed too weak
To the earnest love that laid the swale in rows,
Not without feeble-pointed spikes of flowers
(Pale orchises), and scared a bright green snake.
The fact is the sweetest dream that labor knows.
My long scythe whispered and left the hay to rake.

The Tuft of Flowers

I went to turn the grass once after one
Who mowed it in the dew before the sun.

The dew was gone that made his blade so keen
Before I came to view the leveled scene.

I looked for him behind an isle of trees;
I listened for his whetstone on the breeze.

But he had gone his way, the grass all mown,
And I must be, as he had been, — alone,

"As all must be," I said within my heart,
"Whether they work together or apart."

But as I said it, swift there passed me by
On noiseless wing a bewildered butterfly,

Seeking with memories grown dim over night
Some resting flower of yesterday's delight.

And once I marked his flight go round and round,
As where some flower lay withering on the ground.

And then he flew as far as eye could see,
And then on tremulous wing came back to me.

I thought of questions that have no reply,
And would have turned to toss the grass to dry;

But he turned first, and led my eye to look
At a tall tuft of flowers beside a brook,

A leaping tongue of bloom the scythe had spared
Beside a reedy brook the scythe had bared.

I left my place to know them by their name,
Finding them butterfly-weed when I came.

The mower in the dew had loved them thus,
By leaving them to flourish, not for us,

Nor yet to draw one thought of ours to him,
But from sheer morning gladness at the brim.

The butterfly and I had lit upon,
Nevertheless, a message from the dawn,

That made me hear the wakening birds around,
And hear his long scythe whispering to the ground,

And feel a spirit kindred to my own;
So that henceforth I worked no more alone;

But glad with him, I worked as with his aid,
And weary, sought at noon with him the shade;

And dreaming, as it were, held brotherly speech
With one whose thought I had not hoped to reach.

" Men work together," I told him from the heart,
" Whether they work together or apart."

Mending Wall

Something there is that doesn't love a wall,
That sends the frozen-ground-swell under it,
And spills the upper boulders in the sun;
And makes gaps even two can pass abreast.
The work of hunters is another thing:
I have come after them and made repair
Where they have left not one stone on a stone,
But they would have the rabbit out of hiding,
To please the yelping dogs. The gaps I mean,
No one has seen them made or heard them made,
But at spring mending-time we find them there.
I let my neighbor know beyond the hill;
And on a day we meet to walk the line
And set the wall between us once again.
We keep the wall between us as we go.
To each the boulders that have fallen to each.
And some are loaves and some so nearly balls
We have to use a spell to make them balance;
" Stay where you are until our backs are turned! "
We wear out fingers rough with handling them
Oh, just another kind of outdoor game,
One on a side. It comes to little more:
He is all pine and I am apple-orchard.
My apple trees will never get across
And eat the cones under his pines, I tell him.
He only says, " Good fences make good neighbors."
Spring is the mischief in me, and I wonder
If I could put a notion in his head:
" *Why* do they make good neighbors? Isn't it
Where there are cows? But here there are no cows.
Before I built a wall I'd ask to know

What I was walling in or walling out,
And to whom I was like to give offense.
Something there is that doesn't love a wall,
That wants it down! " I could say " Elves " to him,
But it's not elves exactly, and I'd rather
He said it for himself. I see him there,
Bringing a stone grasped firmly by the top
In each hand, like an old-stone savage armed.
He moves in darkness as it seems to me,
Not of woods only and the shade of trees.
He will not go behind his father's saying,
And he likes having thought of it so well
He says again, " Good fences make good neighbors."

Blue-Butterfly Day

It is blue-butterfly day here in spring,
And with these sky-flakes down in flurry on flurry,
There is more unmixed color on the wing
Than flowers will show for days unless they hurry.

But these are flowers that fly and all but sing;
And now from having ridden out desire,
They lie closed over in the wind and cling
Where wheels have freshly sliced the April mire.

Birches

When I see birches bend to left and right
Across the line of straighter darker trees,
I like to think some boy's been swinging them.
But swinging doesn't bend them down to stay.
Ice-storms do that. Often you must have seen them
Loaded with ice a sunny winter morning
After a rain. They click upon themselves
As the breeze rises, and turn many-colored
As the stir cracks and crazes their enamel.
Soon the sun's warmth makes them shed crystal shells
Shattering and avalanching on the snow-crust —
Such heaps of broken glass to sweep away
You'd think the inner dome of heaven had fallen.

They are dragged to the withered bracken [1] by the load,
And they seem not to break; though once they are bowed
So low for long, they never right themselves:
You may see their trunks arching in the woods
Years afterwards, trailing their leaves on the ground
Like girls on hands and knees that throw their hair
Before them over their heads to dry in the sun.

But I was going to say when Truth broke in
With all her matter-of-fact about the ice-storm,
I should prefer to have some boy bend them
As he went out and in to fetch the cows —
Some boy too far from town to learn baseball,
Whose only play was what he found himself,
Summer or winter, and could play alone.
One by one he subdued his father's trees
By riding them down over and over again
Until he took the stiffness out of them,
And not one but hung limp, not one was left
For him to conquer. He learned all there was
To learn about not launching out too soon
And so not carrying the tree away
Clear to the ground. He always kept his poise
To the top branches, climbing carefully
With the same pains you use to fill a cup
Up to the brim, and even above the brim.
Then he flung outward, feet first, with a swish,
Kicking his way down through the air to the ground.

So was I once myself a swinger of birches;
And so I dream of going back to be.
It's when I'm weary of considerations,
And life is too much like a pathless wood
Where your face burns and tickles with the cobwebs
Broken across it, and one eye is weeping
From a twig's having lashed across it open.
I'd like to get away from earth awhile
And then come back to it and begin over.
May no fate willfully misunderstand me
And half grant what I wish and snatch me away
Not to return. Earth's the right place for love:
I don't know where it's likely to go better.

     1 *bracken:* heavy fern or coarse undergrowth.

I'd like to go by climbing a birch tree,
And climb black branches up a snow-white trunk
Toward heaven, till the tree could bear no more,
But dipped its top and set me down again.
That would be good both going and coming back.
One could do worse than be a swinger of birches.

The Onset

Always the same when on a fated night
At last the gathered snow lets down as white
As may be in dark woods and with a song
It shall not make again all winter long —
Of hissing on the yet uncovered ground, —
I almost stumble looking up and round,
As one who, overtaken by the end,
Gives up his errand and lets death descend
Upon him where he is, with nothing done
To evil, no important triumph won
More than if life had never been begun.

Yet all the precedent is on my side:
I know that winter-death has never tried
The earth but it has failed; the snow may heap
In long storms an undrifted four feet deep
As measured against maple, birch or oak;
It cannot check the Peeper's [1] silver croak;
And I shall see the snow all go down hill
In water of a slender April rill
That flashes tail through last year's withered brake
And dead weed like a disappearing snake.
Nothing will be left white but here a birch
And there a clump of houses with a church.

The Death of the Hired Man

Mary sat musing on the lamp-flame at the table
Waiting for Warren. When she heard his step,
She ran on tiptoe down the darkened passage
To meet him in the doorway with the news

[1] The small shrill frog, especially loud in spring.

And put him on his guard. "Silas is back."
She pushed him outward with her through the door
And shut it after her. "Be kind," she said.
She took the market things from Warren's arms
And set them on the porch, then drew him down
To sit beside her on the wooden steps.
"When was I ever anything but kind to him?
But I'll not have the fellow back," he said.
"I told him so last haying, didn't I?
'If he left then,' I said, 'that ended it.'
What good is he? Who else will harbor him
At his age for the little he can do?
What help he is there's no depending on.
Off he goes always when I need him most.
'He thinks he ought to earn a little pay,
Enough at least to buy tobacco with,
So he won't have to beg and be beholden.'
'All right,' I say, 'I can't afford to pay
Any fixed wages, though I wish I could.'
'Someone else can.' 'Then someone else will have to.'
I shouldn't mind his bettering himself
If that was what it was. You can be certain,
When he begins like that, there's someone at him
Trying to coax him off with pocket-money, —
In haying time, when any help is scarce.
In winter he comes back to us. I'm done."

"Sh! not so loud: he'll hear you," Mary said.

"I want him to: he'll have to soon or late."

"He's worn out. He's asleep beside the stove.
When I came up from Rowe's I found him here,
Huddled against the barn-door fast asleep,
A miserable sight, and frightening, too —
You needn't smile — I didn't recognize him —
I wasn't looking for him — and he's changed.
Wait till you see."

                    "Where did you say he'd been?"

"He didn't say. I dragged him to the house,
And gave him tea and tried to make him smoke.

I tried to make him talk about his travels,
Nothing would do: he just kept nodding off."

" What did he say? Did he say anything? "

" But little."

                " Anything? Mary, confess
He said he'd come to ditch the meadow for me."

" Warren! "

            " But did he? I just want to know."

" Of course he did. What would you have him say?
Surely you wouldn't grudge the poor old man
Some humble way to save his self-respect.
He added, if you really care to know,
He meant to clear the upper pasture, too.
That sounds like something you have heard before?
Warren, I wish you could have heard the way
He jumbled everything. I stopped to look
Two or three times — he made me feel so queer —
To see if he was talking in his sleep.
He ran on Harold Wilson — you remember —
The boy you had in haying four years since.
He's finished school, and teaching in his college.
Silas declares you'll have to get him back.
He says they two will make a team for work:
Between them they will lay this farm as smooth!
The way he mixed that in with other things.
He thinks young Wilson a likely lad, though daft
On education — you know how they fought
All through July under the blazing sun,
Silas up on the cart to build the load,
Harold along beside to pitch it on."

" Yes, I took care to keep well out of earshot."

" Well, those days trouble Silas like a dream.
You wouldn't think they would. How some things linger!
Harold's young college boy's assurance piqued him.

After so many years he still keeps finding
Good arguments he sees he might have used.
I sympathize. I know just how it feels
To think of the right thing to say too late.
Harold's associated in his mind with Latin.
He asked me what I thought of Harold's saying
He studied Latin like the violin
Because he liked it — that an argument!
He said he couldn't make the boy believe
He could find water with a hazel prong —
Which showed how much good school had ever done him.
He wanted to go over that. But most of all
He thinks if he could have another chance
To teach him how to build a load of hay — "

" I know, that's Silas' one accomplishment.
He bundles every forkful in its place,
And tags and numbers it for future reference,
So he can find and easily dislodge it
In the unloading. Silas does that well.
He takes it out in bunches like birds' nests.
You never see him standing on the hay
He's trying to lift, straining to lift himself."

" He thinks if he could teach him that, he'd be
Some good perhaps to someone in the world.
He hates to see a boy the fool of books.
Poor Silas, so concerned for other folk,
And nothing to look backward to with pride,
And nothing to look forward to with hope,
So now and never any different."

Part of a moon was falling down the west,
Dragging the whole sky with it to the hills.
Its light poured softly in her lap. She saw
And spread her apron to it. She put out her hand
Among the harp-like morning-glory strings,
Taut with the dew from garden bed to eaves,
As if she played unheard the tenderness
That wrought on him beside her in the night.
" Warren," she said, " he has come home to die:
You needn't be afraid he'll leave you this time."

"Home," he mocked gently.

                "Yes, what else but home?
It all depends on what you mean by home.
Of course he's nothing to us, any more
Than was the hound that came a stranger to us
Out of the woods, worn out upon the trail."

"Home is the place where, when you have to go there,
They have to take you in."

              "I should have called it
Something you somehow haven't to deserve."

Warren leaned out and took a step or two,
Picked up a little stick, and brought it back
And broke it in his hand and tossed it by.
"Silas has better claim on us, you think,
Than on his brother? Thirteen little miles
As the road winds would bring him to his door.
Silas has walked that far no doubt today.
Why didn't he go there? His brother's rich,
A somebody — director in the bank."

"He never told us that."

          "We know it though."

"I think his brother ought to help, of course.
I'll see to that if there is need. He ought of right
To take him in, and might be willing to —
He may be better than appearances.
But have some pity on Silas. Do you think
If he'd had any pride in claiming kin
Or anything he looked for from his brother,
He'd keep so still about him all this time?"

"I wonder what's between them."

             "I can tell you.
Silas is what he is — we wouldn't mind him —
But just the kind that kinsfolk can't abide.
He never did a thing so very bad.

He don't know why he isn't quite as good
As anyone. He won't be made ashamed
To please his brother, worthless though he is."

" I can't think Si ever hurt anyone."

" No, but he hurt my heart the way he lay
And rolled his old head on that sharp-edged chair-back.
He wouldn't let me put him on the lounge.
You must go in and see what you can do.
I made the bed up for him there tonight.
You'll be surprised at him — how much he's broken.
His working days are done; I'm sure of it."

" I'd not be in a hurry to say that."

" I haven't been. Go, look, see for yourself.
But, Warren, please remember how it is:
He's come to help you ditch the meadow.
He has a plan. You mustn't laugh at him.
He may not speak of it, and then he may.
I'll sit and see if that small sailing cloud
Will hit or miss the moon."

                                        It hit the moon.
Then there were three there, making a dim row,
The moon, the little silver cloud, and she.

Warren returned — too soon, it seemed to her,
Slipped to her side, caught up her hand and waited.

" Warren? " she questioned.

                                " Dead," was all he answered.

The Runaway

Once, when the snow of the year was beginning to fall,
We stopped by a mountain pasture to say " Whose colt? "
A little Morgan had one forefoot on the wall,
The other curled at his breast. He dipped his head
And snorted at us. And then he had to bolt.

We heard the miniatu
And we saw him, or t
Like a shadow against
" I think the little fell
He isn't winter-brok
With the little fellov
I doubt if even his m
It's only weather.' H
Where is his mother
And now he comes
And mounts the wa
And all his tail tha
He shudders his co
" Whoever it is th
When other creat
Ought to be told to come a

Was someth
That no o
Heave
No

171

Nothing Gold Can Stay

Nature's first green is gold,
Her hardest hue to hold.
Her early leaf's a flower;
But only so an hour.
Then leaf subsides to leaf.
So Eden sank to grief.
So dawn goes down to day.
Nothing gold can stay.

The Passing Glimpse

I often see flowers from a passing car
That are gone before I can tell what they are.

I want to get out of the train and go back
To see what they were beside the track.

I name all the kinds I am sure they weren't:
Not fireweed loving where woods have burnt --

Nor bluebells gracing a tunnel mouth —
Nor lupine living on sand and drouth.

ng brushed across my mind
e on earth will ever find?

n gives its glimpses only to those
in position to look too close.

Choose Something Like a Star

O Star (the fairest one in sight),
We grant your loftiness the right
To some obscurity of cloud —
It will not do to say of night,
Since dark is what brings out your light.
Some mystery becomes the proud.
But to be wholly taciturn
In your reserve is not allowed.
Say something to us we can learn
By heart and when alone repeat.
Say something! And it says "I burn."
But say with what degree of heat.
Talk Fahrenheit, talk Centigrade.
Use language we can comprehend.
Tell us what elements you blend.
It gives us strangely little aid,
But does tell something in the end.
And steadfast as Keats' Eremite,[1]
Not even stooping from its sphere,
It asks a little of us here.
It asks of us a certain height,
So when at times the mob is swayed
To carry praise or blame too far,
We may choose something like a star
To stay our minds on and be staid.

To a Young Wretch

As gay for you to take your father's ax
As take his gun — rod — to go hunting — fishing.
You nick my spruce until its fiber cracks;

[1] *Eremite:* a hermit, a solitary being. The reference is to Keats'
sonnet beginning "Bright star, would I were steadfast as thou art.
. . . like nature's patient sleepless Eremite."

It gives up standing straight and goes down swishing.
You link an arm in its arm, and you lean
Across the light snow homeward smelling green.

I could have bought you just as good a tree
To frizzle resin in a candle flame;
And what a saving 'twould have been to me.
But tree by charity is not the same
As tree by enterprise and expedition.
I must not spoil your Christmas with contrition.

It is your Christmases against my woods,
But even where thus opposing interests kill,
They are to be thought of as conflicting goods
Oftener than as conflicting good and ill;
Which makes the war-god seem no special dunce
For always fighting on both sides at once.

And though in tinsel chain and popcorn rope,
My tree, a captive in your window bay,
Has lost its footing on my mountain slope
And lost the stars of heaven, may, oh may,
The symbol star it lifts against your ceiling
Help me accept its fate with Christmas feeling.

Stopping by Woods on a Snowy Evening

Whose woods these are I think I know.
His house is in the village though;
He will not see me stopping here
To watch his woods fill up with snow.

My little horse must think it queer
To stop without a farmhouse near
Between the woods and frozen lake
The darkest evening of the year.

He gives his harness bells a shake
To ask if there is some mistake.
The only other sound's the sweep
Of easy wind and downy flake.

The woods are lovely, dark and deep,
But I have promises to keep,
And miles to go before I sleep,
And miles to go before I sleep.

Come In

As I came to the edge of the woods,
Thrush music — hark!
Now if it was dusk outside,
Inside it was dark.

Too dark in the woods for a bird
By sleight of wing
To better its perch for the night,
Though it still could sing.

The last of the light of the sun
That had died in the west
Still lived for one song more
In a thrush's breast.

Far in the pillared dark
Thrush music went —
Almost like a call to come in
To the dark and lament.

But no, I was out for stars:
I would not come in.
I meant not even if asked,
And I hadn't been.

CARL SANDBURG

Carl (August) Sandburg was born of Swedish stock at Galesburg, Illinois, January 6, 1878. His schooling was haphazard; at thirteen he went to work on a milk wagon. During the next six years he was, in rapid succession, porter in a barbershop, scene-shifter in a cheap theater, truck-handler in a brickyard, turner apprentice in a pottery, dish-washer in Denver and Omaha hotels, harvest hand in Kansas wheat-fields. These tasks in part equipped him to be the laureate of industrial America.

In 1904, Sandburg published a forgotten pamphlet of twenty-two poems, uneven in quality but strangely like the work of the mature Sandburg in feeling. It was twelve years later before the poet became known to the public.

Chicago Poems (1916) is full of ferment; it seethes with poetry surcharged with energy. Here is an exultation that is also an exaltation. Sandburg's speech is simple and powerful; he uses slang as freely as his predecessors used the tongue of their times. Immediately cries of protest were heard; critics said Sandburg was coarse and brutal, his language unrefined, unfit for poetry. His detractors forgot that Sandburg was brutal only when dealing with brutality; beneath his toughness he was one of the tenderest of living poets.

Cornhuskers (1918) is another step forward; it is fully as muscular as its forerunner and far more sensitive. The gain in restraint is evident in the very first poem, a magnificent vision of the prairie. Here is something of the surge of a Norse saga. But the raw violence is restrained; there are, in this volume, delicate perceptions of beauty that astonish those who think Sandburg can write only a big-fisted, roughneck sort of poetry. "Cool Tombs," one of the most poignant lyrics of our time, moves with a new music; "Grass" whispers as quietly as the earlier "Fog" steals in on stealthy, catlike feet.

Smoke and Steel (1920), which divided the Pulitzer Prize, is the sublimation of its predecessors. In this ripest of his collections, Sandburg has fused mood, accent, and image, a fit setting for the title poem, which is an epic of industrialism. Smoke-belching chimneys are here, quarries and great boulders of iron-ribbed rock; here are titanic visions: the dreams of men and machinery. And silence is here — the silence of sleeping tenements and sun-soaked cornfields. *Slabs of the Sunburnt West*, a smaller collection, appeared in 1922. *Selected Poems*, with an introduction by the English critic Rebecca West, was published in 1926. This poetry combined the ordinary and the exquisite; it was, as Sandburg himself wrote in a definition of poetry, "the synthesis of hyacinths and biscuits."

Good Morning, America (1928) is a not always successful unit; lacking integration, it is Sandburg at his best and worst. *The People, Yes* (1936) is a far more comprehensive collection. It assembles folk-tales, tall stories, catch-phrases, fable, gossip, and history, and presents all of these in a native idiom with a panoramic sweep. Moreover, in *The People, Yes* Sandburg passionately affirms his faith in a broad democracy, a democracy of material and spirit. Never, except in Whitman, has the common man been so celebrated; never has there been a greater understanding of "the people's" wisdom and skepticism, their power and their patience.

Besides his poetry, Sandburg has written two volumes of homely but highly imaginative short tales for children: *Rootabaga Stories* (1922) and *Rootabaga Pigeons* (1923). Eight years were spent travelling and studying documents for his remarkable *Abraham Lincoln: The Prairie Years* (1926), and assembling material for his collection of folk-tunes *The American Songbag* (1927). Another ten years prepared him to write *Abraham Lincoln: The War Years*, which won the Pulitzer Prize for history in 1940, the whole work constituting the most impressive presentation of Lincoln ever written. Refusing to age, Sandburg published his first novel at the age of seventy: *Remembrance Rock* (1948), a panoramic account, part fiction and part history of America seen with a poet's vision.

Grass

Pile the bodies high at Austerlitz and Waterloo.
Shovel them under and let me work —
    I am the grass; I cover all.

And pile them high at Gettysburg
And pile them high at Ypres and Verdun.
Shovel them under and let me work.
Two years, ten years, and passengers ask the conductor:
    What place is this?
    Where are we now?

    I am the grass.
    Let me work.

Prayers of Steel

Lay me on an anvil, O God.
Beat me and hammer me into a crowbar.
Let me pry loose old walls;
Let me lift and loosen old foundations.

Lay me on an anvil, O God.
Beat me and hammer me into a steel spike.
Drive me into the girders that hold a skyscraper together.
Take red-hot rivets and fasten me into the central girders.
Let me be the great nail holding a skyscraper through blue
    nights into white stars.

Cool Tombs

When Abraham Lincoln was shoveled into the tombs, he for-
    got the copperheads and the assassin . . . in the dust, in
    the cool tombs.

And Ulysses Grant lost all thought of con men and Wall
    Street, cash and collateral turned ashes . . . in the dust,
    in the cool tombs.

Pocahontas' body, lovely as a poplar, sweet as a red haw [1] in
    November or a pawpaw [2] in May, did she wonder? does
    she remember? . . . in the dust, in the cool tombs?

Take any streetful of people buying clothes and groceries,
    cheering a hero or throwing confetti and blowing tin
    horns . . . tell me if the lovers are losers . . . tell me if
    any get more than the lovers . . . in the dust . . . in
    the cool tombs.

Fog

The fog comes
on little cat feet.
It sits looking
over harbor and city
on silent haunches
and then moves on.

from Smoke and Steel

Smoke of the fields in spring is one,
Smoke of the leaves in autumn another.
Smoke of a steel-mill roof or a battleship funnel,
They all go up in a line with the smokestack,
Or they twist . . . in the slow twist . . . of the wind.

[1] *haw:* the hawthorn tree.
[2] *pawpaw:* the papaya, a juicy, yellow tropical American fruit.

If the north wind comes they run to the south.
If the west wind comes they run to the east.
    By this sign
    all smokes
    know each other.

Smoke of the fields in spring and leaves in autumn,
Smoke of the finished steel, chilled and blue,
By the oath of work they swear: "I know you."

Hunted and hissed from the center
Deep down long ago when God made us over,
Deep down are the cinders we came from —
You and I and our heads of smoke.

Some of the smokes God dropped on the job
Cross on the sky and count our years
And sing in the secrets of our numbers;
Sing their dawns and sing their evenings,
Sing an old log-fire song:
    You may put the damper up,
    You may put the damper down,
    The smoke goes up the chimney just the same.

Smoke of a city sunset skyline,
Smoke of a country dust horizon —
    They cross on the sky and count our years.

    A bar of steel — it is only
Smoke at the heart of it, smoke and the blood of a man.
A runner of fire ran in it, ran out, ran somewhere else,
And left smoke and the blood of a man
And the finished steel, chilled and blue.

So fire runs in, runs out, runs somewhere else again,
And the bar of steel is a gun, a wheel, a nail, a shovel,
A rudder under the sea, a steering-gear in the sky;
And always dark in the heart and through it,
    Smoke and the blood of a man.
Pittsburgh, Youngstown, Gary — they make their steel with
    men.

In the blood of men and the ink of chimneys
The smoke nights write their oaths:

Smoke into steel and blood into steel;
Homestead, Braddock, Birmingham, they make their steel
    with men.
Smoke and blood is the mix of steel.

> The birdmen drone
> In the blue; it is steel
> a motor sings and zooms.

Steel barb-wire around The Works.
Steel guns in the holsters of the guards at the gates of The
    Works.
Steel ore-boats bring the loads clawed from the earth by steel,
    lifted and lugged by arms of steel, sung on its way by
    the clanking clam-shells.
The runners now, the handlers now, are steel; they dig and
    clutch and haul; they hoist their automatic knuckles from
    job to job; they are steel making steel.
Fire and dust and air fight in the furnaces; the pour is timed,
    the billets wriggle; the clinkers are dumped:
Liners on the sea, skyscrapers on the land; diving steel in the
    sea, climbing steel in the sky.

Smoke Rose Gold

The dome of the capitol looks to the Potomac river.
> Out of haze over the sunset,
> Out of a smoke rose gold:
One star shines over the sunset.
Night takes the dome and the river, the sun and the smoke
    rose gold,
The haze changes from sunset to star.
The pour of a thin silver struggles against the dark.
A star might call: It's a long way across.

Jazz Fantasia

Drum on your drums, batter on your banjos, sob on the long
    cool winding saxophones. Go to it, O jazzmen.

Sling your knuckles on the bottoms of the happy tin pans,
    let your trombones ooze, and go husha-husha-hush with
    the slippery sandpaper.

Moan like an autumn wind high in the lonesome treetops, moan soft like you wanted somebody terrible, cry like a racing car slipping away from a motorcycle-cop, bang-bang! you jazzmen, bang altogether drums, traps, banjos, horns, tin cans — make two people fight on the top of a stairway and scratch each other's eyes in a clinch tumbling down the stairs.

Can the rough stuff . . . Now a Mississippi steamboat pushes up the night river with a hoo-hoo-hoo-oo . . . and the green lanterns calling to the high soft stars . . . a red moon rides on the humps of the low river hills . . . Go to it, O jazzmen.

Upstream

The strong men keep coming on.
They go down shot, hanged, sick, broken.
They live on fighting, singing, lucky as plungers.
The strong mothers pulling them on . . .
The strong mothers pulling them from a dark sea, a great prairie, a long mountain.
Call hallelujah, call amen, call deep thanks.
The strong men keep coming on.

Limited

I am riding on a limited express, one of the crack trains of the nation.
Hurtling across the prairie into blue haze and dark air go fifteen all-steel coaches holding a thousand people.
(All the coaches shall be scrap and rust and all the men and women laughing in the diners and sleepers shall pass to ashes.)
I ask a man in the smoker where he is going and he answers: " Omaha."

Finale

(From " Slabs of the Sunburnt West ")

Good night: it is scribbled on the panels
of the cold gray open desert.

Good night; on the big sky blanket over the
Santa Fé trail it is woven in the oldest
Indian blanket songs.

Buffers of land, breakers of sea, say it and
say it, over and over, good night, good night.

Tie your hat to the saddle
and ride, ride, ride, O Rider.
Lay your rails and wires
and ride, ride, ride, O Rider.

The worn tired stars say
you shall die early and die dirty.
The clean cold stars say
you shall die late and die clean.

The runaway stars say
you shall never die at all,
never at all.

Wind Song

Long ago I learned how to sleep,
In an old apple orchard where the wind swept by counting
     its money and throwing it away,
In a wind-gaunt orchard where the limbs forked out and lis-
     tened or never listened at all,
In a passel of trees where the branches trapped the wind into
     whistling, " Who, who are you? "
I slept with my head in an elbow on a summer afternoon and
     there I took a sleep lesson.
There I went away saying: I know why they sleep, I know
     how they trap the tricky winds.
Long ago I learned how to listen to the singing wind and how
     to forget and how to hear the deep whine,
Slapping and lapsing under the day blue and the night stars:
                Who, who are you?

          Who can ever forget
          listening to the wind go by
          counting its money
          and throwing it away?

Yarns of the People
(*From "The People, Yes"*)

They have yarns
Of a skyscraper so tall they had to put hinges
On the two top stories so to let the moon go by,
Of one corn crop in Missouri when the roots
Went so deep and drew off so much water
The Mississippi riverbed that year was dry,
Of pancakes so thin they had only one side,
Of "a fog so thick we shingled the barn and six feet out on the fog,"
Of Pecos Pete straddling a cyclone in Texas and riding it to the west coast where "it rained out under him,"
Of the man who drove a swarm of bees across the Rocky Mountains and the Desert "and didn't lose a bee."
Of a mountain railroad curve where the engineer in his cab can touch the caboose and spit in the conductor's eye,
Of the boy who climbed a cornstalk growing so fast he would have starved to death if they hadn't shot biscuits up to him,
Of the old man's whiskers: "When the wind was with him his whiskers arrived a day before he did,"
Of the hen laying a square egg and cackling, "Ouch!" and of hens laying eggs with the dates printed on them,
Of the ship captain's shadow: it froze to the deck one cold winter night,
Of mutineers on that same ship put to chipping rust with rubber hammers,
Of the sheep-counter who was fast and accurate: "I just count their feet and divide by four,"
Of the man so tall he must climb a ladder to shave himself,
Of the runt so teeny-weeny it takes two men and a boy to see him,
Of mosquitoes: one can kill a dog, two of them a man,
Of a cyclone that sucked cookstoves out of the kitchen, up the chimney flue, and on to the next town,
Of the same cyclone picking up wagon-tracks in Nebraska and dropping them over in the Dakotas,
Of the hook-and-eye snake unlocking itself into forty pieces, each piece two inches long, then in nine seconds flat snapping itself together again,

Of the watch swallowed by the cow: when they butchered
her a year later the watch was running and had the correct time,

Of horned snakes, hoop snakes that roll themselves where
they want to go, and rattlesnakes carrying bells instead
of rattles on their tails,

Of the herd of cattle in California getting lost in a giant red-
wood tree that had been hollowed out,

Of the man who killed a snake by putting its tail in its mouth
so it swallowed itself,

Of railroad trains whizzing along so fast they reached the
station before the whistle,

Of pigs so thin the farmer had to tie knots in their tails to
keep them from crawling through the cracks in their
pens,

Of Paul Bunyan's big blue ox, Babe, measuring between the
eyes forty-two ax-handles and a plug of Star tobacco
exactly,

Of John Henry's hammer and the curve of its swing and his
singing of it as " a rainbow round my shoulder."
They have yarns . . .

Plunger

Empty the last drop.
Pour out the final clinging heartbeat.
Great losers look on and smile.
Great winners look on and smile.

Plunger:
Take a long breath and let yourself go.

ADELAIDE CRAPSEY

Adelaide Crapsey was born September 9, 1878, at Rochester,
New York, where she spent her childhood. She entered Vassar
College in 1897, and was graduated with the class of 1901. In 1905
she went abroad to study archaeology in Rome. After her return
she taught, but failing health compelled her to discontinue, and
though she became instructor in Poetics at Smith College in 1911,
the burden was too great.

In 1913, after her breakdown, she began to write lines which are precise and poignant. She was particularly happy in her "Cinquains," a form that she originated. These five-line stanzas in the strictest possible structure (the lines having, respectively, two, four, six, eight, and two syllables) doubtless owe something to the Japanese *hokku*, but Adelaide Crapsey made them her own. She died at Saranac Lake, New York, on October 8, 1914. Her small volume *Verse* appeared in 1915.

Four Cinquains

November Night

Listen . . .
With faint dry sound,
Like steps of passing ghosts,
The leaves, frost-crisp'd, break from the trees
And fall.

Triad

These be
Three silent things:
The falling snow . . . the hour
Before the dawn . . . the mouth of one
Just dead.

The Warning

Just now,
Out of the strange
Still dusk . . . as strange, as still . . .
A white moth flew. Why am I grown
So cold?

Moon Shadows

Still as
On windless nights
The moon-cast shadows are,
So still will be my heart when I
Am dead.

On Seeing Weather-Beaten Trees

Is it as plainly in our living shown,
By slant and twist, which way the wind hath blown?

(Nicholas) Vachel Lindsay was born in Springfield, Illinois, November 10, 1879. From the window where Lindsay did most of his writing, he saw many Governors come and go, including the martyred John P. Altgeld, whom he celebrated in "The Eagle that is Forgotten," one of his finest poems. He graduated from Springfield High School, attended Hiram College (1897-1900), studied at the Art Institute at Chicago (1900-3) and at the New York School of Art (1904). After two years of lecturing and set- tlement work, he took the first of his long tramps, walking through Florida, Georgia and the Carolinas, preaching "the gospel of beauty," and formulating his plans to make others share his crea- tive enthusiasms. He lectured almost continually and traded on his energy, so much so that he wore himself out before he was fifty- three. Exhausted because he lacked the strength to fulfill his vision, he died December 4, 1931.

Like a true revivalist, he attempted to wake in people a response to beauty; a modern Tommy Tucker, he sang, recited, and chanted for his supper, distributing a pamphlet entitled "Rhymes to be Traded for Bread." But the audiences he was endeavoring to reach did not hear him, even though his collection *General Booth Enters Into Heaven* (1913) struck many a loud and racy note.

Lindsay broadened his effects, and the following year published *The Congo and Other Poems* (1914), an infectious blend of Lind- say's three R's: Rhyme, Religion, and Ragtime. In the title-poem and in the three companion chants Lindsay struck his most power- ful and most popular vein. He gave people that primitive joy in syncopated sound which is the foundation of rhythm and the base of song. He excited audiences and stimulated students. *The Chi- nese Nightingale* (1917) begins with one of the most whimsical pieces Lindsay has ever devised. If the subsequent *The Golden Whales of California* (1920) is less distinctive, it is because the au- thor has written too much and too speedily to be self-critical. It is his peculiar appraisal of loveliness, the rollicking high spirits joined to a stubborn evangelism, that makes Lindsay so representa- tive a product of his environment.

Collected Poems (1923) is a complete exhibit of Lindsay's best and worst. That Lindsay lost whatever faculty of self-criticism he may ever have possessed is evidenced by page after page of flat crudities; entire poems proceed with nothing more creative than mere physical energy whipping up a trivial idea. *Going-to-the-Sun* (1924), *Going-to-the-Stars* (1925), and *The Candle in the Cabin* (1926), following each other in too rapid succession, betray Lind- say's loquacity. These volumes are distinguished chiefly by the whimsical drawings which the poet has scattered among the feeble verses, but the high spirit is unflagging.

Much of Lindsay will die; he will not live as either a prophet or a politician. But the vitality which impels the best of his galloping meters will persist. His innocent wildness of imagination, outlast-ing his naïve programs, will charm even those to whom his brassy declamations (religious at the core) are no longer a novelty. There can be no question about his originality or permanence.

Lindsay also embodied his experiences and meditations on the road in two prose volumes, *A Handy Guide for Beggars* (1916) and *Adventures While Preaching the Gospel of Beauty* (1914), as well as an enthusiastic study of the "silent drama," *The Art of the Moving Picture* (1915). A curious document, half rhapsody, half visionary novel, entitled *The Golden Book of Springfield*, appeared in 1920. A biography, *Vachel Lindsay: A Poet in America* (1935), was written by his friend and fellow-poet, Edgar Lee Masters.

The Eagle That Is Forgotten

(*John P. Altgeld. Born December 30, 1847; died March 12, 1902*) [1]

Sleep softly . . . eagle forgotten . . . under the stone,
Time has its way with you there, and the clay has its own.
"We have buried him now," thought your foes, and in secret
    rejoiced.
They made a brave show of their mourning, their hatred un-
    voiced.
They had snarled at you, barked at you, foamed at you, day
    after day,
Now you were ended. They praised you, . . . and laid you
    away.
The others that mourned you in silence and terror and truth,
The widow bereft of her pittance, the boy without youth,
The mocked and the scorned and the wounded, the lame and
    the poor
That should have remembered forever, . . . remember no
    more.

Where are those lovers of yours, on what name do they call
The lost, that in armies wept over your funeral pall?
They call on the names of a hundred high-valiant ones,
A hundred white eagles have risen, the sons of your sons,
The zeal in their wings is a zeal that your dreaming began,
The valor that wore out your soul in the service of man.

[1] A complete biography of Altgeld did not appear until 1938 when Harry Barnard published "*Eagle Forgotten*": *The Life of John Peter Altgeld.*

Sleep softly, . . . eagle forgotten, . . . under the stone,
Time has its way with you there, and the clay has its own.
Sleep on, O brave hearted, O wise man, that kindled the
  flame —
To live in mankind is far more than to live in a name,
To live in mankind, far, far more . . . than to live in a name.

To a Golden-Haired Girl
in a Louisiana Town

You are a sunrise,
If a star should rise instead of the sun.
You are a moonrise,
If a star should come in the place of the moon.
You are the Spring,
If a face should bloom instead of an apple-bough.
You are my love,
If your heart is as kind
As your young eyes now.

The Traveler

The moon's a devil jester
Who makes himself too free.
The rascal is not always
Where he appears to be.
Sometimes he is in my heart —
Sometimes he is in the sea;
Then tides are in my heart,
And tides are in the sea.

O traveler, abiding not
Where he pretends to be!

The Congo
(*A Study of the Negro Race*)

I. Their Basic Savagery

Fat black bucks in a wine-barrel room,   *A deep rolling*
Barrel-house kings, with feet unstable,   *bass.*
Sagged and reeled and pounded on the
  table,

Pounded on the table,
Beat an empty barrel with the handle of a
    broom,
Hard as they were able,
Boom, boom, Boom,
With a silk umbrella and the handle of a
    broom,
Boomlay, boomlay, boomlay, Boom.

Then I had religion. Then I had a vision.
I could not turn from their revel in de-
    rision.
Then I saw the Congo, creeping through
    the black,
Cutting through the jungle with a
    golden track.
Then along that river-bank
A thousand miles
Tattoed cannibals danced in files;
Then I heard the boom of the blood-lust
    song
And a thigh-bone beating on a tin-pan
    gong.
And "Blood" screamed the whistles and
    the fifes of the warriors,
"Blood" screamed the skull-faced, lean
    witch-doctors,
"Whirl ye the deadly voodoo rattle,
Harry the uplands,
Steal all the cattle,
Rattle-rattle, rattle-rattle,
Bing!
Boomlay, boomlay, boomlay, Boom,"
A roaring, epic, rag-time tune
From the mouth of the Congo
To the Mountains of the Moon.
Death is an Elephant,
Torch-eyed and horrible,
Foam-flanked and terrible.
Boom, steal the pygmies,
Boom, kill the Arabs,
Boom, kill the white men,
Hoo, Hoo, Hoo.

*More deliberate.
Solemnly
chanted.*

*A rapidly
piling climax
of speed and
racket.*

*With a philo-
sophic pause.*

*Shrilly and
with a heavily
accented
meter.*

*Like the wind
in the chimney.*

Listen to the yell of Leopold's [1] ghost
Burning in Hell for his hand-maimed host.
Hear how the demons chuckle and yell.
Cutting his hands off, down in Hell.
Listen to the creepy proclamation,
Blown through the lairs of the forest-nation,
Blown past the white-ants' hill of clay,
Blown past the marsh where the butterflies
    play: —
" Be careful what you do,
Or Mumbo-Jumbo, God of the Congo,
And all of the other
Gods of the Congo,
Mumbo-Jumbo will hoo-doo you,
Mumbo-Jumbo will hoo-doo you,
Mumbo-Jumbo will hoo-doo you."

All the o sounds
very golden.
Heavy accents
very heavy.
Light accents
very light.   Last
line whispered.

II. *Their Irrepressible High Spirits*

Wild crap-shooters with a whoop and a call
Danced the juba in their gambling-hall
And laughed fit to kill, and shook the town,
And guyed the policemen and laughed them
    down
With   a   boomlay,   boomlay,   boomlay,
    Boom. . . .

Rather shrill
and high.

THEN I SAW THE CONGO, CREEPING THROUGH
    THE BLACK,
CUTTING   THROUGH   THE   JUNGLE   WITH   A
    GOLDEN TRACK.

Read exactly as
in first section.

A Negro fairyland swung into view,
A minstrel river
Where dreams come true.
The ebony palace soared on high
Through the blossoming trees to the eve-
    ning sky.
The inlaid porches and casement shone
With gold and ivory and elephant-bone.
And the black crowd laughed till their sides
    were sore

Lay emphasis
on the delicate
ideas.   Keep as
light-footed as
possible.

[1] *Leopold:* King of the Belgians, under whose imperial rule the
Africans were cruelly exploited and tortured.

At the baboon butler in the agate door,
And the well-known tunes of the parrot
    band
That trilled on the bushes of that magic
    land.

A troupe of skull-faced witch-men came   *With pomposity.*
Through the agate doorway in suits of
    flame,
Yea, long-tailed coats with a gold-leaf crust
And hats that were covered with diamond-
    dust.
And the crowd in the court gave a whoop
    and a call
And danced the juba from wall to wall.
But the witch-men suddenly stilled the   *With a great*
    throng   *deliberation and*
                                                ghostliness.
With a stern cold glare, and a stern old
    song: —
" Mumbo-Jumbo will hoo-doo you." . . .
Just then from the doorway, as fat as shotes, *With overwhelm-*
Came the cake-walk princes in their long   *ing assurance,*
    red coats,   *good cheer, and*
                                                pomp.
Shoes with a patent-leather shine,
And tall silk hats that were red as wine.
And they pranced with their butterfly part-   *With growing*
    ners there,   *speed and*
                                                sharply marked
Coal-black maidens with pearls in their   *dance-rhythm.*
    hair,
Knee-skirts trimmed with the jessamine
    sweet,
And bells on their ankles and little black
    feet.
And the couples railed at the chant and the
    frown
Of the witch-men lean, and laughed them
    down.
(O rare was the revel and well worth while
That made those glowering witch-men
    smile.)

The cake-walk royalty then began
To walk for a cake that was tall as a man

To the tune of "Boomlay, boomlay,
    Boom,"
While the witch-men laughed with a sin-
    ister air,
And sang with the scalawags prancing   *With a touch of*
    there: —   *Negro dialect,*
"Walk with care, walk with care,   *and*
Or Mumbo-Jumbo, God of the Congo,   *as rapidly as*
And all of the other   *possible toward*
Gods of the Congo,   *the end.*
Mumbo-Jumbo will hoo-doo you.
Beware, beware, walk with care,
Boomlay, boomlay, boomlay, boom,
Boomlay, boomlay, boomlay, boom,
Boomlay, boomlay, boomlay,
Boom."
Oh, rare was the revel, and well worth   *Slow philo-*
    while   *sophic calm.*
That made those glowering witch-men
    smile.

III. The Hope of Their Religion

A good old Negro in the slums of the town   *Heavy bass.*
Preached at a sister for her velvet gown.   *With a literal*
Howled at a brother for his low-down   *imitation of*
    ways,   *camp-meeting*
His prowling, guzzling, sneak-thief days.   *racket, and*
Beat on the Bible till he wore it out,   *trance.*
Starting the jubilee revival shout.
And some had visions, as they stood on
    chairs,
And sang of Jacob, and the golden stairs,
And they all repented, a thousand strong,
From their stupor and savagery and sin and
    wrong
And slammed their hymn books till they
    shook the room
With "Glory, glory, glory,"
And "Boom, boom, Boom."

THEN I SAW THE CONGO, CREEPING THROUGH   *Exactly as in*
    THE BLACK,   *the first section.*

CUTTING THROUGH THE JUNGLE WITH A
    GOLDEN TRACK.

And the gray sky opened like a new-rent
    veil
And showed the apostles with their coats
    of mail.
In bright white steel they were seated round
And their fire-eyes watched where the
    Congo wound.
And the twelve apostles, from their thrones
    on high,
Thrilled all the forest with their heavenly
    cry: —

Sung to the tune of "Hark, ten thousand harps and voices."

" Mumbo-Jumbo will die in the jungle;
Never again will he hoo-doo you,
Never again will he hoo-doo you."

Then along that river-bank, a thousand
    miles,

With growing deliberation and joy.

The vine-snared trees fell down in files.
Pioneer angels cleared the way
For a Congo paradise, for babes at play,
For sacred capitals, for temples clean.
Gone were the skull-faced witch-men lean.
There, where the wild ghost-gods had
    wailed

In a rather high key — as delicately as possible.

A million boats of the angels sailed
With oars of silver, and prows of blue
And silken pennants that the sun shone
    through.
'Twas a land transfigured, 'twas a new crea-
    tion,
Oh, a singing wind swept the Negro nation;
And on through the backwoods clearing
    flew: —

" Mumbo-Jumbo is dead in the jungle.
Never again will he hoo-doo you.
Never again will he hoo-doo you."

To the tune of "Hark, ten thousand harps and voices."

Redeemed were the forests, the beasts and
    the men,
And only the vulture dared again
By the far, lone mountains of the moon

To cry, in the silence, the Congo tune: —
" Mumbo-Jumbo will hoo-doo you.   *Dying off*
Mumbo-Jumbo will hoo-doo you,   *into a pene-*
                                                   trating,
Mumbo . . . Jumbo . . . will . . . hoo-doo   *terrified*
    . . . you."   *whisper.*

When Lincoln Came to Springfield

When Lincoln came to Springfield,
In the ancient days,
Queer were the streets and sketchy,
And he was in a maze.

Leaving log cabins behind him,
For the mud streets of this place,
Sorrow for Anne Rutledge
Burned in his face.

He threw his muddy saddle bags
On Joshua Speed's floor,
He took off his old hat,
He looked around the store.

He shook the long hair
On his bison-head,
He sat down on the counter,
" Speed, I've moved," he said.

The Apple-Barrel of Johnny Appleseed [1]

On the mountain peak, called " Going-To-The-Sun,"
I saw gray Johnny Appleseed at prayer
Just as the sunset made the old earth fair.
Then darkness came; in an instant, like great smoke,
The sun fell down as though its great hoops broke
And dark rich apples, poured from the dim flame
Where the sun set, came rolling toward the peak,
A storm of fruit, a mighty cider-reek,
The perfume of the orchards of the world,

[1] Nickname of the legendary John Chapman, who scattered
apple-seeds throughout the midwest.

From apple-shadows: red and russet domes
That turned to clouds of glory and strange homes
Above the mountain tops for cloud-born souls: —
Reproofs for men who build the world like moles,
Models for men, if they would build the world
As Johnny Appleseed would have it done —
Praying, and reading the books of Swedenborg [1]
On the mountain top called " Going-To-The-Sun."

ALFRED KREYMBORG

Alfred Kreymborg was born in New York City, December 10, 1883. His education was spasmodic, his childhood being spent beneath the roar of the elevated trains. At ten he was an expert chess player; he supported himself from the age of seventeen to twenty-five by teaching and playing exhibition games. At thirty, he turned to the theater as a medium.

Mushrooms (1916), *Blood of Things* (1920), and *Scarlet and Mellow* (1927) are the work of an apt conjurer and a serious thinker. Humor is in these pages, but it is humor lifted. Here, in spite of what seems a persistence of occasional affectations, is a sensitive imagination. *Puppet Plays* appeared in 1923. Although Kreymborg's marionette-like emotions are often too doll-charming or too doll-tragic, these miniature dramas are appealing.

Less Lonely (1923) is a more conventional collection; there are even thirty orthodox sonnets. As a chronicler, Kreymborg has written part of his autobiography in *Troubadour* (1925) and an outline of American poetry in *Our Singing Strength* (1929).

Old Manuscript

The sky
is that beautiful old parchment
in which the sun
and the moon
keep their diary.
To read it all,
one must be a linguist

[1] *Swedenborg:* the great eighteenth century scientist, philosopher, and religious writer.

more learned than Father Wisdom
and a visionary
more clairvoyant than Mother Dream.
But to feel it,
one must be an apostle:
one who is more than intimate
in having been, always,
the only confidant —
like the earth
or the sea.

The Ditty the City Sang

If a lad's but a lad in the heart of a town,
Is it mad he has grown, or a dunce or a clown,
When he crowns common sights with delights of his own?

He thought he saw ships at the end of the street
With songs that the wind taught the sails to repeat.
But washlines have nothing like ships on their feet.

He thought he saw figures and faces you miss
Coming back to embracing no more than a kiss.
Can the rain that leaves puddles be peopled with this?

He thought he heard bells where the clouds break in two,
With a tone quite as low and clear as it's blue.
But what he heard there not a cloud ever knew.

He thought he touched fingers belonging to kings,
And the crowns and the scepters came tumbling in rings.
But all he felt there is how poverty sings.

WILLIAM CARLOS WILLIAMS

William Carlos Williams was born September 7, 1883, in Rutherford, New Jersey. Educated in New York and Switzerland, he
graduated from the University of Pennsylvania with a medical degree, studied pediatrics in Leipzig, returned to his native Rutherford to practice medicine and to become a modest celebrity.

Williams' first book, *Poems* (1909), was the usual young poet's imitative experiment; his second, *The Tempers* (1913), betrayed the influence of the Imagists. But with *Al Que Quiere* (1917), *Kora in Hell* (1921), and *Sour Grapes* (1922) Williams sounded his own characteristic note. That note is enlarged and emphasized in *Complete Collected Poems: 1906–1938*. More and more freely Williams devotes himself to the swift observation and minute depiction of the American scene. His lines are plain, purposely unadorned and non-melodic; but they intensify ordinary objects with pointed detail and with confident, if clipped, emotion. "Emotion," wrote Williams, "clusters about common things; the pathetic often stimulates the imagination to new patterns — and the job of the poet is to use language effectively, his own language, the only language which is to him authentic." Williams puts intensity into *things*, maintaining that the most ordinary objects have their use and beauty "if the imagination can lighten them." As in "Poem" and "The Poor," the observing eye and the imaginative mind unite to bring all the small but significant details into sharp focus.

Several prose works, notably *In the American Grain* (1925), *White Mule* (1937), and *In the Money* (1940) show Williams as a historian and critic.

Metric Figure

There is a bird in the poplars —
It is the sun!
The leaves are little yellow fish
Swimming in the river;
The bird skims above them —
Day is on his wings.
Phoenix!
It is he that is making
The great gleam among the poplars.
It is his singing
Outshines the noise
Of leaves clashing in the wind.

Poem

By the road to the contagious hospital,
under the surge of the blue
mottled clouds driven from the
northeast — cold wind. Beyond, the

waste of broad, muddy fields,
brown with dried weeds, standing and fallen

patches of standing water,
the scattering of tall trees.

All along the road the reddish,
purplish, forked, upstanding, twiggy
stuff of brushes and small trees
with dead, brown leaves under them
leafless vines —

Lifeless in appearance, sluggish,
dazed spring approaches —

They enter the new world naked,
cold, uncertain of all
save that they enter. All about them
the cold, familiar wind —

Now the grass, tomorrow
the stiff curl of wild-carrot leaf.

One by one objects are defined —
It quickens: clarity, outline of leaf,

But now the stark dignity of
entrance — Still, the profound change
has come upon them; rooted, they
grip down and begin to awaken.

The Poor

It's the anarchy of poverty
delights me, the old
yellow wooden house indented
among the new brick tenements

Or a cast iron balcony
with panels showing oak branches
in full leaf. It fits
the dress of the children

reflecting every stage and
custom of necessity —
Chimneys, roofs, fences of
wood and metal in an unfenced

age and enclosing next to
nothing at all: the old man
in a sweater and soft black
hat who sweeps the sidewalk —

his own ten feet of it —
in a wind that fitfully
turning his corner has
overwhelmed the entire city

SARA TEASDALE

Sara Teasdale was born August 8, 1884, at St. Louis, Missouri, and educated there. After leaving school, she traveled abroad, married, and moved to New York in 1916. Living in seclusion, she became ill and died suddenly January 28, 1933.

Her first book was a slight volume, *Sonnets to Duse* (1907), giving little promise of the rich lyricism which was to follow. *Helen of Troy and Other Poems* (1911) contains the first hints of that delicate craftsmanship which, later, was brought to such a high pitch. *Rivers to the Sea* (1915) emphasizes this poet's epigrammatic skill. The collection contains at least a dozen lyrics in which the words seem to fall into place without art or effort. Seldom employing metaphor or striking imagery, almost bare of ornament, these poems have the magic of folk-song. Theirs is an artlessness that is an art.

Love Songs (1917) is a collection of Sara Teasdale's previous melodies with several new tunes. *Flame and Shadow* (1920) and the more autumnal *Dark of the Moon* (1926) are, however, the best of her books. Here the beauty is fuller and deeper; an almost mystic radiance plays from these starry verses. The words are chosen with a keener sense of their actual as well as their musical values; the rhythms are subtle and varied. *Strange Victory* (1933) is Sara Teasdale's posthumous volume. The poems are sad but not sentimental; though death overshadows the book there is never the cry of frustration nor the melodrama of dying. As in the later lyrics the lines are direct, the emotion unwhipped; the beauty is in the restraint, the compression into essential spirit, into a last serenity. A comprehensive *Selected Poems* appeared in 1937, and revealed the poet's devotion to three themes: love, the loss of love, and the sense of solitude.

Spring Night

The park is filled with night and fog,
 The veils are drawn about the world,
The drowsy lights along the paths
 Are dim and pearled

Gold and gleaming the empty streets,
 Gold and gleaming the misty lake.
The mirrored lights like sunken swords,
 Glimmer and shake.

Oh, is it not enough to be
Here with this beauty over me?
My throat should ache with praise, and I
Should kneel in joy beneath the sky.
O beauty, are you not enough?
Why am I crying after love
With youth, a singing voice, and eyes
To take earth's wonder with surprise?

Why have I put off my pride,
Why am I unsatisfied, —
I, for whom the pensive night
Binds her cloudy hair with light, —
I, for whom all beauty burns
Like incense in a million urns?
O beauty, are you not enough?
Why am I crying after love?

I Shall Not Care

When I am dead and over me bright April
 Shakes out her rain-drenched hair,
Though you should lean above me broken-hearted
 I shall not care.

I shall have peace, as leafy trees are peaceful
  When rain bends down the bough;
And I shall be more silent and cold-hearted
  Than you are now.

Night Song of Amalfi [1]

I asked the heaven of stars
  What should I give my love —
It answered me with silence,
  Silence above.

I asked the darkened sea
  Down where the fishermen go —
It answered me with silence,
  Silence below.

Oh, I could give him weeping,
  Or could give him song —
But how can I give silence
  My whole life long?

Water Lilies

If you have forgotten water lilies floating
  On a dark lake among mountains in the afternoon shade,
If you have forgotten their wet, sleepy fragrance,
  Then you can return and not be afraid.

But if you remember, then turn away forever
  To the plains and the prairies where pools are far apart,
There you will not come at dusk on closing water lilies,
  And the shadow of mountains will not fall on your heart.

Two Songs for Solitude

The Crystal Gazer

I shall gather myself into myself again,
  I shall take my scattered selves and make them one,

[1] *Amalfi:* a beautiful little fishing village in Italy, near Naples.

I shall fuse them into a polished crystal ball
Where I can see the moon and the flashing sun.

I shall sit like a sibyl,[1] hour after hour intent,
Watching the future come and the present go —
And the little shifting pictures of people rushing
In tiny self-importance to and fro.

The Solitary

Let them think I love them more than I do,
Let them think I care, though I go alone,
If it lifts their pride, what is it to me
Who am self-complete as a flower or a stone?

It is one to me that they come or go
If I have myself and the drive of my will,
And strength to climb on a summer night
And watch the stars swarm over the hill.

My heart has grown rich with the passing of years,
I have less need now that when I was young
To share myself with every comer,
Or shape my thoughts into words with my tongue.

ELINOR WYLIE

Elinor (Hoyt) Wylie was born September 7, 1885, in Somerville, New Jersey, but she was, she often protested, of pure Pennsylvania stock. Her girlhood was spent in Washington; the family was a literary one, and it was soon evident that Elinor, the first born, was a prodigy. The facts of her life, if not the personal sufferings, have been recorded by Nancy Hoyt, her youngest sister, in *Elinor Wylie: The Portrait of an Unknown Woman* (1935).

It was in England that her first work was published, a tiny book of forty-three pages entitled *Incidental Numbers* (1912), privately printed and unsigned. It is a tentative collection and she was so sensitive about its "incredible immaturity" that she pleaded with the few who knew of its existence never to refer to it until after her death. Much of it is immature, since most of it was written in her early twenties and some of it in her teens. Yet her character-

[1] *Sibyl:* an ancient prophetess who could foretell coming events.

istic touch — the firm thought matched by the firmly molded line — is already suggested.

She returned to America in 1916, and lived in Boston and Maine. Her poems began to appear in the magazines; she moved to Washington. In 1921 her first "real" volume, *Nets to Catch the Wind*, appeared. It was an instant success. Three years later she was a famous person, the author of two volumes of poems and an extraordinary first novel (*Jennifer Lorn*), married to William Rose Benét, and part of the literary life of New York.

Nets to Catch the Wind impresses immediately because of its brilliance. The brilliance is one which, at first, seems to sparkle without burning. But if the poet seldom allows her verses to grow agitated, she never permits them to remain dull. As a technician, she is always admirable; in "August" the sense of heat is conveyed by tropic luxuriance and contrast; in "The Eagle and the Mole" she lifts moralizing to a proud level. Her auditory effects are scarcely less remarkable; no poem has ever suggested the white silence of snow so effectively as "Velvet Shoes."

Black Armour (1923) exhibits Mrs. Wylie's keenness against a mellower background. The intellect has grown more fiery, the mood has grown warmer, and the craftsmanship is more dazzling than ever. *Trivial Breath* (1928) is the work of a poet in transition. At times the craftsman is uppermost, at times the creative genius. *Angels and Earthly Creatures* (1929) is the very peak of her poetry; a physical beauty and spiritual intensity lift this work above anything the poet had previously written. The whole book is a kind of valedictory, sad and noble. The poet seemed to have a premonition of death; on December 15, 1928, she put her final book together, affixed the motto on the title page, and prepared the last detail for the printer. She died the following day.

A sumptuous *Collected Poems of Elinor Wylie* (1932) was followed by *Collected Prose of Elinor Wylie* (1933), which contains her novels as well as her short stories. But it is as a poet that she excelled, and it is as a poet that she will be remembered.

Velvet Shoes

Let us walk in the white snow
    In a soundless space;
With footsteps quiet and slow,
    At a tranquil pace,
    Under veils of white lace.

I shall go shod in silk,
    And you in wool,
White as a white cow's milk,

More beautiful
Than the breast of a gull.

We shall walk through the still town
    In a windless peace;
We shall step upon white down,
    Upon silver fleece,
    Upon softer than these.

We shall walk in velvet shoes:
    Wherever we go
Silence will fall like dews
    On white silence below.
    We shall walk in the snow.

The Eagle and the Mole

Avoid the reeking herd,
Shun the polluted flock,
Live like that stoic bird,
The eagle of the rock.

The huddled warmth of crowds
Begets and fosters hate;
He keeps, above the clouds,
His cliff inviolate.

When flocks are folded warm,
And herds to shelter run,
He sails above the storm,
He stares into the sun.

If in the eagle's track
Your sinews cannot leap,
Avoid the lathered pack,
Turn from the steaming sheep.

If you would keep your soul
From spotted sight or sound,
Live like the velvet mole;
Go burrow underground.

And there hold intercourse
With roots of trees and stones,
With rivers at their source,
And disembodied bones.

Pegasus Lost [1]

And there I found a gray and ancient ass,
With dull glazed stare, and stubborn wrinkled smile,
Sardonic, mocking my wide-eyed amaze.
A clumsy hulking form in that white place
At odds with the small stable, cleanly, Greek,
The marble manger and the golden oats.
With loathing hands I felt the ass's side,
Solidly real and hairy to the touch.
Then knew I that I dreamed not, but saw truth;
And knowing, wished I still might hope I dreamed.
The door stood wide, I went into the air.
The day was blue and filled with rushing wind,
A day to ride high in the heavens and taste
The glory of the gods who tread the stars.
Up in the mighty purity I saw
A flashing shape that gladly sprang aloft —
My little Pegasus, like a far white bird
Seeking sun-regions, never to return.
Silently then I turned my steps about,
Entered the stable, saddled the slow ass;
Then on its back I journeyed dustily
Between sun-wilted hedgerows into town.

Sea Lullaby

The old moon is tarnished
With smoke of the flood,
The dead leaves are varnished
With color like blood,

---

[1] *Pegasus:* the winged horse of the Grecian myths. He caused
a fountain to spring from a mountain sacred to Apollo and the
Muses. Therefore Pegasus is a symbol of poetry and winged imagination.

A treacherous smiler
With teeth white as milk,
A savage beguiler
In sheathing of silk,

The sea creeps to pillage,
She leaps on her prey;
A child of the village
Was murdered today.

She came up to meet him
In a smooth golden cloak,
She choked him and beat him
To death, for a joke.

Her bright locks were tangled,
She shouted for joy,
With one hand she strangled
A strong little boy.

Now in silence she lingers
Beside him all night
To wash her long fingers
In silvery light.

Puritan Sonnet

Down to the Puritan marrow of my bones
There's something in this richness that I hate.
I love the look, austere, immaculate,
Of landscapes drawn in pearly monotones.
There's something in my very blood that owns
Bare hills, cold silver on a sky of slate,
A thread of water, churned to milky spate
Streaming through slanted pastures fenced with stones.

I love those skies, thin blue or snowy gray,
Those fields sparse-planted, rendering meager sheaves;
That spring, briefer than apple-blossom's breath;
Summer, so much too beautiful to stay;
Swift autumn, like a bonfire of leaves;
And sleepy winter, like the sleep of death.

August

Why should this Negro insolently stride
Down the red noonday on such noiseless feet?
Piled in his barrow, tawnier than wheat,
Lie heaps of smoldering daisies, somber-eyed,
Their copper petals shriveled up with pride,
Hot with a superfluity of heat,
Like a great brazier [1] borne along the street
By captive leopards, black and burning pied. [2]

Are there no water-lilies, smooth as cream,
With long stems dripping crystal? Are there none
Like those white lilies, luminous and cool,
Plucked from some hemlock-darkened northern stream
By fair-haired swimmers, diving where the sun
Scarce warms the surface of the deepest pool?

Nebuchadnezzar [3]

My body is weary to death of my mischievous brain;
I am weary for ever and ever of being brave;
Therefore I crouch on my knees while the cool white rain
Curves the clover over my head like a wave.

The stem and the frosty seed of the grass are ripe;
I have devoured their strength; I have drunk them deep;
And the dandelion is gall in a thin green pipe,
But the clover is honey and sun and the smell of sleep.

[1] *Brazier:* a pan or metal bowl for holding live coals.
[2] *Pied:* two or more colors in spots or blotches.
[3] *Nebuchadnezzar:* the king of Babylon who captured Jerusalem, but who became " as a beast of the field " until he acknowledged the power of God. " And he was driven from men, and did eat grass as oxen, and his body was wet with the dew of heaven." (*The Book of Daniel: Chapter V.*)

Ezra (Loomis) Pound was born at Hailey, Idaho, October 30, 1885. He attended Hamilton College and the University of Pennsylvania and went abroad, seeking fresh material to complete a thesis on Lope de Vega, in 1908. It was in Venice that Pound's first book, *A Lume Spento* (1908), was printed. The following year Pound went to London and the chief poems of the little volume were incorporated in *Personæ* (1909), a small collection containing some of Pound's best and most original work.

Although the young American was a total stranger to the English literary world, his book made a definite impression on critics of all shades. Edward Thomas, the English poet and a careful critic, wrote, " The beauty of it is the beauty of passion, sincerity and intensity, not of beautiful words and suggestions. . . . The thought dominates the words and is greater than they are."

Exultations (1909) was printed in the same year that saw the appearance of *Personæ*. Here Pound begins to be more the archaeologist than the artist. *Canzoni* (1911) and *Ripostes* (1912) both contain much that is sharp and living; they also contain the germs of decay. Pound began to scatter his talents; to start movements which he quickly discarded for new ones; to spend himself in poetic propaganda; to give more and more time to translation. A general collection of his poetry composed before Pound's forty-second year was published under the former title, *Personæ*, in 1927. In this, as in the preceding volumes, Pound was establishing the importance of " speech as song," poetry which could talk as well as chant and declaim. Here can be seen his importance as an Imagist.

He began to publish his *magnum opus* in his fortieth year. The first of the *Cantos* (*Cantos I–XVI*) appeared in 1925. Pound planned to work on a huge scale, contrasting the ancient, the medieval, and the modern world in one hundred poems, each poem to be a " chapter " in an epical work. Up to 1945 eighty-four installments had succeeded in rousing the enthusiasm of a few devotees, but merely baffling most readers with their jumble of archaic records and contemporary headlines, erudite references and current slang, verbal precision and cloudy jokes.

During the Second World War Pound, who had made his home in Italy, became an active supporter of Fascism. Beginning in 1941 he broadcast diatribes against the American system, attacks on Roosevelt, anti-Semitic slurs — all of which were indicated in the later *Cantos* — and acted as a paid propagandist who gave aid and comfort to the enemy. In May, 1945, he was taken prisoner and indicted for treason. Brought to Washington, Pound escaped trial when four psychiatrists testified that he was of unsound mind. After a court hearing on February 14, 1946, Pound was committed to St. Elizabeth's Hospital as an insane person. In 1949 Pound's *Pisan Cantos* was honored by the Bollingen Prize, and a storm of controversy arose. Criticism was directed partly against the giving of the award to a fascist supporter who had acted against his country; and partly against the continued prestige of what was termed "unintelligible" modern poetry, as represented by Pound.

Besides his poetry, Pound wrote a great quantity of critical prose, the best of which can be found in *Make It New* (1935) and *The A B C of Reading* (1934). Too special to achieve permanence, too intellectual to become popular, Pound's contribution should not be underestimated. He was a pioneer of new forms; he formed and led the Imagists; he helped free modern poetry from excessive ornament and vague prettiness. In theory and in the best of his practice he caused poets to consider what was "hard and clean-cut."

A Virginal [1]

No, no! Go from me. I have left her lately.
I will not spoil my sheath with lesser brightness,
For my surrounding air has a new lightness;
Slight are her arms, yet they have bound me straitly
And left me cloaked as with a gauze of ether;
As with sweet leaves; as with a subtle clearness.
Oh, I have picked up magic in her nearness
To sheathe me half in half the things that sheathe her.

No, no! Go from me. I still have the flavor,
Soft as spring wind that's come from birchen bowers.
Green come the shoots, aye April in the branches,
As winter's wound with her sleight hand she stanches,
Hath of the trees a likeness of the savor:
As white their bark, so white this lady's hours.

Ballad for Gloom

For God, our God is a gallant foe
That playeth behind the veil.

I have loved my God as a child at heart
That seeketh deep bosoms for rest,
I have loved my God as a maid to man —
But lo, this thing is best:

[1] *Virginal:* a small spinet, a miniature piano, popular in the six-teenth century. A name also applied to songs written for accompaniment by that instrument. and is so used here.

To love your God as a gallant foe that plays behind the veil;
To meet your God as the night winds meet beyond Arcturus'[1] pale.

I have played with God for a woman,
I have staked with my God for truth,
I have lost to my God as a man, clear-eyed —
  His dice be not of ruth.
For I am made as a naked blade,
  But here ye this thing in sooth:

Who loseth to God as man to man
  Shall win at the turn of the game.
I have drawn my blade where the lightnings meet
  But the ending is the same:
Who loseth to God as the sword blades lose
  Shall win at the end of the game.

For God, our God is a gallant foe that playeth behind the
  veil.
Whom God deigns not to overthrow hath need of triple
  mail.[2]

In a Station of the Metro [3]

The apparition of these faces in the crowd;
Petals on a wet, black bough.

A Girl

The tree has entered my hands,
The sap has ascended my arms,
The tree has grown in my breast
Downward,
The branches grow out of me, like arms.
Tree you are,
Moss you are,

[1] *Arcturus:* a giant fixed star in remote space.
[2] *Mail:* chain armor, a set of small interlocking metal rings used
for protection.
[3] *Metro:* the Paris subway.

You are violets with wind above them.
A child — so high — you are;
And all this is folly to the world.

An Immorality

Sing we for love and idleness,
Naught else is worth the having.

Though I have been in many a land,
There is naught else in living.

And I would rather have my sweet,
Though rose-leaves die of grieving,

Than do high deeds in Hungary
To pass all men's believing.

Greek Epigram

Day and night are never weary,
Nor yet is God of creating
For day and night their torch-bearers
The aube [1] and the crepuscule.[2]

So, when I weary of praising the dawn and the sunset,
Let me be no more counted among the immortals;
But number me amid the wearying ones,
Let me be a man as the herd,
And as the slave that is given in barter.

LOUIS UNTERMEYER

Louis Untermeyer was born October 1, 1885, in New York City, where he lived, except for brief intervals, until 1923. His education was sketchy; his continued failure to comprehend geometry kept him from entering college. He intended to be a composer-pianist,

---

[1] *Aube:* dawn.   [2] *Crepuscule:* twilight.

but he kept music for his diversion instead of a profession. In 1923 he went abroad and, after two years in Europe, returned to devote himself entirely to literature. In 1928 he acquired a farm in the Adirondack Mountains, where he lived until the Second World War, when he became Senior Editor at the Office of War Information and was associated with the Armed Services Editions. Returning to New York and the lecture platform, he admitted that he enjoyed editorializing, loved to talk, and listened with difficulty.

It is not easy for the present compiler to consider this writer as severely as he deserves, the editor not having attained toward the poet that strict detachment which is the goal of criticism. However, it is evident that his work is divided into four kinds: his poetry, his parodies, his translations, and his prose. His initial volume of verse, *First Love* (1911), was a sequence of some seventy lyrics in which the influences of Heine and Housman were not only obvious but crippling; it is significant that when his *Selected Poems* ppeared, just three of the seventy poems were included.

It was with *Challenge* (1914) that the author first declared himself with any sort of definiteness. Although the ghost of Henley haunts many of the pages, poems like " Prayer," " On the Birth of a Child," and " Caliban in the Coal Mines " show " a fresh and lyrical sympathy with the modern world. . . . His vision " (thus *The Boston Transcript*) " is a social vision, his spirit a passionately energized command of the forces of justice." *These Times* (1917), *The New Adam* (1920), *Roast Leviathan* (1923), and *Burning Bush* (1928) were a mixture of fantastic imagination and mere facility. *Food and Drink* (1932) was a riper collection; many of the poems, such as " Long Feud " and " Last Words Before Winter," express serious emotions in a light tone of voice.

The best of his work was gathered in one volume, *Selected Poems and Parodies* (1935), and his early translations from Heine were revised and amplified to form the second volume of his analytical biography, *Heinrich Heine: Paradox and Poet* (1937). By the time he was sixty he had written, compiled, and edited more than fifty volumes, several of which were adopted as textbooks in high-schools and universities. The critical anthologies (*This Singing World, Modern American Poetry, Modern British Poetry,* and *Yesterday and Today*) were issued in various editions. When the *Encyclopædia Britannica* was revised he was chosen to furnish the article on Modern Poetry.

The poet also wrote several volumes of fiction, of which he considers his " novel " *Moses* the best, and several travel books, one of which (*The Donkey of God*) won an award in 1934 for the best book on Italian backgrounds in any language by a non-Italian. His *Treasury of Great Poems* (1942) was followed by *A Treasury of Laughter* (1946) and *The Inner Sanctum Walt Whitman* (1949), which was hailed as a comprehensive reappraisal of " the good gray poet."

Caliban [1] in the Coal Mines

God, we don't like to complain,
  We know that the mine is no lark.
But — there's the pools from the rain;
  But — there's the cold and the dark.

God, You don't know what it is —
  You, in Your well-lighted sky —
Watching the meteors whizz;
  Warm, with the sun always by.

God, if You had but the moon
  Stuck in Your cap for a lamp,
Even You'd tire of it soon,
  Down in the dark and the damp.

Nothing but blackness above
  And nothing that moves but the cars . . .
God, if You wish for our love,
  Fling us a handful of stars!

Long Feud

Where, without bloodshed, can there be
A more relentless enmity
Than the long feud fought silently

Between man and the growing grass.
Man's the aggressor, for he has
Weapons to humble and harass

The impudent spears that charge upon
His sacred privacy of lawn.
He mows them down, and they are gone

Only to lie in wait, although
He builds above and digs below
Where never a root would dare to go.

[1] *Caliban:* the laboring slave, servant to Prospero, in Shakespeare's *The Tempest.*

His are the triumphs till the day
There's no more grass to cut away
And, weary of labor, weary of play,

Having exhausted every whim,
He stretches out each conquering limb.
And then the small grass covers him.

On the Birth of a Child

Lo — to the battle-ground of life,
　Child, you have come, like a conquering shout,
Out of a struggle — into strife;
　Out of a darkness — into doubt.

Girt with the fragile armor of youth,
　Child, you must ride into endless wars,
With the sword of protest, the buckler of truth,
　And a banner of love to sweep the stars.

About you the world's despair will surge;
　Into defeat you must plunge and grope —
Be to the faltering, an urge;
　Be to the hopeless years, a hope!

Be to the darkened world, a flame;
　Be to its unconcern a blow!
For out of its pain and tumult you came,
　And into its tumult and pain you go.

Last Words before Winter

All my sheep
Gather in a heap,
For I spy the woolly, woolly wolf.

Farewell, my flocks,
Farewell. But let me find you
Safe in your stall and barn and box
With your winter's tale behind you.

Farewell, my cattle (both).
I leave you just as loath
As though you were a hundred head,
Instead
Of two-and-a-half.
(Two cows and a calf.)

Farewell, my apple-trees;
You have learned what it is to freeze,
With the drift on your knees.
But, oh, beware
Those first kind days, the snare
Of the too promising air,
The cost
Of over-sudden trust —
And then the killing frost.

Farewell, belovéd acres;
I leave you in the hands
Of one whose earliest enterprise was lands:
Your Maker's.

Yard, hutch, and house, farewell.
It is for you to tell
How you withstood the great white wolf, whose fell
Is softer than a lambkin's, but whose breath
Is death.
Farewell, hoof, claw, and wing,
Finned, furred, and feathered thing,
Till Spring —

All my sheep
Gather in a heap,
For I spy the woolly, woolly, wolf.

Prayer

God, though this life is but a wraith,
  Although we know not what we use,
Although we grope with little faith,
  Give me the heart to fight — and lose.

Ever insurgent let me be,
  Make me more daring than devout;
From sleek contentment keep me free,
  And fill me with a buoyant doubt.

Open my eyes to visions girt
  With beauty, and with wonder lit —
But let me always see the dirt,
  And all that spawn and die in it.

Open my ears to music; let
  Me thrill with Spring's first flutes and drums —
But never let me dare forget
  The bitter ballads of the slums.

From compromise and things half-done,
  Keep me, with stern and stubborn pride;
And when, at last, the fight is won,
  God, keep me still unsatisfied.

WILLIAM ROSE BENÉT

William Rose Benét was born at Fort Hamilton, New York Harbor, February 2, 1886. He was educated at Albany Academy and graduated from Yale in 1907. After various experiences as free-lance writer, publisher's reader, and second lieutenant, Benét became the associate editor of the New York *Post's* "Literary Review" in 1920, resigning in 1923 to become one of the editors of *The Saturday Review of Literature*. Benét died May 4, 1950.

The outstanding feature of Benét's verse is its whimsicality; an oriental imagination riots through his pages. Like the title-poem of his first volume, *Merchants from Cathay* (1913), all of Benét's volumes vibrate with an infectious music; they are full of the sonorous stuff that one rolls out tramping a road alone.

But Benét's charm is not confined to the lift and swing of rollicking choruses. His *The Falconer of God* (1914), *The Great White Wall* (1916), and *The Burglar of the Zodiac* (1918) contain decorations as bold as they are brilliant; they ring with a strange and spicy music evoked from seemingly casual words.

Moons of Grandeur (1920) represents the fullest development of Benét's unusual gifts, a combination of Eastern fantasy and Western vigor. The best of Benét's previous volumes as well as a group of new poems were selected for *Man Possessed* (1927), a volume that reveals a colorful vigor and an extraordinary range of interest. A more critical selection of Benét's poems may be found in his *Golden Fleece* (1935). "Sagacity" is a tribute written after the death of his second wife, the poet Elinor Wylie. *The Dust Which Is God*, an autobiography in verse form, was awarded the Pulitzer Prize in 1942. It was followed by *Day of Deliverance* (1944), a book of wartime poems, and *The Stairway of Surprise* (1947).

Merchants from Cathay [1]

How that They came.

Their heels slapped their bumping mules; their fat chaps glowed.
  Glory unto Mary, each seemed to wear a crown!
Like sunset their robes were on the wide, white road:
  So we saw those mad merchants come dusting into town!

Of their Beasts,

Two paunchy beasts they rode on and two they drove before.
  May the Saints all help us, the tiger-stripes they had!
And the panniers [2] upon them swelled full of stuffs and ore!
  The square buzzed and jostled at a sight so mad.

And their Boast,

They bawled in their beards, and their turbans they wried.
  They stopped by the stalls with curvetting and clatter.
As bronze as the bracken their necks and faces dyed —
  And a stave [3] they sat singing, to tell us of the matter.

[1] *Cathay:* the old name for China. It is used here to convey a fanciful picture; the whole poem is a fantasy of color and movement.

[2] *Panniers:* wicker baskets carried on the backs of horses or other beasts of burden.

[3] *Stave:* a short song.

With its
Burthen

For your silks to Sugarmago! For your dyes
    to Isfahan!
  Weird fruits from the Isle o' Lamaree.
    But for magic merchandise, for treasure-
      trove and spice,
" Here's a catch [1] and a carol to the great,
    grand Chan,
  The King of all the Kings across the sea!

And
Chorus.

" Here's a catch and a carol to the great, grand
    Chan;
For we won through the deserts to his sunset
    barbican; [2]
And the mountains of his palace no Titan's
    reach may span
  Where he wields his seignorie! [3]

A first
Stave
Fearsome,

" Red-as-blood skins of panthers, so bright
        against the sun
On the walls of the halls where his pillared
    state is set
They daze with the blaze no man may look
    upon.
  And with conduits of beverage those floors
    run wet.

And a second
Right hard
To stomach

" His wives stiff with riches, they sit before
        him there.
  Bird and beast at his feast make song and
    clapping cheer.
And jugglers and enchanters, all walking on
    the air,
  Make fall eclipse and thunder — make moons
    and suns appear!

And a third,
Which is a
Laughable
Thing

" Once the Chan, by his enemies sore-prest,
        and sorely spent,
  Lay, so they say, in a thicket 'neath a tree
Where the howl of an owl vexed his foes from
    their intent:

[1] *Catch:* a round, a continuous melody, for several voices.
[2] *Barbican:* a walled town or towering fort.
[3] *Seignorie:* lordship, power and authority.

Then that fowl for a holy bird of reverence
    made he!

We gape to
Hear them end,

    " *A catch and a carol to the great, grand Chan!*
Pastmasters of disasters, our desert caravan
Won through all peril to his sunset barbican,
    Where he wields his seignorie!
And crowns he gave us! We end where we
    began:
A catch and a carol to the great, grand Chan,
    The King of all the Kings across the sea! "

And are in
Terror,

Those   mad,   antic   Merchants! . . . Their
    stripèd beasts did beat
    The market-square suddenly with hooves of
        beaten gold!
The   ground   yawned   gaping   and   flamed be-
    neath our feet!
    They plunged to Pits Abysmal with their
        wealth untold!

And dread
* it is*
Devil's Work.

And some say the Chan himself in anger dealt
    the stroke —
For sharing of his secrets with silly, common
    folk:
But Holy, Blessed Mary, preserve us as you
    may
Lest once more those mad Merchants come
    chanting from Cathay!

Sagacity

We knew so much; when her beautiful eyes could lighten,
Her beautiful laughter follow our phrase;
Or the gaze go hard with pain, the lips tighten,
On the bitterer days.
Oh, ours was all knowing then, all generous displaying.
Such wisdom we had to show!
And now there is merely silence, silence, silence saying
All we did not know.

Jesse James

(A Design in Red and Yellow for a Nickel Library)

Jesse James was a two-gun man,
    (Roll on, Missouri!)
Strong-arm chief of an outlaw clan.
    (From Kansas to Illinois!)
He twirled an old Colt forty-five;
    (Roll on, Missouri!)
They never took Jesse James alive.
    (Roll, Missouri, roll!)

Jesse James was King of the Wes';
    (Cataracts in the Missouri!)
He'd a di'mon' heart in his lef' breas';
    (Brown Missouri rolls!)
He'd a fire in his heart no hurt could stifle;
    (Thunder, Missouri!)
Lion eyes an' a Winchester rifle.
    (Missouri, roll down!)

Jesse James rode a pinto hawse;
Come at night to a water-cawse;
Tetched with the rowel [1] that pinto's flank,
She sprung the torrent from bank to bank.

Jesse rode through a sleepin' town;
Looked the moonlit street both up an' down;
Crack-crack-crack, the street ran flames
An' a great voice cried, " I'm Jesse James! "

Hawse an' afoot they're after Jess!
    (Roll on, Missouri!)
Spurrin' an' spurrin' — but he's gone Wes'.
    (Brown Missouri rolls!)
He was ten foot tall when he stood in his boots;
    (Lightnin' like the Missouri!)
More'n a match fer sich galoots.
    (Roll, Missouri, roll!)

[1] *Tetched with the rowel:* touched the horse with the little pointed wheel on the spur.

Jesse James rode outa the sage;
Roun' the rocks come the swayin' stage;
Straddlin' the road a giant stan's
An' a great voice bellers, " Throw up yer han's! "

Jesse raked in the di'mon' rings,
The big gold watches an' the yuther things;
Jesse divvied 'em then an' thar
With a cryin' child had lost her mar.

They're creepin'; they're crawlin', they're stalkin' Jess;
    (*Roll on, Missouri!*)
They's a rumor he's gone much further Wes';
    (*Roll, Missouri, roll!*)
They's word of a cayuse hitched to the bars
    (*Ruddy clouds on Missouri!*)
Of a golden sunset that busts into stars.
    (*Missouri, roll down!*)

Jesse James rode hell fer leather;
He was a hawse an' a man together;
In a cave in a mountain high up in air
He lived with a rattlesnake, a wolf, an' a bear.

Jesse's heart was as sof' as a woman;
Fer guts an' stren'th he was sooper-human;
He could put six shots through a woodpecker's eye
And take in one swaller a gallon o' rye.

They sought him here an' they sought him there,
    (*Roll on, Missouri!*)
But he strides by night through the ways of the air;
    (*Brown Missouri rolls!*)
They say he was took an' they say he is dead,
    (*Thunder, Missouri!*)
But he ain't — he's a sunset overhead!
    (*Missouri down to the sea!*)

Jesse James was a Hercules.
When he went through the woods he tore up the trees.
When he went on the plains he smoked the groun'
An' the hull lan' shuddered fer miles aroun'.

Jesse James wore a red bandanner
That waved on the breeze like the Star Spangled Banner;
In seven states he cut up dadoes.
He's gone with the buffler an' the desperadoes.

Yes, Jesse James was a two-gun man
     (Roll on, Missouri!)
The same as when this song began;
     (From Kansas to Illinois!)
An' when you see a sunset bust into flames
     (Lightnin' like the Missouri!)
Or a thunderstorm blaze — that's Jesse James!
     (Hear that Missouri roll!)

Night

Let the night keep
What the night takes,
Sighs buried deep,
Ancient heart-aches,
Groans of the lover,
Tears of the lost;
Let day discover not
All the night cost!

Let the night keep
Love's burning bliss,
Drowned in deep sleep
Whisper and kiss,
Thoughts like white flowers
In hedges of May;
Let such deep hours not
Fade with the day!

Monarch is night
Of all eldest things,
Pain and affright,
Rapturous wings;
Night the crown, night the sword
Lifted to smite.
Kneel to your overlord,
Children of night!

John Gould Fletcher, born at Little Rock, Arkansas, January 3, 1886, was educated at Phillips Academy and Harvard. After some years in Massachusetts, he lived in England for twenty years. In 1933 he returned to the family home in Little Rock.

At twenty-seven Fletcher published five books of poems which he has referred to as "his literary wild oats," five small collections of faintly interesting verse. A year later Fletcher joined the Imagists. With H. D. and Amy Lowell he became one of the leaders of this movement and his contributions were among the outstanding features of the anthologies. After the appearance of *Some Imagist Poets,* Fletcher discarded his previous style and emerged as a more arresting poet with *Irradiations – Sand and Spray* (1915). The volume is full of an extraordinary fancy; imagination riots through it, though it is sometimes a bloodless and bodiless imagination. In *Goblins and Pagodas* (1916), Fletcher carries his unrelated harmonies much further. Color dominates him; the set of eleven "color symphonies" is an elaborate design in which the tone as well as the thought is summoned by color-associations, sometimes closely related, sometimes far-fetched. This is illustrated by the selection from "Irradiations," literally "rays of splintered light," which illumine a series of shifting images.

In 1917 Fletcher again began to change in spirit as well as style. He sought for depths rather than surfaces; his "Lincoln" accomplished a closer relation to humanity. A moving mysticism speaks from *The Tree of Life* (1918); the more obviously native *Granite and Breakers* (1921) and *Parables* (1925) contain a prophetic note new to this poet. The later poems reach depths which the preceding verses never attained. A subdued gravity moves through *The Black Rock* (1928), *Branches of Adam* (1926), *XXIV Elegies* (1935), *South Star* (1941), and *The Burning Mountain* (1946).

Fletcher has translated several volumes from the French; his autobiography at the age of fifty was published in 1937 under the title *Life Is My Song. Selected Poems* appeared in 1938 and was awarded the Pulitzer Prize. Fletcher died May 10, 1950.

from Irradiations

I

Over the roof-tops race the shadows of clouds;
Like horses the shadows of clouds charge down the street.

Whirlpools of purple and gold,
Winds from the mountains of cinnabar,[1]

[1] *Cinnabar:* a deep red color.

Lacquered mandarin moments, palanquins [1] swaying and bal-
          ancing
Amid vermilion pavilions, against the jade balustrades,
Glint of the glittering wings of dragon-flies in the light:
Silver filaments, golden flakes settling downwards,
Rippling, quivering flutters, repulse and surrender,
The sun broidered upon the rain,
The rain rustling with the sun.

Over the roof-tops race the shadows of clouds;
Like horses the shadows of clouds charge down the street . . .

III

The trees, like great jade elephants,
Chained, stamp and shake 'neath the gadflies of the breeze;
The trees lunge and plunge, unruly elephants:
The clouds are their crimson howdah-canopies [2];
The sunlight glints like the golden robe of a Shah.
Would I were tossed on the wrinkled backs of those trees.

IV

O seeded grass, you army of little men
Crawling up the long slope with quivering, quick blades of
          steel:
You who storm millions of graves, tiny green tentacles [3] of
          Earth,
Interlace yourselves tightly over my heart,
And do not let me go:
For I would lie here forever and watch with one eye
The pilgrimaging ants in your dull, savage jungles,
The while with the other I see the stiff lines of the slope
Break in mid-air, a wave surprisingly arrested, —
And above them, wavering, dancing, bodiless, colorless, un-
          real,
The long thin lazy fingers of the heat.

[1] *Palanquins:* an enclosed litter large enough for several people,
carried by two to four men.

[2] *Howdah-canopies:* a howdah is a seat or little cushioned rest,
usually covered, on an elephant's back.

[3] *Tentacles:* thin arms, fingers, or " feelers."

London Nightfall

I saw the shapes that stood upon the clouds:
And they were tiger-breasted, shot with light,
And all of them, lifting long trumpets together,
Blew over the city, for the night to come.
Down in the street, we floundered in the mud;
Above, in endless files, gold angels came
And stood upon the clouds, and blew their horns
For night.

Like a wet petal crumpled,
Twilight fell soddenly on the weary city;
The 'busses lurched and groaned,
The shops put up their doors.

But skywards, far aloft,
The angels, vanishing, waved broad plumes of gold,
Summoning spirits from a thousand hills
To pour the thick night out upon the earth.

Lincoln

I

Like a gaunt, scraggly pine
Which lifts its head above the mournful sandhills;
And patiently, through dull years of bitter silence,
Untended and uncared for, begins to grow.

Ungainly, laboring, huge,
The wind of the north has twisted and gnarled its branches;
Yet in the heat of midsummer days, when thunder-clouds
    ring the horizon,
A nation of men shall rest beneath its shade.

And it shall protect them all,
Hold everyone safe there, watching aloof in silence;
Until at last one mad stray bolt from the zenith
Shall strike it in an instant down to earth.

II

There was a darkness in this man; an immense and hollow
   darkness,
Of which we may not speak, nor share with him, nor enter;
A darkness through which strong roots stretched downwards
   into the earth
Towards old things;
Towards the herdman-kings who walked the earth and spoke
   with God,
Towards the wanderers who sought for they knew not what,
   and found their goal at last;
Towards the men who waited, only waited patiently when all
   seemed lost,
Many bitter winters of defeat;
Down to the granite of patience
These roots swept, knotted fibrous roots, prying, piercing,
   seeking,
And drew from the living rock and the living waters about it
The red sap to carry upwards to the sun.
Not proud, but humble,
Only to serve and pass on, to endure to the end through
   service;
For the ax is laid at the root of the trees, and all that bring
   not forth good fruit
Shall be cut down on the day to come and cast into the fire.

III

There is silence abroad in the land today,
And in the hearts of men, a deep and anxious silence;
And, because we are still at last, those bronze lips slowly
   open,
Those hollow and weary eyes take on a gleam of light.

Slowly a patient, firm-syllabled voice cuts through the end-
   less silence
Like laboring oxen that drag a plow through the chaos of
   rude clay-fields:
"I went forward as the light goes forward in early spring
But there were also many things which I left behind.

"Tombs that were quiet;
One, of a mother, whose brief light went out in the darkness,

One, of a loved one, the snow on whose grave is long falling,
One, only of a child, but it was mine.

" Have you forgot your graves? Go, question them in anguish,
Listen long to their unstirred lips. From your hostages to
silence,
Learn there is no life without death, no dawn without sun-
setting,
No victory but to Him who has given all."

IV

The clamor of cannon dies down, the furnace-mouth of the
battle is silent.
The midwinter sun dips and descends, the earth takes on
afresh its bright colors.
But he whom we mocked and obeyed not, he whom we
scorned and mistrusted,
He has descended, like a god, to his rest.

Over the uproar of cities,
Over the million intricate threads of life wavering and cross-
ing,
In the midst of problems we know not, tangling, perplexing,
ensnaring,
Rises one white tomb alone.

Beam over it, stars.
Wrap it round, stripes — stripes red for the pain that he bore
for you —
Enfold it forever, O flag, rent, soiled, but repaired through
your anguish;
Long as you keep him there safe, the nations shall bow to
your law.

Strew over him flowers;
Blue forget-me-nots from the north, and the bright pink
arbutus
From the east, and from the west rich orange blossoms,
But from the heart of the land take the passion-flower.

Rayed, violet, dim,
With the nails that pierced, the cross that he bore and the
circlet,

And beside it there, lay also one lonely snow-white mag-
nolia,
Bitter for remembrance of the healing which has passed.

The Skaters

Black swallows swooping or gliding
In a flurry of entangled loops and curves;
The skaters skim over the frozen river.
And the grinding click of their skates as they impinge upon
the surface,
Is like the brushing together of thin wing-tips of silver.

H. D.

Hilda Doolittle was born September 10, 1886, at Bethlehem,
Pennsylvania. When she was still a child, her father became Director of the Flower Observatory and the family moved to a suburb
in the outskirts of Philadelphia. She attended a private school in
West Philadelphia, entered Bryn Mawr College in 1904, and went
abroad for what was intended to be a short sojourn in 1911. After
a visit to Italy and France, she came to London, joined Ezra
Pound, and helped organize the Imagists. Her work (signed
H. D.) began to appear in a few magazines and its unusual quality
was recognized at once. Her first volume, *Sea Garden*, appeared
in 1916; her second, *Hymen*, was published in 1921.

H. D. is, by all odds, the most important of her group. She is
the only one who has steadfastly held to the letter as well as to the
spirit of its program. She is, in fact, the only true Imagist. Her
poems, capturing the firm delicacy of the Greek models, are like
a set of Tanagra figurines. Here, at first glance, the effect is chill-
ing; beauty seems held in a frozen gesture. But it is in this very
fixation of light, color, and emotion that she achieves intensity.

Observe the tiny poem entitled " Heat." Here, in the fewest
possible words, is something beyond the description of heat — here
is the effect of it. In these lines one feels the very weight and solidity of a midsummer afternoon. The tiny " Oread " paints an
agitated sea in miniature as it might appear to a mountain nymph
who had never seen a great body of water.

Heliodora (1924) and *Collected Poems* (1925) are full of passion, but passion severely controlled. The same combination of
ecstasy and austerity is evident in her later *Red Roses for Bronze*

(1932), in her Greek dramas *Hippolytus Temporizes* (1925), *Ion* (1937), *The Walls Do Not Fall* (1944), and *The Flowering of the Rod* (1946). These works, with their addition of rhyme and regular rhythm, fuse the skill of the early Imagist with the strength of the mature poet.

Oread [1]

Whirl up, sea —
Whirl your pointed pines.
Splash your great pines
On our rocks.
Hurl your green over us —
Cover us with your pools of fir.

Heat

O wind, rend open the heat,
cut apart the heat,
rend it to tatters.

Fruit cannot drop
through this thick air —
fruit cannot fall into heat
that presses up and blunts
the points of pears
and rounds the grapes.

Cut through the heat —
plow through it,
turning it on either side
of your path.

Pear Tree

Silver dust
lifted from the earth,
higher than my arms reach,
you have mounted.
O silver,

[1] *Oread:* a mythological mountain nymph.

higher than my arms reach
you front us with great mass;
no flower ever opened
so stanch a white leaf,
no flower ever parted silver
from such rare silver;
O white pear,
your flower-tufts,
thick on the branch,
bring summer and ripe fruits
in their purple hearts.

Song from Cyprus

Where is the nightingale,
in what myrrh-wood and dim?
ah, let the night come black,
for we would conjure back
all that enchanted him,
        all that enchanted him.

Where is the bird of fire?
in what packed hedge of rose?
in what roofed ledge of flower?
no other creature knows
what magic lurks within,
        what magic lurks within.

Bird, bird, bird, bird, we cry,
hear, pity us in pain;
hearts break in the sunlight,
hearts break in daylight rain,
only night heals again,
        only night heals again.

Lethe [1]

Nor skin nor hide nor fleece
        Shall cover you,
Nor curtain of crimson nor fine

[1] *Lethe:* a river in Hades, the underworld of the Greeks. Lethe's
water when drunk brought forgetfulness.

Shelter of cedar-wood be over you,
    Nor the fir-tree
    Nor the pine.

Nor sight of whin[1] nor gorse
    Nor river-yew,[2]
Nor fragrance of flowering bush,
Nor wailing of reed-bird to waken you.
    Nor of linnet
    Nor of thrush.

Nor word nor touch nor sight
    Of lover, you
Shall long through the night but for this:
The roll of the full tide to cover you
    Without question,
    Without kiss.

JEAN STARR UNTERMEYER

Jean Starr was born at Zanesville, Ohio, May 13, 1886, and educated at the Putnam Seminary in the city of her birth. At sixteen, she came to New York City, pursuing special studies at Columbia. She was married to Louis Untermeyer in 1907, and, except for sojourns abroad, lived in New York.

While not an Imagist, her early work was influenced by that movement with its emphasis on the exact word and the precise image. Precision was almost a passion with her; her first volume, *Growing Pains* (1918), is unusually severe in its definiteness. Self-critical and self-searching, there is, at the same time, a sharp color-sense, a surprising whimsicality, and a translation of ordinary phenomena in terms of the unusually pictorial. The brief "High Tide" and "Clay Hills" establish this; "Autumn," praised by Amy Lowell for its sensitive "painting in words," confirms it.

Dreams Out of Darkness (1921) and *Steep Ascent* (1927) reveal an intensification and ripening of this author's powers with a richer musical undercurrent. *Love and Need* (1940) assembles her other volumes with the addition of new poems in strictly disciplined verse. Her version of Hermann Broch's *The Death of Virgil* (1945) was hailed as a masterpiece of translation.

[1] *Whin:* furze, a kind of gorse, a coarse shrub with yellow flowers.

[2] *River-yew:* an evergreen tree common in Europe.

Clay Hills

It is easy to mold the yielding clay.
And many shapes grow into beauty
Under the facile hand.
But forms of clay are lightly broken:
They will lie shattered and forgotten in a dingy corner.

But underneath the slipping clay
Is rock . . .
I would rather work in stubborn rock
All the years of my life,
And make one strong thing,
And set it in a high clean place,
To recall the granite strength of my desire.

High Tide

I edged back against the night.
The sea growled assault on the wave-bitten shore
And the breakers,
Like young and impatient hounds,
Sprang with rough joy on the shrinking sand.
Sprang, but were pulled back slowly,
With a long, relentless pull,
Whimpering, into the dark.

Then I saw who held them captive;
And I saw how they were bound
With a broad and quivering leash of light,
Held by the moon,
As, calm and unsmiling,
She walked the deep fields of the sky.

Autumn

(*To My Mother*)

How memory cuts away the years,
And how clean the picture comes
Of autumn days, brisk and busy;

Charged with keen sunshine.
And you, stirred with activity,
The spirit of those energetic days.

There was our back-yard,
So plain and stripped of green,
With even the weeds carefully pulled away
From the crooked red bricks that made the walk,
And the earth on either side so black.
Autumn and dead leaves burning in the sharp air.
And winter comforts coming in like a pageant.
I shall not forget them:
Great jars laden with the raw green of pickles,
Standing in a solemn row across the back of the porch,
Exhaling the pungent dill;
And, in the very center of the yard,
You, tending the great catsup kettle of gleaming copper,
Where fat, red tomatoes bobbed up and down
Like jolly monks in a drunken dance.
And there were bland banks of cabbage that came by the
    wagon-load,
Soon to be cut into delicate ribbons
Only to be crushed by the heavy, wooden stompers.
Such feathery whiteness — to come to kraut!
And after, there were grapes that hid their brightness under
    a gray dust,
Then gushed thrilling, purple blood over the fire;
And enameled crab-apples that tricked with their fragrance
But were bitter to taste.
And there were spicy plums and ill-shaped quinces,
And long string beans floating in pans of clear water
Like slim, green fishes.
And there was fish itself,
Salted, silver herring from the city. . . .

And you moved among these mysteries,
Absorbed and smiling and sure;
Stirring, tasting, measuring,
With the precision of a ritual.
I like to think of you in your years of power —
You, now so shaken and so powerless —
High priestess of your home.

(Alfred) Joyce Kilmer was born at New Brunswick, New Jersey, December 6, 1886. He was graduated from Rutgers College in 1904 and received his A.B. from Columbia in 1906. In 1917 Kilmer joined the Officers' Reserve Training Corps; in less than three weeks after America entered the World War, he enlisted as a private in the Seventh Regiment, National Guard, New York. On July 28, 1918, the five-day battle for the mastery of the heights beyond the river Ourcq was begun. Two days later, Kilmer was killed in action.

Death came before the poet had matured his gifts. His first volume, *Summer of Love* (1911), is wholly imitative, full of reflections of a dozen sources. *Trees and Other Poems* (1914) contains the title-poem by which Kilmer is best known and, though various influences are here, a refreshing candor lights up the lines. In *Main Street and Other Poems* (1917) the simplicity is natural and the effect is spontaneous.

Trees

I think that I shall never see
A poem lovely as a tree.

A tree whose hungry mouth is prest
Against the earth's sweet flowing breast;

A tree that looks at God all day,
And lifts her leafy arms to pray;

A tree that may in summer wear
A nest of robins in her hair;

Upon whose bosom snow has lain;
Who intimately lives with rain.

Poems are made by fools like me,
But only God can make a tree.

Martin

When I am tired of earnest men,
    Intense and keen and sharp and clever,
Pursuing fame with brush or pen

Or counting metal disks forever,
Then from the halls of shadowland
    Beyond the trackless purple sea
Old Martin's ghost comes back to stand
    Beside my desk and talk to me.

Still on his delicate pale face
    A quizzical thin smile is showing,
His cheeks are wrinkled like fine lace,
    His kind blue eyes are gay and glowing.
He wears a brilliant-hued cravat,
    A suit to match his soft gray hair,
A rakish stick, a knowing hat,
    A manner blithe and debonair.

How good, that he who always knew
    That being lovely was a duty,
Should have gold halls to wander through
    And should himself inhabit beauty.
How like his old unselfish way
    To leave those halls of splendid mirth
And comfort those condemned to stay
    Upon the bleak and somber earth.

Some people ask: What cruel chance
    Made Martin's life so sad a story?
Martin? Why, he exhaled romance
    And wore an overcoat of glory.
A fleck of sunlight in the street,
    A horse, a book, a girl who smiled, —
Such visions made each moment sweet
    For this receptive, ancient child.

Because it was old Martin's lot
    To be, not make, a decoration,
Shall we then scorn him, having not
    His genius of appreciation?
Rich joy and love he got and gave;
    His heart was merry as his dress.
Pile laurel wreaths upon his grave
    Who did not gain, but was, success.

Robinson Jeffers' condensed autobiography runs as follows: "Born in Pittsburgh in 1887; my parents carried me about Europe a good deal. When I was fifteen I was brought home. Next year my family moved to California and I graduated at eighteen from Occidental College, Los Angeles. After that, desultory years at the University of Southern California, University of Zurich, Medical School in Los Angeles, University of Washington, but with faint interest. I wasn't deeply interested in anything but poetry. I married Una Call Kuster in 1913. We were going to England in the autumn of 1914. But the August news turned us to this village of Carmel instead; and when the stagecoach topped the hill from Monterey, and we looked down through pines and sea-fogs on Carmel Bay, it was evident that we had come without knowing it to our inevitable place."

Flagons and Apples (1912), Jeffers' undistinguished first volume, was followed by *Californians* (1916). In 1925 *Tamar and Other Poems* was brought out by a small printer and caused an overnight sensation. It was reprinted the following year, with the addition of new poems, as *Roan Stallion, Tamar, and Other Poems* (1926). This, it was evident at once, was masculine poetry, stark, even terrible in its intensities. Whatever defects this verse has — and it must be confessed that Jeffers piles on his catastrophes with little humor and less restraint — there is no denying its power. He combines two almost contrary types of strength: the rude American and the stoic Greek.

The Women of Sur Point (1927) again shows how easily Jeffers can swing the long line, how suddenly his phrases soar from the tawdry into the ecstatic. From *Cawdor* (1928) to *Be Angry at the Sun* (1941) and *The Double Axe and Other Poems* (1948), Jeffers deals with themes which are horrifying against settings which are monstrous. Although the shorter poems are quieter and less pessimistic, the prevailing mood is terror with overtones of madness. But if the philosophy is negative, the poetry is vigorous. It is not a pretty poetry, not a poetry we may love, but it is a poetry which is hard to forget. It may move to the extremes of horror or anger, but it never fails to move the reader. *The Selected Poetry of Robinson Jeffers* appeared in 1938 and revealed, beneath the bitterness, a sense of the dignity of age, confidence in survival, and an intense awareness of impersonal beauty.

Several biographies and theses have been written about the poet; two of the best are George Sterling's *Robinson Jeffers* (1926) and Lawrence Powell's *Robinson Jeffers: The Man and His Work* (1934).

Compensation

Solitude that unmakes me one of men
In snowwhite hands brings singular recompense,
Evening me with kindlier natures when
On the needled pinewood the cold dews condense
About the hour of Rigel [1] fallen from heaven
In wintertime, or when the long night tides
Sigh blindly from the sand dune backward driven,
Or when on stormwings of the northwind rides
The foamscud with the cormorants, or when passes
A horse or dog with brown affectionate eyes,
Or autumn frosts are pricked by earliest grasses,
Or whirring from her cover a quail flies.
Why, even in humanity beauty and good
Show, from the mountainside of solitude.

Age in Prospect

Praise youth's hot blood if you will, I think that happiness
Rather consists in having lived clear through
Youth and hot blood, on to the wintrier hemisphere
Where one has time to wait and remember.

Youth and hot blood are beautiful, so is peacefulness.
Youth had some islands in it but age is indeed
An island and a peak; age has infirmities,
Not few, but youth is all one fever.

And there is no possession more sure than memory's;
But if I reach that gray island, that peak,
My hope is still to possess with eyes the homeliness
Of ancient loves, ocean and mountains,

And meditate the sea-mouth of mortality
And the fountain six feet down with a quieter thirst
Than now I feel for old age; a creature progressively
Thirsty for life will be for death too.

[1] *Rigel:* a large and far-distant star in the constellation of Orion.

Joy

Though joy is better than sorrow, joy is not great;
Peace is great, strength is great.
Not for joy the stars burn, not for joy the vulture
Spreads her gray sails on the air
Over the mountain; not for joy the worn mountain
Stands, while years like water
Trench his long sides. " I am neither mountain nor bird
Nor star; and I seek joy."
The weakness of your breed; yet at length quietness
Will cover those wistful eyes.

Hurt Hawks

The broken pillar of the wing jags from the clotted shoulder;
The wing trails like a banner in defeat,
No more to use the sky forever but live with famine
And pain a few days: cat nor coyote
Will shorten the week of waiting for death, there is game
    without talons.

He stands under the oak-bush and waits
The lame feet of salvation; at night he remembers freedom
And flies in a dream, the dawns ruin it.
He is strong and pain is worse to the strong, incapacity is
    worse.
The curs of the day come and torment him
At distance, no one but death the redeemer will humble that
    head,
The intrepid readiness, the terrible eyes.
The wild God of the world is sometimes merciful to those
That ask mercy, not often to the arrogant.
You do not know him, you communal people, or you have
    forgotten him;
Intemperate and savage, the hawk remembers him;
Beautiful and wild, the hawks, and men that are dying re-
    member him . . .

I'd sooner, except the penalties, kill a man than a hawk; but
    the great redtail

Had nothing left but unable misery
From the bone too shattered for mending, the wing that
 trailed under his talons when he moved.
We had fed him six weeks, I gave him freedom,
He wandered over the foreland hill and returned in the eve-
 ning, asking for death,
Not like a beggar, still eyed with the old
Implacable arrogance. I gave him the lead gift in the twi-
 light.
 What fell was relaxed,
Owl-downy, soft feminine feathers; but what
Soared: the fierce rush: the night-herons by the flooded river
 cried fear at its rising
Before it was quite unsheathed from reality.

Gale in April

Intense and terrible beauty, how has our race with the frail
 naked nerves,
So little a craft, swum down from its far launching?
Why now, only because the northwest blows and the headed
 grass billows,
Great seas jagging the west and on the granite
Blanching, the vessel is brimmed, this dancing play of the
 world is too much passion.
A gale in April so overfilling the spirit,
Though his ribs were thick as the earth's, arches of moun-
 tain, how shall one dare to live,
Though his blood were like the earth's rivers and his flesh
 iron,
How shall one dare to live? One is born strong, how do the
 weak endure it?
The strong lean upon death as on a rock,
After eighty years there is shelter and the naked nerves shall
 be covered with deep quietness.
O beauty of things, go on, go on, O torture
Of intense joy, I have lasted out my time, I have thanked
 God and finished,
Roots of millennial trees fold me in the darkness,
Northwest winds shake their tops, not to the root, not to the
 root, I have passed
From beauty to the other beauty, peace, the night splendor.

To the Stone-Cutters

Stone-cutters fighting time with marble, you foredefeated
Challengers of oblivion,
Eat cynical earnings, knowing rock splits, records fall down,
The square-limbed Roman letters
Scale in the thaws, wear in the rain. The poet as well
Builds his monument mockingly;
For man will be blotted out, the blithe earth die, the brave
    sun
Die blind, his heart blackening:
Yet stones have stood for a thousand years, and pained
    thoughts found
The honey of peace in old poems.

ROY HELTON

Roy Helton was born in Washington, D. C., in 1887. He graduated from the University of Pennsylvania in 1908. He studied art, and found he was color-blind. He spent two years at inventions, and found he had no business sense. After a few more experiments he became a schoolmaster in West Philadelphia.

Helton's first volume, *Youth's Pilgrimage* (1915), is a strange, mystical affair, full of vague symbolism. *Outcasts in Beulah Land* (1918) is entirely different in theme and treatment. This is a much starker verse; a poetry of city streets, direct and sharp. Shortly after, Helton spent much of his time in the Appalachian Mountains and became intimately connected with primitive backgrounds. The result was *Lonesome Water* (1930), full of the sense of the Kentucky hills.

"Old Christmas Morning" is one of the poems in the latter collection which is rare in modern verse. It is told as vividly as an old ballad, a ghost story which takes place on the night twelve days after December 25th, on "Old Christmas," which tradition has connected with supernatural events. The story of the feud is heightened not only by the crisp dialogue and the terse stanzas but by the skillful dramatic suspense and the final surprise.

Old Christmas Morning

"Where you coming from, Lomey Carter,
  So airly over the snow?
And what's them pretties you got in your hand
  And where you aiming to go?

"Step in, Honey: Old Christmas morning
  I ain't got nothing much;
Maybe a bite of sweetness and corn bread,
  A little ham meat and such.

"But come in, Honey! Sally Anne Barton's
  Hungering after your face.
Wait till I light my candle up:
  Set down! There's your old place.

"Now where you been so airly this morning?"
  "Graveyard, Sally Anne.
Up by the trace in the salt lick meadows
  Where Taulbe kilt my man."

"Taulbe ain't to home this morning . . .
  I can't scratch up a light:
Dampness gets on the heads of the matches;
  But I'll blow up the embers bright."

"Needn't trouble. I won't be stopping:
  Going a long ways still."
"You didn't see nothing, Lomey Carter,
  Up on the graveyard hill?"

"What should I see there, Sally Anne Barton?"
  "Well, sperits do walk last night."
"There were an elder bush a-blooming
  While the moon still give some light."

"Yes, elder bushes, they bloom, Old Christmas,
  And critters kneel down in their straw.
Anything else up in the graveyard?"
  "One thing more I saw:

" I saw my man with his head all bleeding
Where Taulbe's shot went through."
" What did he say? " " *He stooped and kissed me."*
" What did he say to you? "

" Said, Lord Jesus forguv your Taulbe;
But he told me another word;
He said it soft when he stooped and kissed me.
That were the last I heard."

" Taulbe ain't to home this morning."
" *I know that, Sally Anne,*
For I kilt him, coming down through the meadow
Where Taulbe kilt my man.

" I met him upon the meadow trace
When the moon were fainting fast,
And I had my dead man's rifle gun
And kilt him as he come past."

" But I heard two shots." " *'Twas his was second:*
He shot me 'fore he died:
You'll find us at daybreak, Sally Anne Barton:
I'm laying there dead at his side."

ALAN SEEGER

Alan Seeger was born in New York, June 22, 1888. His boyhood was spent on Staten Island. Later, there were several other
migrations, including a sojourn in Mexico, where Seeger lived the
most impressionable years of his youth. In 1906, he entered Harvard. 1914 came, and the European war had not entered its third
week when, along with some forty of his fellow-countrymen,
Seeger enlisted in the Foreign Legion of France. He was in action
almost continually. On the fourth of July, 1916, ordered to take
the village of Belloy-en-Santerre, Seeger advanced in the first rush
with his squad, which was practically wiped out by hidden machine-gun fire. Seeger fell, mortally wounded, and died the next
morning.

Seeger's literary promise was far greater than his poetic accomplishment. With the exception of his famous (and prophetic)

poem, there is little of importance, though much of charm, in his collected *Poems* published, with an Introduction by William Archer, in 1916.

I Have a Rendezvous with Death

I have a rendezvous with Death
At some disputed barricade,
When Spring comes back with rustling shade
And apple-blossoms fill the air —
I have a rendezvous with Death
When Spring brings back blue days and fair.
It may be he shall take my hand
And lead me into his dark land
And close my eyes and quench my breath —
It may be I shall pass him still.
I have a rendezvous with Death
On some scarred slope of battered hill,
When Spring comes round again this year
And the first meadow-flowers appear.

God knows 'twere better to be deep
Pillowed in silk and scented down,
Where love throbs out in blissful sleep,
Pulse nigh to pulse, and breath to breath,
Where hushed awakenings are dear . . .
But I've a rendezvous with Death
At midnight in some flaming town;
When Spring trips north again this year,
And I to my pledged word am true,
I shall not fail that rendezvous.

T. S. ELIOT

T(homas) S(tearns) Eliot was born in St. Louis, Missouri, September 26, 1888. He was educated at Harvard, at the Sorbonne, and at Oxford. Since 1914 he has lived in England, where he is a member of the publishing firm of Faber & Faber. In 1927 Eliot became a naturalized British subject.

Eliot's *Collected Poems* (1936) contain comparatively few poems besides the long and difficult *The Waste Land* (1922), but these few exercised a great influence upon Eliot's generation. The mood was a mixture of irony and despair; it expressed a world of insecurity and bewilderment. Eliot mirrored an age shell-shocked by war and assaulted by economic uncertainty, an age in which faiths had been shattered and foundations had crumbled. Eliot spoke — or seemed to speak — for those who were hopeless, or helpless, or spiritually dispossessed.

As poetry, Eliot's expression was a bold and successful experiment to some, wholly incomprehensible to others. Certain critics praised it for its suggestiveness and imagination, while others considered it willfully obscure and so meaningless as to belong to a "cult" of unintelligibility. Nevertheless, Eliot's shorter poems and many passages in the longer ones establish a poignant relation between beauty and the commonplace. The very opening of "The Love Song of J. Alfred Prufrock" communicates a mood of irony, disillusion, and defeat, and the ensuing description of the fog is highly imaginative. (It is interesting to compare Eliot's characterization with Sandburg's "Fog" on page 117) "Morning at the Window" and "Prelude" further illustrate Eliot's method of uniting harmony and discords, blending the mysterious with the trivial and tawdry.

"The Hollow Men," one of Eliot's most typical poems, pictures a world which has reached a dead end of doubt. It is, as the title implies, a barren land, a land of stony images, where everything is exhausted — "shape without form, shade without color, paralyzed force, gesture without motion." Men gather on stony soil in a "valley of dying stars." They lean together, lacking initiative. They are without vision; they grope without thought. The confusion is intensified by the juxtaposition of a distorted Nursery Rhyme and a fragment from the Lord's Prayer. The finale completes the despair. Civilization, having lost its ideals and religion, has reached an impasse; man cannot even die heroically. The world ends not with a bang, but with a whimper.

Four Quartets (1943) is a difficult set of poems. Each section bears a subtitle which is the name of a place associated with Eliot's experiences, and each stresses Eliot's main preoccupations: the sense of time, the sense of sin, and the sense of poetry. The style is both simpler and subtler than anything the author had previously written. The language ranges from conversational and flatly prosaic statements to rapt and mystical rhetoric.

A lighter side of Eliot is revealed in *Old Possum's Book of Practical Cats* (1939), a playful volume which includes fourteen amusing tokens of the poet's understanding of kittens, toms, and tabbies. Here are tributes to such fascinating felines as Growltiger, Griddlebone, Mungojerrie, Rumpelteazer, Old Deuteronomy, Mr. Mistoffelees, and the mysterious Macavity. The verse is nimble and the fancies are unsuspectedly whimsical and ingratiating.

In 1948 Eliot was awarded the Nobel Prize " for his work as a trail-blazing pioneer of modern poetry." He had already received the British Order of Merit. Besides his poems, he was the author of several religious plays, notably *The Rock* (1934), *Murder in the Cathedral* (1935), *The Family Reunion* (1939), and several volumes of criticism and interpretation. The best of these are in *Selected Essays: 1917–1932* and *The Use of Poetry* (1933). A statement of Eliot's social philosophy appeared in *Notes Toward a Definition of Culture* (1949).

Many full-length books were devoted to Eliot; one critic remarked that " the poet's rather slender production sometimes seems to be buried under an accumulated mass of glosses and explanations." The best critical studies of his work are *The Achievement of T. S. Eliot* (1935) by F. O. Matthiessen; *T. S. Eliot: A Study of His Writings by Several Hands* (1948) by B. Rajan; *T. S. Eliot: A Selected Critique* (1948) by Leonard Unger; and *T. S. Eliot: The Design of His Poetry* (1949) by Elizabeth Drew.

from The Love Song of J. Alfred Prufrock

Let us go then, you and I,
When the evening is spread out against the sky
Like a patient etherized upon a table;
Let us go, through certain half-deserted streets,
The muttering retreats
Of restless nights in one-night cheap hotels
And sawdust restaurants with oyster-shells:
Streets that follow like a tedious argument
Of insidious intent
To lead you to an overwhelming question. . . .
Oh, do not ask, " What is it? "
Let us go and make our visit.

In the room the women come and go
Talking of Michelangelo.

The yellow fog that rubs its back upon the window-panes,
The yellow smoke that rubs its muzzle on the window-panes,
Licked its tongue into the corners of the evening,
Lingered upon the pools that stand in drains,
Let fall upon its back the soot that falls from chimneys,
Slipped by the terrace, made a sudden leap,
And seeing that it was a soft October night,
Curled once about the house, and fell asleep . . .

Morning at the Window

They are rattling breakfast plates in basement kitchens,
And along the trampled edges of the street
I am aware of the damp souls of housemaids
Sprouting despondently at area gates.

The brown waves of fog toss up to me
Twisted faces from the bottom of the street,
And tear from a passer-by with muddy skirts
An aimless smile that hovers in the air
And vanishes along the level of the roofs.

Prelude

The winter evening settles down
With smells of steaks in passageways.
Six o'clock.
The burnt-out ends of smoky days.
And now a gusty shower wraps
The grimy scraps
Of withered leaves about your feet
And newspapers from vacant lots;
The showers beat
On broken blinds and chimney-pots,
And at the corner of the street
A lonely cab-horse steams and stamps.
And then the lighting of the lamps.

The Hollow Men

I

We are the hollow men
We are the stuffed men
Leaning together
Headpiece filled with straw. Alas!
Our dried voices, when
We whisper together
Are quiet and meaningless

As wind in dry grass
Or rats' feet over broken glass
In our dry cellar

Shape without form, shade without color,
Paralyzed force, gesture without motion:
Those who have crossed
With direct eyes, to death's other Kingdom
Remember us — if at all — not as lost
Violent souls, but only
As the hollow men
The stuffed men.

II

Eyes I dare not meet in dreams
In death's dream kingdom
These do not appear:
There, the eyes are
Sunlight on a broken column
There, is a tree swinging
And voices are
In the wind's singing
More distant and more solemn
Than a fading star.

Let me be no nearer
In death's dream kingdom
Let me also wear
Such deliberate disguises
Rat's coat, crowskin, crossed staves
In a field
Behaving as the wind behaves
No nearer —

Not that final meeting
In the twilight kingdom

III

This is the dead land
This is cactus land
Here the stony images
Are raised, here they receive
The supplication of a dead man's hand
Under the twinkle of a fading star.

Is it like this
In death's other kingdom
Waking alone
At the hour when we are
Trembling with tenderness
Lips that would kiss
Form prayers to broken stone.

IV

The eyes are not here
There are no eyes here
In this valley of dying stars
In this hollow valley
This broken jaw of our lost kingdoms

In this last of meeting places
We grope together
And avoid speech
Gathered on this beach of the tumid river

Sightless, unless
The eyes reappear
As the perpetual star
Multifoliate rose
Of death's twilight kingdom
The hope only
Of empty men.

V

Here we go round the prickly pear
Prickly pear prickly pear
Here we go round the prickly pear
At five o'clock in the morning.

Between the idea
And the reality
Between the motion
And the act
Falls the Shadow
For Thine is the Kingdom

Between the conception
And the creation

Between the emotion
And the response
Falls the Shadow

Life is very long

Between the desire
And the spasm
Between the potency
And the existence
Between the essence
And the descent
Falls the Shadow

For Thine is the Kingdom

For thine is
Life is
For Thine is the

This is the way the world ends
This is the way the world ends
This is the way the world ends
Not with a bang but a whimper.

Macavity: The Mystery Cat

Macavity's a Mystery Cat: he's called The Hidden Paw —
For he's the master criminal who can defy the Law.
He's the bafflement of Scotland Yard, the Flying Squad's de-
spair;
For when they reach the scene of crime — *Macavity's not
there!*

Macavity, Macavity, there's no one like Macavity,
He's broken every human law, he breaks the law of gravity.
His powers of levitation would make a fakir [1] stare,
And when you reach the scene of crime — *Macavity's not
there!*
You may seek him in the basement, you may look up in the
air —
But I tell you once and once again, *Macavity's not there!*

[1] *Fakir:* an Indian magician.

Macavity's a ginger cat, he's very tall and thin;
You would know him if you saw him, for his eyes are sunken
  in.
His brow is deeply lined with thought, his head is highly
  domed;
His coat is dusty from neglect, his whiskers are uncombed.
He sways his head from side to side, with movements like
  a snake;
And when you think he's half asleep, he's always wide awake.

Macavity, Macavity, there's no one like Macavity,
For he's a fiend in feline shape, a monster of depravity.
You may meet him in a by-street, you may see him in the
  square —
But when a crime's discovered, then *Macavity's not there!*

He's outwardly respectable. (They say he cheats at cards.)
And his footprints are not found in any file of Scotland
  Yard's.
And when the larder's looted, or the jewel-case is rifled,
Or when the milk is missing, or another Peke's been stifled,
Or the greenhouse glass is broken, and the trellis past re-
  pair —
Ay, there's the wonder of the thing! *Macavity's not there!*

And when the Foreign Office find a Treaty's gone astray,
Or the Admiralty lose some plans and drawings by the way,
There may be a scrap of paper in the hall or on the stair —
But it's useless to investigate — *Macavity's not there!*
And when the loss has been disclosed, the Secret Service say:
" It *must* have been Macavity! " — but he's a mile away.
You'll be sure to find him resting, or a-licking of his thumbs,
Or engaged in doing complicated long division sums.

Macavity, Macavity, there's no one like Macavity,
There never was a Cat of such deceitfulness and suavity.
He always has an alibi, and one or two to spare:
At whatever time the deed took place — MACAVITY WASN'T
  THERE!
And they say that all the Cats whose wicked deeds are
  widely known

(I might mention Mungojerrie, I might mention Griddle-
 bone)
Are nothing more than agents for the Cat who all the time
Just controls their operations: the Napoleon of Crime!

JOHN CROWE RANSOM

John Crowe Ransom was born in Pulaski, Tennessee, April 30,
1888, of Scotch-Irish descent. Ransom was educated in his own
state and abroad: he received his B.A. at Vanderbilt University in
1909, his B.A. at Oxford in 1913. He taught at Vanderbilt in Nashville, Tennessee, and at Kenyon College, Ohio. He was the chief
inspirer and founder of the Southern group of poets and writers
known as The Fugitives.

Poems About God appeared in 1919, a raw first book with a
tang of bitter humor. *Chills and Fever* (1924) and *Two Gentlemen
in Bonds* (1927) are much more arresting. Here is a fastidiousness,
an almost pedantic precision, rare in American letters. As a craftsman Ransom is fascinating as he shifts from suave whimsicality to
acrid half-rhymes; as a philosopher he is equally original. Even
though his verses are sometimes difficult, there can be no doubt
that these crisp narratives and lyrics will find a definite and distinguished place. Nothing written by any contemporary has succeeded in being so teasing and, at the same time, so tender. "Lady
Lost" and "Here Lies a Lady" combine his gifts. They unite wit
and whimsicality; they surprise the reader by saying serious things
in a mock-serious tone of voice.

Besides his poetry, Ransom has written much philosophical and
critical prose, notably *The World's Body* (1938), which suggests
a system relating to the meaning and psychology of poetry, and
The New Criticism (1941).

Lady Lost

This morning, there flew up the lane
A timid lady-bird to our bird-bath
And eyed her image dolefully as death;
This afternoon, knocked on our windowpane
To be let in from the rain.

And when I caught her eye
She looked aside, but at the clapping thunder

And sight of the whole earth blazing up like tinder
Looked in on us again most miserably,
Indeed as if she would cry.

So I will go out into the park and say,
" Who has lost a delicate brown-eyed lady
In the West End Section? Or has anybody
Injured some fine woman in some dark way,
Last night or yesterday?

" Let the owner come and claim possession,
No questions will be asked. But stroke her gently
With loving words, and she will evidently
Resume her full soft-haired white-breasted fashion,
And her right home and her right passion."

Piazza Piece

— I am a gentleman in a dustcoat trying
To make you hear. Your ears are soft and small
And listen to an old man not at all;
They want the young men's whispering and sighing.
But see the roses on your trellis dying
And hear the spectral singing of the moon —
For I must have my lovely lady soon.
I am a gentleman in a dustcoat trying.

— I am a lady young in beauty waiting
Until my truelove comes, and then we kiss.
But what gray man among the vines is this
Whose words are dry and faint as in a dream?
Back from my trellis, sir, before I scream!
I am a lady young in beauty waiting.

Here Lies a Lady

Here lies a lady of beauty and high degree.
Of chills and fever she died, of fever and chills,
The delight of her husband, her aunts, an infant of three,
And of medicos marveling sweetly on her ills.

For either she burned, and her confident eyes would blaze,
And her fingers fly in a manner to puzzle their heads —
What was she making? Why, nothing; she sat in a maze
Of old scraps of laces, snipped into curious shreds —

Or this would pass, and the light of her fire decline
Till she lay discouraged and cold as a thin stalk white and
    blown,
And would not open her eyes, to kisses, to wine.
The sixth of these states was her last; the cold settled down.

Sweet ladies, long may ye bloom, and toughly I hope ye may
    thole,[1]
But was she not lucky? In flowers and lace and mourning,
In love and great honor we bade God rest her soul
After six little spaces of chill, and six of burning.

MARGARET WIDDEMER

Margaret Widdemer was born at Doylestown, Pennsylvania, and
began writing in her childhood. After graduating from Drexel Institute Library School in 1909, she contributed to various magazines; her first published verse "Factories" became her most
quoted poem.

Miss Widdemer's poetic work has two distinct phases. In the one
mood, she is the protesting poet, the champion of the down-
trodden, the lyricist on fire with angry passion; in the other, she
is the writer of well-made, polite and popular sentimental verse.
Her finest poems are in *Factories with Other Lyrics* (1915), although several of her best songs are in *The Old Road to Paradise*
(1918), which divided, with Sandburg's *Cornhuskers*, the Pulitzer
Poetry Prize in 1918. Miss Widdemer is also the author of several
books of short stories and a score of rather facile novels.

Factories

I have shut my little sister in from life and light
    (For a rose, for a ribbon, for a wreath across my hair),
I have made her restless feet still until the night,

[1] *Thole:* endure.

Locked from sweets of summer and from wild spring air;
I who ranged the meadowlands, free from sun to sun,
    Free to sing and pull the buds and watch the far wings fly,
I have bound my sister till her playing time was done —
    Oh, my little sister, was it I? Was it I?

I have robbed my sister of her day of maidenhood
    (For a robe, for a feather, for a trinket's restless spark),
Shut from love till dusk shall fall, how shall she know good,
    How shall she go scatheless through the sun-lit dark?
I who could be innocent, I who could be gay,
    I who could have love and mirth before the light went by,
I have put my sister in her mating-time away —
    Sister, my young sister, was it I? Was it I?

I have robbed my sister of the lips against her breast,
    (For a coin, for the weaving of my children's lace and
        lawn),
Feet that pace beside the loom, hands that cannot rest —
    How can she know motherhood, whose strength is gone?
I who took no heed of her, starved and labor-worn,
    I, against whose placid heart my sleepy gold-heads lie,
Round my path they cry to me, little souls unborn —
    God of Life! Creator! It was I! It was I!

CONRAD AIKEN

Conrad (Potter) Aiken was born in Savannah, Georgia, August 5, 1889. He attended Harvard, was chosen class-poet, received his A.B. in 1912, married, and moved to Massachusetts. In 1921 he bought a house in Rye, Sussex; he spent his time partly in England, partly in America, until he returned permanently to Massachusetts.

Aiken's early work showed the influence of contemporary poets: *Earth Triumphant and Other Tales in Verse* (1914) is an imitation of Masefield, *Turns and Movies* (1916) is derived from Masters. *The Jig of Forslin* (1916) is more original; the natural musician emerges in languid rhythms and haunting cadences.

The emphasis on melody increases with each subsequent volume: *Nocturne of Remembered Spring* (1917), *The Charnel Rose* (1918), and *The House of Death* (1920) are full of a tired but often beautiful music. Primarily a lyric poet, Aiken frequently condenses an emotion in a few lines; the music of the Morning Song from "Senlin" is rich with subtleties of rhythm. But it is much more than a lyrical movement. Beneath the flowing color of these lines, there is a summoning of the immensities that loom behind the trivial moments of everyday. The poet (in the character of "Senlin") muses in front of the mirror. He starts the day by doing all the ordinary things that everyone does. But even while he ties his tie and winds his watch, he is conscious of the extraordinary things which surround him. Wonder is at his window as the vines climb about it and a robin "chirps in the chinaberry tree." Nothing is commonplace to the poet as he realizes that the earth beneath him is flying through space and that the walls of his house are lit by " a sun far off in a shell of silence." The air rushes above his ceiling; stars and suns revolve beneath his floors. He makes us aware of the entire universe as he casually adjusts his tie and descends the staircase.

Punch, the Immortal Liar (1921), in many ways Aiken's most appealing work, contains this poet's sharpest characterizations as well as his most beautiful symphonic effects. *Priapus and the Pool* (1922) discloses Aiken preeminently as a lyricist. Here are twenty-five songs, several of which are as subtly moving as those by any singer in America today.

The musical advance is established by *Selected Poems* (1929), which won the Pulitzer Prize for that year, *John Deth and Other Poems* (1930), and *Landscape West of Eden* (1933). All these deal with sets of symbols and dream pictures in a limbo of fantasy. The music of such meditative lyrics is pitched lower in the somber " preludes," of which Aiken has written a hundred or more. Sixty-three of these were published in *Preludes for Memnon* (1931). Later books of poetry are *And In The Human Heart* (1940), *Brownstone Eclogues* (1942), and *The Kid* (1947).

Aiken has written a great deal of prose in many veins. The best of his criticism is in *Scepticisms* (1919) and the introduction to *Selected Poems of Emily Dickinson*, published in England in 1924. *Blue Voyage* (1927) is his most striking novel and *Bring! Bring!* (1925) his most successful volume of short stories.

Bread and Music

Music I heard with you was more than music,
And bread I broke with you was more than bread;
Now that I am without you, all is desolate;
All that was once so beautiful is dead.

Your hands once touched this table and this silver,
And I have seen your fingers hold this glass.
These things do not remember you, belovèd,
And yet your touch upon them will not pass.

For it was in my heart you moved among them,
And blessed them with your hands and with your eyes;
And in my heart they will remember always, —
They knew you once, O beautiful and wise.

Miracles

Twilight is spacious, near things in it seem far,
And distant things seem near.
Now in the green west hangs a yellow star.
And now across old waters you may hear
The profound gloom of bells among still trees,
Like a rolling of huge boulders beneath seas.

Silent as thought in evening contemplation
Weaves the bat under the gathering stars.
Silent as dew, we seek new incarnation,
Meditate new avatars.[1]

In a clear dusk like this
Mary climbed up the hill to seek her son,
To lower him down from the cross, and kiss
The mauve wounds, every one.

Men with wings
In the dusk walked softly after her.
She did not see them, but may have felt
The winnowed air around her stir;
She did not see them, but may have known
Why her son's body was light as a little stone.
She may have guessed that other hands were there
Moving the watchful air.

Now, unless persuaded by searching music
Which suddenly opens the portals of the mind,
We guess no angels,
And are contented to be blind.
Let us blow silver horns in the twilight,
And lift our hearts to the yellow star in the green,
To find perhaps, if, while the dew is rising,
Clear things may not be seen.

[1] *Avatar:* passing over from one existence to another.

Morning Song from " Senlin " [1]

It is morning, Senlin says, and in the morning
When the light drips through the shutters like the dew,
I arise, I face the sunrise,
And do the things my fathers learned to do.
Stars in the purple dusk above the rooftops
Pale in a saffron mist and seem to die,
And I myself on a swiftly tilting planet
Stand before a glass and tie my tie.

Vine-leaves tap my window,
Dew-drops sing to the garden stones,
The robin chirps in the chinaberry tree
Repeating three clear tones.

It is morning. I stand by the mirror
And tie my tie once more.
While waves far off in a pale rose twilight
Crash on a white sand shore.
I stand by a mirror and comb my hair;
How small and white my face! —
The green earth tilts through a sphere of air
And bathes in a flame of space.
There are houses hanging above the stars
And stars hung under a sea . . .
And a sun far off in a shell of silence
Dapples my walls for me. . . .

It is morning, Senlin says, and in the morning
Should I not pause in the light to remember God?
Upright and firm I stand on a star unstable,
He is immense and lonely as a cloud.
I will dedicate this moment before my mirror
To him alone, for him I will comb my hair.
Accept these humble offerings, clouds of silence!
I will think of you as I descend the stair.

Vine-leaves tap my window,
The snail-track shines on the stones;

---

[1] *Senlin:* a fictional character which some critics have identified
with the poet.

Dew-drops flash from the chinaberry tree
Repeating two clear tones.

It is morning, I awake from a bed of silence,
Shining I rise from the starless waters of sleep.
The walls are about me still as in the evening,
I am the same, and the same name still I keep.
The earth revolves with me, yet makes no motion,
The stars pale silently in a coral sky.
In a whistling void I stand before my mirror,
Unconcerned, and tie my tie.

There are horses neighing on far-off hills
Tossing their long white manes,
And mountains flash in the rose-white dusk,
Their shoulders black with rains. . . .
It is morning, I stand by the mirror
And surprise my soul once more;
The blue air rushes above my ceiling,
There are suns beneath my floor. . . .

. . . It is morning, Senlin says, I ascend from darkness
And depart on the winds of space for I know not where;
My watch is wound, a key in my pocket,
And the sky is darkened as I descend the stair.
There are shadows across the windows, clouds in heaven,
And a god among the stars; and I will go
Thinking of him as I might think of daybreak
And humming a tune I know. . . .

Vine-leaves tap at the window,
Dew-drops sing to the garden stones,
The robin chirps in the chinaberry tree
Repeating three clear tones.

The Puppet Dreams

There is a fountain in a wood
Where wavering lies a moon:
It plays to the slowly falling leaves
A sleepy tune.

. . . The peach-trees lean upon a wall
Of gold and ivory:
The peacock spreads his tail; the leaves
Fall silently. . . .

There, amid silken sounds and wine
And music idly broken,
The drowsy god observes his world
With no word spoken.

Arcturus,[1] rise! Orion,[2] fall! . . .
The white-winged stars obey. . . .
Or else he greets his Fellow-God;
And there, in the dusk, they play

A game of chess with stars for pawns
And a silver moon for queen:
Immeasurable as clouds, above
A chess-board world they lean

And thrust their hands amid their beards.
And utter words profound
That shake the star-swung firmament
With a fateful sound! . . .

. . . The peach-trees lean upon a wall
Of gold and ivory;
The peacock spreads his tail; the leaves
Fall silently. . . .

EDNA ST. VINCENT MILLAY

Edna St. Vincent Millay was born February 22, 1892, in Rock-land, Maine. Her childhood was spent in her native state, where she wrote her most famous poem ("Renascence"); a sponsor made it possible for her to come to New York and attend Vassar College, from which she was graduated in 1917. She supported

[1] *Arcturus:* a giant star.
[2] *Orion:* a conspicuous constellation named after the mighty hunter in Greek mythology.

herself by writing short stories, by acting, and by translating. After her marriage she moved to a farm in the Berkshires.

Renascence was published in 1917, but the title-poem had been written in 1911, when Miss Millay was nineteen. It was considered an extraordinary product for a young and unknown writer; it remains one of the most remarkable poems of this generation. Beginning like a child's aimless rhyme, it proceeds, with casual simplicity, to an amazing climax. It is as if a child had uttered some elemental truth. The cumulative effect of this poem is surpassed only by its sense of revelation. *A Few Figs from Thistles* (1920) is a more sophisticated booklet. It is a popular collection, but Miss Millay's least commendable performance. It is clever, self-conscious, and facile, a marked contrast to the volumes which preceded and followed it.

Second April (1921), which contains the buoyant "The Poet and His Book" and the unforgettable "Elegy," is an intensification of her lyrical gift touched with increasing sadness. Her poetic play, *Aria da Capo*, first performed by the Provincetown Players in New York, was published in 1920. *The Harp-Weaver and Other Poems* (1924) — the title-poem was awarded the Pulitzer Prize for 1922 — wears its author's heart on its sleeve; often that organ is displayed as a shining toy, a decoration tricked with impudent ribbons. But Miss Millay begins to wear her heart with a difference. No longer brightly egotistic or consciously arch, she speaks with a disillusion that contains more than a tinge of bitterness. Some of the sonnets, which must be numbered among her finest creations, are likely to endure for a long time.

Notes of maturity and gravity grow increasingly with *The Buck in the Snow* (1928), *Fatal Interview* (1931), a quasi-Elizabethan sonnet sequence, *Wine from These Grapes* (1934), and *Conversation at Midnight* (1937). Frequently Miss Millay relies on an old and over-familiar rhetoric, but often the true and original utterance makes itself felt. The passion is intensely personal, the tone is romanticized and, at times, theatrical; but there is no question about the poet's technical mastery, and, beneath the literary skill, there can be heard the tone of authority.

Edna St. Vincent Millay and Her Times (1936) by Elizabeth Atkins is full of biographical information, although it is too exuberant to serve as criticism. She died at her home October 19, 1950.

On Hearing a Symphony of Beethoven

Sweet sounds, oh, beautiful music, do not cease!
Reject me not into the world again.
With you alone is excellence and peace,
Mankind made plausible, his purpose plain.

Enchanted in your air benign and shrewd,
With limbs a-sprawl and empty faces pale,
The spiteful and the stingy and the rude
Sleep like the scullions in the fairy-tale.

This moment is the best the world can give:
The tranquil blossom on the tortured stem.
Reject me not, sweet sounds! oh, let me live,
Till Doom espy my towers and scatter them
A city spell-bound under the aging sun.
Music my rampart, and my only one.

Renascence [1]

All I could see from where I stood
Was three long mountains and a wood;
I turned and looked another way,
And saw three islands in a bay.
So with my eyes I traced the line
Of the horizon, thin and fine,
Straight around till I was come
Back to where I'd started from;
And all I saw from where I stood
Was three long mountains and a wood.
Over these things I could not see;
These were the things that bounded me;
And I could touch them with my hand,
Almost, I thought, from where I stand.

And all at once things seemed so small
My breath came short, and scarce at all.
But, sure, the sky is big, I said;
Miles and miles above my head;
So here upon my back I'll lie
And look my fill into the sky.
And so I looked, and, after all,
The sky was not so very tall.
The sky, I said, must somewhere stop,
And — sure enough! — I see the top!
The sky, I thought, is not so grand;

[1] *Renascence:* a new birth.

I 'most could touch it with my hand!
And, reaching up my hand to try,
I screamed to feel it touch the sky.

I screamed, and — lo! — Infinity
Came down and settled over me;
Forced back my scream into my chest,
Bent back my arm upon my breast,
And, pressing of the Undefined
The definition on my mind,
Held up before my eyes a glass
Through which my shrinking sight did pass
Until it seemed I must behold
Immensity made manifold;
Whispered to me a word whose sound
Deafened the air for worlds around,
And brought unmuffled to my ears
The gossiping of friendly spheres,
The creaking of the tented sky,
The ticking of Eternity.

I saw and heard, and knew at last
The How and Why of all things, past,
And present, and forevermore.
The universe, cleft to the core,
Lay open to my probing sense
That, sickening, I would fain pluck thence
But could not, — nay! But needs must suck
At the great wound, and could not pluck
My lips away till I had drawn
All venom out. — Ah, fearful pawn!
For my omniscience I paid toll
In infinite remorse of soul.
All sin was of my sinning, all
Atoning mine, and mine the gall
Of all regret. Mine was the weight
Of every brooded wrong, the hate
That stood behind each envious thrust,
Mine every greed, mine every lust.
And all the while for every grief,
Each suffering, I craved relief
With individual desire, —
Craved all in vain! And felt fierce fire

About a thousand people crawl;
Perished with each, — then mourned for all!
A man was starving in Capri;
He moved his eyes and looked at me;
I felt his gaze, I heard his moan,
And knew his hunger as my own.
I saw at sea a great fog-bank
Between two ships that struck and sank;
A thousand screams the heavens smote;
And every scream tore through my throat;
No hurt I did not feel, no death
That was not mine; mine each last breath
That, crying, met an answering cry
From the compassion that was I.
All suffering mine, and mine its rod;
Mine, pity like the pity of God.
Ah, awful weight! Infinity
Pressed down upon the finite Me!
My anguished spirit, like a bird,
Beating against my lips I heard;
Yet lay the weight so close about
There was no room for it without.
And so beneath the weight lay I
And suffered death, but could not die.

Long had I lain thus, craving death,
When quietly the earth beneath
Gave way, and inch by inch, so great
At last had grown the crushing weight,
Into the earth I sank till I
Full six feet under ground did lie,
And sank no more, — there is no weight
Can follow here, however great.
From off my breast I felt it roll,
And as it went my tortured soul
Burst forth and fled in such a gust
That all about me swirled the dust.

Deep in the earth I rested now;
Cool is its hand upon the brow
And soft its breast beneath the head
Of one who is so gladly dead.
And all at once, and over all,

The pitying rain began to fall.
I lay and heard each pattering hoof
Upon my lowly, thatchèd roof,
And seemed to love the sound far more
Than ever I had done before.
For rain it hath a friendly sound
To one who's six feet under ground;
And scarce the friendly voice or face:
A grave is such a quiet place.

The rain, I said, is kind to come
And speak to me in my new home.
I would I were alive again
To kiss the fingers of the rain,
To drink into my eyes the shine
Of every slanting silver line,
To catch the freshened, fragrant breeze
From drenched and dripping apple-trees.
For soon the shower will be done,
And then the broad face of the sun
Will laugh above the rain-soaked earth
Until the world with answering mirth
Shakes joyously, and each round drop
Rolls, twinkling, from its grass-blade top.
How can I bear it; buried here,
While overhead the sky grows clear
And blue again after the storm?
O, multi-colored, multiform,
Belovèd beauty over me,
That I shall never, never see
Again! Spring-silver, autumn-gold,
That I shall never more behold!
Sleeping your myriad magics through,
Close-sepulchered away from you!
O God, I cried, give me new birth,
And put me back upon the earth!
Upset each cloud's gigantic gourd
And let the heavy rain, down-poured
In one big torrent, set me free,
Washing my grave away from me!

I ceased; and, through the breathless hush
That answered me, the far-off rush

Of herald wings came whispering
Like music down the vibrant string
Of my ascending prayer, and — crash!
Before the wild wind's whistling lash
The startled storm-clouds reared on high
And plunged in terror down the sky,
And the big rain in one black wave
Fell from the sky and struck my grave.

I know not how such things can be,
I only know there came to me
A fragrance such as never clings
To aught save happy living things;
A sound as of some joyous elf
Singing sweet songs to please himself,
And, through and over everything,
A sense of glad awakening.
The grass, a-tiptoe at my ear,
Whispering to me I could hear;
I felt the rain's cool finger-tips
Brushed tenderly across my lips,
Laid gently on my sealèd sight,
And all at once the heavy night
Fell from my eyes and I could see, —
A drenched and dripping apple-tree,
A last long line of silver rain,
A sky grown clear and blue again.
And as I looked a quickening gust
Of wind blew up to me and thrust
Into my face a miracle
Of orchard-breath, and with the smell, —
I know not how such things can be! —
I breathed my soul back into me.

Ah! Up then from the ground sprang I
And hailed the earth with such a cry
As is not heard save from a man
Who has been dead and lives again.
About the trees my arms I wound;
Like one gone mad I hugged the ground;
I raised my quivering arms on high;
I laughed and laughed into the sky,
Till at my throat a strangling sob

Caught fiercely, and a great heart-throb
Sent instant tears into my eyes.
O God, I cried, no dark disguise
Can e'er hereafter hide from me
Thy radiant identity!
Thou canst not move across the grass
But my quick eyes will see Thee pass,
Nor speak, however silently,
But my hushed voice will answer Thee.
I know the path that tells Thy way
Through the cool eve of every day;
God, I can push the grass apart
And lay my finger on Thy heart!

The world stands out on either side
No wider than the heart is wide;
Above the world is stretched the sky, —
No higher than the soul is high.
The heart can push the sea and land
Farther away on either hand;
The soul can split the sky in two,
And let the face of God shine through.
But East and West will pinch the heart
That cannot keep them pushed apart;
And he whose soul is flat — the sky
Will cave in on him by and by.

The Anguish

I would to God I were quenched and fed
As in my youth
From the flask of song, and the good bread
Of beauty richer than truth.

The anguish of the world is on my tongue.
My bowl is filled to the brim with it; there is more than I
    can eat.
Happy are the toothless old and the toothless young,
That cannot rend this meat.

Pity Me Not

Pity me not because the light of day
At close of day no longer walks the sky;
Pity me not for beauties passed away
From field and thicket as the year goes by·
Pity me not the waning of the moon,
Nor that the ebbing tide goes out to sea,
Nor that a man's desire is hushed so soon,
And you no longer look with love on me.

This have I known always: love is no more
Than the wide blossom which the wind assails;
Than the great tide that treads the shifting shore,
Strewing fresh wreckage gathered in the gales.
Pity me that the heart is slow to learn
What the swift mind beholds at every turn.

Elegy

Let them bury your big eyes
In the secret earth securely,
Your thin fingers, and your fair,
Soft, indefinite-colored hair, —
All of these in some way, surely,
From the secret earth shall rise.
Not for these I sit and stare,
Broken and bereft completely;
Your young flesh that sat so neatly
On your little bones will sweetly
Blossom in the air.

But your voice, — never the rushing
Of a river underground,
Not the rising of the wind
In the trees before the rain,
Not the woodcock's watery call,
Not the note the white-throat utters,
Not the feet of children pushing
Yellow leaves along the gutters
In the blue and bitter fall,

Shall content my musing mind
For the beauty of that sound
That in no new way at all
Ever will be heard again.

Sweetly through the sappy stalk
Of the vigorous weed,
Holding all it held before,
Cherished by the faithful sun,
On and on eternally
Shall your altered fluid run,
Bud and bloom and go to seed.
But your singing days are done;
But the music of your talk
Never shall the chemistry
Of the secret earth restore.
All your lovely words are spoken.
Once the ivory box is broken,
Beats the golden bird no more.

ARCHIBALD MacLEISH

Archibald MacLeish was born in Glencoe, Illinois, May 7,
1892. His career at Yale, from which he graduated with the class
of 1915, was brilliant and versatile. Football and water-polo were
his athletic interests; he was honored by the oldest undergraduate
organizations; he was chairman of the *Yale Literary Monthly* and
a member of Phi Beta Kappa. After college, MacLeish studied
law, became a Lieutenant in the artillery, and returned to graduate
at the head of his class at the Harvard Law School. After a few
years in Boston, he gave up the practice of law to devote his time
to literature. He was, for a while, one of the editors of *Fortune*.
In his mid-forties he was appointed Librarian of Congress; in 1949
he became Professor of Rhetoric and Oratory at Harvard.

Tower of Ivory (1917) gave few hints of the unusual talent that
was revealed in *The Happy Marriage* (1924), *The Pot of Earth*
(1925), and the curious *Nobodaddy* (1925). In these volumes Mac-
Leish shows the influence of several contemporaries, particularly
Aiken, Robinson, Pound, and Eliot, but his own inflection struggles
through.

In *Streets in the Moon* (1926) the complete poet emerges. Here
MacLeish speaks in his recognizable idiom; the subject matter,

conceived in amplitude, conveys an extraordinary sense of space and time, even the "sense of infinity." By the skillful use of assonance, half-rhyme, repetition, and suspense, this poet achieves new effects in the traditional forms, even in so classic a form as the sonnet, "The End of the World." "Ars Poetica" is more than an extension of poetic language; beneath its experiments in timing, interior rhyme and suspension, it says a number of pointed and profound things about poetry.

A growing power and originality are manifest in *The Hamlet of A. MacLeish* (1928), *New Found Land* (1930), *Conquistador* (1932), which won the Pulitzer Prize in 1933, and the carefully selected *Poems 1924–1933*. MacLeish devotes himself more and more to contemporary subjects with increasing success. This is proved by *Public Speech* (1936), the poetic play, *Panic* (1935), *The Fall of the City* (1937), a drama about dictatorship, and *Air Raid* (1938), both written for the radio, *America Was Promises* (1939), and *Actfive and Other Poems* (1948). Through his peculiar blend of narration and meditation, of experiment and accomplishment, MacLeish makes himself one of the most interesting poets of his period.

His service in several public offices (he was for a time Assistant Secretary of State) and his keen awareness of political and social problems make him a poet who is also an active participant in his times. Like Whitman and Sandburg, though his is a different kind of vision, MacLeish seems to see America steadily and whole. His *New Found Land* and particularly *Conquistador* are searchings for an understanding of this vast land born out of time and myth. In the poem "Land of the Free" MacLeish has the speakers, who are impoverished farm workers of depression times, look back over the hard road of Americans' struggle to settle the land and win their freedom.

"You, Andrew Marvell" is an excellent example of MacLeish's individuality. Difficult at first reading, it soon discloses rich and varied effects. The suspense is heightened by the phrases depicting the gradual approach of night; it is intensified by the lack of punctuation; it is sustained by the gathering force of the one long sentence. A further effect is achieved by the choice of words; every epithet is precise and suggestive, neither too vague nor too vivid. The pale, almost colorless light and the unearthly chill of darkness are set off by the warm syllables and colorful associations of Persia, Baghdad, Arabia, Palmyra, Crete, and Kermanshah. Even the title, at first obscure, adds a final overtone to the poem. The seventeenth century poet, Andrew Marvell, addressed a poem "To His Coy Mistress," in which he reminded her that the sun refuses to stand still and that

> . . . at my back I always hear
> Time's wingèd chariot hurrying near.

Soon, says the twentieth century MacLeish, time will pass and the flooding dark will engulf this hill and these hearts again. " You, Andrew Marvell," muses the modern poet, " you, too felt this almost three centuries ago."

Ars Poetica [1]

A poem should be palpable and mute
As a globed fruit

Dumb
As old medallions to the thumb

Silent as the sleeve-worn stone
Of casement ledges where the moss has grown —

A poem should be wordless
As the flight of birds . . .

A poem should be motionless in time
As the moon climbs

Leaving, as the moon releases
Twig by twig the night-entangled trees,

Leaving, as the moon behind the winter leaves,
Memory by memory the mind —

A poem should be motionless in time
As the moon climbs . . .

A poem should be equal to:
Not true

For all the history of grief
An empty doorway and a maple leaf

For love
The leaning grasses and two lights above the sea —

A poem should not mean
But be.

[1] *Ars Poetica:* the art of poetry.

The End of the World

Quite unexpectedly as Vasserot [1]
The armless ambidextrian was lighting
A match between his great and second toe
And Ralph the lion was engaged in biting
The neck of Mme. Sossman while the drum
Pointed, and Teeny was about to cough
In waltz-time swinging Jocko by the thumb —
Quite unexpectedly the top blew off:

And there, there overhead, there, there, hung over
Those thousands of white faces, those dazed eyes,
There in the starless dark, the poise, the hover,
There with vast wings across the canceled skies,
There in the sudden blackness, the black pall
Of nothing, nothing, nothing — nothing at all.

You, Andrew Marvell [2]

And here face down beneath the sun
And here upon earth's noonward height
To feel the always coming on
The always rising of the night

To feel creep up the curving east
The earthly chill of dusk and slow
Upon those under lands the vast
And ever-climbing shadow grow

And strange at Ecbatan the trees
Take leaf by leaf the evening strange
The flooding dark about their knees
The mountains over Persia change

---

[1] *Vasserot:* one of the freaks in the circus side-show described — or suggested — in this poem.

[2] *Andrew Marvell* (1621–1678): See explanatory paragraph on page 208.

And now at Kermanshah the gate
Dark empty and the withered grass
And through the twilight now the late
Few travelers in the westward pass

And Baghdad darken and the bridge
Across the silent river gone
And through Arabia the edge
Of evening widen and steal on

And deepen on Palmyra's street
The wheel-rut in the ruined stone
And Lebanon fade out and Crete
High through the clouds and overblown

And over Sicily the air
Still flashing with the landward gulls
And loom and slowly disappear
The sails above the shadowy hulls

And Spain go under and the shore
Of Africa the gilded sand
And evening vanish and no more
The low pale light across that land

Nor now the long light on the sea —

And here face downward in the sun
To feel how swift how secretly
The shadow of the night comes on . . .

Immortal Autumn

I speak this poem now with grave and level voice
In praise of autumn of the far-horn-winding fall
I praise the flower-barren fields the clouds the tall
Unanswering branches where the wind makes sullen noise

I praise the fall it is the human season now
No more the foreign sun does meddle at our earth
Enforce the green and thaw the frozen soil to birth
Nor winter yet weigh all with silence the pine bough

But now in autumn with the black and outcast crows
Share we the spacious world the whispering year is gone
There is more room to live now the once secret dawn
Comes late by daylight and the dark unguarded goes

Between the mutinous brave burning of the leaves
And winter's covering of our hearts with his deep snow
We are alone there are no evening birds we know
The naked moon the tame stars circle at our eaves

It is the human season on this sterile air
Do words outcarry breath the sound goes on and on
I hear a dead man's cry from autumn long since gone

I cry to you beyond this bitter air.

from Land of the Free

We wonder whether the dream of American liberty
Was two hundred years of pine and hardwood
And three generations of the grass

And the generations are up: the years over

We don't know

It was two hundred years from the smell of the tidewater
Up through the Piedmont: on through the piney woods:
Till we came out
With our led calves and our lean women
In the oak openings of Illinois

It was three generations from the oak trees —
From the islands of elm and the islands of oak in the prairie —
Till we heeled out with our plows and our steel harrows
On the grass-drowned reef bones of the Plains

  "Four score and seven years" said the Orator

We remember it differently: we remember it
Kansas: Illinois: Ohio: Connecticut.
We remember it Council Bluffs: St. Louis:
Wills Creek: the Cumberland: Shenandoah —

The long harangues of the grass in the wind are our histories

We tell our freedom backward by the land
We tell our past by the gravestones and the apple trees

We wonder whether the great American dream
Was the singing of locusts out of the grass to the west and the
West is behind us now:
The west wind's away from us:

We wonder if the liberty is done:
The dreaming is finished

We can't say

We aren't sure

Of if there's something different men can dream
Or if there's something different men can mean by
Liberty

Or if there's liberty a man can mean that's
Men: not land

We wonder

We don't know

We're asking

ELIZABETH COATSWORTH

Elizabeth Coatsworth was born in 1893 in Buffalo, New York. After extended travels she returned to America, where she divided her time between Maine and an old house overlooking the harbor of Hingham, Massachusetts.

Miss Coatsworth made her debut with *Fox Footprints* (1921), a group of images and studies in the Oriental mood. *Atlas and Beyond* (1924) is a far more original work, although it, too, finds its subjects overseas. *Compass Rose* (1929) contains not only her most native but her most winning poetry. Most of the verses are highly suggestive; the author is one for whom the fact is but the means to a fantastic end. Often, as in " A Lady Comes to an Inn," she suggests an odd or faintly terrifying story without telling the details; she is content to whisper the illuminating " hints " and let the reader's imagination fill in the alluring outline.

Miss Coatsworth is also the author of novels and many books for young people, her prose being liberally interspersed with rhymes. *Maine Ways* (1947) reflects her love for her favorite state. *The Creaking Stair* (1949) contains the best of her ghost-haunted poems.

A Lady Comes to an Inn

Three strange men came to the inn,
One was a black man pocked and thin,
One was brown with a silver knife,
And one brought with him a beautiful wife.

That lovely woman had hair as pale
As French champagne or finest ale,
That lovely woman was long and slim
As a young white birch or a maple limb.

Her face was like cream, her mouth was a rose,
What language she spoke nobody knows,
But sometimes she'd scream like a cockatoo
And swear wonderful oaths that nobody knew.

Her great silk skirts like a silver bell
Down to her little bronze slippers fell,
And her low-cut gown showed a dove on its nest
In blue tattooing across her breast.

Nobody learned the lady's name
Nor the marvelous land from which they came,
But no one in all the countryside
Has forgotten those men and that beautiful bride.

Calling in the Cat

Now from the dark, a deeper dark,
The cat slides,
Furtive and aware,

His eyes still shine with meteor spark
The cold dew weights his hair.
Suspicious,
Hesitant, he comes
Stepping morosely from the night,
Held but repelled,
Repelled but held,
By lamp and firelight.

Now call your blandest,
Offer up
The sacrifice of meat,
And snare the wandering soul with greeds,
Give him to drink and eat,
And he shall walk fastidiously
Into the trap of old
On feet that still smell delicately
Of withered ferns and mould.

DOROTHY PARKER

Dorothy Rothschild was born in West End, New Jersey, August 22, 1893. Her father was Jewish, her mother Scotch. She attended Miss Dana's School in Morristown, New Jersey, and the Blessed Sacred Convent in New York. She says that the only thing she learned was that if you spit on a pencil eraser it will erase ink.

She came to New York, wrote verse and short stories, married Edwin Pond Parker, became a dramatic critic and book-reviewer, and was quoted widely (and often falsely) for her witty thrusts and malicious epigrams. After a divorce from Parker, she married Alan Campbell, the actor, with whom she wrote scenarios in Hollywood. She is "slightly over five feet in height, dark, with somewhat weary eyes and a sad mouth. She is superstitious and hates to be alone; flowers and a good cry are said to be among her favorite diversions."

Her first book of prose, *Laments for the Living* (1930), contains several remarkable short stories, one of which ("Big Blonde") won the O. Henry Memorial prize. But it is as a poet that she is best known. The contents of her three volumes — *Enough Rope* (1927), *Sunset Gun* (1928), and *Death and Taxes* (1931) — were collected in *Not So Deep as a Well* (1936). Most of this poetry plays bitter variations on the theme of frustrated love, but the lines are so neatly turned, the twists so surprising, that the reader is always amused and often charmed. Mrs. Parker has a way of expressing heartbreak by a "wisecrack"; when she is most caustic she is often most convincing. Although her self-dramatizing tends to fall into a formula, the best of her work turns wry grimaces into genuine lyrics.

Love Song

My own dear love, he is strong and bold
 And he cares not what comes after.
His words ring sweet as a chime of gold,
 And his eyes are lit with laughter.
He is jubilant as a flag unfurled;
 Oh, a girl, she'd not forget him.
My own dear love, he is all my world —
 And I wish I'd never met him.

My love, he's mad, and my love, he's fleet,
 And a wild young wood-thing bore him.
The ways are fair to his roaming feet,
 And the skies are sunlit for him.
As sharply sweet to my heart he seems
 As the fragrance of acacia.
My own dear love, he is all my dreams —
 And I wish he were in Asia.

My love runs by like a day in June,
 And he makes no friends of sorrows.
He'll tread his galloping rigadoon
 In the pathway of the morrows.
He'll live his days where the sunbeams start
 Nor could storm nor wind uproot him.
My own dear love, he is all my heart —
 And I wish somebody'd shoot him.

Autumn Valentine

In May my heart was breaking —
 Oh, wide the wound, and deep!
And bitter it beat at waking,
 And sore it split in sleep.

And when it came November,
I sought my heart, and sighed,
" Poor thing, do you remember? "
" What heart was that? " it cried.

LOUIS GINSBERG

Louis Ginsberg was born October 1, 1896, at Newark, New Jersey. He attended Rutgers and Columbia University, and received his M.A. in 1924. After graduation, he divided his time between writing and teaching high-school English in Paterson, New Jersey.

The Attic of the Past (1920) and *The Everlasting Minute* (1937) show various influences, none of which fail to hide the lyrist. Ginsberg's recent poems are not only swifter in technique but clearer in the communication of " the glory of the commonplace." The poem here reprinted illustrates that gift; it is interesting to compare Ginsberg's treatment of the theme with Sandburg's (page 117) and Eliot's (page 185) use of the same subject.

Fog

Here in this world of fog like amethyst,
Harshness has now been sponged away by mist.

The hardest, sternest lines relent and cease
Their cruelty, while angels cradle peace.

The blurry walks are sown with phantom feet,
While glamor drizzles slowly on the street.

As glory smolders through the foggy veil,
A trolley crawls, a phosphorescent snail.

Tall buildings once so arrogant to see
Wilt to a white and gossamer frailty.

This mist can make the meanest side street be
Password and threshold for a mystery.

Blest is this mist that muffles sense and sound;
For, lest a cruel, heedless sun should pound

Merciless deserts of a blinding light,
Fog will bestow its gift of second sight!

STEPHEN VINCENT BENÉT

Stephen Vincent Benét, the younger brother of William Rose Benét, was born at Bethlehem, Pennsylvania, in July, 1898. He was educated in various parts of the country, and graduated from Yale in 1919. He died of a heart ailment March 13, 1943.

At seventeen he published a small book containing six dramatic portraits, *Five Men and Pompey* (1915), a set of monologs little short of astounding, coming from a schoolboy. In Benét's next volume, *Young Adventure* (1918), one hears something more than the speech of an infant prodigy; the precocious facility has developed into undoubted vigor. *Heavens and Earth* (1920) and *Tiger Joy* (1925) have a wider imaginative sweep. The latter volume contains several vigorous and wholly American ballads. This native quality is the outstanding feature of *John Brown's Body* (1928), the book which made Benét famous and which was awarded the Pulitzer Prize. Here is a long narrative poem so varied in style and treatment that it reads as easily as a novel. No single passage can be cited as great poetry, but the speed and activity of the whole give the work a continual stimulation and no little power.

Benét left several uncompleted works, notably *Western Star* (1943), which was posthumously awarded the Pulitzer Prize. He was also the author of a few novels and some famous short stories, the best of which were collected in *Thirteen O'Clock*.

Portrait of a Boy

After the whipping, he crawled into bed;
Accepting the harsh fact with no great weeping.
How funny uncle's hat had looked striped red!
He chuckled silently. The moon came, sweeping
A black frayed rag of tattered cloud before
In scorning; very pure and pale she seemed,
Flooding his bed with radiance. On the floor
Fat motes danced. He sobbed; closed his eyes and dreamed.

Warm sand flowed round him. Blurts of crimson light
Splashed the white grains like blood. Past the cave's mouth
Shone with a large fierce splendor, wildly bright,
The crooked constellations of the South;
Here the Cross swung; and there, affronting Mars,
The Centaur [1] stormed aside a froth of stars.
Within, great casks like wattled aldermen
Sighed of enormous feasts, and cloth of gold
Glowed on the walls like hot desire. Again,
Beside webbed purples from some galleon's hold,
A black chest bore the skull and bones in white
Above a scrawled " Gunpowder! " By the flames,
Decked out in crimson, gemmed with syenite,[2]
Hailing their fellows by outrageous names
The pirates sat and diced. Their eyes were moons.
" Doubloons! " they said. The words crashed gold. " Dou-
     bloons! "

1935

All night they marched, the infantrymen under pack,
But the hands gripping the rifles were naked bone
And the hollow pits of the eyes stared, vacant and black,
When the moonlight shone.

The gas mask lay like a blot on the empty chest,
The slanting helmets were spattered with rust and mold,
But they burrowed the hill for the machine-gun nest
As they had of old.

And the guns rolled, and the tanks, but there was no sound,
Never the gasp or rustle of living men
Where the skeletons strung their wire on disputed ground. . . .
I knew them, then.

" It is seventeen years," I cried. " You must come no more.
We know your names. We know that you are the dead.
Must you march forever from France and the last, blind
     war? "
" *Fool! From the next!* " they said.

[1] *Centaur:* a southern constellation, so called because it was
thought to resemble the mythical animal which was half-horse and
half-man.
[2] *Syenite:* brilliant, fiery stones.

Nancy Hanks [1]

If Nancy Hanks
Came back as a ghost,
Seeking news
Of what she loved most,
She'd ask first
" Where's my son?
What's happened to Abe?
What's he done?

" Poor little Abe,
Left all alone
Except for Tom,
Who's a rolling stone;
He was only nine
The year I died;
I remember still
How hard he cried.

" Scraping along
In a little shack,
With hardly a shirt
To cover his back,
And a prairie wind
To blow him down,
Or pinching times
If he went to town.

" You wouldn't know
About my son?
Did he grow tall?
Did he have fun?
Did he learn to read?
Did he get to town?
Do you know his name?
Did he get on? "

[1] From *A Book of Americans*, a collaboration by Stephen Vincent Benét and his wife, Rosemary Carr Benét; copyright, 1933. Nancy Hanks was the mother of Lincoln.

Léonie Adams was born in Brooklyn, New York, December 9,
1899. She was a member of the class of 1922 at Barnard College,
where she wrote her first published poems " in secret." It was only
through the persuasion of three of her friends that her volume,
Those Not Elect (1925), was made ready for the press. The author's own evasion of " realism " is apparent in all her poetry. The
poems themselves are of two sorts: the younger and simpler verses,
full of a shy ecstasy, and the later, more metaphysical expressions
of a rare and not so easily communicated wonder. Whatever her
style, there is no mistaking either her restraint or the beauty of
her suggestions.

In 1928 Miss Adams was awarded a fellowship by the Guggen-
heim Foundation and went abroad for two years; after her return
she taught at New York University and Bennington College. Her
second volume, *High Falcon* (1929), carries on the tradition of a
poetry which is so pure that it is almost abstract.

Home-Coming

When I stepped homeward to my hill
   Dusk went before with quiet tread;
The bare laced branches of the trees
   Were as a mist about its head.

Upon its leaf-brown breast, the rocks
   Like great gray sheep lay silent-wise;
Between the birch trees' gleaming arms,
   The faint stars trembled in the skies.

The white brook met me half-way up
   And laughed as one that knew me well,
To whose more clear than crystal voice
   The frost had joined a crystal spell.

The skies lay like pale-watered deep.
   Dusk ran before me to its strand
And cloudily leaned forth to touch
   The moon's slow wonder with her hand.

Lullaby

Hush, lullay,
Your treasures all
          Encrust with rust.
Your trinket pleasures
          Fall
To dust.
Beneath the sapphire arch
Upon the grassy floor
Is nothing more
          To hold,
And play is over old.
Your eyes
          In sleepy fever gleam,
Your lids droop
          To their dream.
You wander late alone,
The flesh frets on the bone,
Your love fails
          In your breast.
Here is the pillow.
          Rest.

ELMA DEAN

Elma Dean was born October 2, 1899, in Beaver Falls, Pennsylvania, but has spent much of her time in California. She writes poetry about animals and the outdoors, but says she would almost rather garden than write. Her poems have appeared in magazines as popular as *The Saturday Evening Post* and as special as *Poetry*. "The Elder Brother" first appeared in *The New Yorker*. In its deft and economical lines the poem has an ironical and yet gentle humor.

The Elder Brother
(POEM FOR ALL GOOD AND LOYAL DOGS)

After Light and the shaping of Land he came,
The four small footmarks on immaculate green.

Imagine him, bearing whatever name,
Taking his form from mist, being first seen
By his Maker, who must have called him **Good**;
Imagine the lifted muzzle trying the sweet
New air, finding the earth-provided food:
Surely now God's Eden was complete.

But, seeing His creature lonely, He made that other,
Who walked upright and glistened in the sun;
And the animal chose him for god and brother,
A deity to touch and love and own —
To go with gladly from that forbidden place,
Adoring through the many falls from Grace.

DOROTHY E. REID

Dorothy E. Reid was born in 1900 in Bucyrus, Ohio. At Ohio State University, from which she was graduated in 1925, she won the annual Vandewater Prize and was editor-in-chief of *The Candle*, a magazine of "revolt against opinionless student life." After school teaching and journalism, she turned to advertising.

Coach Into Pumpkin (1925) is the work of a beginner, but a beginner with charm and sensitivity. The unusual turn of phrase is evident even in her less successful poems; the poet possesses a "point of view" which is as different as her personal blend of observation and fantasy. This combination grows firmer in her later work which fluctuates between lightness and poignance.

Mrs. Winkelsteiner

Mrs. Winkelsteiner
  Made songs in her head;
You went to borrow eggs,
  You got songs instead,

Or a song about eggs
  And the eggs in a sack;
It wasn't very long
  Till you hurried right back.

Mrs. Winkelsteiner
  Sat around the room;
Her three brown daughters
  Were handy with the broom,

And handy with the iron,
  And handy with the bread;
But Mrs. Winkelsteiner
  Made songs in her head.

"*Little birdie in the tree,
Chirp a song to me.*"

"*Red cow sitting in the sun,
Waiting for farmer to come.*"

"*Egg so smooth and round,
Hens lay them on the ground.*"

Mrs. Winkelsteiner's
  Been a long time dead,
And all the songs she knew
  Are cold in her head.

You go after eggs
  And the eggs are in a sack,
It isn't very often
  That you want to go back

Where the birds still chirp,
  And the hens still call,
And the three brown daughters
  Never sing at all.

Men

I like men.
  They stride about,
They reach in their pockets
  And pull things out;

They look important,
  They rock on their toes,
They lose all the buttons
  Off their clothes;

They throw away pipes,
  They find them again.
Men are queer creatures;
  I like men.

LANGSTON HUGHES

Langston Hughes was born February 1, 1902, in Joplin, Missouri, was graduated from Central High School in Cleveland, and at eighteen became a teacher of English in Mexico. He spent a year at Columbia University and some time as a ship's hand on the high seas. After ten months in France, he worked his way through Italy and Spain, and returned to New York with twenty-five cents. Working as a busboy in Washington, he was discovered by Vachel Lindsay, who read several of his poems to a fashionable audience in the very hotel in which Hughes carried trays of dishes.

The Weary Blues, Hughes' first volume, appeared in 1926. One of the poems had already won first prize in a magazine which fostered creative work by Negroes. Hughes' poetry, appearing at the same time as Countee Cullen's, justified those who claimed we were witnessing a revival of Negro art. Hughes was the first to express the spirit of the blues in words. In his note to his second volume, *Fine Clothes to the Jew* (1927), he writes, "The *Blues,* unlike the *Spirituals,* have a strict poetic pattern: one long line repeated and a third line to rhyme with the first two. . . . The mood of the *Blues* is almost always despondency, but when they are sung people laugh."

Although at least half of Hughes' work centers about the Blues, much of his poetry is grim. His portraits of Negro workmen are more memorable than those produced by any of his compatriots. *Dear Lovely Death* (1931) is a proof that Hughes can turn from the popular to the proletarian and still remain on the level of poetry. His play, *Mulatto*, produced early in 1936, was followed by *Shakespeare in Harlem* (1942) and *Fields of Wonder* (1947). With Arna Bontemps, Hughes compiled a large anthology, *The Poetry of the Negro* (1949).

Homesick Blues

De railroad bridge's
A sad song in de air.
De railroad bridge's
A sad song in de air.
Every time de trains pass
I wants to go somewhere.

I went down to de station;
Ma heart was in ma mouth.
Went down to de station;
Heart was in ma mouth.
Lookin' for a box car
To roll me to de South.

Homesick blues, Lawd,
'S a terrible thing to have.
Homesick blues is
A terrible thing to have.
To keep from cryin'
I opens ma mouth an' laughs.

Brass Spittoons

Clean the spittoons, boy.
    Detroit,
    Chicago,
    Atlantic City,
    Palm Beach.
Clean the spittoons.
The steam in hotel kitchens,
And the smoke in hotel lobbies,
And the slime in hotel spittoons:
Part of my life.
    Hey, boy!
    A nickel,
    A dime,
    A dollar,
Two dollars a day.

Hey, boy!
A nickel,
A dime,
A dollar,
Two dollars
Buys shoes for the baby.
House rent to pay.
Church on Sunday.
          My God!

Babies and church
and women and Sunday
all mixed up with dimes and
dollars and clean spittoons
and house rent to pay.
          Hey, boy!

A bright bowl of brass is beautiful to the Lord.
Bright polished brass like the cymbals
Of King David's dancers,
Like the wine cups of Solomon.
          Hey, boy!
A clean spittoon on the altar of the Lord.
A clean bright spittoon all newly polished,
At least I can offer that.
          Com'mere, boy!

OGDEN NASH

Ogden Nash was born August 19, 1902, in Rye, New York, of a distinguished and, seemingly, ubiquitous family. He claims to have had ten thousand cousins in North Carolina; his great-great-grandfather was Revolutionary Governor of the State, and the latter's brother, General Francis Nash, gave his name to Nashville, Tennessee. Ogden Nash entered Harvard in the class of 1924, but left after one year. He spent another year at St. George's School in Rhode Island, where, he says, he lost his entire nervous system carving lamb for a table of fourteen-year-olds.

To continue his biography in his own words: "Came to New York to make my fortune as a bond salesman; in two years I sold one bond — to my godmother. However, I saw a lot of good movies. Next went to work writing car cards. After two years of that I landed in the advertising department of Doubleday. That was 1925, and I Doubledayed until 1931." After 1931 Nash engaged in a succession of varied activities: he was on the staff of *The New Yorker*, became associated with two publishing firms, married and lived in Baltimore, had two daughters and moved to Hollywood, where he wrote — or rewrote — scenarios, returned to New York and composed hundreds of lyrics, many of them for musical comedies.

The best of Nash is in *Free Wheeling* (1931), *The Bad Parent's Garden of Verse* (1936), *I'm a Stranger Here Myself* (1938), *The Face Is Familiar* (1940), *Good Intentions* (1942), and *Versus* (1949), but all his volumes are characterized by rollicking spirits, shrewd satire, and a slightly insane manner. The style is bantering, but the end is often a kind of social criticism. For most readers, however, Nash's charm lies in his irresponsible absurdities, in the impudent rhymes which do not quite rhyme, and his way of giving a new twist to an old subject. He can be witty, surprising, satirical, and nonsensical at the same time.

The Rhinoceros

The rhino is a homely beast,
For human eyes he's not a feast,
But you and I will never know
Why nature chose to make him so.
Farewell, farewell, you old rhinoceros,
I'll stare at something less prepoceros!

Adventures of Isabel

Isabel met an enormous bear;
Isabel, Isabel, didn't care.
The bear was hungry, the bear was ravenous,
The bear's big mouth was cruel and cavernous.
The bear said, Isabel, glad to meet you,
How do, Isabel, now I'll eat you!
Isabel, Isabel, didn't worry,
Isabel didn't scream or scurry.
She washed her hands and she straightened her hair up,
Then Isabel quietly ate the bear up.

Once on a night as black as pitch
Isabel met a wicked old witch.
The witch's face was cross and wrinkled,
The witch's gums with teeth were sprinkled.
Ho, ho, Isabel! the old witch crowed,
I'll turn you into an ugly toad!
Isabel, Isabel, didn't worry,
Isabel didn't scream or scurry.
She showed no rage and she showed no rancor,
But she turned the witch into milk and drank her.

Isabel met a hideous giant,
Isabel continued self-reliant.
The giant was hairy, the giant was horrid,
He had one eye in the middle of his forehead.
Good morning, Isabel, the giant said,
I'll grind your bones to make my bread.
Isabel, Isabel, didn't worry,
Isabel didn't scream or scurry.
She nibbled the zwieback that she always fed off,
And when it was gone, she cut the giant's head off.

Isabel met a troublesome doctor,
He punched and he poked till he really shocked her.
The doctor's talk was of coughs and chills
And the doctor's satchel bulged with pills.
The doctor said unto Isabel,
Swallow this, it will make you well.
Isabel, Isabel, didn't worry,
Isabel didn't scream or scurry.
She took those pills from the pill-concocter,
And Isabel calmly cured the doctor.

The Purist

I give you now Professor Twist,
A conscientious scientist.
Trustees exclaimed, " He never bungles! "
And sent him off to distant jungles.
Camped on a tropic riverside,
One day he missed his loving bride.
She had, the guide informed him later,

Been eaten by an alligator.
Professor Twist could not but smile.
" You mean," he said, " a crocodile."

COUNTEE CULLEN

Countee Cullen was born in New York City, May 30, 1903. He was educated in the New York schools and New York University, was graduated with the class of 1925, and received his M.A. at Harvard in 1926.

Beginning in 1924, poems by this hitherto unknown Negro began appearing in various magazines; within a year his name had reached the literary circles. A firmness of execution, a boldness of style, and a gift of epigram were apparent in his work. Cullen's first volume, *Color*, was published in 1925 and disclosed a brilliance which makes one willing to overlook the poet's imitativeness. Although this volume and the subsequent *Copper Sun* (1927) reveal little that is definitely Negro in idiom or rhythm (differing greatly from Langston Hughes), Cullen's background has, to some extent, conditioned his subject matter.

The Ballad of the Brown Girl (1927) appeared in the same year as his anthology of Negro verse, *Caroling Dusk*. Cullen selected the best of his poems for *On These I Stand* (1947) shortly before his death, January 8, 1946.

Simon the Cyrenian Speaks [1]

He never spoke a word to me,
And yet he called my name.
He never gave a sign to see,
And yet I knew and came.

At first I said, " I will not bear
His cross upon my back —
He only seeks to place it there
Because my skin is black."

[1] *Simon the Cyrenian:* a Negro who carried the cross of Jesus up the hill of Golgotha. "And . . . they found a man of Cyrene, Simon by name; him they compelled to bear his cross." (*St. Matthew* 27:32)

But He was dying for a dream,
And He was very meek;
And in His eyes there shone a gleam
Men journey far to seek.

It was Himself my pity bought;
I did for Christ alone
What all of Rome could not have wrought
With bruise of lash or stone.

From the Dark Tower

We shall not always plant while others reap
The golden increment of bursting fruit,
Nor always countenance, abject and mute,
That lesser men should hold their brothers cheap;
Not everlastingly while others sleep
Shall we beguile their limbs with mellow flute,
Not always bend to some more subtle brute.
We were not made eternally to weep.

The night, whose sable breast relieves the stark,
White stars, is no less lovely being dark;
And there are buds that cannot bloom at all
In light, but crumple, piteous, and fall.
So in the dark we hide the heart that bleeds,
And wait, and tend our agonizing needs.

THEODORE SPENCER

Born July 4, 1903, in Villa Nova, Pennsylvania, Theodore
Spencer seemed destined to become a scholar and a teacher. Educated at Princeton and Harvard, in 1927 he became a tutor in
English at Harvard, and taught there until his premature death,
due to a heart attack, January 18, 1949.

Spencer's first publication was *A Garland for John Donne*
(1931), a collection of essays celebrating the three hundredth an-
niversary of Donne's death. His original poetry appeared in *The
Paradox in the Circle* (1941), *An Act of Life* (1944), *Collected
Poems, 1941–1947*, and the posthumous *An Acre in the Seed* (1949).

Nothing Spencer wrote was careless or commonplace. He had an unusual gift of communication, an ability to say much in a little space. His condensations give his verse a clean edge, and his lines have a quality that is tart and tender, and usually memorable. "A Narrative" is typical of Spencer's playful philosophizing.

A Narrative

Bill dug a well
And knelt down to it;
Frank bought a telescope
And stared up through it;
Both looking for truth
Since nobody knew it.
Bill sought dark,
No light reflected;
Frank sought light,
With dark neglected.
One looked up,
One looked down;
And a long-drawn fight
Began in our town.
Was Bill in the right
Looking down his well?
Was Frank our hope,
With his telescope?
We could not tell.

But when Frank said
"I find that dark
Is what makes light,"
Bill raised his head:
"I can't find night
Without a spark,"
Was what Bill said.
"Let's look at your well,"
Said Frank to Bill;
And Bill looked up
Through the telescope.
"What do you see?"
Said Bill to Frank.
"Stars and an echo of dark," said Frank
"What do you see?"

Said Frank to Bill.
" Dark and the echo of stars," said Bill.

One looked up,
One looked down;
And the fight goes on
All over our town.
Was Bill our hope
At the telescope?
Did Frank do right
To take Bill's well?
No one can tell.
They're at it still.

MERRILL MOORE

Merrill Moore was born September 11, 1903, in Columbia, Tennessee. He received his B.A. at Vanderbilt University, Nashville, in 1924, and his M.D. in 1928. At Vanderbilt he was a member of the now famous group of poets known as " The Fugitives," but he served his internship in Boston, practiced there, served with the Army during the Second World War in New Zealand and China, received his honorable discharge as Colonel, and returned to practice psychiatry in Boston.

One of the busiest men of his day, he is also the most prolific writer of sonnets. At thirty-five he had already written more sonnets than any man who ever lived; in 1938 the editor made a rough count of about 40,000, and the total is steadily mounting. Four volumes of these sonnets have appeared: *The Noise That Time Makes* (1929), *Six Sides to a Man* (1935), *M* (1938), justifying its title with one thousand poems, and *Clinical Sonnets* (1949).

As a sonneteer, Moore does not adhere to the orthodox form. The rhyme-schemes are haphazard and irregular, the rhythms are uncertain; the stanzas divide themselves arbitrarily. But the ideas are continually fresh, the lines are alert with exact images, the rhythms are based on the rise and fall of the breath. Never has there been a more spontaneous poetry. Moreover, in breaking through the rigidity of the old form, Moore has fashioned a sonnet which is as distinctly American as Petrarch's was Italian. Naturally, in such energetic quantity, this is far from a poetry of perfection. But the best of Moore's sonnets are keen in insight, sharp in observation, rich in the tone of conversation, and always surprising in subject and treatment.

How She Resolved to Act

" I shall be careful to say nothing at all
About myself or what I know of him
Or the vaguest thought I have — no matter how dim,
Tonight if it so happen that he call."

And not ten minutes later the door-bell rang,
And into the hall he stepped as he always did,
With a face and a bearing that quite poorly hid
His brain that burned and his heart that fairly sang,
And his tongue that wanted to be rid of the truth.

As well as she could, for she was very loath
To signify how she felt, she kept very still,
But soon her heart cracked loud as a coffee mill,
And her brain swung like a comet in the dark,
And her tongue raced like a squirrel in the park.

No Envy, John Carter

Some night, John Carter, you will dream of hands,
Hands that are dead now, or as good as dead,
That you killed, or as good as made them die
Along the road that you have prospered by;
And I will never envy you the dread
With which you must awake then, as you see
Hands stretched towards you, striving, piteously
Stretched, beseeching, grasping at what was taken,

Hands by pain and grievance sorely shaken
And pointed at you while your agents keep
The power you've gained in this and other lands —
Some night, Mr. Carter, you will dream.
But it will not be an untroubled dream,
And, oh, I shall not envy you your sleep.

The Book of How

After the stars were all hung separately out
For mortal eyes to see that care to look,
The one who did it sat down and wrote a book

On how he did it.
                    It took him about
As long to write the book as to do the deed,
But he said, " It's things like this we mostly need."
And the angels approved but the devils screamed with laugh-
    ter,
For they knew exactly what would follow after.

For somehow he managed entirely to omit
The most important facts in accomplishing it:
Where he got the ladder to reach the stars;
And how he lighted them, especially Mars;
And what he hung them on when he got them there,
Eternally distant and luminous in the air.

Answer

Here are three ways to get your answer to me:
One, loose your pigeons, for they know my roof.
Tie the message to their legs with a tiny band
And they will bring, but will not understand
The words that one who holds herself aloof
Has written on rice paper with black ink;
That is the quickest way to do, I think,
Others I know but none as instantly.

Or tie a ribbon to the white swan's neck,
Red for yes or very blue for no,
They pass by here for water. If they go
Three days unribboned I'll know that you walk
In your rose garden waiting for the fall
To tell me by blowing dead leaves over my wall.

PHYLLIS McGINLEY

Phyllis McGinley was born in 1905 in Ontario, Oregon, brought
up in Colorado, and educated in Utah. After leaving the university
at Salt Lake City, she taught English in New Rochelle, worked in
an advertising agency, helped edit *Town and Country*, and moved

to a Westchester suburb because she had found a lot of Victorian furniture and wanted a Victorian house to put it in.

She intended to be a serious poet, but she soon discovered that light-verse writers get more butter on their bread. Being unusually fond of butter, Miss McGinley turned more and more to dexterous rhymes and agile verse. Her first volume, *On the Contrary* (1934), was followed by *One More Manhattan* (1937), *A Pocketful of Wry* (1940), and *Stories from a Glass House* (1946). The tone is deceptive. Mild enough on the surface, it is far from innocuous; a gently smiling manner conceals the teeth, and the slyness hides a satire that bites often and deeply. The technique is part of the wit, comic in its twists but always tipped with a critical point.

Intimations of Mortality [1]
(*On Being Told by the Dentist "This will be over soon."*)

Indeed, it will soon be over. I shall be done
   With the querulous drill, the forceps, the clove-smelling
     cotton.
I can go forth into fresher air, into sun,
   This narrow anguish forgotten.

In twenty minutes, or forty, or half an hour,
   I shall be easy, and proud of my hard-got gold.
But your apple of comfort is eaten by worms, and sour.
   Your consolation is cold.

This will not last, and the day will be pleasant after.
   I shall dine tonight with a witty and favorite friend.
No doubt tomorrow I shall rinse my mouth with laughter.
   And also that will end.

The handful of time that I am charily granted
   Will likewise pass, to oblivion duly apprenticed.
Summer will blossom and autumn be faintly enchanted.
   Then time for the grave, or the dentist.

Because you are shrewd, my man, and your hand is clever,
   You must not believe your words have a charm to spell me.
There was never a half of an hour that lasted forever.
   Be quiet. You need not tell me.

[1] The title is a humorous variation from the title of Wordsworth's famous poem *Ode: Intimations of Immortality;* it means, literally, " hints of eventual death."

Elizabeth Bishop was born February 8, 1911, in Worcester, Massachusetts. Brought up in New England and Nova Scotia, she was graduated from Vassar College and has traveled widely. For some time she spent part of each year in Key West, which may account for the peculiar quality of her images which combine New England severity with tropical floridity. In 1946 she received the Houghton Mifflin Literary Fellowship for a book of poems, *North & South*.

At first glance Miss Bishop appears to be a painter, an impressionist who, with a line here, a stroke there, evokes a continual play of substance and shadow. But the visual effects are largely intellectual, and Miss Bishop is seen to be both a colorist and a wit. Irony lurks behind many of the images, but they do not depend on technique and intellect only. "The Fish," a miniature Moby Dick, combines unusually careful observation and a vividly alert imagination.

The Fish

I caught a tremendous fish
and held him beside the boat
half out of water, with my hook
fast in a corner of his mouth.
He didn't fight.
He hadn't fought at all.
He hung a grunting weight,
battered and venerable
and homely. Here and there
his brown skin hung in strips
like ancient wall-paper,
and its pattern of darker brown
was like wall-paper:
shapes like full-blown roses
stained and lost through age.
He was speckled with barnacles,
fine rosettes of lime,
and infested
with tiny white sea-lice,
and underneath two or three
rags of green weed hung down.
While his gills were breathing in
the terrible oxygen
— the frightening gills

fresh and crisp with blood,
that can cut so badly —
I thought of the coarse white flesh
packed in like feathers,
the big bones and the little bones,
the dramatic reds and blacks
of his shiny entrails,
and the pink swim-bladder
like a big peony.
I looked into his eyes
which were far larger than mine
but shallower, and yellowed,
the irises backed and packed
with tarnished tinfoil
seen through the lenses
of old scratched isinglass.
They shifted a little, but not
to return my stare.
— It was more like the tipping
of an object toward the light.
I admired his sullen face,
the mechanism of his jaw,
and then I saw
that from his lower lip
— if you could call it a lip —
grim, wet, and weapon-like,
hung five old pieces of fish-line,
or four and a wire leader
with the swivel still attached,
with all their five big hooks
grown firmly in his mouth.
A green line, frayed at the end
where he broke it, two heavier lines,
and a fine black thread
still crimped from the strain and snap
when it broke and he got away.
Like medals with their ribbons
frayed and wavering,
a five-haired beard of wisdom
trailing from his aching jaw.
I stared and stared
and victory filled up
the little rented boat,

from the pool of bilge
where oil had spread a rainbow
around the rusted engine
to the bailer rusted orange,
the sun-cracked thwarts,
the oarlocks on their strings,
the gunnels — until everything
was rainbow, rainbow, rainbow!
And I let the fish go.

NATHALIA CRANE

Nathalia Clara Ruth Crane was born in New York City, August 11, 1913. Through her father she is descended from John and Priscilla Alden; on her mother's side she inherits the gifts of a famous family of Spanish Jews who were poets, musicians, and ministers of state. Nathalia began to write when she was eight years old. At nine she sent some verses to *The New York Sun* and they were accepted wholly on their merit, the poetry editor having no idea that the lines were written by a child.

Nathalia's first volume, *The Janitor's Boy*, appeared when its author was ten and a half, in 1924. It became one of the most discussed publications of the year. Some of the critics explained the work by insisting that Nathalia was some sort of instrument unaware of what was played; others ridiculed the idea that a child could have written verses so smooth in execution and so remarkable in overtones.

Lava Lane (1925), *The Singing Crow* (1926), and *Venus Invisible* (1928) are more sedate; these volumes are almost wholly serious, and the growth is obvious. In November, 1927, Nathalia won first prize ($500) in a contest for the best poem celebrating Lindbergh's flight across the Atlantic. During her attendance at New Jersey College for Women and at Barnard she was kept from publishing, but at twenty-two she assembled another collection of verse that remains peculiarly her own style, half-childish and half-pedantic. This book was *Swear by the Night* (1936), with a foreword by the editor. In the end one forgets who may have written such condensations as " Destiny " and " The Colors." The appeal of these lines is not that they have been written by a child but by a poet.

The Janitor's Boy

Oh, I'm in love with the janitor's boy,
  And the janitor's boy loves me;
He's going to hunt for a desert isle
  In our geography.

A desert isle with spicy trees
  Somewhere near Sheepshead Bay;
A right nice place, just fit for two,
  Where we can live alway.

Oh, I'm in love with the janitor's boy,
  He's busy as he can be;
And down in the cellar he's making a raft
  Out of an old settee.

He'll carry me off, I know that he will,
  For his hair is exceedingly red,
And the only thing that occurs to me
  Is to dutifully shiver in bed.

The day that we sail, I shall leave this brief note,
  For my parents I hate to annoy:
" I have flown away to an isle in the bay
  With the janitor's red-haired boy."

Destiny

The wind doth wander up and down,
Forever seeking for a crown;
The rose, in stillness on a stem,
Inherits love's own diadem.

The Dust

Crumbling a pyramid, humbling a rose,
The dust has its reasons wherever it goes.

Treating the sword blade the same as the staff,
Turning the chariot wheel into chaff.

Toppling a pillar and nudging a wall,
Building a sand pile to counter each fall.

Yielding to nothing, not even the rose,
The dust has its reasons wherever it goes.

The Colors

You cannot choose your battlefield,
The gods do that for you,
But you can plant a standard
Where a standard never flew.

KARL SHAPIRO

Karl (Jay) Shapiro was born November 10, 1913, in Baltimore, Maryland. He attended the University of Virginia and Johns Hopkins University. In 1941 he was inducted into the Army and, during the Second World War, served as a sergeant overseas. From 1942 until 1945, he was stationed in the South Pacific; his first two books were put together while he was there.

Person, Place and Thing (1942) was hailed as one of the most startling first books of the period. Shapiro's brusque and sometimes tortured irony was matched by a sensitivity which, though understanding, was never sentimental. Mark Van Doren praised his "acute sense of form and a wit that never fails"; Selden Rodman acclaimed him as "a true spokesman of our generation." His hatred of injustice and resentment against the traditional "romantic" attitude matured into *V-Letter and Other Poems* (1944), which was awarded the Pulitzer Prize. *Essay on Rime* (1945) is a threefold examination of the confusion in modern poetry: the confusion in prosody, the confusion in language, and the confusion in belief. The unknowing reader might think this work of more than two thousand lines the labor of a dusty academician amassing data for his Ph.D.; actually it was written by a soldier thousands of miles away from any library. *Trial of a Poet and Other Poems* (1947) shows Shapiro's concern with the poet's function in the world and comes to the conclusion that the poet is both an onlooker and a critic, usually at odds with his times.

Although it is not specifically a war poem, "The Leg" is a reflection of the atmosphere of war. Shapiro has turned the horror

of the subject into something which is both whimsical and noble.
"Travelogue for Exiles" expresses the results of war with tragic
rony.

Travelogue for Exiles

Look and remember. Look upon this sky;
Look deep and deep into the sea-clean air,
The unconfined, the terminus of prayer.
Speak now and speak into the hallowed dome.
What do you hear? What does the sky reply?
The heavens are taken: this is not your home.

Look and remember. Look upon this sea;
Look down and down into the tireless tide.
What of a life below, a life inside,
A tomb, a cradle in the curly foam?
The waves arise; sea-wind and sea agree
The waters are taken: this is not your home.

Look and remember. Look upon this land,
Far, far across the factories and the grass.
Surely, there, surely, they will let you pass.
Speak then and ask the forest and the loam.
What do you hear? What does the land command?
The earth is taken: this is not your home.

The Leg

Among the iodoform, in twilight-sleep,
What have I lost? he first inquires,
Peers in the middle distance where a pain,
Ghost of a nurse, hastily moves, and day,
Her blinding presence pressing in his eyes
And now his ears. They are handling him
With rubber hands. He wants to get up.

One day beside some flowers near his nose
He will be thinking, *When will I look at it?*
And pain, still in the middle distance, will reply
At what? and he will know it's gone,
O where! and begin to tremble and cry.
He will begin to cry as a child cries
Whose puppy is mangled under a screaming wheel.

Later, as if deliberately, his fingers
Begin to explore the stump. He learns a shape
That is comfortable and tucked in like a sock.
This has a sense of humor, this can despise
The finest surgical limb, the dignity of limping,
The nonsense of wheel-chairs. Now he smiles to the wall:
The amputation becomes an acquisition.

For the leg is wondering where he is (all is not lost)
And surely he has a duty to the leg;
He is its injury, the leg is his orphan,
He must cultivate the mind of the leg,
Pray for the part that is missing, pray for peace
In the image of man, pray, pray for its safety,
And after a little it will die quietly.

The body, what is it, Father, but a sign
To love the force that grows us, to give back
What in Thy palm is senselessness and mud?
Knead, knead the substance of our understanding
Which must be beautiful in flesh to walk,
That if Thou take me angrily in hand
And hurl me to the shark, I shall not die!

RANDALL JARRELL

Randall Jarrell was born May 6, 1914, in Nashville, Tennessee,
spent his childhood in California, and, after that, lived in Arizona,
Texas, and Tennessee. Educated at Vanderbilt University he made
his living by teaching English at a number of colleges. In 1942 he
enlisted in the Air Force, flew for a while, was "washed out" and
spent most of the war as CNT (Celestial Navigation Trainer)
operator at a field in Arizona, where he trained B-29 crews.

Blood for a Stranger (1942) is a first book in which the critic
is controlled by the sensitive poet. Jarrell alternates suave measures
with brusque rhythms and achieves a wry music without straining for effect. This unforced intensity grows steadily in *Little
Friend, Little Friend* (1945) and *Losses* (1948). The poems vibrate
with an emotion which is tender and tragic, full of unsentimental
pity which can smolder with bitter outrage. In " A Camp in the
Prussian Forest " Jarrell describes a visit to a former prison-

camp, and displays irony and compassion in reflecting on the horrible murders committed by the Nazis. Whatever Jarrell touches is given a precise impact. John Crowe Ransom wrote that Jarrell had " an angel's velocity and range with language "; the late Theodore Spencer said that his " energy, satiric bitterness, and weight prove him to be one of the most interesting poets of his generation."

A Camp in the Prussian Forest

I walk beside the prisoners to the road.
Load on puffed load,
Their corpses, stacked like sodden wood,
Lie barred or galled with blood

By the charred warehouse. No one comes today
In the old way
To knock the fillings from their teeth;
The dark, coned, common wreath

Is plaited for their grave — a kind of grief.
The living leaf
Clings to the planted profitable
Pine if it is able;

The boughs sigh, mile on green, calm, breathing mile,
From this dead file
The planners ruled for them . . . One year
They sent a million here:

Here men were drunk like water, burnt like wood.
The fat of good
And evil, the breast's star of hope
Were rendered into soap.

I paint the star I sawed from yellow pine —
And plant the sign
In soil that does not yet refuse
Its usual Jews

Their first asylum. But the white, dwarfed star —
This dead white star —
Hides nothing, pays for nothing; smoke
Fouls it, a yellow joke,

The needles of the wreath are chalked with ash,
A filmy trash
Litters the black woods with the death
Of men; and one last breath

Curls from the monstrous chimney . . . I laugh aloud
Again and again;
The star laughs from its rotting shroud
Of flesh. O star of men!

PETER VIERECK

Peter Viereck was born August 5, 1916, in New York City. He attended Horace Mann School and, at twenty-one, was graduated *summa cum laude* from Harvard, where he was Phi Beta Kappa. During 1937–38 he was a Fellow at Christ Church, Oxford, and, a few years later, was awarded the M.A. and Ph.D. in history from Harvard. During the Second World War he served overseas in the African and Italian campaigns and, later, taught at the " G. I. University " at Florence. After receiving his honorable discharge in 1945, he returned to Harvard, where he was Instructor in Literature and German. He became Assistant Professor at Smith and Associate Professor at Mount Holyoke.

Viereck's first work was a book of political essays: *Metapolitics: From the Romantics to Hitler* (1941), a brilliant analysis of the cultural backgrounds of Fascism. Viereck's astonishing range of manner and material was enlarged in *Terror and Decorum* (1948), a book of energetic and, at times, exuberant poems. Whatever Viereck touches takes on freshness and excitement. He puts the scrawled phrase " Kilroy was here " into rhyme with epic spirit by comparing the mythical American roamer to the great adventurers of history: the wandering Ulysses; Columbus, " the Cathay-drunk Genoese "; Chaucer's lusty Miller; the tragically driven Orestes; Icarus, who tried to fly into the sun — all those who did not hesitate (did not say " Perhaps " or " Better Not ") but followed their destiny. He is an experimenter who respects tradition without being submerged by it, a genuine wit who is, at the same time, a poet of emotional power. *Terror and Decorum* was awarded the Pulitzer Prize. It was followed by *Conservatism Revisited* (1949), a philosophical attempt to reconcile the differences between the liberal and conservative points of view in politics and society.

Kilroy

[An example of an unfaked epic spirit emerging from the war was the expression " Kilroy was here," scribbled everywhere by American soldiers and implying that nothing was too adventurous or remote. See explanatory sentence in the paragraph above.]

Also Ulysses once — that other war.
     (Is it because we find his scrawl
     Today on every privy door
     That we forget his ancient role?)
Also was there — he did it for the wages —
When a Cathay-drunk Genoese set sail.
Whenever " longen folk to goon on pilgrimages,"
Kilroy is there;
        he tells The Miller's Tale.

At times he seems a paranoiac [1] king
Who stamps his crest on walls and says " My Own! "
But in the end he fades like a lost tune,
Tossed here and there, whom all the breezes sing.
" Kilroy was here "; these words sound wanly gay,
     Haughty yet tired with long marching.
He is Orestes — guilty of what crime? —
     For whom the Furies still are searching;
     When they arrive, they find their prey
(Leaving his name to mock them) went away.
Sometimes he does not flee from them in time:
" Kilroy was — "
       (with his blood a dying man
     Wrote half the phrase out in Bataan.

Kilroy, beware. " HOME " is the final trap
That lurks for you in many a wily shape:
In pipe-and-slippers plus a Loyal Hound
     Or fooling around, just fooling around.
Kind to the old (their warm Penelope)
But fierce to boys,
        thus " home " becomes that sea,
Horribly disguised, where you were always drowned —
     (How could suburban Crete condone

---

[1] *Paranoiac:* self-deluded, mentally disordered.

The yarns you would have V-mailed from the sun?) —
And folksy fishes sip Icarian tea.

One stab of hopeless wings imprinted your
                    Exultant Kilroy-signature
Upon sheer sky for all the world to stare:
            " I was there! I was there! I was there! "

God is like Kilroy. He, too, sees it all;
That's how He knows of every sparrow's fall;
That's why we prayed each time the tightropes cracked
On which our loveliest clowns contrived their act.
The G. I. Faustus who was
                              everywhere
Strolled home again. " What was it like outside? "
Asked Can't, with his good neighbors Ought and But
And pale Perhaps and grave-eyed Better Not;
For " Kilroy " means: the world is very wide.
            He was there, he was there, he was there!

And in the suburbs Can't sat down and cried.

Modern British Poetry

PREFACE

British poetry has undergone less radical change in form and content during the past century than the American; and it is therefore more difficult to determine who are, in spirit as well as in writing, the first important " modern " British poets. We may perhaps logically begin with Thomas Hardy, a pioneer of candor and a poet who clearly anticipated the forthright, direct speech of the contemporary generation. Hardy wrote during the reign of Queen Victoria but lived a quarter century beyond it, so it can be said that he takes his departure, as does modern British poetry generally, from the period known as Victorianism.

THE END OF VICTORIANISM

The age commonly called Victorian came to an end in England about 1880. It was an age distinguished by many true idealists and many false ideals. It was, in spite of notable artists, on an entirely different level from the epoch preceding. Its poetry was, in the main, not universal but parochial; its romanticism was gilt and tinsel; its realism was kin to the artificial backgrounds, the red plush and fancy knickknacks. The period was full of pessimistic resignation (the note popularized by Fitzgerald's Omar Khayyám), a negation which, refusing to see any glamour in the present world, turned to the Middle Ages, to King Arthur, to the legend of Troy — to the soft surroundings of a dream-world instead of the hard edges of actual experience.

The poets of a generation before this time were fired with ideas of freedom, an insatiable hunger for truth in all its forms and manifestations. The characteristic poets of the Victorian Era, says Max Plowman, " wrote under the dominance of churchliness, of 'sweetness and light,' and a thousand lesser theories that have not truth but comfort for their end." The revolt against the tawdriness of the period had already begun; the best of Victorianism can be found not in men who were typically Victorian, but in pioneers like Browning, Swinburne, William Morris, and Thomas Hardy, who were completely out of sympathy with their time.

THOMAS HARDY

Hardy knew nature too intimately to be sentimental about it. Refusing to consider life as a Victorian compound of " sweetness and light," he saw the grim warfare of the farmer, the persistent tragedies of drought and disease. Like his follower, the American Edwin Arlington Robinson, Hardy was especially sympathetic to failures, possibly because he sometimes thought of himself as one. He had begun with poetry but, in the hope of making a living, had turned to the writing of novels. The early stories had been roughly criticized; his two masterpieces, *Tess of the D'Urbervilles* and *Jude the Obscure*, were violently attacked. Critics maliciously called the latter " Jude the Obscene." After years of antagonism, Hardy gave up fiction entirely and returned to poetry, his first and last love. It took a long time for the public to discover Hardy's significance. Part of no school or tendency, Hardy was a movement by himself. He was largely responsible for the swing from pallid romanticism to robust reality. Where others avoided troublesome depths, Hardy probed desperately, even in darkness. Dubious about human importance, Hardy was stirred by the endless strivings of humanity. Even in defeat, there was nobility as well as hope, a hope heard by the poet in a frail and storm-tossed bird (" The Darkling Thrush ") who had chosen to fling his song and his soul through unrelieved gloom.

RISE AND DECLINE
OF THE ESTHETIC PHILOSOPHY

A further, if more limited, revolt was instigated by Oscar Wilde. Wilde's was, in the most outspoken manner, the first use of estheticism as a slogan; the battle-cry of the group was the now outworn but then revolutionary " Art for Art's sake "! And, so sick were people of the Victorian heavy platitudes and dull moralizing that the slogan won. At least, temporarily.

The Yellow Book (1894–1897), the organ of the younger writers, represented a reasoned reaction. The Rhymers' Club was the nucleus, and its members — among them Ernest Dowson, Lionel Johnson, Arthur Symons, William Butler Yeats — met at the Cheshire Cheese where, over their cakes and ale, they fondly hoped to restore the spirit of the Elizabethan age. Unfortunately they lacked the gusto of their Mermaid Tavern models. Where the Elizabethans were all for size, the sad young men were all for subtlety; instead of being large and carefree, they were small and self-conscious. They wrote with one eye on the British public which they hoped to startle, and the other on the French poets whom they hoped to impress.

Almost the first act of the " new " men was to rouse and outrage their immediate predecessors. This end-of-the-century desire to shock has a place of its own — especially as an antidote, a harsh corrective. Mid-Victorian propriety and self-satisfaction crumbled under the audacities of the sensational young authors and artists. The old walls fell; the public, once indifferent to *belles lettres,* was more than attentive to every phase of experimentation. The last decade of the nineteenth century was so tolerant of novelty in art and ideas that it would seem, says Holbrook Jackson in his penetrative summary, *The Eighteen-Nineties,* " as though the declining century wished to make amends for several decades of artistic monotony. It may indeed be something more than a coincidence that placed this decade at the close of a century, and *fin de siècle* may have been at once a swan song and a deathbed repentance."

Later on, the movement, surfeited with its own excesses, fell into the mere poses of revolt; it degenerated into a defense not of Art but of Artificiality.

WILLIAM ERNEST HENLEY

Henley repudiated languid aestheticism; he scorned an art which was out of touch with the world. His was a large and sweeping affirmation. He felt that mere existence was glorious; life was difficult, often dangerous and dirty, but splendid at the heart. Art, he knew, could not be separated from the dreams and hungers of man; it could not flourish only on its own technical accomplishments. To live, poetry would have to share the fears, hopes, and struggles of the prosaic world. So Henley came like a swift salt breeze blowing through a perfumed and heavily screened studio. He sang loudly (often too loudly) of the joy of living and the courage of the " unconquerable soul." He was a powerful influence not only as a poet but as a critic and editor. A pioneer and something of a prophet, he was one of the first to champion the writings of Stevenson, the paintings of Whistler, and the genius of the sculptor Rodin.

If at times Henley's verse is imperialistic, over-muscular and strident, his noisy moments are redeemed not only by his delicate lyrics but by his passionate enthusiasm for nobility in whatever cause it is joined.

THE CELTIC REVIVAL AND J. M. SYNGE

In 1889, William Butler Yeats published his *Wanderings of Oisin;* in the same year Douglas Hyde, the scholar and folklorist who was elected President of the Irish Republic in 1938, brought out his *Book of Gaelic Stories.*

The revival of Gaelic and the renascence of Irish literature may be said to date from the publication of those two books. The fundamental idea of both men and their followers was the same. It was to create a literature which would express the national consciousness of Ireland through a purely national art. This community of fellowship and aims is to be found in the varied but allied work of William Butler Yeats, " Æ " (George W. Russell), Moira O'Neill, Lionel Johnson, Katharine Tynan, Padraic Colum, and others. These writers began to reflect the strange background of dreams, politics, suffering, and heroism that is immortally Irish. The first fervor gone, a short period of dullness set in. After reanimating the old myths with a new significance, it seemed that the movement would lose itself in a literary mysticism. But there followed an increasing concern with the peasant, the migratory laborer, the tramp — an interest that was something of a reaction against the influence of Yeats and his mystic otherworldliness.

In 1904 the Celtic Revival reached its height with John Millington Synge, who was not only the greatest dramatist of the Irish Theatre, but one of the greatest dramatists who have written in English. Synge's poetry, brusque and all too small in quantity, was a minor occupation with him, yet the quality and power of it is unmistakable. The raw vigor in it was to serve as a bold banner for the younger men of the following period.

Although Synge's poetry numbered only twenty-four original pieces and eighteen translations, it had a surprising effect. It marked a point of departure, a reaction against the over-rhetorical verse of his immediate predecessors and the dehumanized mysticism of his associates. In a memorable preface to his *Poems* he wrote a *credo* for all that might be called the "new" poetry. "I have often thought," it begins, "that at the side of poetic diction, which everyone condemns, modern verse contains a great deal of poetic material, using 'poetic' in the same special sense. The poetry of exaltation will be always the highest; but when men lose their poetic feeling for ordinary life and cannot write poetry of ordinary things, their exalted poetry is likely to lose its strength of exaltation in the way that men cease to build beautiful churches when they have lost happiness in building shops. . . . Even if we grant that exalted poetry can be kept successfully by itself, the strong things of life are needed in poetry also, to show that what is exalted or tender is not made by feeble blood."

RUDYARD KIPLING

While Synge was publishing his proofs of the poetry in everyday life, Kipling was illuminating, in a totally different manner, the wealth of poetic material in things regarded as too unpoetic for poetry. Before literary England had recovered from its surfeit of Victorian priggishness and later, aesthetical delicacy, Kipling came along with a great tide of life, sweeping all before him. An obscure Anglo-Indian journalist, the publication of his *Barrack-room Ballads* in 1892 brought him sudden notice. By 1895 he was internationally famous. Brushing over the pallid attempts to revive a faded past, he rode triumphantly on a wave of buoyant and sometimes brutal joy in the present. Kipling gloried in the material world; he did more — he glorified it. He pierced the coarse exteriors of seemingly prosaic things — things like machinery, bridge-building, cockney soldiers, slang, steam, the dirty by-products of science — and uncovered their hidden glamour. "Romance is gone," sighed most of his contemporaries; but, added Kipling;

> ". . . all unseen
> Romance brought up the nine-fifteen."

That sentence is the key to Kipling's attitude and the idiom which helped rejuvenate English verse.

Kipling, with his perception of ordinary people in terms of ordinary life, was one of the strongest links between the Wordsworth-Browning era and the apostles of realism. There are serious defects in his work. Frequently he falls into a journalistic ease that tends to turn into jingle; he is fond of a militaristic drum-banging. But a burning if sometimes too simple faith shines through his achievement. Kipling's best work reveals an intensity that crystallizes into beauty what was tawdry; it lifts the incidental and vulgar to the plane of the universal.

JOHN MASEFIELD

All art is a twofold revivifying — a recreation of subject and a reanimating of form. Poetry becomes perennially " new " by returning to the old with a greater awareness. In 1911, when art was again searching for novelty, John Masefield created something startling and new by going back to 1385 and *The Canterbury Pilgrims!* Employing the Chaucerian model and a form similar to the almost forgotten Byronic stanza, Masefield wrote, in rapid succession, *The Everlasting Mercy* (1911), *The Widow in the Bye Street* (1912), *Dauber* (1912), *The Daffodil Fields* (1913) — four astonishing rhymed narratives and four of the most remarkable poems of his generation. Expressive of the more rugged phases of life, these poems responded to Synge's proclamation that " the strong things of life are needed in poetry also . . . and it may almost be said that before verse can be human again it must be brutal."

Masefield brought back to poetry that mixture of beauty and brutality which, as Chaucer proved and Synge maintained, is one of its most human and enduring qualities. He brought back that rich animation which is the lifeblood of Chaucer, of Shakespeare, of Burns, of Heine — and of all those who were not only great artists but great humanists. As a purely descriptive poet, Masefield can take his place with the masters of seascape and landscape. As an imaginative realist, he showed men that they themselves were wilder and far more thrilling than anything in the world — or out of it. Few things in contemporary poetry are as powerful as the regeneration of Saul Kane (in *The Everlasting Mercy*) or the story of *Dauber*, the legend of a dreaming youth who wanted to be a painter. The vigorous description of rounding Cape Horn in the latter poem is superbly done, a masterpiece in itself. Masefield's later volumes are quieter in tone, more measured in technique. But the firm line is there, a strength that leaps through all his work from *Salt Water Ballads* (1902) to *Reynard the Fox* (1919).

THE WAR AND THE GEORGIANS

There is no sharp line of demarcation between Masefield and the realists who succeeded him. W. W. Gibson had already sounded the " return to actuality " by turning from his preoccupation with shining knights, faultless queens, ladies in distress, and all the paraphernalia of hackneyed medieval romances, to write about ferrymen, berry-pickers, stone-cutters, farmers, printers, circus-men, carpenters — dramatizing (though sometimes theatricalizing) the primitive emotions of uncultured and ordinary people.

The first volume of the biennial *Georgian Poetry* had just appeared when the First World War caught up the youth of England in a great gust of national fervor. Not only the young men but their seniors joined what seemed then to be " the Great Adventure," only to find that it was, as one of them has since called it, " the Great Nightmare." After the early flush of romanticism had passed, the voices of disillusion were heard. Not at first, for the censorship was omnipresent. But Siegfried Sassoon's fierce satires and burning denunciations could not be stilled, the mocking lines of Robert Graves began to be quoted, and Wilfred Owen's posthumous poems painted a picture the very opposite of the journalistic jingo verses which attempted to depict civilization's greatest tragedy in bright and heroic colors.

Robert Graves summarized the part which the soldier-poets played. He pointed out that those who celebrated war were either far from the front or saw little actual fighting, that not more than four or five poets saw the war through to the end, that these " unanimously vilified rather than celebrated the war, and of these only Siegfried Sassoon published his verse while the war was still on."

The effect of the war on the older poets was disastrous. With the exception of Yeats, all the poets suffered a loss of faith and force; some of them, like Hodgson and Housman, ceased to write at all. Peace brought back only a few of the younger poets. English literature received a setback on all fronts; the shock affected writers of every school; it diverted where it did not arrest the current of contemporary verse. A false pastoral note crept in. Horrified by the death-dealing machine, many of the poets turned from destructive ingenuities to " primal simplicities." Following the example of that genuinely bucolic poet, W. H. Davies, a small group began to sing exclusively about the charms of childhood, sunsets, lambs, and other rural delights. Walter de la Mare continued to write of experiences beyond reality, of a lost world of curious music and delicate dreams. James Stephens elaborated his odd whimsicalities in an inflection which was a cross between wisdom and banter. Charlotte Mew and Anna Wickham found a new turn to feminism and struck many arresting notes. Humbert Wolfe composed in experimental and dissonant harmonies. But most of the younger men, fearing to be false and hating to be " pretty," turned to an unhappy form of expression — a literature of nerves.

THE LITERATURE OF NERVES

Headed by the three Sitwells (Edith, Osbert, and Sachererell) a poetry emerged which took the form of satire. Sometimes the burlesque was broad, but usually the allusions were so private that only a few " insiders " found them intelligible. The Sitwells advertised themselves liberally, bellowed their verses through megaphones, declaimed them against a background of modernistic music, and even capitalized their unpopularity. Although the Sitwells and their followers wrote some brilliant lines, most of their work is high-pitched, nervous, exasperated and (as a not unnatural result) exasperating. Too often their art is a kind of personal sport, a game played in code, a sort of intimate charade.

Such work was bound to cause another revulsion in taste. A new group of poets spoke up against the unreason and aimlessness of the literature of nerves.

POETS OF THE 1930'S

In the early 1930's several poets emerged who had more than mere contemporaneousness in common. Their vocabulary, their taste, their technique, most of all their social and political convictions, were in the greatest possible contrast to those of the Georgians and the Sitwellians. They owed much to the American T. S. Eliot, who so strongly influenced English poetry at the beginning of the twentieth century. Eliot prepared the way for them, celebrating and satirizing the end of a cycle, the cultural decay of a period and a system. But such poets as Stephen Spender, W. H. Auden, and Louis MacNeice refused to follow Eliot's evasions and defeatism. They claimed to be revolutionaries; Eliot was credited with having shown them the way to new techniques and a greater freedom, but nothing more. Nevertheless, the poetic art in England received a sudden increase in vitality impelled by a social fervor. It came with such exuberance that even those who challenged its philosophy could not dispute its stimulating and affirmative force.

"THE AGE OF ANXIETY"

At the end of the nineteen thirties, the hopes and affirmations of humanity were dashed by a universal denial. The horror of the Second World War which began in September, 1939, threatened all contemporary culture. Dictatorships upset the balance of power; the military state — a state of mind as well as a form of misgovernment — violated nations and betrayed humanity. The feeling of tension increased as the war grew in length and intensity. The arts seemed haunted by ghosts of undefined but devastating guilt. Poetry echoed the mind's despair and the heart's apprehension. W. H. Auden characterized his time in a bitter book-length poem entitled "The Age of Anxiety."

The impact of the war increasingly affected the psychology of civilians as well as soldiers; but even universal disorganization found expression in poetry. The spirit of man, dismayed and temporarily defeated, could not be destroyed. Constructive power is inexhaustible; creation, not chaos, is a constant. Poets like Edith Sitwell turned from preoccupations with techniques and textures to write poems of grave significance. Stephen Spender's work grew larger in concept and nobler in tone. So did C. Day Lewis's. W. H. Auden, the most versatile poet of his generation, amplified his brilliance and wit with searching and religious depths.

The flight from reality had ended. The battle for freedom

of expression had been won. New ideas, new images gave metaphor a speed and power beyond conventional logic. Intuition, strengthened by experience, produced a poetry which was dynamic, immediate, and intense. Once again, the poet fulfilled his function. He sharpened the reader's perceptions, increased his appreciation, and heightened his awareness of life in all its simple commonplaces and changing complexities.

THOMAS HARDY

Thomas Hardy was born in the village of Upper Bockhampton, near Dorchester, in Wessex, June 2, 1840. His father was a stone-mason, and young Hardy was apprenticed to an architect. He studied in London, won a prize from the Royal Institute of Architects at the age of twenty-three, and, at the age of thirty-one, published the first of his many novels. The book, *Desperate Remedies*, was a failure, and little attention was paid to the writer until the publication of *Under the Greenwood Tree*, in which he mirrored his native Wessex background. Between the ages of thirty-four and fifty-seven Hardy wrote eleven novels and three collections of short stories, most of them somber in tone and adding a note of social criticism to the pictures of men forever struggling in a heedless or hostile world. Only a few critics understood Hardy's intense honesty; most of the reviewers were antagonistic. *Tess of the D'Urbervilles* was severely condemned; *Jude the Obscure* was so savagely attacked that Hardy stopped writing fiction.

At sixty he returned to the writing of poetry — " my first love," he wrote to an editor — after devoting more than twenty years to prose, a form he never really liked. He said he had been " *compelled* to give up verse for prose " in order to support himself by printing " potboilers." Besides composing hundreds of lyrics, many of them condensed dramas, Hardy produced *The Dynasts*, a huge drama of the Napoleonic wars in three books, nineteen acts, and one hundred and thirty scenes.

The last half of Hardy's life was spent at Max Gate, a home which he had designed for himself and where he lived in semi-seclusion. (A picture, half-truth and half-caricature, of this period is presented in Somerset Maugham's novel *Cakes and Ale*.) He died in his eighty-eighth year, " the grand old man of English letters," January 11, 1928. His ashes were placed in Westminster Abbey, but his heart was buried, at his own request, on Egdon Heath, in the churchyard he had made famous and the soil he loved so faithfully.

Hardy's *Collected Poems*, several times revised, and his posthumous *Winter Words in Various Moods* (1929) prove that Hardy's power increased as he grew older. He wrote in almost every manner and meter. At one moment he is tragically ironic, as in the " Satires of Circumstance," the next moment he is lightly lyrical, as in " When I Set Out for Lyonnesse," one of Hardy's own favorites. Although he was often labelled a pessimist, he was a man whose heart bled for the sufferings of humanity and who never lost hope in mankind. Hardy felt that man struggled against vast and unequal odds, but the very futility of his struggle — and his persistence in striving — made him noble. In poetry Hardy's genius for condensation was at its highest; time and again he captured in a single stanza a whole countryside with its people laboring against a quiet but fiercely alive landscape.

In Time of " The Breaking of Nations " [1]

Only a man harrowing clods
    In a slow silent walk,
With an old horse that stumbles and nods
    Half asleep as they stalk.

Only thin smoke without flame
    From the heaps of couch-grass:
Yet this will go onward the same
    Though Dynasties pass.

Yonder a maid and her wight [2]
    Come whispering by;
War's annals will fade into night
    Ere their story die.

The Darkling Thrush

I leaned upon a coppice gate
    When Frost was specter-gray,
And Winter's dregs made desolate
    The weakening eye of day.
The tangled vine-stems scored the sky
    Like strings from broken lyres,
And all mankind that haunted nigh
    Had sought their household fires.

The land's sharp features seemed to be
    The Century's corpse outleant;
His crypt the cloudy canopy,
    The wind his death-lament.
The ancient pulse of germ and birth

[1] " *The Breaking of Nations* ": a time of upheaval and war.
[2] *Wight*: a man.

Was shrunken hard and dry,
And every spirit upon earth
  Seemed fervorless as I.

At once a voice burst forth among
  The bleak twigs overhead
In a full-hearted evensong
  Of joy unlimited;
An aged thrush, frail, gaunt and small,
  In blast-beruffled plume,
Has chosen thus to fling his soul
  Upon the growing gloom.

So little cause for carolings
  Of such ecstatic sound
Was written on terrestrial things
  Afar or nigh around,
That I could think there trembled through
  His happy good-night air
Some blessed hope, whereof he knew
  And I was unaware.

When I Set Out for Lyonnesse

When I set out for Lyonnesse,
  A hundred miles away,
    The rime was on the spray,[1]
And starlight lit my lonesomeness
When I set out for Lyonnesse
  A hundred miles away.

What could bechance at Lyonnesse
  While I should sojourn there
    No prophet durst declare,
Nor did the wisest wizard guess
What would bechance at Lyonnesse
  While I should sojourn there.

When I came back from Lyonnesse
  With magic in my eyes,
    All marked with mute surmise

[1] *Rime on the spray:* frost on the branch.

My radiance rare and fathomless,
When I came back from Lyonnesse
With magic in my eyes.

A Satire of Circumstance

" I stood at the back of the shop, my dear,
    But you did not perceive me.
Well, when they deliver what you were shown
    I shall know nothing of it, believe me! "

And he coughed and coughed as she paled and said,
    " O, I didn't see you come in there —
Why couldn't you speak? " — " Well, I didn't. I left
    That you should not notice I'd been there.

" You were viewing some lovely things. ' Soon required
    For a widow, of latest fashion ';
And I knew 'twould upset you to meet the man
    Who had to be cold and ashen

" And screwed in a box before they could dress you
    ' In the last new note in mourning,'
As they defined it. So, not to distress you,
    I left you to your adorning."

The Prospect

The twigs of the birch imprint the December sky
Like branching veins upon a thin old hand;
I think of summer-time, yes, of last July,
When she was beneath them, greeting a gathered band
Of the urban and bland.

Iced airs wheeze through the skeletoned hedge from the
        north,
With steady snores, and a numbing that threatens snow,
And skaters pass; and merry boys go forth
To look for slides. But well, well do I know
Whither I would go!

Waiting Both

A star looks down at me,
And says: "Here I and you
Stand, each in our degree:
What do you mean to do —
    Mean to do?"

I say: "For all I know,
Wait, and let Time go by,
Till my change come." — "Just so,"
The star says: "So mean I —
    So mean I."

AUSTIN DOBSON

(Henry) Austin Dobson was born at Plymouth, in 1840, and was educated in Wales and on the Continent. In 1856 he received a clerkship in the government and was in official office most of his life.

Vignettes in Rhyme (1873) attracted attention by the ease with which the author managed his dexterous and difficult effects. With *Proverbs in Porcelain* (1877) and *At the Sign of the Lyre* (1885), it was evident that a new master of light verse had arisen.

During the latter part of his life, Dobson devoted himself to semi-biographical essays, intended to immortalize some nearly or wholly forgotten celebrity. His prose is scarcely less distinctive than his verse; his charmingly dispensed knowledge of the time of Queen Anne gives a special flavor of "archaic gentility."

Although most of his rhymes are charming rather than profound, certain pages, like "Before Sedan," are memorable for their serious clarity. Dobson died September 3, 1921.

In After Days

In after days when grasses high
O'ertop the stone where I shall lie,
    Though ill or well the world adjust
    My slender claim to honored dust,
I shall not question or reply.

I shall not see the morning sky;
I shall not hear the night-wind's sigh;
　　I shall be mute, as all men must
　　　　In after days!

But yet, now living, fain were I
That someone then should testify,
　　Saying — " He held his pen in trust
　　To Art, not serving shame or lust."
Will none? — Then let my memory die
　　　　In after days!

Before Sedan [1]

" The dead hand clasped a letter."
　　　— Special Correspondence.

Here in this leafy place
　　Quiet he lies,
Cold with his sightless face
　　Turned to the skies;
'Tis but another dead;
All you can say is said.

Carry his body hence, —
　　Kings must have slaves;
Kings climb to eminence
　　Over men's graves:
So this man's eye is dim; —
Throw the earth over him.

What was the white you touched,
　　There, at his side?
Paper his hand had clutched
　　Tight ere he died; —
Message or wish, may be;
Smooth the folds out and see.

Hardly the worst of us
　　Here could have smiled!
Only the tremulous

[1] *Sedan:* a French city on the River Meuse, the site of a decisive
battle in the Franco-Prussian war of 1870.

Words of a child;
Prattle, that has for stops
Just a few ruddy drops.

Look. She is sad to miss,
    Morning and night,
His — her dead father's — kiss;
    Tries to be bright,
Good to mamma, and sweet.
That is all. " Marguerite."

Ah, if beside the dead
    Slumbered the pain!
Ah, if the hearts that bled
    Slept with the slain!
If the grief died — but no.
Death will not have it so.

GERARD MANLEY HOPKINS

Gerard Manley Hopkins was born in Essex, July 28, 1844, became a Jesuit, and taught Greek and Greek meters at University College in Dublin. He was, in addition, a painter and a musician of no little ability, and his various gifts equipped him to be an innovator in poetic structure. Although he wrote much during an intensely spiritual life, none of his poetry appeared during his lifetime, and it was not until thirty years after his death that his extraordinary verse was collected. Hopkins died in 1889 and the world was not given the *Poems of Gerard Hopkins, Now First Published, with Notes by Robert Bridges* until 1918. The book was twice enlarged; a third augmented edition appeared in 1948. *Gerard Manley Hopkins: A Biography* (1930) by G. F. Lahey shed further light on Hopkins' rich personality.

A reader of Hopkins should expect obstacles when reading Hopkins for the first time; he must be prepared for difficulties that seem insuperable. He must be willing to accept a series of packed and harsh sounds; he must penetrate obscurities which are cloudy to the point of confusion. But he will be rewarded. Behind the tortured constructions and heaped-up epithets there is magnificence. In spite of the verbal excesses and oddities there is an originality of vision which is nothing less than startling. Like the things he loved most, Hopkins was " counter, original, spare, strange," possibly the most original genius of his generation. Everywhere in his work there is a new extravagance of metaphor. The opulence is not carefully built up; it is reckless, as though the poet could not lay his hands on figures rich and rapid enough to express the speed of his intuitions. To Hopkins everything was happy and magnificent. The world was not merely colorful but prodigal, "barbarous in beauty."

Heaven-Haven

A Nun Takes the Veil

I have desired to go
  Where springs not fail,
To fields where flies no sharp and sided hail,
  And a few lilies blow.

And I have asked to be
  Where no storms come,
Where the green swell is in the havens dumb
  And out of the swing of the sea.

Pied Beauty

Glory be to God for dappled things —
  For skies as couple-colored as a brindled cow;
    For rose-moles all in stipple upon trout that swim;
Fresh-firecoal chestnut-falls; finches' wings;
  Landscapes plotted and pieced — fold, fallow, and plow;
    And all trades, their gear and tackle and trim.
All things counter, original, spare, strange;
  Whatever is fickle, freckled (who knows how?)
    With swift, slow; sweet, sour; adazzle, dim;
He fathers-forth whose beauty is past change:
      Praise Him.

Thou Art Indeed Just, Lord

Thou art indeed just, Lord, if I contend
With thee; but, sir, so what I plead is just.
Why do sinners' ways prosper? and why must
Disappointment all I endeavour end?

Wert thou my enemy, O thou my friend,
How wouldst thou worse, I wonder, than thou dost
Defeat, thwart me? Oh, the sots and thralls of lust
Do in spare hours more thrive than I that spend,
Sir, life upon thy cause. See, banks and brakes
Now, leavèd how thick! lacèd they are again
With fretty chervil,[1] look, and fresh wind shakes
Them; birds build — but not I build; no, but strain,
Time's eunuch, and not breed one work that wakes.
Mine, O thou lord of life, send my roots rain.

ROBERT BRIDGES

Robert (Seymour) Bridges was born in 1844 and educated at Eton and Corpus Christi College, Oxford. He studied medicine in London and practiced until 1882. Most of his poems, like his occasional plays, are classical in tone as well as treatment. He was appointed poet laureate in 1913, following Alfred Austin. His command of the secrets of rhythm, especially exemplified in *Shorter Poems* (1894), gives his lines a subtle but firm delicacy of pattern.

Bridges' *Poetical Works*, excluding his dramas, appeared in 1913, but it was not until Bridges was eighty-five that *The Testament of Beauty* was published. This lengthy philosophical poem was acclaimed by critics who had previously neglected or belittled the poet. Although many readers found the work diffuse and difficult, it was conceded to be his major effort. Bridges died, after a short illness, April 21, 1930.

Winter Nightfall

The day begins to droop —
    Its course is done:
But nothing tells the place
    Of the setting sun.

The hazy darkness deepens,
    And up the lane
You may hear, but cannot see,
    The homing wain.[2]

---

[1] *Chervil:* a plant with lacy, aromatic leaves.   [2] *Wain:* wagon.

An engine pants and hums
  In the farm hard by:
Its lowering smoke is lost
  In the lowering sky.

The soaking branches drip,
  And all night through
The dropping will not cease
  In the avenue.

A tall man there in the house
  Must keep his chair:
He knows he will never again
  Breathe the spring air:

His heart is worn with work;
  He is giddy and sick
If he rise to go as far
  As the nearest rick: [1]

He thinks of his morn of life,
  His hale, strong years;
And braves as he may the night
  Of darkness and tears.

ARTHUR O'SHAUGHNESSY

Arthur (William Edgar) O'Shaughnessy was born in London
in 1844, and was connected, for a while, with the British Museum.
His first literary success, *Epic of Women* (1870), promised a splendid future for the young poet, a promise strengthened by his *Music and Moonlight* (1874). Always delicate in health, his hopes
were dashed by illness and an early death in London in 1881.

The poem here reprinted, like all of O'Shaughnessy's, owes
much to its editor. The "Ode," which has become one of the
classics of the age, originally had seven verses, the last four being
mere versifying. When Palgrave compiled his *Golden Treasury*,
he recognized the great difference between the first three inspired
stanzas and the others — and calmly and courageously dropped the
final four.

[1] *Rick:* a stack or pile of hay.

Ode

We are the music-makers,
  And we are the dreamers of dreams,
Wandering by lone sea-breakers,
  And sitting by desolate streams;
World-losers and world-forsakers,
  On whom the pale moon gleams:
Yet we are the movers and shakers
  Of the world forever, it seems.

With wonderful deathless ditties
We built up the world's great cities,
  And out of a fabulous story
  We fashion an empire's glory:
One man with a dream, at pleasure,
  Shall go forth and conquer a crown;
And three with a new song's measure
  Can trample an empire down.

We, in the ages lying
  In the buried past of the earth,
Built Nineveh [1] with our sighing,
  And Babel [2] itself with our mirth;
And o'erthrew them with prophesying
  To the old of the new world's worth;
For each age is a dream that is dying,
  Or one that is coming to birth.

WILLIAM ERNEST HENLEY

  William Ernest Henley was born August 23, 1849, and was educated at Gloucester. From childhood he was afflicted with a tuberculous disease which necessitated, in later life, the amputation of a foot. His *Hospital Verses*, vivid forerunners of free verse are a record of the time when he was at the infirmary at Edinburgh;

  [1] *Nineveh:* an ancient city of Assyria.
  [2] *Babel:* the site of the famous tower mentioned in the Bible which was the scene of a confusion of voices and languages.

they are sharp with the sights, sensations, and the smells of the sick-room. In spite (or, more probably, because) of his continued poor health, Henley never ceased to worship strength and energy; courage and a triumphant belief shine out of the athletic *London Voluntaries* (1892) and the light lyrics in *Hawthorn and Lavender* (1898). In contrast to his free verse Henley wrote many poems in the strict French forms, of which the rondeau, "What Is to Come," is an excellent example.

After a brilliant and varied career, devoted mostly to journalism, Henley died in 1903.

Invictus [1]

Out of the night that covers me,
    Black as the Pit from pole to pole,
I thank whatever gods may be
    For my unconquerable soul.

In the fell clutch of circumstance
    I have not winced nor cried aloud.
Under the bludgeonings of chance
    My head is bloody, but unbowed.

Beyond this place of wrath and tears
    Looms but the Horror of the shade,
And yet the menace of the years
    Finds, and shall find, me unafraid.

It matters not how strait the gate,
    How charged with punishments the scroll,
I am the master of my fate:
    I am the captain of my soul.

The Blackbird

The nightingale has a lyre of gold,
    The lark's is a clarion call,
And the blackbird plays but a boxwood flute,
    But I love him best of all.

[1] *Invictus:* Unconquerable.

For his song is all of the joy of life,
  And we in the mad, spring weather,
We two have listened till he sang
  Our hearts and lips together.

Margaritæ Sorori [1]

A late lark twitters from the quiet skies;
And from the west,
Where the sun, his day's work ended,
Lingers as in content,
There falls on the old, gray city
An influence luminous and serene,
A shining peace.
The smoke ascends
In a rosy-and-golden haze. The spires
Shine, and are changed. In the valley
Shadows rise. The lark sings on. The sun,
Closing his benediction,
Sinks, and the darkening air
Thrills with a sense of the triumphing night—
Night with her train of stars
And her great gift of sleep.

So be my passing!
My task accomplished and the long day done,
My wages taken, and in my heart
Some late lark singing,
Let me be gathered to the quiet west,
The sundown splendid and serene,
Death.

What Is to Come

What is to come we know not. But we know
That what has been was good; was good to show,
Better to hide, and best of all to bear.
We are the masters of the days that were:
We have lived, we have loved, we have suffered. Even so.

[1] *Margaritæ Sorori:* Sister Margaret; written in memory of
Henley's wife's sister.

Shall we not take the ebb who had the flow?
Life was our friend. Now if it be our foe —
Dear, though it spoil and break us! — need we care
　　　　　　　　　　What is to come?

Let the great winds their worst and wildest blow,
Or the gold weather round us mellow slow;
We have fulfilled ourselves, and we can dare
And we can conquer, though we may not share
In the rich quiet of the afterglow
　　　　　　　　　　What is to come.

ROBERT LOUIS STEVENSON

Robert Louis Stevenson was born at Edinburgh in 1850. He was trained to be a lighthouse engineer, following the profession of his family. Instead, he studied law, was admitted to the bar in 1875, and abandoned law for literature a few years later. His poor health made him leave England; he lived, at various times, in Switzerland and the United States, and finally settled in the South Seas, where he died, in Samoa, in 1894.

Primarily a novelist, Stevenson has left one immortal book of poetry which is equally at home in the nursery and the library: *A Child's Garden of Verses* (first published in 1885) is second only to Mother Goose's own collection in its lyrical simplicity and universal appeal. *Underwoods* (1887) and *Ballads* (1890) complete his entire poetic output. As a genial essayist, Stevenson is worthy to be ranked with Lamb. As a romancer, his fame rests on *Kidnapped*, the unfinished *Weir of Hermiston, Dr. Jekyll and Mr. Hyde*, and that eternal classic of youth, *Treasure Island*.

Romance

I will make you brooches and toys for your delight
Of bird-song at morning and star-shine at night.
I will make a palace fit for you and me,
Of green days in forests and blue days at sea.

I will make my kitchen, and you shall keep your room,
Where white flows the river and bright blows the broom,[1]

---

[1] *Broom:* a shrub with showy yellow flowers.

And you shall wash your linen and keep your body white
In rainfall at morning and dewfall at night.

And this shall be for music when no one else is near,
The fine song for singing, the rare song to hear!
That only I remember, that only you admire,
Of the broad road that stretches and the roadside fire.

Requiem

Under the wide and starry sky
   Dig the grave and let me lie:
Glad did I live and gladly die,
   And I laid me down with a will.

This be the verse you 'grave for me:
   Here he lies where he long'd to be;
Home is the sailor, home from the sea,
   And the hunter home from the hill.

Go, Little Book

Go, little book, and wish to all
Flowers in the garden, meat in the hall,
A bin of wine, a spice of wit,
A house with lawns enclosing it,
A living river by the door,
A nightingale in the sycamore.

OSCAR WILDE

Oscar Wilde was born in Dublin, Ireland, in 1856. As an undergraduate at Oxford he was marked for a brilliant career; when he was twenty-one he won the Newdigate Prize with his poem *Ravenna*. Giving himself almost entirely to prose, Wilde became known as a writer of brilliant epigrammatic essays and even more brilliant paradoxical plays. His flippancies were quoted everywhere; his fame as a wit was only surpassed by his notoriety as a professional aesthete.

Most of his " poems in prose " (such as *The Birthday of the In-fanta* and *The Fisherman and His Soul*) are more imaginative and richly colored than his verse; but in one long poem, written while he was in prison, *The Ballad of Reading Gaol* (1898), he sounded his deepest, simplest, and most enduring note. Prison was, in many ways, a regeneration for Wilde. It not only produced the lengthy *Ballad of Reading Gaol* but made possible his most poignant piece of writing, *De Profundis*, only a part of which has been published.

Wilde died at Paris, an unhappy exile, November 30, 1900.

Requiescat [1]

Tread lightly, she is near
    Under the snow,
Speak gently, she can hear
    The daisies grow.

All her bright golden hair
    Tarnished with rust,
She that was young and fair
    Fallen to dust.

Lily-like, white as snow,
    She hardly knew
She was a woman, so
    Sweetly she grew.

Coffin-board, heavy stone,
    Lie on her breast;
I vex my heart alone,
    She is at rest.

Peace, peace; she cannot hear
    Lyric or sonnet;
All my life's buried here,
    Heap earth upon it.

Requiescat: a prayer for the repose of a dead person.

Born in 1857 at Ashton, Lancashire, Francis Thompson was educated at Owen's College, Manchester. He tried all manner of ways of earning a living. He was, at various times, assistant in a boot-shop, medical student, collector for a bookseller, and homeless vagabond; there was a period in his life when he sold matches on the streets of London. He was discovered in terrible poverty, ill with tuberculosis and suffering from the effects of opium, by Wilfrid Meynell, editor of a magazine to which he had sent some verses.

Supported and befriended by Wilfrid and Alice Meynell, Thompson broke off his opium habits (although he never regained complete health) and started to write with renewed energy. Almost immediately thereafter he became famous. His exalted mysticism is seen at its purest in "The Hound of Heaven." Coventry Patmore, the distinguished poet of an earlier period, says of this rapt poem (unfortunately too long to quote in this collection), "It is one of the very few *great* odes of which our language can boast."

Sister Songs appeared in 1895, *New Poems* in 1897. Thompson's prose, containing the famous essay on Shelley, was not collected until many years later. He was never anyone but himself; a mystic unaware of any world but the world within him, as much enraptured by strange colors, curious words (he delighted in the sound of archaic syllables), and quaint symbols as a child.

Thompson died in November, 1907. Various collected editions of his poems were issued shortly after his death. His poetry, like the snowflake which he celebrated in one of his most characteristic poems, was "insculped and embossed," pure and frail, but "fashioned surely."

To a Snowflake

What heart could have thought you? —
Past our devisal
(O filigree petal!)
Fashioned so purely,
Fragilely, surely,
From what Paradisal
Imagineless metal,
Too costly for cost?
Who hammered you, wrought you,
From argentine [1] vapor? —
" God was my shaper.

[1] *Argentine:* silvery; from *argentum,* silver.

Passing surmisal,
He hammered, He wrought me,
From curled silver vapor,
To lust of his mind: —
Thou couldst not have thought me!
So purely, so palely,
Tinily, surely,
Mightily, frailly,
Insculped and embossed,
With His hammer of wind,
And His graver of frost."

Daisy

Where the thistle lifts a purple crown
    Six foot out of the turf,
And the harebell shakes on the windy hill —
    O breath of the distant surf! —

The hills look over on the South,
    And southward dreams the sea;
And with the sea-breeze hand in hand
    Came innocence and she.

Where 'mid the gorse the raspberry
    Red for the gatherer springs;
Two children did we stray and talk
    Wise, idle, childish things.

She listened with big-lipped surprise,
    Breast-deep 'mid flower and spine:
Her skin was like a grape whose veins
    Run snow instead of wine.

She knew not those sweet words she spake,
    Nor knew her own sweet way;
But there's never a bird, so sweet a song
    Thronged in whose throat all day.

Oh, there were flowers in Storrington
    On the turf and on the spray;
But the sweetest flower on Sussex hills
    Was the Daisy-flower that day!

Her beauty smoothed earth's furrowed face.
  She gave me tokens three: —
A look, a word of her winsome mouth,
  And a wild raspberry.

A berry red, a guileless look,
  A still word, — strings of sand!
And yet they made my wild, wild heart
  Fly down to her little hand.

For standing artless as the air,
  And candid as the skies,
She took the berries with her hand,
  And the love with her sweet eyes.

The fairest things have fleetest end,
  Their scent survives their close:
But the rose's scent is bitterness
  To him that loved the rose.

She looked a little wistfully,
  Then went her sunshine way: —
The sea's eye had a mist on it,
  And the leaves fell from the day.

She went her unremembering way,
  She went and left in me
The pang of all the partings gone,
  And partings yet to be.

She left me marvelling why my soul
  Was sad that she was glad;
At all the sadness in the sweet,
  The sweetness in the sad.

Still, still I seem to see her, still
  Look up with soft replies,
And take the berries with her hand,
  And the love with her lovely eyes.

Nothing begins, and nothing ends,
  That is not paid with moan,
For we are born in other's pain,
  And perish in our own.

Alfred Edward Housman was born in Worcestershire, March 26, 1859, and, after a classical education, was, for ten years, a Higher Division Clerk in H. M. Patent Office. Later in life, he became a teacher, one of the leading authorities on the Latin poets and dramatists whose crisp utterance he himself surpassed.

Housman's first book, *A Shropshire Lad* (1896), is known wherever English poetry is read. Underneath its ironies, there is a bitter humor that has many subtle variations. From a melodic standpoint, *A Shropshire Lad* is a collection of exquisite and memorable songs. After a silence of twenty-six years, a second volume, significantly entitled *Last Poems*, appeared in 1922. Here, once more, we have the note of pessimism sung in a jaunty rhythm and an incongruously jolly key. The Shropshire lad lives again to pipe his tunes of betrayal, singing of lovesick lads, deserted girls, and suicides with enviable simplicity and a flawless command of his instrument.

Housman refused to collect his prose, but in 1933 he printed *The Name and Nature of Poetry*, a teasing and thought-provoking lecture which he delivered at Cambridge. He was planning a third small collection of poems when he died, May 1, 1936. This third collection, *More Poems* (1936), contained a short preface by his brother Laurence Housman and was followed by a memoir. *More Poems* is the Shropshire lad's farewell to the world. The three thin books actually form one volume. *The Collected Poems of A. E. Housman* (1940) emphasizes the poet's combination of definite power, delicate humor, and lyric perfection.

Oh, When I Was in Love with You

Oh, when I was in love with you,
Then I was clean and brave,
And miles around the wonder grew
How well did I behave.

And now the fancy passes by,
And nothing will remain,
And miles around they'll say that I
Am quite myself again.

Bredon Hill

In summertime on Bredon
  The bells they sound so clear;
Round both the shires they ring them
  In steeples far and near,
  A happy noise to hear.

Here of a Sunday morning
  My love and I would lie,
And see the colored counties,
  And hear the larks so high
  About us in the sky.

The bells would ring to call her
  In valleys miles away:
"Come all to church, good people;
  Good people, come and pray."
  But here my love would stay.

And I would turn and answer
  Among the springing thyme,
"Oh, peal upon our wedding,
  And we will hear the chime,
  And come to church in time."

But when the snows at Christmas
  On Bredon top were strown,
My love rose up so early
  And stole out unbeknown
  And went to church alone.

They tolled the one bell only,
  Groom there was none to see,
The mourners followed after,
  And so to church went she,
  And would not wait for me.

The bells they sound on Bredon,
  And still the steeples hum.
"Come all to church, good people, —"
  Oh, noisy bells, be dumb;
  I hear you, I will come.

Reveillé [1]

Wake! The silver dusk returning
　　Up the beach of darkness brims,
And the ship of sunrise burning
　　Strands upon the eastern rims.

Wake! The vaulted shadow shatters,
　　Trampled to the floor it spanned,
And the tent of night in tatters
　　Straws the sky-pavilioned land.

Up, lad! Up! 'Tis late for lying:
　　Hear the drums of morning play;
Hark, the empty highways crying
　　" Who'll beyond the hills away? "

Towns and countries woo together;
　　Forelands beacon, belfries call;
Never lad that trod on leather
　　Lived to feast his heart with all.

Up, lad! Thews that lie and cumber
　　Sunlit pallets never thrive;
Morns abed and daylight slumber
　　Were not meant for man alive.

Clay lies still, but blood's a rover;
　　Breath's a ware that will not keep.
Up, lad! When the journey's over
　　There'll be time enough to sleep.

Say, Lad, Have You Things to Do

Say, lad, have you things to do?
　　Quick then, while your day's at prime.
Quick, and if 'tis work for two,
　　Here am I, man: now's your time.

[1] *Reveillé:* a signal, usually a bugle-call, rousing sleepers to the
day's work.

Send me now, and I shall go;
  Call me, I shall hear you call;
Use me ere they lay me low
  Where a man's no use at all;

Ere the wholesome flesh decay,
  And the willing nerve be numb,
And the lips lack breath to say,
  "No, my lad, I cannot come."

The Carpenter's Son

" Here the hangman stops his cart:
Now the best of friends must part.
Fare you well, for ill fare I:
Live, lads, and I will die.

" Oh, at home had I but stayed
'Prenticed to my father's trade,
Had I stuck to plane and adze,
I had not been lost, my lads.

" Then I might have built perhaps
Gallows-trees for other chaps,
Never dangled on my own,
Had I but left ill alone.

" Now, you see, they hang me high,
And the people passing by
Stop to shake their fists and curse;
So 'tis come from ill to worse.

" Here hang I, and right and left
Two poor fellows hang for theft;
All the same's the luck we prove,
Though the midmost hangs for love.

" Comrades all, that stand and gaze,
Walk henceforth in other ways;
See my neck and save your own:
Comrades all, leave ill alone.

"Make some day a decent end,
Shrewder fellows than your friend.
Fare you well, for ill fare I:
Live, lads, and I will die."

From Far, from Eve and Morning

From far, from eve and morning
   And yon twelve-winded sky,[1]
The stuff of life to knit me
   Blew hither: here am I.

Now — for a breath I tarry
   Nor yet disperse apart —
Take my hand quick and tell me
   What have you in your heart.

Speak now, and I will answer;
   How shall I help you, say;
Ere to the wind's twelve quarters
   I take my endless way.

Loveliest of Trees

Loveliest of trees, the cherry now
Is hung with bloom along the bough,
And stands about the woodland ride
Wearing white for Eastertide.

Now, of my threescore years and ten,
Twenty will not come again,
And take from seventy springs a score,
It only leaves me fifty more.

And since to look at things in bloom
Fifty springs are little room,
About the woodlands I will go
To see the cherry hung with snow.

---

[1] *Twelve-winded sky:* it was once supposed that there were twelve different winds in the heavens.

On the Idle Hill of Summer

On the idle hill of summer,
  Sleepy with the flow of streams,
Far I hear the steady drummer
  Drumming like a noise in dreams.

Far and near and low and louder
  On the roads of earth go by,
Dear to friends and food for powder,
  Soldiers marching, all to die.

East and west on fields forgotten
  Bleach the bones of comrades slain,
Lovely lads, all dead and rotten;
  None that go return again.

Far the calling bugles hollo,
  High the screaming fife replies,
Gay the files of scarlet follow:
  Woman bore me, I will rise.

To an Athlete Dying Young

The time you won your town the race
We chaired you through the market-place;
Man and boy stood cheering by,
And home we brought you shoulder-high.

Today, the road all runners come,
Shoulder-high we bring you home,
And set you at your threshold down,
Townsman of a stiller town.

Smart lad, to slip betimes away
From fields where glory does not stay,
And early though the laurel grows,
It withers quicker than the rose.

Eyes the shady night has shut
Cannot see the record cut,
And silence sounds no worse than cheers
After earth has stopped the ears:

Now you will not swell the rout
Of lads that wore their honors out,
Runners whom renown outran
And the name died before the man.

So set, before its echoes fade,
The fleet foot on the sill of shade,
And hold to the low lintel up
The still-defended challenge-cup.

And round that early-laureled head
Will flock to gaze the strengthless dead,
And find unwithered on its curls
The garland briefer than a girl's.

When I Was One-and-Twenty

When I was one-and-twenty
    I heard a wise man say,
" Give crowns and pounds and guineas
    But not your heart away;
Give pearls away and rubies
    But keep your fancy free."
But I was one-and-twenty,
    No use to talk to me.

When I was one-and-twenty
    I heard him say again,
" The heart out of the bosom
    Was never given in vain;
'Tis paid with sighs a-plenty
    And sold for endless rue."
And I am two-and-twenty,
    And oh, 'tis true, 'tis true.

ARTHUR SYMONS

Arthur Symons was born in Wales in 1865 and began imitating
the French Symbolist writers in his youth. His early volumes of
poetry — notably *Days and Nights* (1889) and *London Nights*
(1895) — are artificial in tone but unusually fine in technique.

The best of Symons' poems have a rare delicacy of touch; they breathe an intimacy in which the sophistication is definite but restrained. His various collections of essays and stories reflect the same blend of intellectuality and romanticism that one finds in his *Collected Poems* (1907). They show various influences, but less dependence on literature than the preceding volumes. It is interesting to compare the poet's longing for the quiet countryside in Symons' " In the Wood of Finvara " with Yeats's " The Lake Isle of Innisfree " on page 286.

Symons died January 22, 1945.

In the Wood of Finvara

I have grown tired of sorrow and human tears;
Life is a dream in the night, a fear among fears,
A naked runner lost in a storm of spears.

I have grown tired of rapture and love's desire;
Love is a flaming heart, and its flames aspire
Till they cloud the soul in the smoke of a windy fire.

I would wash the dust of the world in a soft green flood;
Here between sea and sea, in the fairy wood,
I have found a delicate, wave-green solitude.

Here, in the fairy wood, between sea and sea,
I have heard the song of a fairy bird in a tree,
And the peace that is not in the world has flown to me.

WILLIAM BUTLER YEATS

William Butler Yeats was born in Sandymount, near Dublin, in 1865, was educated in England and his native Ireland, studied art abroad, made his home at intervals in Paris and on the Italian Riviera, but always returned to the country of which he was so vital a recorder. He attained prominence not only as poet and dramatist, but as journalist and politician. He helped establish the Irish National Theatre and served the Irish Free State as senator. He was one of the leaders in the Celtic revival, a patriot in the widest sense. He was one of the few men in literature who made not only his nation's laws but also its songs. He died January 28, 1939.

Mosada (1886), a poem of which less than 100 copies were printed, was Yeats's first work, but it was not until *The Land of Heart's Desire* (1894), that Yeats became identified with the national movement. His *Plays for an Irish Theatre* contain some of the most characteristic romantic writing of the period, symbolic, spiritual, yet simple and natural. The same combination of simplicity and symbolism is evident in the early poems. Apart from the exquisite music and haunting phrases, the lines have a flavor utterly unlike that achieved by any of Yeats's contemporaries. For sheer charm the verses in the early *The Wind Among the Reeds* (1899) are among his most popular.

In the later poetry Yeats's tone is more sinewy, even more severe. The poet no longer deals with shadowy waters and mystical Gaelic gods, but with the actualities of the present. With this change, the images are more direct and the poet uses a stripped rather than an embroidered speech. His *Collected Poems*, published in 1933, containing many revisions, *The King of the Great Clock Tower* (1935), and the posthumous *Last Poems and Plays* (1940) show the increasing sharpness of the poet's mind. But even in the most rigorous lines Yeats never sacrifices music; the work of his seventies is more arresting than the work of his youth. Just before his sixtieth year Yeats was awarded the Nobel Prize for literature, for his colorful and " consistently emotional " poetry.

Yeats has pictured himself and discussed his aims and theories in more detail than have most poets. His two rich books of autobiography, republished in one comprehensive volume in 1938, are an indispensable source-book for students, as is Richard Ellmann's intensive study, *Yeats: The Man and the Masks* (1948), and Donald A. Stauffer's *The Golden Nightingale* (1949).

The Lake Isle of Innisfree [1]

I will arise and go now, and go to Innisfree,
And a small cabin build there, of clay and wattles [2] made;
Nine bean rows will I have there, a hive for the honey bee,
    And live alone in the bee-loud glade.

And I shall have some peace there, for peace comes dropping
        slow,
Dropping from the veils of the morning to where the cricket
        sings;
There midnight's all a glimmer, and noon a purple glow,
    And evening full of the linnet's wings.

[1] An island in a lake in the county of Sligo, Ireland.
[2] *Wattles:* woven twigs or stalks holding the clay together.

I will arise and go now, for always night and day
I hear lake water lapping with low sounds by the shore;
While I stand on the roadway, or on the pavements gray,
  I hear it in the deep heart's core.

An Old Song Resung

Down by the salley gardens [1] my love and I did meet;
She passed the salley gardens with little snow-white feet.
She bid me take love easy, as the leaves grow on the tree;
But I, being young and foolish, with her would not agree.

In a field by the river my love and I did stand,
And on my leaning shoulder she laid her snow-white hand.
She bid me take life easy, as the grass grows on the weirs;
But I was young and foolish, and now am full of tears.

The Song of the Old Mother

I rise in the dawn, and I kneel and blow
Till the seed of the fire flicker and glow.
And then I must scrub, and bake, and sweep,
Till stars are beginning to blink and peep;
But the young lie long and dream in their bed
Of the matching of ribbons, the blue and the red,
And their day goes over in idleness,
And they sigh if the wind but lift up a tress,
While I must work, because I am old
And the seed of the fire gets feeble and cold.

When You Are Old

When you are old and gray and full of sleep,
And nodding by the fire, take down this book,
And slowly read, and dream of the soft look
Your eyes had once, and of their shadows deep;

[1] *Salley gardens:* pleasure gardens, usually with willow trees.

How many loved your moments of glad grace,
And loved your beauty with love false or true;
But one man loved the pilgrim soul in you,
And loved the sorrows of your changing face.

And bending down beside the glowing bars
Murmur, a little sadly, how love fled
And paced upon the mountains overhead
And hid his face amid a crowd of stars.

Aedh [1] Wishes for the Cloths of Heaven

Had I the heavens' embroidered cloths,
Enwrought with golden and silver light,
The blue and the dim and the dark cloths
Of night and light and the half-light,
I would spread the cloths under your feet:
But I, being poor, have only my dreams;
I have spread my dreams under your feet;
Tread softly because you tread on my dreams.

The Fiddler of Dooney [2]

When I play on my fiddle in Dooney,
Folk dance like a wave of the sea;
My cousin is priest in Kilvarnet,
My brother in Moharabuiee.

I passed by brother and cousin:
They read in their books of prayer;
I read in my book of songs
I bought at the Sligo fair.

When we come at the end of time,
To Peter sitting in state,
He will smile on the three old spirits,
But call me first through the gate;

[1] Aedh is the narrator in several of Yeats's poems. The name is also used as a symbol of burning imagination. "Aedh," wrote Yeats, "whose name is not merely the Irish form of Hugh, but the Irish for fire, is fire burning by itself."

[2] Dooney and the other places mentioned in this poem are little villages on the west coast of Ireland.

For the good are always the merry,
Save by an evil chance,
And the merry love the fiddle
And the merry love to dance:

And when the folk there spy me,
They will all come up to me,
With ' Here is the fiddler of Dooney! '
And dance like a wave of the sea.

The Ballad of Father Gilligan

The old priest Peter Gilligan
Was weary night and day;
For half his flock were in their beds,
Or under green sods lay.

Once, while he nodded on a chair,
At the moth-hour of eve,
Another poor man sent for him,
And he began to grieve.

" I have no rest, nor joy, nor peace,
" For people die and die ";
And after cried he, " God forgive!
" My body spake, not I."

He knelt, and leaning on the chair
He prayed and fell asleep;
And the moth-hour went from the fields,
And stars began to peep.

They slowly into millions grew,
And leaves shook in the wind;
And God covered the world with shade,
And whispered to mankind.

Upon the time of sparrow chirp
When the moths came once more,
The old priest Peter Gilligan
Stood upright on the floor.

"Mavrone, mavrone![1] the man has died,
"While I slept on the chair";
He roused his horse out of its sleep
And rode with little care.

He rode now as he never rode,
By rocky lane and fen;
The sick man's wife opened the door;
"Father! You come again!"

"And is the poor man dead?" he cried.
"He died an hour ago."
The old priest Peter Gilligan
In grief swayed to and fro.

"When you were gone, he turned and died
"As merry as a bird."
The old priest Peter Gilligan
He knelt him at that word.

"He who hath made the night of stars
"For souls, who tire and bleed,
"Sent one of His great angels down
"To help me in my need.

"He who is wrapped in purple robes,
"With planets in His care,
"Had pity on the least of things
"Asleep upon a chair."

RUDYARD KIPLING

Rudyard Kipling was born December 30, 1865, in Bombay, India, of English parents, and was educated in England. In youth he returned to India, where he took a position on the *Lahore Civil and Military Gazette*. He wrote some of his most famous short tales for that paper, many of them collected in *Soldiers Three* and *Plain Tales from the Hills*. His experiences in India also formed the background for the more sensitive stories, *Under the Deodars* and *The Phantom 'Rickshaw*, as well as his famous *Departmental*

[1] *Mavrone!:* Alas! Woe's me!

Ditties and *Barrack-Room Ballads*, which won him recognition as a poet.

In 1892 Kipling married an American, Carolyn Balestier, and came to Vermont. It appears that Kipling intended to make America his permanent home, but he quarreled violently with his brother-in-law, was aggravated into going to court, and finally was driven back to England. Except for a short visit to New York, Kipling stayed away from the States, and the facts were not revealed until almost forty years later when, in 1937, a neighbor of Balestier's published *Rudyard Kipling's Vermont Feud*. Nevertheless, Kipling collaborated with his American brother-in-law on a novel, *The Naulahka*, and it was in Vermont that he wrote the immortal *Jungle Books* and the *Just-So Stories*.

After returning to England, Kipling isolated himself in a Sussex village, was awarded the Nobel Prize for literature in 1907, and died January 17, 1936. Upon his death he was praised throughout the world for such masterpieces as *Kim* and for the ballads which entitle him to be known as a " people's poet."

Considered solely as a poet, Kipling is one of the most vital figures of the period. He combines the world of the worker and the world of the dreamer; the spirit of romance surges under his realities. His brisk lines communicate the tang of a countryside, the tingle of salt spray, the rough sentiment of unsentimental nature, the snapping of a banner, the untutored, unbroken spirit of common man. Yet it is not merely realism which makes Kipling popular. What attracts the average reader to this poetry is the author's attitude to everyday existence. At a time when others sang of perfumed lilies and idyllic leisure, Kipling celebrated difficulties, duty, hard labor; where others attempted to evoke Greek gods and literary figures, Kipling hailed bridge-builders, engineers, soldiers, sweating stokers, sea-captains — all those who not only existed in the world of work but exulted in the job. The best of Kipling's verse, hearty and, in the best sense, wholesome, is in the comprehensive *Poems: Inclusive Edition*, an indispensable part of any library.

Gunga Din

You may talk o' gin an' beer
When you're quartered safe out 'ere,
An' you're sent to penny-fights an' Aldershot [1] it;
But when it comes to slaughter
You will do your work on water,
An' you'll lick the bloomin' boots of 'im that's got it.
Now in Injia's sunny clime,

[1] *Aldershot:* a famous training camp in England.

Where I used to spend my time
A-servin' of 'Er Majesty the Queen,
Of all them black-faced crew
The finest man I knew
Was our regimental *bhisti*,[1] Gunga Din.

    It was " Din! Din! Din!
    You limping lump o' brick-dust, Gunga Din!
    Hi! *slippy hitherao!* [2]
    Water, get it! *Panee lao!* [3]
    You squidgy-nosed old idol, Gunga Din! "

The uniform 'e wore
Was nothin' much before,
An' rather less than 'arf o' that be'ind,
For a twisty piece o' rag
An' a goatskin water-bag
Was all the field-equipment 'e could find.
When the sweatin' troop-train lay
In a sidin' through the day,
Where the 'eat would make your bloomin' eyebrows crawl,
We shouted " *Harry By!* " [4]
Till our throats were bricky-dry,
Then we wopped 'im 'cause 'e couldn't serve us all.

    It was " Din! Din! Din!
    You 'eathen, where the mischief 'ave you been?
    You put some *juldee* [5] in it,
    Or I'll *marrow* [6] you this minute,
    If you don't fill up my helmet, Gunga Din! "

'E would dot an' carry one
Till the longest day was done,
An' 'e didn't seem to know the use o' fear.
If we charged or broke or cut,
You could bet your bloomin' nut,

[1] The *bhisti*, or native water-carrier, attached to regiments in India.
[2] Hurry up!
[3] Bring water swiftly.
[4] Tommy Atkins' equivalent for " O Brother! "
[5] Speed.
[6] Hit you.

'E'd be waitin' fifty paces right flank rear.
With 'is *mussick* [1] on 'is back,
'E would skip with our attack,
An' watch us till the bugles made " Retire."
An' for all 'is dirty 'ide,
'E was white, clear white, inside
When 'e went to tend the wounded under fire!

It was " Din! Din! Din! "
With the bullets kickin' dust-spots on the green.
When the cartridges ran out,
You could 'ear the front-files shout:
" Hi! ammunition-mules an' Gunga Din! "

I sha'n't forgit the night
When I dropped be'ind the fight
With a bullet where my belt-plate should 'a' been.
I was chokin' mad with thirst,
An' the man that spied me first
Was our good old grinnin', gruntin' Gunga Din.
'E lifted up my 'ead,
An' 'e plugged me where I bled,
An' 'e guv me 'arf-a-pint o' water — green;
It was crawlin' an' it stunk,
But of all the drinks I've drunk,
I'm gratefulest to one from Gunga Din.

It was " Din! Din! Din! "
'Ere's a beggar with a bullet through 'is spleen;
'E's chawin' up the ground an' 'e's kickin' all around:
For Gawd's sake, git the water, Gunga Din! "

'E carried me away
To where a *dooli* [2] lay,
An' a bullet come an' drilled the beggar clean.
'E put me safe inside,
An' just before 'e died:
" I 'ope you liked your drink," sez Gunga Din.
So I'll meet 'im later on
In the place where 'e is gone —
Where it's always double drill and no canteen;

1 Water-skin.　　　　　　　　[2] Stretcher.

'E'll be squattin' on the coals
Givin' drink to pore damned souls,
An' I'll get a swig in Hell from Gunga Din!

Din! Din! Din!
You Lazarushian-leather [1] Gunga Din!
Tho' I've belted you an' flayed you,
By the livin' Gawd that made you,
You're a better man than I am, Gunga Din!

The Return

Peace is declared, and I return
    To 'Ackneystadt,[2] but not the same,
Things 'ave transpired which made me learn
    The size and meanin' of the game.
I did no more than others did,
    I don't know where the change began;
I started as an average kid,
    I finished as a thinkin' man.

If England was what England seems
    An' not the England of our dreams,
But only putty, brass, an' paint,
    'Ow quick we'd drop 'er! But she ain't!

Before my gappin' mouth could speak
    I 'eard it in my comrade's tone;
I saw it on my neighbor's cheek
    Before I felt it flush my own.
An' last it come to me — not pride,
    Nor yet conceit, but on the 'ole
(If such a term may be applied),
    The makin's of a bloomin' soul.

Rivers at night that cluck an' jeer,
    Plains which the moonshine turns to sea,
Mountains that never let you near,

---

[1] *Lazarushian-leather:* Lazarus was a poor beggar. Here the word also refers to Gunga Din's leather-like color.

[2] *'Ackneystadt:* London. Hackney is a London borough. Spoken half-scornfully by a soldier just returned from the Boer war in South Africa.

An' stars to all eternity;
An' the quick-breathin' dark that fills
  The 'ollows of the wilderness,
When the wind worries through the 'ills —
  These may 'ave taught me more or less.

Towns without people, ten times took,
  An' ten times left an' burned at last;
An' starvin' dogs that come to look
  For owners when a column passed;
An' quiet, 'omesick talks between
  Men, met by night, you never knew
Until — 'is face — by shellfire seen —
  Once — an' struck off. They taught me, too.

The day's lay-out — the mornin' sun
  Beneath your 'at-brim as you sight;
The dinner-'ush from noon till one,
  An' the full roar that lasts till night;
An' the pore dead that look so old
  An' was so young an hour ago,
An' legs tied down before they're cold —
  These are the things which make you know.

Also Time runnin' into years —
  A thousand Places left be'ind —
An' men from both two 'emispheres
  Discussin' things of every kind;
So much more near than I 'ad known,
  So much more great than I 'ad guessed —
An' me, like all the rest, alone —
  But reachin' out to all the rest!

So 'ath it come to me — not pride,
  Nor yet conceit, but on the 'ole
(If such a term may be applied),
  The makin's of a bloomin' soul.
But now, discharged, I fall away
  To do with little things again. . . .
Gawd, 'oo knows all I cannot say,
  Look after me in Thamesfontein! [1]

[1] *Thamesfontein:* London, the city on the Thames — another half-jesting reference by the returned soldier; *stadt* and *fontein* being South African Dutch terms for town or village.

> *If England was what England seems*
>   *An' not the England of our dreams,*
> *But only putty, brass, an' paint,*
>   *'Ow quick we'd chuck 'er!* But she ain't!

Danny Deever

" What are the bugles blowin' for? " said Files-on-Parade.

" To turn you out, to turn you out," the Color-Sergeant said.

" What makes you look so white, so white? " said Files-on-
    Parade.

" I'm dreadin' what I've got to watch," the Color-Sergeant
    said.

    " For they're hangin' Danny Deever, you can 'ear the Dead
       March play,

    The regiment's in 'ollow square — they're hangin' him to-
       day;

    They've taken of his buttons off an' cut his stripes away,

    An' they're hangin' Danny Deever in the mornin'."

" What makes the rear-rank breathe so 'ard? " said Files-on-
    Parade.

" It's bitter cold, it's bitter cold," the Color-Sergeant said.

" What makes that front-rank man fall down? " says Files-
    on-Parade.

" A touch of sun, a touch of sun," the Color-Sergeant said.

    " They are hangin' Danny Deever, they are marchin' of
       'im round.

    They 'ave 'alted Danny Deever by 'is coffin on the ground:

    An 'e'll swing in 'arf a minute for a sneakin' shootin'
       hound —

    O they're hangin' Danny Deever in the mornin'! "

" 'Is cot was right-'and cot to mine," said Files-on-Parade.

" 'E's sleepin' out an' far tonight," the Color-Sergeant said.

" I've drunk 'is beer a score o' times," said Files-on-Parade.

" 'E's drinkin' bitter beer alone," the Color-Sergeant said.

    " They are hangin' Danny Deever, you must mark 'im to 'is
       place,

    For 'e shot a comrade sleepin' — you must look 'im in the
       face;

    Nine 'undred of 'is county an' the regiment's disgrace,

    While they're hangin' Danny Deever in the mornin'."

"What's that so black agin the sun?" said Files-on-Parade.
"It's Danny fightin' 'ard for life," the Color-Sergeant said.
"What's that that whimpers over 'ead?" said Files-on-Parade.
"It's Danny's soul that's passin' now," the Color-Sergeant
said.
    "For they're done with Danny Deever, you can 'ear the
        quickstep play,
    The regiment's in column, an' they're marchin' us away;
    Ho! the young recruits are shakin', an' they'll want their
        beer today,
    After hangin' Danny Deever in the mornin'."

"Tommy"

I went into a public-'ouse to get a pint o' beer,
The publican 'e up an' sez, "We serve no redcoats here."
The girls be'ind the bar they laughed an' giggled fit to die,
I outs into the street again, an' to myself sez I:
    O, it's Tommy this, an' Tommy that, an' "Tommy go
        away";
    But it's "Thank you, Mister Atkins," when the band
        begins to play,
    The band begins to play, my boys, the band begins to
        play,
    O, it's "Thank you, Mister Atkins," when the band be-
        gins to play.

I went into a theater as sober as could be,
They give a drunk civilian room, but 'adn't none for me;
They sent me to the gallery or round the music-'alls,
But when it comes to fightin', Lord! they'll shove me in the
    stalls.[1]
    For it's Tommy this, an' Tommy that, an' "Tommy
        wait outside";
    But it's "Special train for Atkins," when the trooper's
        on the tide,
    The troopship's on the tide, my boys, etc.

O, makin' mock o' uniforms that guard you while you sleep
Is cheaper than them uniforms, an' they're starvation cheap;
An' hustlin' drunken sodgers when they're goin' large a bit

       [1] *stalls:* best places for the show.

Is five times better business than paradin' in full kit.
      Then it's Tommy this, an' Tommy that, an' "Tommy,
        'ow's yer soul?"
      But it's "Thin red line of 'eroes" when the drums be-
        gin to roll,
      The drums begin to roll, my boys, etc.

We aren't no thin red 'eroes, nor we aren't no blackguards
   too,
But single men in barricks, most remarkable like you;
An' if sometimes our conduck isn't all your fancy paints,
Why, single men in barricks don't grow into plaster saints.
      While it's Tommy this, an' Tommy that, an' "Tommy
        fall be'ind";
      But it's "Please to walk in front, sir," when there's
        trouble in the wind,
      There's trouble in the wind, my boys, etc.

You talk o' better food for us, an' schools, an' fires, an' all:
We'll wait for extry rations if you treat us rational.
Don't mess about the cook-room slops, but prove it to our
   face,
The Widow's [1] uniform is not the soldier-man's disgrace.
      For it's Tommy this, an' Tommy that, an' "Chuck him
        out, the brute!"
      But it's "Savior of 'is country" where the guns begin
        to shoot;
      An' it's Tommy this, an' Tommy that, an' anything
        you please;
      An' Tommy ain't a bloomin' fool—you bet that
        Tommy sees!

An Astrologer's Song

To the Heavens above us
  O look and behold
The Planets that love us
  All harnessed in gold!
What chariots, what horses
  Against us shall bide
While the Stars in their courses
  Do fight on our side?

[1] Queen Victoria was often referred to as "The Widow."

All thoughts, all desires,
  That are under the sun,
Are one with their fires,
  As we also are one:
All matter, all spirit,
  All fashion, all frame,
Receive and inherit
  Their strength from the same.

(Oh, man that deniest
  All power save thine own,
Their power in the highest
  Is mightily shown.
Not less in the lowest
  That power is made clear.
Oh, man, if thou knowest,
  What treasure is here!)

Earth quakes in her throes
  And we wonder for why!
But the blind planet knows
  When her ruler is nigh;
And, attuned since Creation
  To perfect accord,
She thrills in her station
  And yearns to her Lord.

The waters have risen,
  The springs are unbound —
The floods break their prison,
  And ravin [1] around.
No rampart withstands 'em,
  Their fury will last,
Till the Sign that commands 'em
  Sinks low or swings past.

Through abysses unproven
  And gulfs beyond thought,
Our portion is woven,
  Our burden is brought.
Yet They that prepare it,

    [1] *ravin:* seize things violently.

Whose Nature we share,
Make us who must bear it
Well able to bear.

Though terrors o'ertake us
We'll not be afraid.
No power can unmake us,
Save that which has made.
Nor yet beyond reason
Or hope shall we fall —
All things have their season,
And Mercy crowns all!

Then, doubt not, ye fearful —
The Eternal is King —
Up, heart, and be cheerful,
And lustily sing:
What chariots, what horses
Against us shall bide
While the Stars in their courses
Do fight on our side?

Recessional [1]

God of our fathers, known of old,
Lord of our far-flung battle-line,
Beneath whose awful hand we hold
Dominion over palm and pine —
Lord God of Hosts, be with us yet,
Lest we forget — lest we forget!

The tumult and the shouting dies;
The captains and the kings depart:
Still stands Thine ancient sacrifice,
An humble and a contrite heart.
Lord God of Hosts, be with us yet,
Lest we forget — lest we forget!

[1] The recessional is a hymn sung toward the end of a church service. This hymn, written during the Diamond Jubilee of Queen Victoria, took courage to publish when poets and politicians alike were glorifying the "deathless power" of the British Empire.

Far-called, our navies melt away;
   On dune and headland sinks the fire:
Lo, all our pomp of yesterday
   Is one with Nineveh and Tyre! [1]
Judge of the Nations, spare us yet,
Lest we forget — lest we forget!

If, drunk with sight of power, we loose
   Wild tongues that have not Thee in awe,
Such boastings as the Gentiles use,
   Or lesser breeds without the Law —
Lord God of Hosts, be with us yet,
Lest we forget — lest we forget!

For heathen heart that puts her trust
   In reeking tube and iron shard,[2]
All valiant dust that builds on dust,
   And guarding, calls not Thee to guard,
For frantic boast and foolish word —
Thy Mercy on Thy People, Lord!

L'Envoi [3]

What is the moral? Who rides may read.
   When the night is thick and the tracks are blind
A friend at a pinch is a friend indeed;
   But a fool to wait for the laggard behind;
Down to Gehenna [4] or up to the Throne
He travels the fastest who travels alone.

White hands cling to the tightened rein,
   Slipping the spur from the booted heel,
Tenderest voices cry, " Turn again."
   Red lips tarnish the scabbarded steel,
High hopes faint on a warm hearthstone —
He travels the fastest who travels alone.

[1] *Nineveh and Tyre:* ancient cities of Assyria and Phoenicia, long since destroyed.
[2] *reeking tube and iron shard:* smoking guns and bursting bombshells.
[3] *L'Envoi:* last words or " message."
[4] *Gehenna:* hell.

One may fall but he falls by himself —
   Falls by himself with himself to blame;
One may attain and to him is the pelf,
   Loot of the city in Gold or Fame:
Plunder of earth shall be all his own:
He travels the fastest who travels alone.

ERNEST DOWSON

Ernest Dowson was born at Belmont Hill in Kent, August 2,
1867. His great-uncle was Alfred Domett (Browning's "War-
ing"), who was at one time Prime Minister of New Zealand. Dowson, practically an invalid all his life, hid himself in miserable surroundings; for almost two years he lived in sordid supper-houses
known as "cabmen's shelters." He literally drank himself to death
in 1900.

His delicate and fantastic poetry was an attempt to escape from
a reality too brutal for him. His passionate lyric, "I have been
faithful to thee, Cynara! in my fashion," a triumph of despair and
disillusion, is an outburst in which Dowson epitomized himself;
and the two shorter poems which follow are equally characteristic.

To One in Bedlam [1]

With delicate, mad hands, behind his sordid bars,
Surely he hath his posies, which they tear and twine;
Those scentless wisps of straw that, miserable, line
His strait, caged universe, whereat the dull world stares.

Pedant and pitiful. O, how his rapt gaze wars
With their stupidity! Know they what dreams divine
Lift his long, laughing reveries like enchanted wine,
And make his melancholy germane to the stars'?

O lamentable brother! if those pity thee,
Am I not fain of all thy lone eyes promise me;
Half a fool's kingdom, far from men who sow and reap,

[1] *Bedlam:* a corrupt pronunciation of Bethlehem. Here it refers
to a madhouse, for the hospital of St. Mary of Bethlehem in London was used as an asylum for lunatics in the fifteenth century.

All their days, vanity? Better than mortal flowers,
Thy moon-kissed roses seem: better than love or sleep,
The star-crowned solitude of thine oblivious hours!

Envoy

They are not long, the weeping and the laughter,
    Love and desire and hate;
I think they have no portion in us after
        We pass the gate.

They are not long, the days of wine and roses:
    Out of a misty dream
Our path emerges for a while, then closes
        Within a dream.

To Cynara

Non Sum Qualis Eram Bonae Sub Regno Cynarae [1]

Last night, ah, yesternight, betwixt her lips and mine
There fell thy shadow, Cynara! thy breath was shed
Upon my soul between the kisses and the wine;
And I was desolate and sick of an old passion,
    Yea, I was desolate and bowed my head:
I have been faithful to thee, Cynara! in my fashion.

All night upon mine heart I felt her warm heart beat,
Night-long within mine arms in love and sleep she lay;
Surely the kisses of her bought red mouth were sweet;
But I was desolate and sick of an old passion,
    When I awoke and found the dawn was gray:
I have been faithful to thee, Cynara! in my fashion.

I have forgot much, Cynara! gone with the wind,
Flung roses, roses riotously with the throng,
Dancing, to put thy pale, lost lilies out of mind;
But I was desolate and sick of an old passion,
    Yea, all the time, because the dance was long:
I have been faithful to thee, Cynara! in my fashion.

[1] Non Sum. . . . Cynarae: "I am not what I was during the
reign of the good Cynara." The quotation is from Dowson's favorite poet, Horace. Cynara, in the poem, is the poet's true love

I cried for madder music and for stronger wine,
But when the feast is finished and the lamps expire,
Then falls thy shadow, Cynara! the night is thine;
And I am desolate and sick of an old passion,
    Yea, hungry for the lips of my desire:
I have been faithful to thee, Cynara! in my fashion.

" Æ "

George William Russell was born April 10, 1867, in the little town of Lurgan, in the north of Ireland. He intended to become a painter, moved to Dublin, formed a close friendship with William Butler Yeats and James Stephens, and was one of those who instigated the Irish revival. He wrote articles for the papers, using the diphthong " Æ " as his pen name. Like Yeats he became active in Irish politics, and spent much of his time establishing co-operative societies and editing local journals. He was particularly interested in poetry, painting, and farming. The best of his work is in *Collected Poems* (1914) from which there emanates a mystical breath of earth. Yeats has spoken of these poems as " revealing a kind of scented flame consuming them from within."

After Russell's death, which occurred July 17, 1935, critics united to praise his aims if not all his poetry. His contemporaries considered him one of the noblest spirits of his day, one who believed not only in the immortality of man but in man's present dignity, and one who labored to improve the lot of humanity. Two illuminating books appeared in 1938: *The Living Torch*, a selection of his prose articles, edited by Monk Gibbon, and *A Memoir of " Æ "* by John Eglinton.

Continuity

No sign is made while empires pass.
The flowers and stars are still His care,
The constellations hid in grass,
The golden miracles in air.

Life in an instant will be rent,
Where death is glittering blind and wild --
The Heavenly Brooding is intent
To that last instant on Its child.

It breathes the glow in brain and heart,
Life is made magical. Until
Body and spirit are apart,
The Everlasting works Its will.

In that wild orchid that your feet
In their next falling shall destroy,
Minute and passionate and sweet
The Mighty Master holds His joy.

Though the crushed jewels droop and fade,
The Artist's labors will not cease,
And of the ruins shall be made
Some yet more lovely masterpiece.

The Unknown God

Far up the dim twilight fluttered
    Moth-wings of vapor and flame:
The lights danced over the mountains,
    Star after star they came.

The lights grew thicker unheeded,
    For silent and still were we;
Our hearts were drunk with a beauty
    Our eyes could never see.

ANTHONY C. DEANE

Anthony C. Deane was born in 1870. He was the Seatonian prize-man in 1905 at Clare College, Cambridge, and was Vicar of All Saints, Ennismore Gardens, after 1916. His long list of light verse and essays includes many excellent parodies; the most delightful are in his *New Rhymes for Old* (1901), a volume that deserves to be better known.

The Ballad to the *Billycock*

It was the good ship *Billycock*, with thirteen men aboard,
 Athirst to grapple with their country's foes, —
A crew, 'twill be admitted, not numerically fitted
 To navigate a battleship in prose.

It was the good ship *Billycock* put out from Plymouth Sound,
 While lustily the gallant heroes cheered,
And all the air was ringing with the merry bo'sun's singing,
 Till in the gloom of night she disappeared.

But when the morning broke on her, behold, a dozen ships,
 A dozen ships of France around her lay,
(Or, if that isn't plenty, I will gladly make it twenty),
 And hemmed her close in Salamander Bay.

Then to the Lord High Admiral there spake a cabin-boy:
 " Methinks," he said, " the odds are somewhat great,
And, in the present crisis, a cabin-boy's advice is
 That you and France had better arbitrate! "

" Pooh! " said the Lord High Admiral, and slapped his
 manly chest,
 " Pooh! That would be both cowardly and wrong;
Shall I, a gallant fighter, give the needy ballad-writer
 No suitable material for song?

" Nay — is the shorthand-writer here? — I tell you, one and
 all,
 I mean to do my duty, as I ought;
With eager satisfaction let us clear the decks for action
 And fight the craven Frenchmen! " So they fought.

And (after several stanzas which as yet are incomplete,
 Describing all the fight in epic style)
When the *Billycock* was going, she'd a dozen prizes towing
 (Or twenty, as above) in single file!

Ah, long in glowing English hearts the story will remain,
 The memory of that historic day,
And, while we rule the ocean, we will picture with emotion
 The *Billycock* in Salamander Bay!

P.S. I've lately noticed that the critics — who, I think,
 In praising *my* productions are remiss —
Quite easily are captured, and profess themselves enraptured,
 By patriotic ditties such as this,

For making which you merely take some dauntless English-
       men,
 Guns, heroism, slaughter, and a fleet —
Ingredients you mingle in a meter with a jingle,
 And there you have your masterpiece complete!

Why, then, with labor infinite, produce a book of verse
 To languish on the " All for Twopence " shelf?
The ballad bold and breezy comes particularly easy —
 I mean to take to writing it myself!

CHARLOTTE MEW

Charlotte (Mary) Mew was born in London in 1870, the daughter of an architect who died while she was still a child. Brought
up in poverty and obscurity, her life was complicated by a long
illness which finally overcame her. She was extremely self-critical,
published little, and destroyed a great quantity of her work before
she died March 24, 1928.

She published only one book during her lifetime — *The Farmer's Bride* (1916), reissued, with eleven poems added, in America as
Saturday Market (1921) — yet that volume contains some of the
finest poetry of the period. Thomas Hardy considered her the
best woman poet of her time and other poets added their tributes
during her life. She did not exploit her emotion, she scarcely ex-
hibited it; one might say that she distilled emotion and kept it in
a secret vial. Her shorter lyrics are simple and intense; her longer
work is in dramatic narratives and poignant monologs such as the
powerful meditation " Madeleine in Church." *The Rambling
Sailor*, a gathering of unpublished work, appeared in 1929, a year
after her death.

Sea Love

Tide be runnin' the great world over:
 'Twas only last June month I mind that we
Was thinkin' the toss and the call in the breast of the lover
 So everlastin' as the sea.

Heer's the same little fishes that sputter and swim,
  Wi' the moon's old glim on the gray, wet sand;
An' him no more to me nor me to him
  Than the wind goin' over my hand.

Again

One day, not here, you will find a hand
Stretched out to you as you walk down some heavenly street;
You will see a stranger scarred from head to feet;
But when he speaks to you you will not understand,
Nor yet who wounded him nor why his wounds are sweet.
  And saying nothing, letting go his hand,
  You will leave him in the heavenly street —
    So we shall meet!

Beside the Bed

Someone has shut the shining eyes, straightened and folded
  The wandering hands quietly covering the unquiet breast:
So, smoothed and silenced you lie, like a child, not again to
    be questioned or scolded;
  But, for you, not one of us believes that this is rest.

Not so to close the windows down can cloud and deaden
  The blue beyond: or to screen the wavering flame subdue
    its breath:
Why, if I lay my cheek to your cheek, your gray lips, like
    dawn, would quiver and redden,
  Breaking into the old, odd smile at this fraud of death.

Because all night you have not turned to us or spoken,
  It is time for you to wake; your dreams were never very
    deep:
I, for one, have seen the thin, bright, twisted threads of them
    dimmed suddenly and broken.
  This is only a most piteous pretense of sleep!

William Henry Davies was born April 20, 1870, in Monmouthshire, of poor Welsh parents. Apprenticed to various trades, he ran away and became a wanderer; he was, until the dramatist Bernard Shaw discovered him, a cattleman, a day-laborer, a berry-picker, a pan-handler, a "super-tramp," as he described himself. At the age of thirty-four he began to write poetry. In a preface to Davies' *The Autobiography of a Super-Tramp*, Shaw describes how he happened to see the poems:

"In 1905 I received a volume of poems by one William H. Davies, whose address was The Farm House, Kennington. The author, as far as I could guess, had walked into a printer's or stationer's shop; handed in his manuscript; and ordered his book as he might have ordered a pair of boots. It was marked 'price, half a crown.' An accompanying letter asked me very civilly if I required a half-crown book of verses; and if so, would I please send the author the half crown: if not, would I return the book. This was attractively simple and sensible. I opened the book, and was more puzzled than ever; before I had read three lines I perceived that the author was a real poet. His work was not in the least strenuous or modern; there was indeed no sign of his ever having read anything otherwise than as a child reads."

It is this seeming childlikeness, this artlessness, which distinguishes the poems of Davies. He writes of cows and lambs, birds and butterflies as though he had never seen them before — as though no one had even heard of them before. Untouched by current fashions in verse, he continued to compose songs which are strangely simple and spontaneous, songs which remind the reader of a more casual Blake. In Davies' *Collected Poems* (revised four times since their first publication in 1916) good and bad are uncritically mingled. Davies wrote too much and too hastily — more than twenty volumes of poems were published between 1907 and 1938 — and the poet never had sufficiently severe standards to separate the genuine vision from the uninspired statement. Davies was planning a new collection of happy and homely verse when he died at his home in Gloucestershire, September 26, 1940.

If Davies is too diffuse, the poet's quaint touch is unmistakable and, at its best, unforgettable. If the world is not as innocent and lovely as Davies makes it seem, he almost persuades us it should be.

The Hour of Magic

This is the hour of magic, when the Moon
  With her bright wand has charmed the tallest tree
To stand stone-still with all his million leaves!
  I feel around me things I cannot see;

I hold my breath, as Nature holds her own.
   And do the mice and birds, the horse and cow,
Sleepless in this deep silence, so intense,
   Believe a miracle has happened now,
And wait to hear a sound they'll recognize,
To prove they still have life with earthly ties?

The Villain

While joy gave clouds the light of stars,
   That beamed where'er they looked;
And calves and lambs had tottering knees,
   Excited, while they sucked;
While every bird enjoyed his song,
Without one thought of harm or wrong —
I turned my head and saw the wind,
   Not far from where I stood,
Dragging the corn by her golden hair,
   Into a dark and lonely wood.

The Moon

Thy beauty haunts me heart and soul,
   O thou fair Moon, so close and bright;
Thy beauty makes me like the child
   That cries aloud to own thy light:
The little child that lifts each arm
To press thee to her bosom warm.

Though there are birds that sing this night
   With thy white beams across their throats,
Let my deep silence speak for me
   More than for them their sweetest notes:
Who worships thee till music fails
It greater than thy nightingales.

Days Too Short

When primroses are out in Spring,
   And small, blue violets come between;
   When merry birds sing on boughs green,
And rills, as soon as born, must sing;

When butterflies will make side-leaps,
  As though escaped from Nature's hand
  Ere perfect quite; and bees will stand
Upon their heads in fragrant deeps;

When small clouds are so silvery white
  Each seems a broken rimmèd moon —
  When such things are, this world too soon,
For me, doth wear the veil of Night.

The White Cascade

What happy mortal sees that mountain now,
The white cascade that's shining on its brow?

The white cascade that's both a bird and star,
That has a ten-mile voice and shines so far?

Though I may never leave this land again,
Yet every spring my mind must cross the main

To hear and see that water-bird and star
That on the mountain sings, and shines so far.

A Greeting

Good morning, Life — and all
Things glad and beautiful.
My pockets nothing hold;
But he that owns the gold,
The Sun, is my great friend —
His spending has no end.

Hail to the morning sky,
Which bright clouds measure high;
Hail to you birds whose throats
Would number leaves by notes;
Hail to you shady bowers,
And you green fields of flowers.

Hail to you women fair,
That make a show so rare
In cloth as white as milk —
Be't calico or silk:
Good morning, Life — and all
Things glad and beautiful.

HILAIRE BELLOC

Joseph Hilaire Pierre Belloc was born in 1870 near Paris, France. Four of his great-uncles were generals under Napoleon; his father was a French lawyer; his mother, an Englishwoman, was prominent in the feminist movement which secured votes for women. Belloc was brought up in Sussex, married a Californian, became a naturalized Englishman in 1903. As an eminent Roman Catholic he was made a Knight Commander of the Order of St. Gregory; as a politician he was a Liberal Member of Parliament; as a writer he was controversial.

Although Belloc has written in every form and on almost every subject — at sixty-seven he had published about one hundred volumes — he began with poetry. From the early *Verses and Sonnets* (1896) to his latest biography Belloc pursued a tempestuous career with vigor and versatility, grimly ironic and, as in *The Bad Child's Book of Beasts* and *Cautionary Tales for Children* (1908), delightfully nonsensical. "Tarantella" echoes the lively pace of the folk-dance which gives the poem its name, and the quickly shifting rhythms are emphasized by the rapid internal rhymes, reminiscent of the castanets and tambourines which accompany the dancing measures. Belloc died at the age of eighty-three, July 16, 1953.

Tarantella

Do you remember an Inn,
  Miranda?
Do you remember an Inn?
And the treading and the spreading
Of the straw for a bedding,
And the fleas that tease in the High Pyrenees,
And the wine that tasted of the tar?
And the cheers and the jeers of the young muleteers
(Under the vine of the dark veranda)?

Do you remember an Inn, Miranda,
Do you remember an Inn?
And the cheers and the jeers of the young muleteers
Who hadn't got a penny,
And who weren't paying any,
And the hammer at the doors and the din?
And the *hip! hop! hap!*
Of the clap
Of the hands to the twirl and the swirl
Of the girl gone chancing,
Glancing,
Dancing,
Backing and advancing,
Snapping of the clapper to the spin
Out and in —
And the *ting, tong, tang* of the guitar!
Do you remember an Inn,
    Miranda?
Do you remember an Inn?

Never more,
    Miranda,
Never more.
Only the high peaks hoar:
And Aragon [1] a torrent at the door.
No sound
In the walls of the halls where falls
The tread
Of the feet of the dead to the ground.
No sound:
But the boom
Of the far waterfall like doom.

Epitaph on the Politician

Here richly, with ridiculous display,
The Politician's corpse was laid away.
While all of his acquaintance sneered and slanged
I wept: for I had longed to see him hanged.

[1] *Aragon:* a medieval kingdom, a province of Spain.

John Millington Synge was born at Rathfarnham, near Dublin, in 1871. As a child in Wicklow, he was already fascinated by the strange idioms and the rhythmic speech he heard there, a native utterance which was to be rich material for his work.

For some time, Synge's career was uncertain. He went to Germany, intending to become a professional musician. There he studied the theory of music, perfecting himself meanwhile in Gaelic and Hebrew. Yeats found him in France and advised him to go to the Aran Islands, to live there as if he were one of the people. "Express a life," said Yeats, "that has never found expression."

The result of this close contact was four of the greatest poetic prose dramas not only of Synge's own generation, but of several generations preceding it. In *Riders to the Sea* (1903), *The Well of the Saints* (1905), and *The Playboy of the Western World* (1907) there is a richness of imagery, a new language startling in its vigor, a wildness and passion that contrast strangely with the mysticism and spirituality of his associates in the Irish Theatre. The same earthiness is manifest in his *Poems and Translations* (1910), issued a year after his death. Synge died after an operation March 24, 1909.

Prelude

Still south I went and west and south again,
Through Wicklow from the morning till the night,
And far from cities and the sights of men,
Lived with the sunshine and the moon's delight.

I knew the stars, the flowers, and the birds,
The gray and wintry sides of many glens,
And did but half remember human words,
In converse with the mountains, moors and fens.

A Translation from Petrarch [1]

(*He is Jealous of the Heavens and the Earth*)

What a grudge I am bearing the earth that has its arms about her, and is holding that face away from me, where I was finding peace from great sadness.

What a grudge I am bearing the Heavens that are after

[1] *Petrarch:* Italian poet (1304–1374), particularly noted for the sonnets to his dead — and ideal — love, Laura.

taking her, and shutting her in with greediness, the Heavens that do push their bolts against so many.

What a grudge I am bearing the blessed saints that have got her sweet company, that I am always seeking; and what a grudge I am bearing against Death, that is standing in her two eyes, and will not call me with a word.

A Translation from Villon [1]

(*Prayer of the Old Woman, Villon's Mother*)

Mother of God that's Lady of the Heavens, take myself, the poor sinner, the way I'll be along with them that's chosen.

Let you say to your own Son that He'd have a right to forgive my share of sins, when it's the like He's done, many's the day, with big and famous sinners. I'm a poor aged woman, was never at school, and is no scholar with letters, but I've seen pictures in the chapel with Paradise on one side, and harps and pipes in it, and the place on the other side, where sinners do be boiled in torment; the one gave me great joy, the other a great fright and scaring; let me have the good place, Mother of God, and it's in your faith I'll live always.

It's yourself that bore Jesus, that has no end or death, and He the Lord Almighty, that took our weakness and gave Himself to sorrows, a young and gentle man. It's Himself is our Lord surely, and it's in that faith I'll live always.

Beg-Innish

Bring Kateen-beug and Maurya Jude [2]
To dance in Beg-Innish, [3]
And when the lads (they're in Dunquin)
Have sold their crabs and fish,
Wave fawny shawls and call them in,
And call the little girls who spin,
And seven weavers from Dunquin,
To dance in Beg-Innish.

[1] *Villon:* French lyric poet (1431–1464?), known as the vagabond poet, fictional hero of *The Vagabond King.*

[2] *Kateen-beug and Maurya Jude:* two Irish girls.

[3] *Beg-Innish:* a small town in Ireland; the accent is on the last syllable.

I'll play you jigs, and Maurice Kean,
Where nets are laid to dry,
I've silken strings would draw a dance
From girls are lame or shy;
Four strings I've brought from Spain and France
To make your long men skip and prance,
Till stars look out to see the dance
Where nets are laid to dry.

We'll have no priest or peeler in
To dance in Beg-Innish;
But we'll have drink from M'riarty Jim
Rowed round while gannets [1] fish,
A keg with porter to the brim,
That every lad may have his whim,
Till we up sails with M'riarty Jim
And sail from Beg-Innish.

RALPH HODGSON

Ralph Hodgson was born in Yorkshire, in 1872, one of the shy-
est of English lyric poets. Although he is extremely reticent con-
cerning his life, it has been learned that Hodgson was at various
times a journalist, a professional cartoonist, a breeder of bull ter-
riers, a traveler in America, and a teacher. In 1924 Hodgson became lecturer in English literature at Sendai University, Japan,
returned to the Orient several times, and, in 1939, came to America,
where he found a retreat near Canton, Ohio.

As a poet, Hodgson shares many of Housman's traits. Like
Housman he has written comparatively little — most of his work is
gathered in a small collection entitled simply *Poems* — and, also
like Housman, his poems are on an unusually high level. His style
is delicate but firm, and his poems are full of a love for all natural
things, particularly the small and helpless, a love that goes out to
. . . an idle rainbow
No less than laboring seas.

Although Hodgson's short lyrics are among the freshest of the
period, the longer verses are beautifully sustained, an almost per-

---

[1] *Gannets:* large sea fowl, expert flyers who catch fish by diving
for them.

fect combination of meaning and magic. One succumbs to the
charm of "Eve" at the first reading; here is the oldest of legends
told with a strange simplicity which is, in itself, a novelty. This
Eve is neither the conscious sinner nor the traditional mother of
men; she is, in these seemingly artless lines, a young country girl,
regarding the world and evil itself with a frank, childlike wonder.
Such snatches of music as this and "Time, You Old Gypsy Man"
seem destined for a long life.

Time, You Old Gypsy Man

Time, you old gypsy man,
　Will you not stay,
Put up your caravan
　Just for one day?

All things I'll give you
Will you be my guest,
Bells for your jennet [1]
Of silver the best,
Goldsmiths shall beat you
A great golden ring,
Peacocks shall bow to you,
Little boys sing,
Oh, and sweet girls will
Festoon you with may.
Time, you old gypsy,
Why hasten away?

Last week in Babylon,
Last night in Rome,
Morning, and in the crush
Under Paul's dome;
Under Paul's dial
You tighten your rein —
Only a moment,
And off once again;
Off to some city
Now blind in the womb,
Off to another
Ere that's in the tomb.

[1] *Jennet*: a female donkey, or jenny.

Time, you old gypsy man,
  Will you not stay,
Put up your caravan
  Just for one day?

The Birdcatcher [1]

When flighting time is on, I go
With clap-net and decoy,
A-fowling after goldfinches
And other birds of joy;

I lurk among the thickets of
The Heart where they are bred,
And catch the twittering beauties as
They fly into my Head.

Stupidity Street

I saw with open eyes
Singing birds sweet
Sold in the shops
For the people to eat,
Sold in the shops of
Stupidity Street.

I saw in a vision
The worm in the wheat,
And in the shops nothing
For people to eat:
Nothing for sale in
Stupidity Street.

Eve

Eve, with her basket, was
Deep in the bells and grass,
Wading in bells and grass
Up to her knees.

[1]. The Birdcatcher is a symbol of the poet.

Picking a dish of sweet
Berries and plums to eat,
Down in the bells and grass
Under the trees.

Mute as a mouse in a
Corner the cobra lay,
Curled round a bough of the
Cinnamon tall. . . .
Now to get even and
Humble proud heaven and
Now was the moment or
Never at all.

"Eva!" Each syllable
Light as a flower fell,
"Eva!" he whispered the
Wondering maid,
Soft as a bubble sung
Out of a linnet's lung,
Soft and most silvery
"Eva!" he said.

Picture that orchard sprite;
Eve, with her body white,
Supple and smooth to her
Slim finger tips;
Wondering, listening,
Listening, wondering,
Eve with a berry
Half-way to her lips.

Oh, had our simple Eve
Seen through the make-believe!
Had she but known the
Pretender he was!
Out of the boughs he came,
Whispering still her name,
Tumbling in twenty rings
Into the grass.

Here was the strangest pair
In the world anywhere,

Eve in the bells and grass
Kneeling, and he
Telling his story low. . . .
Singing birds saw them go
Down the dark path to
The Blasphemous Tree.

Oh, what a clatter when
Titmouse and Jenny Wren
Saw him successful and
Taking his leave!
How the birds rated him,
How they all hated him!
How they all pitied
Poor motherless Eve!

Picture her crying
Outside in the lane,
Eve, with no dish of sweet
Berries and plums to eat,
Haunting the gate of the
Orchard in vain. . . .
Picture the lewd delight
Under the hill tonight —
" Eva! " the toast goes round,
" Eva! " again.

The Mystery

He came and took me by the hand
    Up to a red rose tree,
He kept His meaning to Himself
    But gave a rose to me.

I did not pray Him to lay bare
    The mystery to me,
Enough the rose was Heaven to smell,
    And His own face to see.

John McCrae was born in Guelph, Ontario, Canada, in 1872. He was graduated in arts in 1894 and in medicine in 1898, finished his studies at Johns Hopkins in Baltimore and returned to Canada. He was a lieutenant of artillery in South Africa (1899–1900) and was in charge of the Medical Division of the McGill Canadian General Hospital during World War I. After serving two years, he died of pneumonia, January, 1918, his volume *In Flanders Fields* (1919) appearing posthumously.

Few who read the title-poem of his book, possibly the most widely-read poem produced by the war, realize that it is a perfect rondeau, one of the loveliest and strictest of the French forms.

In Flanders Fields

In Flanders fields the poppies blow
Between the crosses, row on row,
    That mark our place; and in the sky
    The larks, still bravely singing, fly
Scarce heard amid the guns below.

We are the Dead. Short days ago
We lived, felt dawn, saw sunset glow,
    Loved and were loved, and now we lie
    In Flanders fields.

Take up our quarrel with the foe:
To you from failing hands we throw
    The torch; be yours to hold it high.
    If ye break faith with us who die
We shall not sleep, though poppies grow
    In Flanders fields.

WALTER DE LA MARE

Walter de la Mare was born in Kent in 1873, but lived in and around London most of his life. For many years he was employed in a clerical position by the English branch of the Standard Oil Company, but he hated "the drudgery at the desk's dead wood."

De la Mare was almost thirty before he ventured to publish his first volume, *Songs of Childhood* (1902), and even then he published it under a pseudonym, "Walter Ramal." Succeeding volumes, beginning with *Peacock Pie* (1913), proved he was, as Harold Williams wrote, essentially "the singer of a young and romantic world, a singer even for children, understanding and perceiving as a child." De la Mare paints scenes of miniature loveliness; he uses thin-spun fragments of fairylike delicacy and gives them solidity and strength. An astonishing joiner of words, he surprises us by transforming what began as a child's nonsense-rhyme into a thrilling snatch of music. The trick of revealing the ordinary in whimsical colors, of catching the commonplace off its guard, is part of De la Mare's charm.

The poet's other gift is his sense of the supernatural, of the fantastic world that lies on the edge of consciousness. *The Listeners* (1912) is a book that is full of half-heard whispers. Moonlight and mystery seem soaked in the lines, and a cool wind from Nowhere blows over them. The magical title-poem is an example. In this poem there is an uncanny splendor; here is the effect, the thrill, the overtones of a ghost story rather than the narrative itself. "The Listeners" may be the tale of a traveler coming at dusk upon a haunted house, daring to summon its dread occupants; it may be a spirit returning to the scene of weird adventures; it may be a symbol of mankind, surrounded by sinister shadows, but bravely challenging whatever is present or to come. The important thing about the poem, however, is its very suggestiveness; never have silence and creeping darkness been so subtly communicated.

Later works, such as *The Veil* (1921), *The Fleeting and Other Poems* (1934), that extraordinary novel, *Memoirs of a Midget* (1921), and *The Burning Glass* (1945), show a more somber strain. There is a weariness in the poems of this period, but the harmonies in *Collected Poems 1901–1918* are always delicate and continually explore the worlds which remain beyond the reach of reality.

Silver

Slowly, silently, now the moon
Walks the night in her silver shoon;
This way, and that, she peers, and sees
Silver fruit upon silver trees;
One by one the casements catch
Her beams beneath the silvery thatch;
Couched in his kennel, like a log,
With paws of silver sleeps the dog;
From their shadowy cote the white breasts peep
Of doves in a silver-feathered sleep;
A harvest mouse goes scampering by,

With silver claws and a silver eye;
And moveless fish in the water gleam,
By silver reeds in a silver stream.

The Listeners

"Is there anybody there?" said the Traveler,
  Knocking on the moonlit door;
And his horse in the silence champed the grasses
  Of the forest's ferny floor.
And a bird flew up out of the turret,
  Above the Traveler's head:
And he smote upon the door again a second time;
  "Is there anybody there?" he said.
But no one descended to the Traveler;
  No head from the leaf-fringed sill
Leaned over and looked into his gray eyes,
  Where he stood perplexed and still.
But only a host of phantom listeners
  That dwelt in the lone house then
Stood listening in the quiet of the moonlight
  To that voice from the world of men:
Stood thronging the faint moonbeams on the dark stair,
  That goes down to the empty hall,
Hearkening in an air stirred and shaken
  By the lonely Traveler's call.
And he felt in his heart their strangeness,
  Their stillness answering his cry,
While his horse moved, cropping the dark turf,
  'Neath the starred and leafy sky;
For he suddenly smote on the door, even
  Louder, and lifted his head: —
"Tell them I came, and no one answered,
  That I kept my word," he said.
Never the least stir made the listeners,
Though every word he spake
Fell echoing through the shadowiness of the still house
  From the one man left awake:
Ay, they heard his foot upon the stirrup,
  And the sound of iron on stone,
And how the silence surged softly backward,
  When the plunging hoofs were gone.

An Epitaph

Here lies a most beautiful lady,
Light of step and heart was she;
I think she was the most beautiful lady
That ever was in the West Country.

But beauty vanishes; beauty passes;
However rare — rare it be;
And when I crumble, who will remember
This lady of the West Country?

Summer Evening

The sandy cat by the Farmer's chair
Mews at his knee for dainty fare;
Old Rover in his moss-greened house
Mumbles a bone, and barks at a mouse.
In the dewy fields the cattle lie
Chewing the cud 'neath a fading sky.
Dobbin at manger pulls his hay:
Gone is another summer's day.

Old Susan

When Susan's work was done, she'd sit
With one fat guttering candle lit,
And window opened wide to win
The sweet night air to enter in;
There, with a thumb to keep her place,
She'd read, with stern and wrinkled face.
Her mild eyes gliding very slow
Across the letters to and fro,
While wagged the guttering candle flame
In the wind that through the window came.

And sometimes in the silence she
Would mumble a sentence audibly,
Or shake her head as if to say,
" You silly souls, to act this way! "
And never a sound from night I'd hear,

Unless some far-off cock crowed clear;
Or her old shuffling thumb should turn
Another page; and rapt and stern,
Through her great glasses bent on me
She'd glance into reality;
And shake her round old silvery head,
With — " You! — I thought you was in bed! " —
Only to tilt her book again,
And rooted in Romance remain.

Chicken

Clapping her platter stood plump Bess,
   And all across the green
Came scampering in, on wing and claw
   Chicken fat and lean: —
Dorking, Spaniard, Cochin China,
   Bantams sleek and small,
Like feathers blown in a great wind,
   They came at Bessie's call.

There Blooms No Bud in May

There blooms no bud in May
Can for its white compare
With snow at break of day,
On fields forlorn and bare.

For shadow it hath rose,
Azure, and amethyst;
And every air that blows
Dies out in beauteous mist.

It hangs the frozen bough
With flowers on which the night
Wheeling her darkness through
Scatters a starry light.

Fearful of its pale glare
In flocks the starlings rise;
Slide through the frosty air,
And perch with plaintive cries.

Only the inky rook,
Hunched cold in ruffled wings,
Its snowy nest forsook,
Caws of unnumbered Springs.

Peace

Night arches England, and the winds are still;
Jasmine and honeysuckle steep the air;
Softly the stars that are all Europe's fill
Her heaven-wide dark with radiancy fair;
That shadowed moon now waxing in the west,
Stirs not a rumor in her tranquil seas;
Mysterious sleep has lulled her heart to rest,
Deep even as theirs beneath her churchyard trees.

Secure, serene; dumb now the nighthawk's threat;
The guns' low thunder drumming o'er the tide;
The anguish pulsing in her stricken side . . .
All is at peace. Ah, never, heart, forget
For this her youngest, best and bravest died,
These bright dews once were mixed with bloody sweat.

Sam

When Sam goes back in memory,
　　It is to where the sea
Breaks on the shingle, emerald-green,
　　In white foam, endlessly;
He says — with small brown eye on mine —
　　"I used to keep awake,
And lean from my window in the moon,
　　Watching those billows break.
And half a million tiny hands,
　　And eyes, like sparks of frost,
Would dance and come tumbling into the moon,
　　On every breaker tossed.
And all across from star to star,
　　I've seen the watery sea,
With not a single ship in sight,
　　Just ocean there, and me;

And heard my father snore. And once,
  As sure as I'm alive,
Out of those wallowing, moon-flecked waves
  I saw a mermaid dive;
Head and shoulders above the wave,
  Plain as I now see you,
Combing her hair, now back, now front,
  Her two eyes peeping through;
Calling me, 'Sam!' — quietlike — 'Sam!' . . .
  But me . . . I never went,
Making believe I kind of thought
  'Twas someone else she meant . . .
Wonderful lovely there she sat,
  Singing the night away,
All in the solitudinous sea
  Of that there lonely bay.
P'raps," and he'd smooth his hairless mouth,
  " P'raps, if 'twere now, my son,
P'raps, if I heard a voice say, 'Sam!'
  Morning would find me gone."

G. K. CHESTERTON

Gilbert Keith Chesterton was born in Kensington, London, May 29, 1874. He began his literary life by reviewing books on art, and soon became known as one of the most versatile writers of his day. He was an energetic force as journalist, novelist, dramatist, essayist, parodist, publicist, and lyricist. He produced books on religion and detective novels with equal facility and conviction. Whether he wrote serious biographies, such as his *Charles Dickens* (1906), or wildly fantastic narratives, such as *The Club of Queer Trades* (1905) and *The Flying Inn* (1914), he was witty, usually surprising and always stimulating. Chesterton died June 14, 1936.

As a poet, he suffered sometimes from his very buoyancy and love of paradox. From his first volume of verse, *The Wild Knight and Other Poems* (1900) to *New and Collected Poems* (1929) the lines are swift, full of banging rhymes and tramping rhythms. The criticism he made of Elizabeth Barrett Browning's style applies with equal force to him: "Whenever her verse is bad, it is bad from some extravagance of imagery, some kind of debauch of cleverness." Yet the best of his ballads and lyrics are not only swinging but inspiring, even when they are sad or satirical.

"Lepanto" is one of the most rousing of modern ballad narratives. Anticipating Vachel Lindsay's "The Congo" and other chants of modern poetry, Chesterton retells the story of the Crusaders under the leadership of Don John, who commanded the combined Christian navies in 1571 and broke the power of the Turks; he revivifies the details, changing them from dry historical data into drama. The syllables beat as though on brass; the armies sing, the feet tramp, the drums snarl, and the tides of marching crusaders roll resonantly out of the lines.

No discussion of Chesterton would be complete without a tribute to his epigrammatic power. "The Donkey" and "Elegy in a Country Churchyard" are noteworthy examples of such condensation. As a politician and paradoxical essayist, Chesterton will have an interest for future critics, but Chesterton the poet will outlive his period.

Lepanto [1]

White founts falling in the Courts of the sun,
And the Soldan of Byzantium is smiling as they run;
There is laughter like the fountains in that face of all men
    feared,
It stirs the forest darkness, the darkness of his beard;
It curls the blood-red crescent, the crescent of his lips;
For the inmost sea of all the earth is shaken with his ships.
They have dared the white republics up the capes of Italy,
They have dashed the Adriatic round the Lion of the Sea,
And the Pope has cast his arms abroad for agony and loss,
And called the kings of Christendom for swords about the
    Cross.
The cold queen of England is looking in the glass;
The shadow of the Valois is yawning at the Mass;
From evening isles fantastical rings faint the Spanish gun,
And the Lord upon the Golden Horn [2] is laughing in the sun.

Dim drums throbbing, in the hills half heard,
Where only on a nameless throne a crownless prince has
    stirred,
Where, risen from a doubtful seat and half attainted stall,
The last knight of Europe takes weapons from the wall.
The last lingering troubadour to whom the bird has sung,

---

[1] For a background to "Lepanto" see page lv.
[2] The pagan Lord, Sultan (Soldan) of Turkey.

That once went singing southward when all the world was
    young.
In that enormous silence, tiny and unafraid,
Comes up along a winding road the noise of the Crusade.

Strong gongs groaning as the guns boom far,
Don John of Austria is going to the war,
Stiff flags straining in the night-blasts cold
In the gloom black-purple, in the glint old-gold;
Torchlight crimson on the copper kettle-drums,
Then the tuckets,[1] then the trumpets, then the cannon, and
    he comes.
Don John laughing in the brave beard curled,
Spurning of his stirrups like the thrones of all the world,
Holding his head up for a flag of all the free.
Love-light of Spain — hurrah!
Death-light of Africa!
Don John of Austria
Is riding to the sea.

Mahound [2] is in his paradise above the evening star,
(*Don John of Austria is going to the war.*)
He moves a mighty turban on the timeless houri's knees,
His turban that is woven of the sunsets and the seas.
He shakes the peacock gardens as he rises from his ease,
And he strides among the tree-tops and is taller than the
    trees;
And his voice through all the garden is a thunder sent to
    bring
Black Azrael and Ariel and Ammon [3] on the wing.
Giants and the Genii,
Multiplex of wing and eye,
Whose strong obedience broke the sky
When Solomon was king.

They rush in red and purple from the red clouds of the
    morn,
From the temples where the yellow gods shut up their eyes
    in scorn;

[1] *Tuckets:* blasts of martial music; fanfares.
[2] *Mahound:* Mohammed.
[3] These are demons and powerful spirits of the heathen.

They rise in green robes roaring from the green hells of the
    sea
Where fallen skies and evil hues and eyeless creatures be,
On them the sea-valves cluster and the gray sea-forests curl,
Splashed with a splendid sickness, the sickness of the pearl;
They swell in sapphire smoke out of the blue cracks of the
    ground, —
They gather and they wonder and give worship to Mahound.
And he saith, " Break up the mountains where the hermit-
    folk can hide,
And sift the red and silver sands lest bone of saint abide,
And chase the Giaours [1] flying night and day, not giving rest,
For that which was our trouble comes again out of the west.
We have set the seal of Solomon on all things under sun,
Of knowledge and of sorrow and endurance of things done.
But a noise is in the mountains, in the mountains, and I know
The voice that shook our palaces — four hundred years ago:
It is he that saith not ' Kismet '; [2] it is he that knows not Fate;
It is Richard, it is Raymond, it is Godfrey at the gate!
It is he whose loss is laughter when he counts the wager
    worth.
Put down your feet upon him, that our peace be on the
    earth."
For he heard drums groaning and he heard guns jar,
(*Don John of Austria is going to the war.*)
Sudden and still — hurrah!
Bolt from Iberia! [3]
Don John of Austria
Is gone by Alcalar.

St. Michael's on his Mountain in the sea-roads of the north
(*Don John of Austria is girt and going forth.*)
Where the gray seas glitter and the sharp tides shift
And the sea-folk labor and the red sails lift.
He shakes his lance of iron and he claps his wings of stone;
The noise is gone through Normandy; the noise is gone
    alone;
The North is full of tangled things and texts and aching eyes,
And dead is all the innocence of anger and surprise,
And Christian killeth Christian in a narrow dusty room,

    [1] *Giaours:* Christians.
    [2] *Kismet:* destiny, fate.
    [3] *Iberia:* the ancient name of the Spanish peninsula.

And Christian dreadeth Christ that hath a newer face of
    doom,
And Christian hateth Mary that God kissed in Galilee, —
But Don John of Austria is riding to the sea.
Don John calling through the blast and the eclipse
Crying with the trumpet, with the trumpet of his lips,
Trumpet that sayeth *ha!*
          Domino gloria! [1]
Don John of Austria
Is shouting to the ships.

The Pope was in his chapel before day or battle broke,
(*Don John of Austria is hidden in the smoke.*)
The hidden room in man's house where God sits all the year,
The secret window whence the world looks small and very
    dear.
He sees as in a mirror on the monstrous twilight sea
The crescent of his cruel ships whose name is mystery;
They fling great shadows foe-wards, making Cross and
    Castle dark,
They veil the plumèd lions on the galleys of St. Mark; [2]
And above the ships are palaces of brown, black-bearded
    chiefs,
And below the ships are prisons, where with multitudinous
    griefs,
Christian captives sick and sunless, all a laboring race repines
Like a race in sunken cities, like a nation in the mines.
They are lost like slaves that swat, [3] and in the skies of morn-
    ing hung
The stair-ways of the tallest gods when tyranny was young.
They are countless, voiceless, hopeless as those fallen or
    fleeing on
Before the high Kings' horses in the granite of Babylon.
And many a one grows witless in his quiet room in hell
Where a yellow face looks inward through the lattice of his
    cell,
And he finds his God forgotten, and he seeks no more a
    sign —
(*But Don John of Austria has burst the battle-line!*)

[1] *Domino gloria!:* Glory to God!
[2] *Cross . . . Castle . . . plumèd lions on the galleys of St.
Mark:* these are the emblems on the flags of the Christian fleet.
[3] *swat:* old form for "sweat."

Don John pounding from the slaughter-painted poop,
Purpling all the ocean like a bloody pirate's sloop,
Scarlet running over on the silvers and the golds,
Breaking of the hatches up and bursting of the holds,
Thronging of the thousands up that labor under sea
White for bliss and blind for sun and stunned for liberty.
Vivat Hispania! [1]
Domino Gloria!
Don John of Austria
Has set his people free!

Cervantes [2] on his galley sets the sword back in the sheath
(*Don John of Austria rides homeward with a wreath.*)
And he sees across a weary land a straggling road in Spain,
Up which a lean and foolish knight forever rides in vain,
And he smiles, but not as Sultans smile, and settles back the
    blade. . . .
(**But Don John of Austria rides home from the Crusade.**)

The Donkey

When fishes flew and forests walked
    And figs grew upon thorn,
Some moment when the moon was blood,
    Then surely I was born;

With monstrous head and sickening cry
    And ears like errant wings,
The devil's walking parody
    On all four-footed things.

The tattered outlaw of the earth,
    Of ancient crooked will;
Starve, scourge, deride me: I am dumb,
    I keep my secret still.

Fools! For I also had my hour;
    One far fierce hour and sweet:
There was a shout about my ears,
    And palms before my feet.

    [1] *Vivat Hispania!:* Hurrah for Spain!
    [2] *Cervantes:* Spanish novelist, author of *Don Quixote.* See page
lvi.

Elegy in a Country Churchyard

The men that worked for England
They have their graves at home;
And bees and birds of England
About the cross can roam.

But they that fought for England,
Following a falling star,
Alas, alas, for England
They have their graves afar.

And they that rule in England
In stately conclave met,
Alas, alas, for England
They have no graves as yet.

JOHN MASEFIELD

John Masefield was born in Ledbury, in the western county of Herefordshire, June 1, 1878. His father was a lawyer, but the son craved the sea even as a child. At fourteen young Masefield was apprenticed as a cabin boy; at seventeen he made his first trip to America. In 1895 he landed in New York with less than five dollars in his pocket, hoping to become a writer, to express the music of the sea, the wind in the rigging, and the men "hard-palmed from tallying on to whips." He had already fallen in love with the vigor and humanity of Chaucer — " it was Chaucer who made me realize what poetry could be " — but he was as yet unable to capture the spirit of the sea and put it into verse. For a while he worked in a Greenwich Village saloon as bus-boy, cuspidor-cleaner, emergency waiter, and bouncer; then he found a job in a carpet factory in Yonkers. He returned to England where his first book, *Salt Water Ballads* (1902), was published in his twenty-fourth year. By the time he was fifty-five he had written more than sixty volumes.

The early books reflect his wanderings; the poems in *Ballads* (1903) and the prose in *A Mainsail Haul* (1905) may be crude, but there is no doubt about the vitality and human feeling. Here, as in the succeeding works, Masefield speaks up for the "men with the broken heads and the blood running into their eyes," not for the rulers and princes, but the scorned and the rejected. He celebrates the brave souls who always

> . . . will prefer the wild,
> Long after life is meek and mild.

Although Masefield continued to sing about strenuous action and the communion of hearty spirits, it was not until *The Everlasting Mercy* (1911) that he became famous. Here, as in the other long narrative poems, *The Widow in the Bye Street* (1912), the autobiographical *Dauber* (1912), and *The Daffodil Fields* (1913), there is a frank pleasure in "the mere living," a rough joy which could not be communicated by soft phrases and delicate images.

Reynard the Fox (1919) is probably the most national of Masefield's works, and it is said to have done more than any other poem to win Masefield the office of poet laureate which was awarded to him in 1930. His later work is quieter and more questioning in tone. Although after 1930 Masefield produced too much undistinguished work in too many forms — novels, essays, plays, books for young people, adaptations of old legends — his enlarged *Collected Poems* (1935) exhibits his main theme: the mystery of life and the "joy of trying for beauty," a vivid combination of physical exulting and spiritual exaltation.

A Consecration

Not of the princes and prelates with periwigged charioteers [1]
Riding triumphantly laureled to lap the fat of the years, —
Rather the scorned — the rejected — the men hemmed in with
  the spears;

The men of the tattered battalion which fights till it dies,
Dazed with the dust of the battle, the din and the cries.
The men with the broken heads and the blood running into
  their eyes.

Not the bemedaled Commander, beloved of the throne,
Riding cock-horse to parade when the bugles are blown,
But the lads who carried the koppie [2] and cannot be known.
Not the ruler for me, but the ranker, the tramp of the road,
The slave with the sack on his shoulders pricked on with the
  goad,
The man with too weighty a burden, too weary a load.

[1] *Periwigged charioteers:* decorated drivers and attendants with fancy wigs.

[2] A corruption of "kopje," a South African term for a small hill. The line refers to the unknown privates who stormed and captured the hills in the Boer War.

The sailor, the stoker of steamers, the man with the clout,
The chantyman bent at the halliards [1] putting a tune to the
    shout,
The drowsy man at the wheel and the tired look-out.

Others may sing of the wine and the wealth and the mirth,
The portly presence of potentates goodly in girth; —
Mine be the dirt and the dross, the dust and scum of the
    earth!

Theirs be the music, the color, the glory, the gold;
Mine be a handful of ashes, a mouthful of mold.
Of the maimed, of the halt and the blind in the rain and
    the cold —
Of these shall my songs be fashioned, my tales be told.

                                     AMEN.

Sea-Fever

I must down to the seas again, to the lonely sea and the sky,
And all I ask is a tall ship and a star to steer her by,
And the wheel's kick and the wind's song and the white sail's
    shaking,
And a gray mist on the sea's face and a gray dawn breaking.

I must down to the seas again, for the call of the running
    tide
Is a wild call and a clear call that may not be denied;
And all I ask is a windy day with the white clouds flying,
And the flung spray and the blown spume, and the sea-gulls
    crying.

I must down to the seas again to the vagrant gypsy life.
To the gull's way and the whale's way where the wind's like
    a whetted knife;
And all I ask is a merry yarn from a laughing fellow-rover,
And quiet sleep and a sweet dream when the long trick's
    over.

[1] The sailor who led the songs (or "chantys") while the men
pulled rhythmically on the halliards (or "haulyards") to raise or
lower sail.

Laugh and Be Merry

Laugh and be merry, remember, better the world with a song,
Better the world with a blow in the teeth of a wrong.
Laugh, for the time is brief, a thread the length of a span.
Laugh, and be proud to belong to the old proud pageant of
    man.

Laugh and be merry: remember, in olden time,
God made Heaven and Earth for joy He took in a rhyme,
Made them, and filled them full with the strong red wine of
    His mirth,
The splendid joy of the stars: the joy of the earth.

So we must laugh and drink from the deep blue cup of the
    sky,
Join the jubilant song of the great stars sweeping by,
Laugh, and battle, and work, and drink of the wine outpoured
In the dear green earth, the sign of the joy of the Lord.

Laugh and be merry together, like brothers akin,
Guesting awhile in the rooms of a beautiful inn,
Glad till the dancing stops, and the lilt of the music ends.
Laugh till the game is played; and be you merry, my friends.

Rounding the Horn
(From " Dauber ")

Then came the cry of " Call all hands on deck! "
The Dauber [1] knew its meaning; it was come:
Cape Horn, that tramples beauty into wreck,
And crumples steel and smites the strong man dumb.
Down clattered flying kites and staysails; some
Sang out in quick, high calls: the fair-leads skirled,[2]
And from the south-west came the end of the world . . .

    [1] *The Dauber:* the central figure in the poem by that name, a
painter, supposed to be a semi-autobiographical portrait. This passage is a small section of a much longer poem, a stormy epic of
the sea.
    [2] *The fair-leads skirled:* the blocks which guide the ropes
whirled through the air.

"Lay out!" the Bosun yelled. The Dauber laid
Out on the yard, gripping the yard, and feeling
Sick at the mighty space of air displayed
Below his feet, where mewing birds were wheeling.
A giddy fear was on him; he was reeling.
He bit his lip half through, clutching the jack.
A cold sweat glued the shirt upon his back.

The yard was shaking, for a brace was loose.
He felt that he would fall; he clutched, he bent,
Clammy with natural terror to the shoes
While idiotic promptings came and went.
Snow fluttered on a wind-flaw and was spent;
He saw the water darken. Someone yelled,
"Frap [1] it; don't stay to furl! Hold on!" He held.

Darkness came down — half darkness — in a whirl;
The sky went out, the waters disappeared.
He felt a shocking pressure of blowing hurl
The ship upon her side. The darkness speared
At her with wind; she staggered, she careered;
Then down she lay. The Dauber felt her go,
He saw her yard tilt downwards. Then the snow

Whirled all about — dense, multitudinous, cold —
Mixed with the wind's one devilish thrust and shriek,
Which whiffled out men's tears, defeated, took hold,
Flattening the flying drift against the cheek.
The yards buckled and bent, man could not speak.
The ship lay on her broadside; the wind's sound
Had devilish malice at having got her downed.

. . . .

How long the gale had blown he could not tell,
Only the world had changed, his life had died.
A moment now was everlasting hell.
Nature an onslaught from the weather side,
A withering rush of death, a frost that cried,
Shrieked, till he withered at the heart; a hail
Plastered his oilskins with an icy mail. . . .

[1] *Frap:* tighten, wrap around with rope

" Up! " yelled the Bosun; " up and clear the wreck! "
The Dauber followed where he led; below
He caught one giddy glimpsing of the deck
Filled with white water, as though heaped with snow.
He saw the streamers of the rigging blow
Straight out like pennons from the splintered mast,
Then, all sense dimmed, all was an icy blast.

Roaring from nether hell and filled with ice,
Roaring and crashing on the jerking stage,
An utter bridle given to utter vice,
Limitless power mad with endless rage
Withering the soul; a minute seemed an age.
He clutched and hacked at ropes, at rags of sail,
Thinking that comfort was a fairy tale,

Told long ago — long, long ago — long since
Heard of in other lives — imagined, dreamed —
There where the basest beggar was a prince.
To him in torment where the tempest screamed,
Comfort and warmth and ease no longer seemed
Things that a man could know; soul, body, brain,
Knew nothing but the wind, the cold, the pain.

Tomorrow

Oh yesterday the cutting edge drank thirstily and deep,
The upland outlaws ringed us in and herded us as sheep,
They drove us from the stricken field and bayed us into keep;
    But tomorrow,
    By the living God, we'll try the game again!

Oh yesterday our little troop was ridden through and
    through,
Our swaying, tattered pennons fled, a broken, beaten few,
And all a summer afternoon they hunted us and slew;
    But tomorrow,
    By the living God, we'll try the game again!

And here upon the turret-top the bale-fire glowers red,
The wake-lights burn and drip about our hacked, disfigured
    dead,

And many a broken heart is here and many a broken head;
   But tomorrow,
By the living God, we'll try the game again!

W. W. GIBSON

Wilfrid Wilson Gibson was born in 1878 in Hexam among the gaunt Northumberland hills. His early work was imitative, derived from the romantic Victorians, sentimental in tone. The titles suggest the manner: *Urlyn the Harper* (1902), *The Queen's Vigil* (1903), and *The Nets of Love*.

Influenced by Masefield and the growing realism of the period, Gibson executed a complete right about face in his thirtieth year. With *Daily Bread* (1910), *Fires* (1912), *Borderlands* (1914), and *Livelihood* (1917) Gibson wrote a series of dramatic poems expressing the dreams, the labors, and the fears of common humanity. At his best in the dramatic monolog, Gibson justifies his title in England as "the poet of contemporary industrial life."

Gibson's later work suffers from a thinning out of power; facility is evident in *Krindlesyke* (1922) and *Kestrel Edge* (1924) but little else. Best and worst are combined in *Collected Poems: 1905–1925*, in which such poems as those here reprinted have a particular vitality.

The White Dust

I felt no tremor and I caught no sound;
But a fresh crack scored my ceiling: white dust dropped,
Sprinkling my polished table . . .
                         Underground,
Fathoms beneath my comfortable room,
In the pit's dripping gloom,
A new drift's rock-roof, insecurely propped,
Had settled; and, in settling, crushed just then
The life out of six men:
Six hearts had stopped . . .

But I, unguessing, looked up fretfully
At the fresh crack; and rose impatiently
To wipe the dust from my mahogany.

The Stone

" And will you cut a stone for him,
To set above his head?
And will you cut a stone for him —
A stone for him? " she said.

Three days before, a splintered rock
Had struck her lover dead —
Had struck him in the quarry dead,
Where, careless of the warning call,
He loitered, while the shot was fired —
A lively stripling, brave and tall,
And sure of all his heart desired . . .
A flash, a shock,
A rumbling fall . . .
And, broken 'neath the broken rock,
A lifeless heap, with face of clay;
And still as any stone he lay,
With eyes that saw the end of all.

I went to break the news to her;
And I could hear my own heart beat
With dread of what my lips might say.
But some poor fool had sped before;
And flinging wide her father's door,
Had blurted out the news to her,
Had struck her lover dead for her,
Had struck the girl's heart dead in her,
Had struck life, lifeless, at a word,
And dropped it at her feet:
Then hurried on his witless way,
Scarce knowing she had heard.

And when I came, she stood, alone
A woman, turned to stone:
And, though no word at all she said,
I knew that all was known.

Because her heart was dead,
She did not sigh nor moan,
His mother wept:

She could not weep.
Her lover slept:
She could not sleep.
Three days, three nights,
She did not stir:
Three days, three nights,
Were one to her,
Who never closed her eyes
From sunset to sunrise,
From dawn to evenfall:
Her tearless, staring eyes,
That seeing naught, saw all.

The fourth night when I came from work,
I found her at my door.
" And will you cut a stone for him? "
She said and spoke no more:
But followed me, as I went in,
And sank upon a chair;
And fixed her gray eyes on my face,
With still, unseeing stare.
And, as she waited patiently,
I could not bear to feel
Those still, gray eyes that followed me,
Those eyes that plucked the heart from me,
Those eyes that sucked the breath from me
And curdled the warm blood in me,
Those eyes that cut me to the bone,
And pierced my marrow like cold steel.

And so I rose, and sought a stone;
And cut it, smooth and square:
And, as I worked, she sat and watched,
Beside me, in her chair.
Night after night, by candlelight,
I cut her lover's name:
Night after night, so still and white,
And like a ghost she came;
And sat beside me in her chair;
And watched with eyes aflame.

She eyed each stroke;
And hardly stirred:

She never spoke
A single word:
And not a sound or murmur broke
The quiet, save the mallet-stroke.
With still eyes ever on my hands,
With eyes that seemed to burn my hands,
My wincing, overwearied hands,
She watched, with bloodless lips apart,
And silent, indrawn breath:
And every stroke my chisel cut,
Death cut still deeper in her heart:
The two of us were chiseling,
Together, I and death.

And when at length the job was done,
And I had laid the mallet by,
As if, at last, her peace were won,
She breathed his name; and, with a sigh,
Passed slowly through the open door:
And never crossed my threshold more.

Next night I labored late, alone,
To cut her name upon the stone.

Sight

By the lamplit stall I loitered, feasting my eyes
On colors ripe and rich for the heart's desire —
Tomatoes, redder than Krakatao's [1] fire,
Oranges like old sunsets over Tyre,
And apples golden-green as the glades of Paradise.

And as I lingered, lost in divine delight,
My heart thanked God for the goodly gift of sight
And all youth's lively senses keen and quick . . .
When suddenly, behind me in the night,
I heard the tapping of a blind man's stick.

[1] *Krakatao:* a great volcano near Java.

(Philip) Edward Thomas was born in 1878, was educated at Oxford, and supported himself for many years by writing reviews, travel-books, biographies, and odd literary jobs "to keep the pot boiling." It was only when Robert Frost came to England and took up his residence near the Thomas home that the English writer, influenced by the American, turned to poetry.

Loving, like Frost, the commonplaces of existence, the quaint and casual turn of ordinary life, Thomas caught the magic of the English countryside in its unpoetic aspects. *Poems* (1917), dedicated to Robert Frost, is full of Thomas's fidelity to little things, things as unglorified as the unfreezing of the "rock-like mud," a list of quaint-sounding villages, birds' nests uncovered by the autumn wind, dusty nettles. His lines glow with a deep reverence for the soil. *Last Poems* (published posthumously in 1919) is full of evidences that Thomas knew the life and landscapes of the country "from the inside." As Henry Newbolt has written, "He did not so much inhabit England as haunt it."

Thomas was killed at Arras, at an observatory outpost, on Easter Monday, 1917. His *Collected Poems* appeared in 1929 with an introduction by Walter de la Mare.

Tall Nettles

Tall nettles cover up, as they have done
These many springs, the rusty harrow, the plow
Long worn out, and the roller made of stone:
Only the elm butt tops the nettles now.

This corner of the farmyard I like most:
As well as any bloom upon a flower
I like the dust on the nettles, never lost
Except to prove the sweetness of a shower.

If I Should Ever by Chance

If I should ever by chance grow rich
I'll buy Codham, Cockridden, and Childerditch,
Roses, Pyrgo, and Lapwater,[1]
And let them all to my elder daughter.

[1] *Codham, Cockridden, Childerditch . . . Lapwater:* places in rural England. Thomas chose them because of the music in the names.

The rent I shall ask of her will be only
Each year's first violets, white and lonely,
The first primroses and orchises —
She must find them before I do, that is.
But if she finds a blossom on furze [1]
Without rent they shall all forever be hers,
Codham, Cockridden, and Childerditch,
Roses, Pyrgo, and Lapwater, —
I shall give them all to my elder daughter.

Cock-Crow

Out of the wood of thoughts that grows by night
To be cut down by the sharp ax of light, —
Out of the night, two cocks together crow,
Cleaving the darkness with a silver blow:
And brought before my eyes twin trumpeters stand,
Heralds of splendor, one at either hand,
Each facing each as in a coat of arms: —
The milkers lace their boots up at the farms.

Thaw

Over the land freckled with snow half-thawed
The speculating rooks at their nests cawed,
And saw from elm-tops, delicate as flower of grass,
What we below could not see, Winter pass.

HAROLD MONRO

Harold (Edward) Monro was born in 1879 in Brussels, was educated at Cambridge, scorned poetry as an undergraduate, but began writing verse soon after he was graduated. In 1912 Monro founded The Poetry Bookshop, an establishment which became a London literary center, and edited the quarterly *Poetry and Drama*, which became the organ of the younger men. His own volumes, *Before Dawn* (1911) and *Children of Love* (1914), were

[1] *Furze:* a spiny shrub with yellow flowers.

important contributions to the Georgian movement. Monro died March 16, 1932.

Monro's later poetry, notably in *Strange Meetings* (1917) and *Real Property* (1922), reveals a mysticism which depicts the play between the world of reality and the world of fantasy. Even the most whimsical ideas attain intensity in Monro's curious and original lines. No writer has done more with " still life," or with the passing event and its effect upon the mind. " Every Thing " is an excellent illustration of Monro's power of animating the inanimate. The bed " sighs," the kettle puffs and breathes and complains, the copper basin rattles and seems to cry as it tumbles, the gas jet flares suddenly, the rafters creak of their own will, a door swings open by itself, the clock " stirs all its body " and strikes the hour. The whole poem is a sort of humorous hymn to the common " Teraphim," to the ordinary utensils and furnishings, which are not only man's household goods but his unacknowledged household gods.

Wind in the Dusk

So wayward is the wind tonight
'Twill send the planets tumbling down;
And all the roaring trees are dight [1]
In gauzes wafted from the moon.

Faint, streaky wisps of roaming cloud
Are swiftly from the mountain swirled;
The wind is like a floating shroud
Wound lightly round a shivering world.

I think I see a little star
Entangled in a knotty tree,
As trembling fishes captured are
In nets from the eternal sea.

There seems a bevy in the air
Of spirits from the sparkling skies;
There seems a maiden with her hair
All tumbled in my blinded eyes.

Blow! Scatter even if you will
The stars like spray about my eyes!
Wind, overturn the goblet, spill
On me the everlasting skies!

> [1] *dight:* an old form of " clothed " or " adorned."

Every Thing

Since man has been articulate,
Mechanical, improvidently wise,
(Servant of Fate),
He has not understood the little cries
And foreign conversations of the small
Delightful creatures that have followed him
Not far behind;
Has failed to hear the sympathetic call
Of Crockery and Cutlery, those kind
Reposeful Teraphim [1]
Of his domestic happiness; the Stool
He sat on, or the Door he entered through:
He has not thanked them, overbearing fool!
What is he coming to?

But you should listen to the talk of these.
Honest they are, and patient they have kept;
Served him without his Thank you or his Please . .
I often heard
The gentle Bed, a sigh between each word,
Murmuring, before I slept.
The Candle, as I blew it, cried aloud,
Then bowed,
And in a smoky argument
Into the darkness went.

The Kettle puffed a tentacle of breath: —
"Pooh! I have boiled his water, I don't know
Why; and he always says I boil too slow.
He never calls me 'Sukie, dear,' and oh,
I wonder why I squander my desire
Sitting submissive on his kitchen fire."

Now the old Copper Basin suddenly
Rattled and tumbled from the shelf,
Bumping and crying: "I can fall by myself;

[1] Seraphim, mentioned in the Bible, are angels, celestial beings.
Teraphim, on the other hand, are earthly objects of reverence —
terra: earth. In this sense, and in this poem, they are household
gods.

Without a woman's hand
To patronize and coax and flatter me,
I understand
The lean and poise of gravitable land."
It gave a raucous and tumultuous shout,
Twisted itself convulsively about,
Rested upon the floor, and, while I stare,
It stares and grins at me.
The old impetuous Gas above my head
Begins irascibly to flare and fret,
Wheezing into its epileptic jet,
Reminding me I ought to go to bed.

The Rafters creak; and Empty-Cupboard door
Swings open; now a wild Plank of the floor
Breaks from its joist, and leaps behind my foot.
Down from the chimney, half a pound of Soot
Tumbles and lies, and shakes itself again.
The Putty cracks against the window-pane.
A piece of Paper in the basket shoves
Another piece, and toward the bottom moves.
My independent Pencil, while I write,
Breaks at the point: the ruminating Clock
Stirs all its body and begins to rock,
Warning the waiting presence of the Night,
Strikes the dead hour, and tumbles to the plain
Ticking of ordinary work again.

You do well to remind me, and I praise
Your strangely individual foreign ways.
You call me from myself to recognize
Companionship in your unselfish eyes.
I want your dear acquaintances, although
I pass you arrogantly over, throw
Your lovely sounds, and squander them along
My busy days. I'll do you no more wrong.

Purr for me, Sukie, like a faithful cat.
You, my well-trampled Boots, and you, my Hat,
Remain my friends: I feel, though I don't speak,
Your touch grow kindlier from week to week.
It well becomes our mutual happiness
To go toward the same end more or less.

There is not much dissimilarity,
Not much to choose, I know it well, in fine,
Between the purposes of you and me,
And your eventual Rubbish Heap, and mine.

The Guest

(*A Christmas Prayer*)

Tall, cool and gentle, you are here
To turn the water into wine.
Now, at the ebbing of the year,
Be you the sun we need to shine.

It is the birthday of your word;
And we are gathered. Will you come?
Let not your spirit be a sword,
O, luminous delightful lord.

ALFRED NOYES

Alfred Noyes was born at Staffordshire, September 16, 1880, and educated at Exeter College, Oxford. He is one of the few contemporary poets who have been fortunate enough to write a kind of poetry that is not only salable but popular with many classes of people.

His first book, *The Loom of Years* (1902), was published when he was twenty-two years old, and *Poems* (1904) intensified his promise. Unfortunately, Noyes has not developed his gifts as deeply as his admirers have hoped. His poetry, extremely straightforward and rhythmical, has often degenerated into sentimentalities; it has also attempted to express profundities far beyond Noyes's power.

What is most appealing about Noyes is his ease and heartiness; his gift lies in the almost personal bond established between the poet and his public. People have so good a time reading his vivacious lines because Noyes had so good a time writing them. Noyes's own gusto quickens glees and catches like *Forty Singing Seamen* (1907), the lusty choruses in *Tales of the Mermaid Tavern* (1913), and the inspired nonsense of *The Forest of Wild Thyme* (1905).

Eight volumes were assembled in 1913 and published in two books of *Collected Poems;* a third collection appeared in 1920; a fourth in 1927. Although many of these pages are doomed to an early death — are, in fact, already extinct — Noyes will remain a poet pleasant to read because of the melodious "Sherwood," the lilt of "The Barrel-Organ," the gallop of "The Highwayman," and a handful of other ballads.

The Barrel-Organ

There's a barrel-organ caroling across a golden street
   In the City as the sun sinks low;
And the music's not immortal; but the world has made it
   sweet
   And fulfilled it with the sunset glow;
And it pulses through the pleasures of the City and the pain
   That surround the singing organ like a large eternal light;
And they've given it a glory and a part to play again
   In the Symphony that rules the day and night.

And now it's marching onward through the realms of old ro-
   mance,
   And trolling out a fond familiar tune,
And now it's roaring cannon down to fight the King of
   France,
   And now it's prattling softly to the moon.
And all around the organ there's a sea without a shore
   Of human joys and wonders and regrets;
To remember and to recompense the music evermore
   For what the cold machinery forgets . . .

        Yes; as the music changes,
          Like a prismatic glass,
        It takes the light and ranges
          Through all the moods that pass;
        Dissects the common carnival
          Of passions and regrets,
        And gives the world a glimpse of all
          The colors it forgets.

        And there *La Traviata* sighs
          Another sadder song;

And there *Il Trovatore* [1] cries
   A tale of deeper wrong;
And bolder knights to battle go
   With sword and shield and lance,
Than ever here on earth below
   Have whirled into — a dance!

Go down to Kew in lilac-time, in lilac-time, in lilac-time;
   Go down to Kew in lilac-time (it isn't far from London!)
And you shall wander hand in hand with love in summer's
     wonderland;
   Go down to Kew in lilac-time (it isn't far from London!)

The cherry-trees are seas of bloom and soft perfume and
     sweet prefume,
   The cherry-trees are seas of bloom (and oh, so near to
     London!)
And there they say, when dawn is high and all the world's a
     blaze of sky
   The cuckoo, though he's very shy, will sing a song for
     London.
The nightingale is rather rare and yet they say you'll hear
     him there
   At Kew, at Kew in lilac-time (and oh, so near to London!)
The linnet and the throstle, too, and after dark the long
     halloo
   And golden-eyed *tu-whit, tu-whoo* of owls that ogle
     London.

For Noah hardly knew a bird of any kind that isn't heard
   At Kew, at Kew in lilac-time (and oh, so near to London!)
And when the rose begins to pout and all the chestnut spires
     are out
   You'll hear the rest, without a doubt, all chorusing for
     London: —

Come down to Kew in lilac-time, in lilac-time, in lilac-time;
   Come down to Kew in lilac-time (it isn't far from
     London!)

[1] *La Traviata* (The Lost One) and *Il Trovatore* (The Troubadour) are two of Verdi's most popular operas. The former is
based on Dumas' touching tale, *La Dame aux Camélias* (" Ca-
mille "); both operas were first heard in 1853.

And you shall wander hand in hand with love in summer's
wonderland;
  Come down to Kew in lilac-time (it isn't far from
  London!)

And then the troubadour begins to thrill the golden street,
  In the City as the sun sinks low;
And in all the gaudy busses there are scores of weary feet
Marking time, sweet time, with a dull mechanic beat,
And a thousand hearts are plunging to a love they'll never
      meet,
Through the meadows of the sunset, through the poppies
      and the wheat,
  In the land where the dead dreams go.

Verdi, Verdi, when you wrote *Il Trovatore* did you dream
  Of the City when the sun sinks low,
Of the organ and the monkey and the many-colored stream
On the Piccadilly pavement, of the myriad eyes that seem
To be litten for a moment with a wild Italian gleam
As *A che la morte* [1] parodies the world's eternal theme
  And pulses with the sunset-glow?

There's a thief, perhaps, that listens with a face of frozen
      stone
  In the City as the sun sinks low;
There's a portly man of business with a balance of his own,
There's a clerk and there's a butcher of a soft reposeful tone,
And they're all of them returning to the heavens they have
      known:
They are crammed and jammed in busses and — they're each
      of them alone
  In the land where the dead dreams go.

There's a laborer that listens to the voices of the dead
  In the City as the sun sinks low;
And his hand begins to tremble and his face is rather red
As he sees a loafer watching him and — there he turns his
      head

[1] *A che la morte:* a phrase which is heard near the end of the
famous "Miserere" in Verdi's opera, *Il Trovatore.* The sentence,
of which the phrase is a part, means "Ah, how slow is death to
him who wants to die."

And stares into the sunset where his April love is fled,
For he hears her softly singing and his lonely soul is led
  Through the land where the dead dreams go . . .

There's a barrel-organ caroling across a golden street
  In the City as the sun sinks low;
Though the music's only Verdi there's a world to make it
    sweet
Just as yonder yellow sunset where the earth and heaven
    meet
Mellows all the sooty City! Hark, a hundred thousand feet
Are marching on to glory through the poppies and the wheat
  In the land where the dead dreams go.

            So it's Jeremiah, Jeremiah,
              What have you to say
            When you meet the garland girls
              Tripping on their way?
            All around my gala hat
              I wear a wreath of roses
            (A long and lonely year it is
              I've waited for the May!)
            If anyone should ask you,
              The reason why I wear it is —
            My own love, my true love is coming
                home today.

And it's buy a bunch of violets for the lady
  (*It's lilac-time in London; its lilac-time in London!*)
Buy a bunch of violets for the lady;
  While the sky burns blue above:

On the other side the street you'll find it shady
  (*It's lilac-time in London; it's lilac-time in London!*)
But buy a bunch of violets for the lady,
  And tell her she's your own true love.

There's a barrel-organ caroling across a golden street
  In the City as the sun sinks glittering and slow;
And the music's not immortal; but the world has made it
    sweet
And enriched it with the harmonies that make a song com-
    plete

In the deeper heavens of music where the night and morning
    meet,
  As it dies into the sunset glow;
And it pulses through the pleasures of the City and the pain
  That surround the singing organ like a large eternal light,
And they've given it a glory and a part to play again
  In the Symphony that rules the day and night.

> And there, as the music changes,
>   The song runs round again;
> Once more it turns and ranges
>   Through all its joy and pain:
> Dissects the common carnival
>   Of passions and regrets;
> And the wheeling world remembers all
>   The wheeling song forgets.

Come down to Kew in lilac-time, in lilac-time, in lilac-time;
  Come down to Kew in lilac-time (it isn't far from
    London!)
And you shall wander hand in hand with Love in summer's
  wonderland,
  Come down to Kew in lilac-time (it isn't far from
    London!)

PADRAIC COLUM

Padraic Colum was born at Longford, Ireland (in the same
county as Oliver Goldsmith), December 8, 1881, and was educated
at the local schools. At twenty he was a member of a group that
created the Irish National Theatre. He has lived in America since
1914, mostly in New York City.

Colum began as a dramatist with *Broken Soil* (1904) and *The
Land* (1905), and this early dramatic tendency has colored much
of his work. *Wild Earth*, his most notable collection of verse, first
appeared in 1909, and an amplified edition of it was published in
America in 1916. His *Dramatic Poems* appeared in 1922, *Creatures*,
beautifully illustrated, in 1927. These were followed by *Old Pastures* (1930) and *Flower Pieces* (1939). Colum is also successful
as an adapter, sensitive as a critic, and deservedly popular as a
teller of tales for children.

"The Plower" is a kind of companion-piece to Edwin Markham's "The Man with the Hoe" on page 62. Here, too, the figure of the laborer, etched against the sunset, is enlarged into something symbolic. In both poems the dumb, driven toiler is revealed as one who is capable not only of drudgery but dreams, the "upward looking and the light" (in Markham's poem) and, in Colum's lines, "the height up to heaven and the thrones of the gods."

The Plower

Sunset and silence! A man: around him earth savage, earth
      broken;
Beside him two horses — a plow!

Earth savage, earth broken, the brutes, the dawn man there
      in the sunset,
And the Plow that is twin to the Sword, that is founder of
      cities!

"Brute-tamer, plow-maker, earth-breaker! Can'st hear?
      There are ages between us.
"Is it praying you are as you stand there alone in the
      sunset?

"Surely our sky-born gods can be naught to you, earth child
      and earth master?
"Surely your thoughts are of Pan, or of Wotan, or Dana? [1]

"Yet, why give thought to the gods? Has Pan led your brutes
      where they stumble?
"Has Dana numbled pain of the child-bed, or Wotan put
      hands to your plow?

"What matter your foolish reply! O, man, standing lone and
      bowed earthward,
"Your task is a day near its close. Give thanks to the night-
      giving God." . . .

Slowly the darkness falls, the broken lands blend with the
      savage;

[1] Pan, Wotan, and Dana are mythological gods, all earth-bound spirits, often identified in myths with the fruits and toil of the earth. Pan is Greek, Wotan is Scandinavian, Dana is Irish.

The brute-tamer stands by the brutes, a head's breadth only
    above them.

A head's breadth? Ay, but therein is hell's depth, and the
    height up to heaven,
And the thrones of the gods and their halls, their chariots,
    purples, and splendors.

JOSEPH CAMPBELL

Joseph Campbell was born in Belfast in 1881, and is not only a
poet but an artist; he made the illustrations for *The Rushlight*
(1906), a volume of his own poems. Writing under the Gaelic
form of his name, Seosamh MacCathmhaoil, he has published half
a dozen books of verse, the most striking of which is *The Moun-
tainy Singer*, first published in Dublin in 1909. *Earth of Cualann*
(1917) is a more substantial offering.

The Old Woman

As a white candle
   In a holy place,
So is the beauty
   Of an aged face.

As the spent radiance
   Of the winter sun,
So is a woman
   With her travail done.

Her brood gone from her,
   And her thoughts as still
As the waters
   Under a ruined mill.

James Stephens was born in Dublin, February, 1882, in humble surroundings. He had no formal education; he spent his youth in poverty, wandering about Ireland, frequently on the verge of starvation. Even in early manhood, after he had obtained a position as typist, he supported a wife and child for years on less than seven dollars a week. Finally one of his contributions to a magazine was noticed by George Russell (" Æ "), who encouraged Stephens and finally rescued him from clerical slavery.

Everything Stephens has written, from the early verses in *Insurrections* (1909) to *Strict Joy* (1931), from the imaginative and poetic novel *The Crock of Gold* (1912) to the somber short stories in *Etched in Moonlight* (1928), reveals a mind which is both fantastic and philosophic. Even when Stephens is most amusing he is meaningful. A poem such as " To the Four Courts, Please " is ironic but touching; " The Shell " turns from the imaginary world to the realistic everyday world in the sudden contrast of the last two lines.

The chief fault of his verse is Stephens' fondness for making his simple people a little too simple and ultra-poetic; but the main effect of his prose and verse is to help form a new basis of Irish legendry, to give his native land a mythology as dramatic and as dignified as the mythology of the ancient classic world. A cumulative picture of Stephens' growth is offered in his *Collected Poems* (1926). Stephens died December 26, 1950.

The Shell

And then I pressed the shell
Close to my ear
And listened well,
And straightway like a bell
Came low and clear
The slow, sad murmur of the distant seas,
Whipped by an icy breeze
Upon a shore
Wind-swept and desolate.
It was a sunless strand that never bore
The footprint of a man,
Nor felt the weight
Since time began
Of any human quality or stir
Save what the dreary winds and waves incur.
And in the hush of waters was the sound
Of pebbles rolling round,

Forever rolling with a hollow sound.
And bubbling sea-weeds as the waters go,
Swish to and fro
Their long, cold tentacles of slimy gray.
There was no day,
Nor ever came a night
Setting the stars alight
To wonder at the moon:
Was twilight only and the frightened croon,
Smitten to whimpers, of the dreary wind
And waves that journeyed blind —
And then I loosed my ear. . . . O, it was sweet
To hear a cart go jolting down the street.

To the Four Courts, Please

The driver rubbed at his nettly chin
With a huge, loose forefinger, crooked and black,
And his wobbly, violet lips sucked in,
And puffed out again and hung down slack:
One fang shone through his lop-sided smile,
In his little pouched eye flickered years of guile.

And the horse, poor beast, it was ribbed and forked,
And its ears hung down, and its eyes were old,
And its knees were knuckly, and as we talked
It swung the stiff neck that could scarcely hold
Its big, skinny head up — then I stepped in,
And the driver climbed to his seat with a grin.

God help the horse and the driver too,
And the people and beasts who have never a friend,
For the driver easily might have been you,
And the horse be me by a different end.
And nobody knows how their days will cease,
And the poor, when they're old, have little of peace.

Little Things

Little things that run and quail
And die in silence and despair:

Little things that fight and fail
And fall on earth and sea and air;

All trapped and frightened little things,
The mouse, the coney,[1] hear our prayer.

As we forgive those done to us,
The lamb, the linnet, and the hare,

Forgive us all our trespasses,
Little creatures everywhere.

What Tomas An Buile Said in a Pub [2]

I saw God. Do you doubt it?
  Do you dare to doubt it?
I saw the Almighty Man. His hand
Was resting on a mountain, and
He looked upon the World and all about it:
I saw him plainer than you see me now,
  You mustn't doubt it.

He was not satisfied;
  His look was all dissatisfied.
His beard swung on a wind far out of sight
Behind the world's curve, and there was light
Most fearful from His forehead, and He sighed,
" That star went always wrong, and from the start
  I was dissatisfied."

He lifted up His hand —
  I say He heaved a dreadful hand
Over the spinning Earth. Then I said, " Stay,
You must not strike it, God; I'm in the way;
And I will never move from where I stand."
He said, " Dear child, I feared that you were dead,"
  And stayed His hand.

[1] *Coney:* rabbit.

[2] Tomas An Buile is one of Stephens' most imaginative creations. A great drinker and boaster, Tomas stands at the bar of a pub (saloon) and spins a mighty yarn in which he pictures himself and God on intimate terms.

Good and Bad

Good and bad and right and wrong,
Wave the silly words away:
This is wisdom to be strong,
This is virtue to be gay:
Let us sing and dance until
We shall know the final art,
How to banish good and ill
With the laughter of the heart.

JOHN DRINKWATER

John Drinkwater was born at Leytonstone, Essex, in 1882. Although he is best known as a dramatist, and particularly for his *Abraham Lincoln* (1918), a play founded on Lord Charnwood's biography, he began with verse and continually returned to it. Drinkwater was one of the group known as the Georgians (see p. 255), and his own volumes carry out their program, being mildly pastoral in setting and meditative in mood. His books of poems number about thirty; the best of his verses were chosen for *Selected Poems* (1922). Drinkwater died in 1937.

A Town Window

Beyond my window in the night
  Is but a drab inglorious street,
Yet there the frost and clean starlight
  As over Warwick woods are sweet.

Under the gray drift of the town
  The crocus works among the mold
As eagerly as those that crown
  The Warwick spring in flame and gold.

And when the tramway down the hill
  Across the cobbles moans and rings,
There is about my window-sill
  The tumult of a thousand wings.

Reciprocity

I do not think that skies and meadows are
Moral, or that the fixture of a star
Comes of a quiet spirit, or that trees
Have wisdom in their windless silences.
Yet these are things invested in my mood
With constancy, and peace, and fortitude;
That in my troubled season I can cry
Upon the wide composure of the sky,
And envy fields, and wish that I might be
As little daunted as a star or tree.

ANNA WICKHAM

Anna Wickham was born in Wimbledon, Surrey, in 1883. She
went to Australia at six, returned when she was twenty-one,
studied for opera in Paris with De Reszke and suddenly, after a
few years of marriage, became a poet. In a burst of creative energy
she wrote nine hundred poems in four years.

Her first two books were republished in America in one volume, *The Contemplative Quarry* (1921). The most casual reading
of Anna Wickham's work reveals the strength of her candor. The
poems could scarcely be put in the category of " charming " verse;
they are sometimes harsh, gnarled by their own changes of mood.
Her lines present the picture of woman struggling between dreams
and domesticity; they are acutely sensitive, restless, analytical. The
very tone of her poetry reflects the disturbed music and the
nervous intensity of the poet and her age. But, even when this
poet is most perturbed by her problems, she does not forget to
sing

Song

I was so chill, and overworn, and sad,
To be a lady was the only joy I had.
I walked the street as silent as a mouse,
Buying fine clothes, and fittings for the house.

But since I saw my love
I wear a simple dress,
And happily I move
Forgetting weariness.

Domestic Economy

I will have few cooking-pots,
They shall be bright;
They shall reflect to blinding
God's straight light.
I will have four garments,
They shall be clean;
My service shall be good,
Though my diet be mean.
Then I shall have excess to give to the poor,
And right to counsel beggars at my door.

The Singer

If I had peace to sit and sing,
Then I could make a lovely thing;
But I am stung with goads and whips,
So I build songs like iron ships.

Let it be something for my song,
If it is sometimes swift and strong.

Envoi

God, thou great symmetry,
Who put a biting lust in me
From whence my sorrows spring,
For all the frittered days
That I have spent in shapeless ways,
Give me one perfect thing.

D(avid) H(erbert) Lawrence was born September 17, 1885, in the mining town of Eastwood. Both his parents were workers. Lawrence gives a graphic picture of his boyhood in *Sons and Lovers* (1913); several other novels return to the scene of his youth. Lawrence obtained a scholarship, became a clerk, then a teacher, and published his first book, *The White Peacock*, in his twenty-fifth year.

Known chiefly for his highly poetic prose, Lawrence cared more for his vividly colored and passionate poetry. His volumes of verse were gathered in the two-volume *Collected Poems* (1929), which are an extended autobiography of the flesh and spirit. Many of the poems are slight — " Green " shows why, for a time, Lawrence joined the Imagists — but almost all speak eloquently with " the hot blood's blindfold art."

After a struggle of many years, Lawrence succumbed to tuberculosis and died in France, March 2, 1930. In less than ten years after his death, there appeared ten different biographies, portraits, and interpretations — and almost as many quarrels among the interpreters.

Piano

Softly, in the dusk, a woman is singing to me;
Taking me back down the vista of years, till I see
A child sitting under the piano, in the boom of the tingling strings
And pressing the small, poised feet of a mother who smiles as she sings.

In spite of myself, the insidious mastery of song
Betrays me back, till the heart of me weeps to belong
To the old Sunday evenings at home, with winter outside
And hymns in the cozy parlor, the tinkling piano our guide.

So now it is vain for the singer to burst into clamor
With the great black piano appassionato. The glamour
Of childish days is upon me, my manhood is cast
Down in the flood of remembrance, I weep like a child for the past.

Green

The dawn was apple-green,
The sky was green wine held up in the sun,
The moon was a golden petal between.

She opened her eyes, and green
They shone, clear like flowers undone
For the first time, now for the first time seen.

A White Blossom

A tiny moon as small and white as a single jasmine flower
Leans all alone above my window, on night's wintry bower,
Liquid as lime-tree blossom, soft as brilliant water or rain
She shines, the first white love of my youth, passionless and
     in vain.

HUMBERT WOLFE

Humbert Wolfe was born at Milan, Italy, January 5, 1885. As
he himself declared, he "lost no time in crossing to Bradford in
Yorkshire, which town he reached during the same year, and remained there till he left it for Oxford some eighteen years later.
Wrote increasingly unsatisfactory verse from the age of sixteen till
his appointment to the British Civil Service in 1909. This appointment naturally induced in him a more restrained outlook upon
life, and, beyond a few casual poems and a rejected novel, he had
no literary output or recognition till after the War in 1919. In that
year, he published *London Sonnets*, followed by *Shylock Reasons
with Mr. Chesterton.*"

After 1923 Wolfe's output increased rapidly. Between that year
and 1938 he published eighteen volumes, all but three of them in
verse. The outstanding quality, from the delicate *Kensington
Gardens* (1924) to the somber *Requiem* (1927), is the combination
of grace and gravity. Sometimes the seriousness weighs down the
light fancy; sometimes the charm seems out of place against a
grimly serious background. But, generally, Wolfe's touch is sure,
sensitive, and skillful. From the craftsman's standpoint Wolfe is
most interesting for his technical innovations, his curiously divided
lines, and his use of "suspended" rhyme. But every reader can

relish the wit and whimsicality which distinguish this versatile poet.

In addition to his other activities, Wolfe edited two anthologies and a series of poetry pamphlets, made a sequence of paraphrases from the Greek Anthology, *Others Abide* (1927), and published his Greek translations at the same time as his *Cursory Rhymes* (1927), a set of sophisticated burlesques for children. Wolfe died of a heart attack in 1940.

The Gray Squirrel

Like a small gray
coffee-pot,
sits the squirrel.
He is not

all he should be,
kills by dozens
trees, and eats
his red-brown cousins.

The keeper, on the
other hand
, who shot him, is
a Christian, and

loves his enemies,
which shows
the squirrel was not
one of those.

Green Candles

" There's someone at the door," said gold candlestick:
" Let her in quick, let her in quick! "
" There is a small hand groping at the handle.
Why don't you turn it? " asked green candle.

" Don't go, don't go," said the Hepplewhite chair,
" Lest you find a strange lady there."
" Yes, stay where you are," whispered the white wall:
" There is nobody there at all."

"I know her little foot," gray carpet said:
"Who but I should know her light tread?"
"She shall come in," answered the open door,
"And not," said the room, "go out any more."

Love in Jeopardy [1]

Here by the rose-tree
   they planted once
of Love in Jeopardy
   an Italian bronze.

Not love the conqueror,
   not love with wings,
but a boy waiting for
   perilous things:

his bow unstrung,
   unsounded the zither,
and the delicate young
   hands clasped together.

As grave as the first
   boy with the first maiden,
outside of the curst
   closed gates of Eden.

But they have ravished
   away this love,
and he is not cherished
   nor spoken of,

save, whenas fluted
   from Eden, blows
for two the transmuted
   phrase of the rose,

thorn-note, blossom-note,
   note of the petal,
cool as the rain, but
   trembling a little

[1] *Love in Jeopardy:* see page xxxvi.

as though, brought hither
   from far, one sung
to a mute zither,
   with bow unstrung,

how by a rose-tree
   they planted once
of Love in Jeopardy
   an Italian bronze.

The Lilac

Who thought of the lilac?
" I," dew said,
" I made up the lilac
out of my head."

" She made up the lilac!
Pooh! " trilled a linnet,
and each dew-note had a
lilac in it.

FRANCES CORNFORD

Frances (Darwin) Cornford, a granddaughter of Charles Darwin, was born in Cambridge in 1886. She married Francis Macdonald Cornford, Lecturer of Trinity College, Cambridge, in 1909. Among her volumes the most distinctive are *Spring Morning* (1915) and *Autumn Midnight* (1923), which include the simple and spontaneous " A Wasted Day " and the delightfully mocking triolet (one of the most delicate of the French forms) " To a Fat Lady Seen from the Train."

A Wasted Day

I spoiled the day;
   Hotly, in haste
All the calm hours
   I gashed and defaced.

Let me forget,
   Let me embark
— Sleep for my boat —
   And sail through the dark.

Till a new day
   Heaven shall send,
Whole as an apple,
   Kind as a friend.

To a Fat Lady Seen from the Train

O why do you walk through the fields in gloves,
   Missing so much and so much?
O fat white woman whom nobody loves,
Why do you walk through the fields in gloves,
When the grass is soft as the breast of doves
   And shivering sweet to the touch?
O why do you walk through the fields in gloves,
   Missing so much and so much?

SIEGFRIED SASSOON

Siegfried (Lorraine) Sassoon was born September 8, 1886. Educated at Marlborough and Clare College, Cambridge, Sassoon spent his youth fox-hunting and verse-making. His early life as a country gentleman was to be strongly contrasted with his later war experiences, although in recent years Sassoon has become well-known for his chronicles of the graceful days of Edwardian England. Between 1906 and 1915 Sassoon privately printed several volumes which were unconsciously imitative of Tennyson and Rossetti. With *The Old Huntsman* (1917) Sassoon found his own idiom and was hailed as "one of England's most brilliant rising stars." The first poem, a long monolog obviously inspired by Masefield, gave little evidence of what was to come. Immediately following it came a series of war poems full of tragedy and bitterness. Every line of these quivering stanzas bore the mark of a sensitive and outraged nature; there was scarcely a phrase that did not protest against the "glorification" and false glamour of war.

In the First World War, Sassoon was a captain in the Royal

Welsh Fusileers; he served three times in France, once in Palestine, and was awarded the Military Cross for bringing in wounded under fire. His poems written in the trenches sounded an entirely new note, an outcry of anguish which was often disguised in irony. *Counter-Attack* appeared in 1918. In this volume Sassoon turned completely to the gigantic brutality of war. The bloody years twisted his tenderness till what was stubborn and satiric in him forced its way to the top. In *Counter-Attack* Sassoon found his angry outlet. Most of these poems are choked with passion; many of them are torn out, roots and all, from the very core of an intense conviction.

Early in 1920 Sassoon visited America. At the same time he brought out *Picture Show* (1920), a vigorous answer to those who feared that Sassoon had "written himself out." *Recreations* (1923), a privately distributed volume, shows Sassoon in a more playfully intellectual vein. Less direct than his deeper notes, these poems display another side of Sassoon's genius. *Satirical Poems*, a collection of this *genre*, was published in 1926. A comprehensive *Collected Poems* appeared in 1949.

Sassoon's slightly disguised autobiography consisted of several volumes, beginning with *Memoirs of a Fox-Hunting Man* (1928), which was awarded two coveted English literary prizes, and included *Memoirs of an Infantry Officer* (1930), *Sherston's Progress* (1936) and *The Old Century and Seven More Years* (1938).

The Dug-Out

Why do you lie with your legs ungainly huddled,
And one arm bent across your sullen, cold,
Exhausted face? It hurts my heart to watch you,
Deep-shadowed from the candle's guttering gold;
And you wonder why I shake you by the shoulder;
Drowsy, you mumble and sigh and turn your head. . . .
You are too young to fall asleep forever;
And when you sleep you remind me of the dead.

Dreamers

Soldiers are citizens of death's gray land,
    Drawing no dividend from time's tomorrows.
In the great hour of destiny they stand,
    Each with his feuds, and jealousies, and sorrows.
Soldiers are sworn to action: they must win

Some flaming, fatal climax with their lives.
Soldiers are dreamers; when the guns begin
   They think of firelit homes, clean beds, and wives.

I see them in foul dug-outs, gnawed by rats,
   And in the ruined trenches, lashed with rain,
Dreaming of things they did with balls and bats,
   And mocked by hopeless longing to regain
Bank-holidays, and picture shows, and spats,
   And going to the office in the train.

The Rear-Guard

Groping along the tunnel, step by step,
He winked his prying torch with patching glare
From side to side, and sniffed the unwholesome air.

Tins, boxes, bottles, shapes too vague to know,
A mirror smashed, the mattress from a bed;
And he, exploring fifty feet below
The rosy gloom of battle overhead.
Tripping, he grabbed the wall; saw someone lie
Humped at his feet, half-hidden by a rug,
And stooped to give the sleeper's arm a tug.
" I'm looking for headquarters." No reply.
" God blast your neck! " (For days he'd had no sleep.)
" Get up and guide me through this stinking place."
Savage, he kicked a soft, unanswering heap,
And flashed his beam across the livid face
Terribly glaring up, whose eyes yet wore
Agony dying hard ten days before;
And fists of fingers clutched a blackening wound.
Alone he staggered on until he found
Dawn's ghost that filtered down a shafted stair
To the dazed, muttering creatures underground
Who hear the boom of shells in muffled sound.
At last, with sweat of horror in his hair,
He climbed through darkness to the twilight air,
Unloading hell behind him step by step.

Does It Matter?

Does it matter? — losing your leg? . . .
For people will always be kind,
And you need not show that you mind
When the others come in after hunting
To gobble their muffins and eggs.

Does it matter? — losing your sight? . . .
There's such splendid work for the blind;
And people will always be kind,
As you sit on the terrace remembering
And turning your face to the light.

Do they matter? — those dreams from the pit? . . .
You can drink and forget and be glad,
And people won't say that you're mad;
For they'll know that you've fought for your country
And no one will worry a bit.

Base Details

If I were fierce and bald and short of breath,
　　I'd live with scarlet Majors at the Base,
And speed glum heroes up the line to death.
　　You'd see me with my puffy petulant face,
Guzzling and gulping in the best hotel,
　　Reading the Roll of Honor. "Poor young chap,"
I'd say — "I used to know his father well.
　　Yes, we've lost heavily in this last scrap."
And when the war is done and youth stone dead,
I'd toddle safely home and die — in bed.

Aftermath

Have you forgotten yet? . . .
For the world's events have rumbled on since those gagged
　　days,
Like traffic checked awhile at the crossing of city ways:
And the haunted gap in your mind has filled with thoughts
　　that flow

Like clouds in the lit heavens of life; and you're a man re-
      prieved to go,
Taking your peaceful share of Time, with joy to spare.

But the past is just the same,— and War's a bloody
      game. . . .
Have you forgotten yet? . . .
Look down, and swear by the slain of the War that you'll
      never forget.

Do you remember the dark months you held the sector at
      Mametz, —
The night you watched and wired and dug and piled sand-
      bags on parapets?
Do you remember the rats; and the stench
Of corpses rotting in front of the front-line trench, —
And dawn coming, dirty-white, and chill with a hopeless
      rain?
Do you ever stop and ask, " Is it all going to happen again? "

Do you remember that hour of din before the attack, —
And the anger, the blind compassion that seized and shook
      you then
As you peered at the doomed and haggard faces of your
      men?
Do you remember the stretcher-cases lurching back
With dying eyes and lolling heads, those ashen-gray
Masks of the lads who once were keen and kind and gay?

Have you forgotten yet? . . .
Look up, and swear by the green of the Spring that you'll
      never forget.

Everyone Sang [1]

      Everyone suddenly burst out singing;
      And I was filled with such delight
      As prisoned birds must find in freedom
      Winging wildly across the white
      Orchards and dark green fields; on; on;
            and out of sight.

      This poem expresses the feeling released by the armistice, the
sudden joy after what seemed an eternity of war and darkness.

Everyone's voice was suddenly lifted,
And beauty came like the setting sun.
My heart was shaken with tears, and horror
Drifted away. . . . O, but every one
Was a bird; and the song was wordless; the
singing will never be done.

The Wisdom of the World

The wisdom of the world is this; to say " *There is
No other wisdom but to gulp what time can give* " . . .
To guard no inward vision winged with mysteries;
To hear no voices haunt the hurrying hours we live;
To keep no faith with ghostly friends; never to know
Vigils of sorrow crowned when loveless passions fade . . .
From wisdom such as this to find my gloom I go,
Companioned by those powers who keep me unafraid.

RUPERT BROOKE

Possibly the most famous of the younger Georgians, Rupert
(Chawner) Brooke, was born at Rugby in August, 1887, and educated at King's College, Cambridge. As a youth, Brooke was keenly
interested in all forms of athletics; playing cricket, football, tennis,
and swimming as well as most professionals. He was six feet tall,
his finely molded head topped with a crown of loose hair of
lively brown; " a golden young Apollo," said Edward Thomas.
Another friend of his wrote, " To look at, he was part of the
youth of the world."

At the very outbreak of the war, Brooke enlisted, fired with an
idealism that conquered his skepticism. After seeing service in
Belgium, 1914, he spent the following winter in a training-camp in
Dorsetshire and sailed with the British Mediterranean Expedition-
ary Force in February, 1915, to take part in the Dardanelles
Campaign.

Brooke never reached his destination. He died of blood-poison
at Skyros, April 23, 1915. His early death was one of England's
great literary losses; *Collected Poems*, issued posthumously, appeared a few months after. *The Complete Poems of Rupert Brooke*
(1932) reveals the full measure of his contradictory cynicism and
romanticism.

Brooke's sonnet-sequence, *1914*, which, with prophetic irony, appeared a few weeks before his death, contains the accents of immortality. His playful satire and his nostalgic tenderness are combined in " The Great Lover," of which Lascelles Abercrombie has written, " It is life he loves, and not in any abstract sense, but all the infinite little familiar details of life, remembered and catalogued with delightful zest."

Sonnet

Oh! Death will find me, long before I tire
   Of watching you; and swing me suddenly
Into the shade and loneliness and mire
   Of the last land! There, waiting patiently,
One day, I think, I'll feel a cool wind blowing,
   See a slow light across the Stygian [1] tide,
And hear the dead about me stir, unknowing,
   And tremble. And I shall know that you have died.

And watch you, a broad-browed and smiling dream,
   Pass, light as ever, through the lightless host,
Quietly ponder, start, and sway, and gleam —
   Most individual and bewildering ghost! —
And turn, and toss your brown delightful head
Amusedly, among the ancient dead.

The Great Lover

I have been so great a lover: filled my days
So proudly with the splendor of Love's praise,
The pain, the calm, and the astonishment,
Desire illimitable, and still content,
And all dear names men use, to cheat despair,
For the perplexed and viewless streams that bear
Our hearts at random down the dark of life.
Now, ere the unthinking silence on that strife
Steals down, I would cheat drowsy Death so far,
My night shall be remembered for a star
That outshone all the suns of all men's days.

[1] *Stygian:* pertaining to the river Styx, in Greek mythology the dark river of death.

Shall I not crown them with immortal praise
Whom I have loved, who have given me, dared with me
High secrets, and in darkness knelt to see
The inenarrable [1] godhead of delight?
Love is a flame: — we have beaconed the world's night.
A city: — and we have built it, these and I.
An emperor: — we have taught the world to die.
So, for their sakes I loved, ere I go hence,
And the high cause of Love's magnificence,
And to keep loyalties young, I'll write those names
Golden forever, eagles, crying flames,
And set them as a banner, that men may know,
To dare the generations, burn, and blow
Out on the wind of Time, shining and streaming. . . .

These I have loved:
   White plates and cups, clean-gleaming,
Ringed with blue lines; and feathery, faëry dust;
Wet roofs, beneath the lamp-light; the strong crust
Of friendly bread; and many-tasting food;
Rainbows; and the blue bitter smoke of wood;
And radiant raindrops couching in cool flowers;
And flowers themselves, that sway through sunny hours
Dreaming of moths that drink them under the moon;
Then, the cool kindliness of sheets, that soon
Smooth away trouble; and the rough male kiss
Of blankets; grainy wood; live hair that is
Shining and free; blue-massing clouds; the keen
Unpassioned beauty of a great machine;
The benison [2] of hot water; furs to touch;
The good smell of old clothes; and other such —
The comfortable smell of friendly fingers,
Hair's fragrance, and the musty reek that lingers
About dead leaves and last year's ferns. . . .
        Dear names
And thousand others throng to me! Royal flames;
Sweet water's dimpling laugh from tap or spring;
Holes in the ground; and voices that do sing:
Voices in laughter, too; and body's pain,
Soon turned to peace; and the deep-panting train;
Firm sands; the little dulling edge of foam
That browns and dwindles as the wave goes home;

---

[1] *Inenarrable:* indescribable. [2] *Benison:* blessing.

And washen stones, gay for an hour; the cold
Graveness of iron; moist black earthen mold;
Sleep; and high places; footprints in the dew;
And oaks; and brown horse-chestnuts, glossy-new;
And new-peeled sticks; and shining pools on grass; —
All these have been my loves. And these shall pass,
Whatever passes not, in the great hour,
Nor all my passion, all my prayers, have power
To hold them with me through the gate of Death.
They'll play deserter, turn with the traitor breath,
Break the high bond we made, and sell Love's trust
And sacramental covenant to the dust.
— Oh, never a doubt but, somewhere, I shall wake,
And give what's left of love again, and make
New friends now strangers. . . .
                              But the best I've known
Stays here, and changes, breaks, grows old, is blown
About the winds of the world, and fades from brains
Of living men, and dies.
                    Nothing remains.
O dear my loves, O faithless, once again
This one last gift I give: that after men
Shall know, and later lovers, far-removed
Praise you, " All these were lovely "; say, " He loved."

The Soldier

If I should die, think only this of me;
    That there's some corner of a foreign field
That is forever England. There shall be
    In that rich earth a richer dust concealed;
A dust whom England bore, shaped, made aware,
    Gave, once, her flowers to love, her ways to roam,
A body of England's breathing English air,
    Washed by the rivers, blest by suns of home.

And think, this heart, all evil shed away,
    A pulse in the eternal mind, no less
        Gives somewhere back the thoughts by England given
Her sights and sounds; dreams happy as her day;
    And laughter, learnt of friends; and gentleness,
        In hearts at peace, under an English heaven.

Edith Sitwell, daughter of Sir George and Lady Ida Sitwell, granddaughter of the Earl of Londesborough and sister of the two writers Osbert and Sacheverell, was born at Scarborough, Yorkshire, in 1887. She was educated, as she puts it, " in secrecy," and in 1914 came to London, where she has lived ever since.

In 1916 she began the editing of *Wheels*, a determinedly " modern " anthology which outraged most of the conservative critics. Her own poems provided an even greater series of shocks. After a mild and undistinguished debut — *The Mother and Other Poems* (1915) — Miss Sitwell published, in a succession so speedy as to seem little less than rapid-fire: *Clowns' Houses* (1918), *The Wooden Pegasus* (1920), *Façade* (1922), *Bucolic Comedies* (1923). In these volumes — particularly in the last two — Miss Sitwell limits her gamut; but, within her range, there is no poet quite like her. Many of her early poems are, as she herself has said, " abstract " poems — that is, they are " patterns in sound," just as certain " abstract " paintings are patterns in color rather than representations of objects we recognize. These early exercises in strange rhythms and unexpected rhymes are technically difficult. The later poems are not only more " human " but are emotional and often deeply religious.

Hers is a queer vocabulary, a curious collection of epithets in which the trees are " stag-antlered," the morning light " creaks down," the fire has a " furry warmth," " bird-blood " leaps within the veins, and the world itself is " like a bare egg laid by the feathered air." As a result much of Miss Sitwell's work sounds like nonsense, but it is nonsense with a point, even with a purpose. In " Aubade," for example, Miss Sitwell wants to show the " sad stupidity " of a plain girl on a country farm, neglected and " not quite bright," coming down to light the fire. The girl imagines each drop of rain hardening into a " dull blunt wooden stalactite "; she faces daily chores of weeding (" eternities " of kitchen-garden) where the flowers " cluck " (since most of them are cockscombs) and mock at her; even the flames remind her of the carrots and turnips which she is continually cleaning and cooking; her spirits hang limp as the " milk's weak mind." Here, and elsewhere, as in " The Old Nurse's Song," her verse has the charming inconsequence of a glorified nursery rhyme.

The readers who were waiting for Miss Sitwell to " humanize " her hard, bright idiom were rewarded by *The Sleeping Beauty* (1924), *Troy Park* (1926), *Street Song* (1942), and *The Song of the Cold* (1948). In these volumes, and in her severely selected *Canticle of the Rose* (1949), she achieves a unity, a sustained intensity, which her earlier work never expressed.

Interlude

Amid this hot green glowing gloom
A word falls with a raindrop's boom.

Like baskets of ripe fruit in air
The bird-songs seem, suspended where

Those goldfinches — the ripe warm lights
Peck slyly at them — take quick flights.

My feet are feathered like a bird
Among the shadows scarcely heard;

I bring you branches green with dew
And fruits that you may crown anew

Your whirring waspish-gilded hair
Amid this cornucopia —

Until your warm lips bear the stains
And bird-blood leap within your veins.

Aubade [1]

Jane, Jane,
Tall as a crane,
The morning light creaks down again.

Comb your cockscomb-ragged hair;
Jane, Jane, come down the stair.

Each dull blunt wooden stalactite
Of rain creaks, hardened by the light,

Sounding like an overtone
From some lonely world unknown.

But the creaking empty light
Will never harden into sight,

[1] *Aubade:* morning song.

Will never penetrate your brain
With overtones like the blunt rain.

The light would show (if it could harden)
Eternities of kitchen-garden,

Cockscomb flowers that none will pluck,
And wooden flowers that 'gin to cluck.

In the kitchen you must light
Flames as staring, red and white

As carrots or as turnips, shining
Where the cold dawn light lies whining.

Cockscomb hair on the cold wind
Hangs limp, turns the milk's weak mind. . . .

    Jane, Jane,
    Tall as a crane,
    The morning light creaks down again!

Solo for Ear Trumpet [1]

The carriage brushes through the bright
Leaves (violent jets from life to light).
Strong polished speed is plunging, heaves
Between the showers of bright hot leaves.
The window-glasses glaze our faces
And jar them to the very bases, —
But they could never put a polish
Upon my manners, or abolish
My most distinct disinclination
For calling on a rich relation!
In her house, — bulwark built between
The life man lives and visions seen, —
The sunlight hiccups white as chalk,
Grown drunk with emptiness of talk,
And silence hisses like a snake,
Invertebrate and rattling ache. . . .

[1] The title is ironic, for an " ear-trumpet " is not an instrument but a hearing device. The poet is the speaker, and her rich deaf relative regards everything, even the trumpet which heralds Judgment Day, as an intrusion on her privacy.

Till suddenly, Eternity
Drowns all the houses like a sea,
And down the street the Trump of Doom
Blares, — barely shakes this drawing-room,
Where raw-edged shadows sting forlorn
As dank dark nettles. Down the horn
Of her ear-trumpet I convey
The news that: " It is Judgment Day! "
" Speak louder; I don't catch, my dear! "
I roared: " *It is the Trump we hear!* "
" The *What?* " — " The T R U M P ! " . . .
    " I shall complain —
Those boy-scouts practicing again! "

The Old Nurse's Song

Ptolemy, poor Ptolemy,
In a dusty room doth lie —
Beggars for his bedfellows,
Pence upon his eye.
The old men spend his money,
The nursemaids eat his honey —
But no one knows at all, my dear,
Where Ptolemy doth lie.

The moon, a milk-white unicorn,[1]
She chased me round the town:
She chased me up — and chased me down —
She whistled through her horn:
" Go and listen at the keyhole
When the cold wind blows —
It's Ptolemy, poor Ptolemy,
A-snoring through his nose."

Song

Now that Fate is dead and gone
And that Madness reigns alone,
Still the Furies shake the fires

[1] *Unicorn:* a fabled animal, a kind of horse, with one horn in the center of its forehead.

Of their torches in the street
Of my blood. . . . And still they stand
In the city's street that tires
Of the tread of Man.

Three old rag-pickers are they —
Clothed with grandeur by the light
As a queen, but blind as Doom
Fumbling for the rag of Man
In an empty room.

Now they take the place of Fate
In whom the flames of Madness ran
Since her lidless eyes were cursed
With the world-expunging sight
Of the heart of Man.

How simple was the time of Cain
Before the latter Man-made Rain [1]
Washed away all loss and gain
And the talk of right and wrong —
Murdered now and gone!

And the Ghost of Man is red
From the sweep of the world's blood
In this late equality
Would you know the Ghost of Man
From the Ghost of the Flea?

But still the fires of the great Spring
In the desolate fields proclaim
Eternity . . . those wild fires shout
Of Christ the New Song.

Run those fires from field to field;
I walk alone and ghostily
Burning with Eternity's
Fires, and quench the Furies' song
In flame that never tires.

[1] *Man-made Rain:* bombs dropped from airplanes.

Irene Rutherford McLeod, born August 21, 1891, has written several volumes of vigorous verse, the best of which may be found in *Songs to Save a Soul* (1915) and *Before Dawn* (1918). "Lone Dog" has proved to be her most popular poem.

Lone Dog

I'm a lean dog, a keen dog, a wild dog, and lone;
I'm a rough dog, a tough dog, hunting on my own;
I'm a bad dog, a mad dog, teasing silly sheep;
I love to sit and bay the moon, to keep fat souls from sleep.

I'll never be a lap dog, licking dirty feet,
A sleek dog, a meek dog, cringing for my meat,
Not for me the fireside, the well-filled plate,
But shut door, and sharp stone, and cuff and kick and hate.

Not for me the other dogs, running by my side,
Some have run a short while, but none of them would bide.
O mine is still the lone trail, the hard trail, the best,
Wide wind, and wild stars, and hunger of the quest!

RICHARD ALDINGTON

Richard Aldington was born in Hampshire in 1892, and educated at Dover College and London University. His first poems were published in 1909; *Images Old and New* appeared in 1915. Aldington, H. D., Amy Lowell, and John Gould Fletcher are considered the finest of the Imagist poets; their sensitive, firm, and clean-cut lines put to shame their imitators. Aldington's *War and Love* (1918) and *Exile and Other Poems* (1923) are somewhat more regular in pattern, more humanized in tone.

Aldington's first novel, *Death of a Hero* (1929), was written in fifty-two days. This panoramic novel, which deals with three English generations, was followed by several others, the best of which are *Roads to Glory* (1931) and *All Men are Enemies* (1933). A collected *Poems of Richard Aldington* was published in 1934. An eminent translator, Aldington is also the editor of *The Viking Book of Poetry*.

Images

I

Like a gondola of green scented fruits
Drifting along the dank canals of Venice,
You, O exquisite one,
Have entered into my desolate city.

II

The blue smoke leaps
Like swirling clouds of birds vanishing.
So my love leaps forth toward you,
Vanishes and is renewed.

III

A rose-yellow moon in a pale sky
When the sunset is faint vermilion
In the mist among the tree-boughs
Art thou to me, my beloved.

IV

A young beech tree on the edge of the forest
Stands still in the evening,
Yet shudders through all its leaves in the light air
And seems to fear the stars —
So are you still and so tremble.

V

The red deer are high on the mountain,
They are beyond the last pine trees.
And my desires have run with them.

VI

The flower which the wind has shaken
Is soon filled again with rain;
So does my heart fill slowly with tears,
O Foam-Driver, Wind-of-the-Vineyards,
Until you return.

All Lovely Things

Hide from me all lovely things
Whether of skies or starry flowers;
Let me not see the grace of women
Nor look in children's eyes.

Give me things harsh and cruel
In a grim derelict land,
For these can only kill,
While beauty tortures alive.

WILFRED OWEN

Wilfred Owen was born at Oswestry, March 18, 1893, was educated at the Birkenhead Institute, matriculated at London University in 1910, and obtained a private tutorship in 1913 near Bordeaux. In 1915, in spite of delicate health, he joined the Artist's Rifles, served in France from 1916 to June, 1917, when he was invalided home. Fourteen months later, he returned to the Western Front, was awarded the Military Cross for gallantry in October, and was killed a week before the armistice, on November 4, 1918, while trying to get his men across the Sambre Canal.

Owen's name was unknown to the world until his friend Siegfried Sassoon unearthed his posthumous *Poems* (1920), to which Sassoon wrote the introduction. It was evident at once that here was one of the most important contributions to the literature of the First World War, expressed by a poet whose courage was only surpassed by his integrity. The restrained passion as well as the pitiful outcries in Owen's poetry have a spiritual kinship with Sassoon's stark verses. They reflect that stage of the war when the easy patriotics have a sardonic sound on the battlefront. "He never." writes Sassoon, "wrote his poems (as so many war-poets did) to make the effect of a personal gesture. He pitied others; he did not pity himself." An enlarged *Poems of Wilfred Owen* (1931) emphasized the authenticity and even nobility of these poems, even though they are not concerned with the usual subject matter of poetry. The subject is war, as Owen declared, "war and the pity of war. The poetry is in the pity."

Although Owen's work was unknown during his lifetime, it has been repeatedly "discovered," especially by the post-war poets. Critics have ranked him among the finest spirits of his time.

Anthem for Doomed Youth

What passing-bells for these who die as cattle?
Only the monstrous anger of the guns.
Only the stuttering rifles' rapid rattle
Can patter out their hasty orisons.[1]
No mockeries for them; no prayers nor bells,
Nor any voice of mourning save the choirs, —
The shrill, demented choirs of wailing shells;
And bugles calling for them from sad shires.[2]

What candles may be held to speed them all?
Not in the hands of boys, but in their eyes
Shall shine the holy glimmers of good-bys.
The pallor of girls' brows shall be their pall;
Their flowers the tenderness of patient minds,
And each slow dusk a drawing-down of blinds.

Futility

Move him into the sun —
Gently its touch woke him once,
At home, whispering of fields unsown,
Always it woke him, even in France,
Until this morning and this snow.
If anything might rouse him now
The kind old sun will know.

Think how it wakes the seeds —
Woke, once, the clay of a cold star.
Are limbs so dear-achieved, are sides
Full-nerved — still warm — too hard to stir?
Was it for this the clay grew tall?
— Oh, what made fatuous sunbeams toil
To break earth's sleep at all!

[1] *Orisons:* prayers.   [2] *Shires:* counties, countrysides.

Apologia Pro Poemate Meo [1]

I, too, saw God through mud —
    The mud that cracked on cheeks when wretches smiled.
    War brought more glory to their eyes than blood,
    And gave their laughs more glee than shakes a child.

Merry it was to laugh there —
    Where death becomes absurd and life absurder.
    For power was on us as we slashed bones bare
    Not to feel sickness or remorse of murder.

I, too, have dropped off fear —
    Behind the barrage, dead as my platoon,
    And sailed my spirit surging, light and clear,
    Past the entanglement where hopes lay strewn;

And witnessed exultation —
    Faces that used to curse me, scowl for scowl,
    Shine and lift up with passion of oblation,[2]
    Seraphic for an hour, though they were foul.

I have made fellowships —
    Untold of happy lovers in old song.
    For love is not the binding of fair lips
    With the soft silk of eyes that look and long,

By Joy, whose ribbon slips —
    But wound with war's hard wire whose stakes are strong;
    Bound with the bandage of the arm that drips;
    Knit in the welding of the rifle-thong.

I have perceived much beauty
    In the hoarse oaths that kept our courage straight;
    Heard music in the silentness of duty;
    Found peace where shell-storms spouted reddest spate.

Nevertheless, except you share
    With them in hell the sorrowful dark of hell,
    Whose world is but the trembling of a flare,
    And heaven but as the highway for a shell,

[1] *Apologia Pro Poemate Meo:* Excuse (or Reason) for My Poems.

[2] *Oblation:* a sacrifice, a religious offering.

You shall not hear their mirth:
> You shall not come to think them well content
> By any jest of mine. These men are worth
> Your tears: You are not worth their merriment.

SYLVIA TOWNSEND WARNER

Sylvia Townsend Warner was born at Harrow-on-the-Hill, December, 1893. A writer of extremely sensitive verse, she was unknown until the publication of her fantastic novel, *Lolly Willowes, or The Passionate Huntsman* (1926). Her volume of poetry, *The Espalier* (1925), had already prepared a few readers for work of a particularly distinguished kind. There is not a mediocre sentiment nor a slipshod line in this volume, whether Miss Warner is writing in the broad bucolic vein or fashioning epitaphs which reveal her as a master of condensation. This concentrated quality is again manifest in the delightful *Mr. Fortune's Maggot* (1927), *The Salutation* (1932), and the verses in *Time Importuned* (1928). *More Joy in Heaven* (1935) and *A Garland of Straw* (1943) are collections of short stories; *The Cat's Cradle Book* (1940) contains subtle and mischievous fables; *Summer Will Show* (1936), *After the Death of Don Juan* (1938), and *The Corner That Held Them* (1948) are novels quaint but powerful.

Country Thought

> Idbury bells are ringing
> And Westcote has just begun,
> And down in the valley
> Ring the bells of Bledington.[1]
>
> To hear all the church-bells
> Ring-ringing together,
> Chiming so pleasantly
> As if nothing were the matter,
>
> The notion might come
> To some religious thinker
> That The Lord God Almighty
> Is a traveling tinker,

[1] Idbury, Westcote, and Bledington are adjoining villages in England.

Who travels through England
From north to south,
And sits him at the roadside
With a pipe in his mouth,

A-tinkling and a-tinkering
To mend up the souls
That week-day wickedness
Has worn into holes.

And yet there is not
One tinker, but Three —
One at Westcote, One at Bledington
And One at Idbury.

Four Epitaphs

John Bird, a laborer, lies here,
Who served the earth for sixty year
With spade and mattock, drill and plow;
But never found it kind till now.

I, an unwedded wandering dame,
For quiet into the country came:
Here, hailed it; but did not foretell
I'd stay so long and rest so well.

I, Richard Kent, beneath these stones,
Sheltered my old and trembling bones;
But my best manhood, quick and brave,
Lies buried in another grave.

Her grieving parents cradled here
Ann Monk, a gracious child and dear.
Lord, let this epitaph suffice:
Early to Bed and Early to Rise.

Elizabeth

"Elizabeth the Beloved" —
So much says the stone
That is all with weather defaced,
With moss overgrown.

But if to husband or child,
Brother or sire, most dear
Is past deciphering.
This only is clear:

That once she was beloved,
Was Elizabeth,
And is now beloved no longer,
If it be not of Death.

CHARLES HAMILTON SORLEY

Charles Hamilton Sorley was born at Old Aberdeen, May 15, 1895. He studied at Marlborough College and University College, Oxford. He was finishing his studies abroad and was on a walking-tour along the banks of the Moselle when war came. Sorley returned home to receive a commission in the 7th Battalion of the Suffolk Regiment. In August, 1915, at the age of twenty, he was made a captain. On October 13, 1915, he was killed in action near Hulluch.

Sorley left only one book, *Marlborough and Other Poems*. The verse contained in it is sometimes rough but never rude. Tolerance and a dignity unusual for a boy of twenty distinguish his poetry. There is scarcely a line here, from the restrained sonnets which foreshadow death, to the buoyant "Song of the Ungirt Runners," which is not vivid and deeply felt.

Two Sonnets

I

Saints have adored the lofty soul of you.
Poets have whitened at your high renown.
We stand among the many millions who
Do hourly wait to pass your pathway down.
You, so familiar, once were strange: we tried
To live as of your presence unaware.
But now in every road on every side
We see your straight and steadfast signpost there.

I think it like the signpost in my land
Hoary and tall, which pointed me to go
Upward, into the hills, on the right hand,
Where the mists swim and the winds shriek and blow,
A homeless land and friendless, but a land
I did not know and that I wished to know.

II

Such, such is death: no triumph: no defeat:
Only an empty pail, a slate rubbed clean,
A merciful putting away of what has been.
And this we know: Death is not Life effete,
Life crushed, the broken pail. We who have seen
So marvelous things know well the end not yet.
Victor and vanquished are a-one in death:
Coward and brave: friend, foe. Ghosts do not say,
" Come, what was your record when you drew breath? "
But a big blot has hid each yesterday
So poor, so manifestly incomplete.
And your bright Promise, withered long and sped,
Is touched; stirs, rises, opens and grows sweet
And blossoms and is you, when you are dead.

The Song of the Ungirt Runners

We swing ungirded [1] hips,
And lightened are our eyes,
The rain is on our lips,
We do not run for prize.
We know not whom we trust
Nor whitherward we fare,
But we run because we must
   Through the great wide air.

The waters of the seas
Are troubled as by storm.
The tempest strips the trees
And does not leave them warm.
Does the tearing tempest pause?
Do the tree tops ask it why?
So we run without a cause
   'Neath the big bare sky.

   [1] *ungirded:* unbound, free.

The rain is on our lips,
We do not run for prize.
But the storm the water whips
And the wave howls to the skies.
The winds arise and strike it
And scatter it like sand,
And we run because we like it
    Through the broad bright land.

ROBERT GRAVES

Robert (Ranke) Graves was born in England of mixed Irish.
Scottish, and German stock, July 26, 1895. He was educated at
Charterhouse and Oxford, after which he joined the British Ex-
peditionary Force and served three times in France, in the same
regiment as Siegfried Sassoon. Like Sassoon, Graves reacts against
the storm of fury and blood-lust, but, fortified by a lighter and
more whimsical spirit, where Sassoon is violent, Graves is volatile,
where Sassoon is bitter, Graves is almost blithe. An infectious
gayety rises from *Fairies and Fusiliers* (1917); in *Country Sentiment* (1919) Graves turns to a more serious simplicity. *Country
Sentiment* was, so Graves says, "an endeavor to escape from a
painful war neurosis into an Arcadia of amatory fancy."

After forty, Graves gave himself energetically to reappraisals
of history, legend, and myth. The best-selling novels, *I, Claudius*
(1934) and *Claudius the God* (1935), were followed by the biography, *Wife to Mr. Milton* (1943), *Hercules, My Shipmate*
(1945), the controversial *King Jesus* (1946), the erudite *The White
Goddess* (1948), and *Watch the Northwind Rise* (1949), a witty
fantasy of a future Utopia run by witchcraft. The poet was always
apparent in all these books and, more obviously, in *Poems: 1938–
1945* and the comprehensive *Collected Poems: 1914–1947*.

It's a Queer Time

It's hard to know if you're alive or dead
When steel and fire go roaring through your head.
One moment you'll be crouching at your gun
Traversing, mowing heaps down half in fun:
The next, you choke and clutch at your right breast --
No time to think — leave all — and off you go . . .

To Treasure Island where the Spice winds blow,
To lovely groves of mango, quince, and lime —
Breathe no good-by, but ho, for the Red West!
> It's a queer time.

You're charging madly at them yelling "Fag!"
When somehow something gives and your feet drag.
You fall and strike your head; yet feel no pain
And find . . . you're digging tunnels through the hay
In the Big Barn, 'cause it's a rainy day.
Oh, springy hay, and lovely beams to climb!
You're back in the old sailor suit again.
> It's a queer time.

Or you'll be dozing safe in your dug-out —
A great roar — the trench shakes and falls about —
You're struggling, gasping, struggling, then . . . *hullo!*
Elsie comes tripping gaily down the trench,
Hanky to nose — that lyddite [1] makes a stench —
Getting her pinafore all over grime.
Funny! because she died ten years ago!
> It's a queer time.

The trouble is, things happen much too quick;
Up jump the Boches,[2] rifles thump and click,
You stagger, and the whole scene fades away:
Even good Christians don't like passing straight
From Tipperary or their Hymn of Hate
To Alleluiah-chanting, and the chime
Of golden harps . . . and . . . I'm not well today . . .
> It's a queer time.

Neglectful Edward

Nancy

Edward, back from the Indian Sea,
"What have you brought for Nancy?"

[1] *Lyddite:* a high explosive; so named because it was first made in Lydd, England.
[2] *Boches:* slang for Germans.

Edward

" A rope of pearls and a gold earring,
And a bird of the East that will not sing.
A carven tooth, a box with a key — "

Nancy

" God be praised you are back," says she,
" Have you nothing more for your Nancy? "

Edward

" Long as I sailed the Indian Sea
I gathered all for your fancy:
Toys and silk and jewels I bring,
And a bird of the East that will not sing:
What more can you want, dear girl, from me? '

Nancy

" God be praised you are back," said she,
" Have you nothing better for Nancy? "

Edward

" Safe and home from the Indian Sea,
And nothing to take your fancy? "

Nancy

" You can keep your pearls and your gold earring,
And your bird of the East that will not sing,
But, Ned, have you nothing more for me
Than heathenish gew-gaw toys? " says she,
" Have you nothing better for Nancy? "

The Traveler's Curse After Misdirection

(*From the Welsh*)

May they wander stage by stage
Of the same vain pilgrimage,
Stumbling on, age after age,
Night and day, mile after mile,
At each and every step, a stile;
At each and every stile, withal,
May they catch their feet and fall;

At each and every fall they take,
May a bone within them break;
And may the bones that break within
Not be, for variation's sake,
Now rib, now thigh, now arm, now shin
But always, without fail, *the neck!*

L. A. G. STRONG

Leonard A. G. Strong was born March 8, 1896 in Devon. After graduating from Wadham College, Oxford, he taught at Summer Fields, a famous preparatory school. Although his first books were books of verse, Strong became known as a successful novelist both in America and England. *Selected Poems* appeared in 1935.

As a poet Strong's reputation rests on his lyrics which summon the spirit of the English countryside, sometimes in the local dialect, sometimes in suggestive descriptions of the landscape.

A Moment

The winter afternoon
Is clear and still,
And Time sits thinking
On this frozen hill.

Stand high upon the rocks,
Take horn and blow.
Far out across the moor
The long notes go.

Pure, unassailable
And cold they fly,
Like silver javelins
Against the sky.

The rabbit suddenly
Attentive sits,
No stir about him but
His little wits.

Her hunger all forgot,
A speckled bird
Ponders with head on side
What she has heard.

Old Dan'l

Out of his cottage to the sun
Bent double comes old Dan'l,
His chest all over cotton wool,
His back all over flannel.

"Winter will finish him," they've said
Each winter now for ten:
But come the first warm day of Spring
Old Dan'l's out again.

Epitaph on a Sentry

The snare of sleep held fast his struggling will.
They found him — and he now may sleep his fill.

C. DAY LEWIS

C. (Cecil) Day Lewis was born at Ballintubber, Ireland,
April 27, 1904. He was educated at Sherburne School and Wadham College, Oxford, where he became affiliated with Stephen
Spender and W. H. Auden. He taught at the Junior School of
Cheltenham College and wrote with increasing rapidity in various
mediums, from poetry to murder mysteries.

Transitional Poem (1929) was Lewis's first serious bid for notice.
His social vision was amplified in *From Feathers to Iron* (1931)
and *The Magnetic Mountain* (1933). The three volumes were
assembled in *Poems: 1929–1933,* published in the United States in
1935, approximately at the same time as the American debut of
Auden and Spender. Lewis failed to integrate his gifts. He fluctuated between an old tradition which he distrusted and a new
technique which his mind approved but his imagination had not
yet accepted. Nevertheless, from the conflict several illuminating

lyrics, half scornful, half serene, were born. *A Time to Dance* (1935), *Short Is The Time* (1944) and *Poems: 1933–1947* are full of poetry which is enthusiastic and often electric — electricity being one of Lewis's favorite symbols. Sometimes the lines substitute exuberance for intensity, but Lewis is rarely without verbal power and moral purpose. "When They Have Lost" is as strict in form as any classic sonnet, but it is modern not only in feeling but in its social implications. Its message is as imperative as the summons in the ironic and angry "Newsreel."

Lewis also wrote a book-length essay entitled *A Hope for Poetry*, which is an excellent analysis of recent poetry. Besides his poetry and criticism, Lewis has written in many other veins: a novel, books for boys, and several keenly constructed detective stories — the best of which are *Minute for Murder* and *Head of a Traveler* — written under the pseudonym of Nicholas Blake.

Nearing Again the Legendary Isle [1]

Nearing again the legendary isle
Where sirens sang and mariners were skinned,
We wonder now what was there to beguile
That such stout fellows left their bones behind.

Those chorus-girls are surely past their prime,
Voices grow shrill and paint is wearing thin,
Lips that sealed up the sense from gnawing time
Now beg the favor with a graveyard grin.

We have no flesh to spare and they can't bite,
Hunger and sweat have stripped us to the bone;
A skeleton crew we toil upon the tide
And mock the theme-song meant to lure us on:

No need to stop the ears, avert the eyes
From purple rhetoric of evening skies.

[1] The "legendary isle" is the island of Calypso as described in Homer's *Odyssey*. The hero, Odysseus, had escaped the Sirens, whose songs "crazed the wits of every mortal who hears them," and he and his shipmates are one stage nearer home. Lewis takes the same theme and modernizes it; he turns the magic of the ancient Sirens ("those chorus-girls") into mockery.

When They Have Lost

When they have lost the little that they looked for,
The poor allotment of ease, custom, fame:
When the consuming star their fathers worked for
Has guttered into death, a fatuous flame:
When love's a cripple, faith a bed-time story,
Hope eats her heart out and peace walks on knives,
And suffering men cry an end to this sorry
World of whose children want alone still thrives:
Then shall the mounting stages of oppression
Like mazed and makeshift scaffolding torn down
Reveal his unexampled, best creation —
The shape of man's necessity full-grown.
Built from their bone, I see a power-house stand
To warm men's hearts again and light the land.

Newsreel

Enter the dream-house, brothers and sisters, leaving
Your debts asleep, your history at the door:
This is the home for heroes, and this loving
Darkness a fur you can afford.

Fish in their tank electrically heated
Nose without envy the glass wall: for them
Clerk, spy, nurse, killer, prince, the great and the defeated
Move in a mute day-dream.

Bathed in this common source, you gape incurious
At what your active hours have willed —
Sleep-walking on that silver wall, the furious
Sick shapes and pregnant fancies of your world.

There is the mayor opening the oyster season:
A society wedding: the autumn hats look swell:
An old crock's race, and a politician
In fishing-waders to prove that all is well.

Oh, look at the warplanes! Screaming hysteric treble
In the long power-dive, like gannets they fall steep.

But what are they to trouble —
These silver shadows to trouble your watery, womb-deep
    sleep?

See the big guns, rising, groping, erected
To plant death in your world's soft womb.
Fire-bud, smoke-blossom, iron seed projected —
Are these exotics? They will grow nearer home:

Grow near home — and out of the dream-house stumbling
One night into a strangling air and the flung
Rags of children and thunder of stone niagaras tumbling,
You'll know you slept too long.

LOUIS MacNEICE

Louis MacNeice was born September 12, 1907, in the north of
Ireland. He was educated at Merton College, Oxford, became a
professor of classics in London, and was one of the group known
as the "post-war poets." His first volume, *Blind Fireworks* (1929),
showed talent and some originality, but it was not until the publication of *Poems* (1937) that MacNeice revealed his characteristic
idiom. His speech mingled the prosaic and the exalted, and turned
from a contemplation of the past to a "modernistic" interpretation of nature, particularly in its mechanical phases. In this poetry
observation is often expressed in irony. "Sunday Morning" and
"Morning Sun" record the mood and all its details — details which
are exact and yet imaginative.

Poems: 1925–1940 is a mingling of the delicate lyrics which
MacNeice wrote as a youth and the semi-jazz derivations which
he composed in his thirties. In the later poems he often relies on
a complacently casual tone. The ideas suffer correspondingly, and
the style becomes a loose set of statements dropped haphazardly
into verse. *Springboard* (1945) and *Holes in the Sky* (1948) over-
use the offhand manner, but MacNeice frequently sharpens his
idiom and shoots phrases which rankle but lodge in the mind.

MacNeice also wrote *Out of the Picture* (1937) a verse play;
a sensible, if not inspired, examination entitled *Modern Poetry*
(1938); and a searching summary of *The Poetry of W. B. Yeats*
(1941).

Sunday Morning

Down the road someone is practicing scales,
The notes like little fishes vanish with a wink of tails,
Man's heart expands to tinker with his car
For this is Sunday morning, Fate's great bazaar.
Regard these means as ends, concentrate on this Now,
And you may grow to music or drive beyond Hindhead any-
    how,
Take corners on two wheels until you go so fast
That you can clutch a fringe or two of the windy past,
That you can abstract this day and make it to the week of
    time
A small eternity, a sonnet self-contained in rhyme.

But listen, up the road, something gulps; the church spire
Opens its eight bells out, skulls' mouths which will not tire
To tell how there is no music or movement which secures
Escape from the weekday time. Which deadens and endures.

Morning Sun

Shuttles of trains going north, going south, drawing threads
    of blue
The shining of the lines of trams like swords
Thousands of posters asserting a monopoly of the good, the
    beautiful, the true
Crowds of people all in the vocative, you and you,
The haze of the morning shot with words.

Yellow sun comes white off the wet streets but bright
Chromium yellows in the gay sun's light
Filleted sun streaks the purple mist,
Everything is kissed and reticulated with sun
Scooped-up and cupped in the open fronts of shops
And bouncing on the traffic which never stops.

And the street fountain blown across the square
Rainbow-trellises the air and sunlight blazons
The red butcher's and scrolls of fish on marble slabs
Whistled bars of music crossing silver sprays

And horns of cars, touché, touché,[1] rapiers' retort, a moving
   cage,
A turning page of shine and sound, the day's maze.

But when the sun goes out, the streets go cold, the hanging
   meat
And tiers of fish are colorless and merely dead
And the hoots of cars neurotically repeat and the tiptoed feet
Of women hurry and falter whose faces are dead
And I see in the air but not belonging there
The blown gray powder of the fountain gray as the ash
That forming on a cigarette covers the red.

W. H. AUDEN

W(ystan) H(ugh) Auden was born in York, February 21, 1907.
He was educated at Gresham's School, Holt, and Christ Church,
Oxford. From 1930 to 1935 he taught school at Malvern. He was
with the G. P. O. Film Unit from 1935 to 1936. In 1939 he came to
America and took out citizenship papers.

By the time Auden was thirty he had already been the center
of several controversies, an English magazine had brought out a
special Auden number; an entire movement seems to have stemmed
from his energy and versatility. At thirty-three he had written and
compiled four books of poetry, three plays, a collection of prose
fiction, two books of travel, and two anthologies. *Poems* (1930)
and *The Orators* (1932) were published, together with the supple-
mentary *Dance of Death*, in a one-volume American edition severely entitled *Poems* (1934).

The outstanding feature of Auden's poetry is its combination
of variety and originality. When Auden uses traditional forms, he
imposes a new pattern upon them, from archaic ballads to street-
corner " blues." No contemporary poet has a greater natural command of language; he makes rhetoric out of banal jargon, and
summons eloquence without raising his voice. It has been said
with some justice that Auden is self-divided. By nature he is a
patrician, but by instinct he is a champion of the common people.
He speaks for those who are bullied into war and exploited in
peace, but he is not wholly one of them. *On This Island* (1940)
and *The Double Man* (1941) made it apparent that Auden was

   [1] *Touché:* literally touched, or hit. A term used originally in
fencing.

the most provocative poet of his generation. He managed to unite opposites, to combine the latest findings in science with man's oldest dreams.

The Collected Poetry of W. H. Auden (1945) defines an epoch. Such a long poem as " The Sea and the Mirror " is a startling modern commentary on Shakespeare's " The Tempest." Other later poems show that, although Auden wrote poetry of increasing seriousness, he did not lose his unpredictable wit. His growing concern with religion helped him find a faith and enlarged his scope as well as his audience.

The Age of Anxiety (1947), which received the Pulitzer Prize in 1948, is another long stride in Auden's progress. Technically it is a prime example of his virtuosity; using the language of the 1940's, it employs the severely stressed poetic form of the Anglo-Saxons, the tough, triply alliterative line of *Beowulf*. Thus Auden established himself as a protean poet: a capricious artist delighting in straight-face frivolities and a probing spirit torn between agnosticism and blind belief; a superb rhetorician rich in learning and a lover of extravagant oddities; a dramatic lyricist and a natural dialectician — in short, a poet who is equally adept at sheer fooling and pure enchantment.

Versatile enough in his own right, Auden had to resort to collaborators in order to keep pace with his own energetic career. With John Garrett he compiled an anthology, *The Poet's Tongue* (1935); with Louis MacNeice he composed *Letters from Iceland* (1937); with Christopher Isherwood he wrote two plays, *The Dog Beneath the Skin* (1935), a satire, and *On the Frontier* (1938), a melodrama, and *Journey to a War* (1939), an account of a trip through war-torn China.

Fish in the Unruffled Lakes

> Fish in the unruffled lakes
> The swarming colors wear,
> Swans in the winter air
> A white perfection have,
> And the great lion walks
> Through his innocent grove;
> Lion, fish, and swan
> Act, and are gone
> Upon Time's toppling wave.
>
> We till shadowed days are done,
> We must weep and sing
> Duty's conscious wrong,

The Devil in the clock,
The Goodness carefully worn
For atonement or for luck;
We must lose our loves;
On each beast and bird that moves
Turn an envious look.

Sighs for folly said and done
Twist our narrow days:
But I must bless, I must praise
That you, my swan, who have
All gifts that to the swan
Impulsive Nature gave,
The majesty and pride,
Last night should add
Your voluntary love.

from " In Memory of W. B. Yeats "

Earth, receive an honored guest;
William Yeats is laid to rest:
Let the Irish vessel lie
Emptied of its poetry.

Time that is intolerant
Of the brave and innocent,
And indifferent in a week
To a beautiful physique,

Worships language and forgives
Everyone by whom it lives;
Pardons cowardice, conceit,
Lays its honors at their feet.

Time that with this strange excuse
Pardoned Kipling and his views,
And will pardon Paul Claudel,[1]
Pardons him for writing well.

[1] *Paul Claudel:* French poet and essayist, born in 1868, whose work grew increasingly mystical.

In the nightmare of the dark
All the dogs of Europe bark,
And the living nations wait,
Each sequestered in its hate;

Intellectual disgrace
Stares from every human face,
And the seas of pity lie
Locked and frozen in each eye.

Follow, poet, follow right
To the bottom of the night,
With your unconstraining voice
Still persuade us to rejoice;

With the farming of a verse
Make a vineyard of the curse,
Sing of human unsuccess
In a rapture of distress;

In the deserts of the heart
Let the healing fountain start,
In the prison of his days
Teach the free man how to praise.

Stop All the Clocks

Stop all the clocks, cut off the telephone,
Prevent the dog from barking with a juicy bone,
Silence the pianos and with muffled drum
Bring out the coffin, let the mourners come.

Let aeroplanes circle moaning overhead
Scribbling on the sky the message He Is Dead,
Put crêpe bows round the white necks of the public doves,
Let the traffic policemen wear black cotton gloves.

He was my North, my South, my East and West,
My working week and my Sunday rest,
My noon, my midnight, my talk, my song;
I thought that love would last for ever: I was wrong.

The stars are not wanted now; put out every one:
Pack up the moon and dismantle the sun;
Pour away the ocean and sweep up the woods:
For nothing now can ever come to any good.

Who's Who

A shilling life will give you all the facts:
How Father beat him, how he ran away,
What were the struggles of his youth, what acts
Made him the greatest figure of his day:
Of how he fought, fished, hunted, worked all night;
Though giddy, climbed new mountains; named a sea:
Some of the last researchers even write
Love made him weep his pints like you and me.

With all his honors on, he sighed for one
Who, say astonished critics, lived at home;
Did little jobs about the house with skill
And nothing else; could whistle; would sit still
Or potter round the garden; answered some
Of his long marvellous letters, but kept none.

STEPHEN SPENDER

Stephen Spender was born February 28, 1909, near London. The son of a famous journalist, he was first interested in painting; at seventeen he supported himself by printing chemists' labels. He attended University College, Oxford, left without taking his degree, but formed a friendship with Louis MacNeice and other young poets who composed the post-war group a few years later. At eighteen he printed on his own press *Nine Experiments* (1928), in which his unique phrasing was already apparent.

Poems (1933) shows Spender as one of the most forceful exponents of modern social forces and the machine age. To him the rose is less romantic than the railroad train; " The Express " glides from the station " after the first powerful manifesto, the black statement of pistons," more majestic than any queen, and she goes on her journey wrapped " in music no bird-song, nor bough breaking with honey buds, shall ever equal." Splender's images are startling and sometimes obscure, but they are compelled by an ardent imagination and by a deep concern for humanity.

Spender's "Not Palaces" discloses the intensity of his imagination and his social vision. Here an eager nature declares itself in lines which are a call to youth, a call to understand and co-operate with the vast changes now taking place. It is too late, he says, to dream of fairy palaces or moon over the past with its outworn caste system ("family pride") and remnants of old-world traditions of prettiness: "beauty's filtered dusts." We must live vitally, drawing our energy as from an electric battery, the symbol of the age. All our faculties must enter into the new world — eye, that quick-darting "gazelle," ear which "suspends the spirit," touch — all the faculties must contribute toward a greater humanity where men shall not be starved and exploited, but where Man, "bringing light to life," shall become his greater self.

Ruins and Visions (1942), *Poems of Dedication* (1947) and *The Edge of Being* (1949) reveal Spender's limitations, his heavily burdened lines and his total lack of humor. But they also reveal his desperate sincerity, the intense voice of one who feels something with great passion and purpose. It is the voice that speaks up for "the palpable and obvious love of man," an utterance which, achieving the high level of the lines beginning "I think continually of those who were truly great," is exalted and often noble. This poem is one of the most eloquent of the period. Out of the shaken world which surrounds us, Spender reminds us of the unsung champions, the strugglers and pioneers who were inflamed with a burning belief in humanity, "the soul's history." Soldiers on forgotten fields of battle, scientists in makeshift laboratories, stubborn idealists fighting to save a lost cause, teachers who would not be intimidated, tireless doctors, the anonymous army of dreamers and doers — all these by their very living fought for everyone. They sacrificed hours of ease for our casual comforts; they gave up safety for our security. It is these fire-bringers, children of light — "born of the sun" — who brought light out of darkness, and, leaving "the vivid air signed with their honor," conferred upon us their heritage of hope.

The Express

After the first powerful plain manifesto
The black statement of pistons, without more fuss
But gliding like a queen, she leaves the station.
Without bowing and with restrained unconcern
She passes the houses which humbly crowd outside,
The gasworks and at last the heavy page

Of death, printed by gravestones in the cemetery.
Beyond the town there lies the open country
Where, gathering speed, she acquires mystery,
The luminous self-possession of ships on ocean.
It is now she begins to sing — at first quite low
Then loud, and at last with a jazzy madness —
The song of her whistle screaming at curves,
Of deafening tunnels, brakes, innumerable bolts.
And always light, aerial, underneath
Goes the elate meter of her wheels.
Steaming through metal landscape on her lines
She plunges new eras of wild happiness
Where speed throws up strange shapes, broad curves
And parallels clean like the steel of guns.
At last, further than Edinburgh or Rome,
Beyond the crest of the world, she reaches night
Where only a low streamline brightness
Of phosphorus on the tossing hills is white.
Ah, like a comet through flames she moves entranced
Wrapt in her music no bird song, no, nor bough
Breaking with honey buds, shall ever equal.

Mask

The face of the landscape is a mask
Of bone and iron lines where time
Has plowed its character.
I look and look to read a sign,
Through errors of light and eyes of water
Beneath the land's will, of a fear
And the memory of a struggle,
As man behind his mask still wears a child.

Not Palaces

Not palaces, an era's crown
Where the mind dreams, intrigues, rests;
The architectural gold-leaved flower
From people ordered like a single mind,
I build. This only what I tell:
It is too late for rare accumulation,

For family pride, for beauty's filtered dusts;
I say, stamping the words with emphasis,
Drink from here energy and only energy,
As from the electric charge of a battery,
To will this time's change.
Eye, gazelle, delicate wanderer,
Drinker of horizon's fluid line;
Ear that suspends on a chord
The spirit drinking timelessness;
Touch, love — all senses —
Leave your gardens, your singing feasts,
Your dreams of suns circling before our sun,
Of heaven after our world.
Instead, watch images of flashing brass
That strike the outward sense, the polished will,
Flag of our purpose which the wind engraves.
No spirit seek here rest. But this: No man
Shall hunger; Man shall spend equally.
Our goal which we compel: Man shall be man.

The program of the antique Satan
Bristling with guns on the indented page,
With battleship towering from hilly waves:
For what? Drive of a ruining purpose,
Destroying all but its age-long exploiters.
Our program like this, yet opposite,
Death to the killers, bringing light to life.

Thoughts During an Air Raid

Of course, the entire effort is to put myself
Outside the ordinary range
Of what are called statistics. A hundred are killed
In the outer suburbs. Well, well, I carry on.
So long as the great " I " is propped upon
This girdered bed which seems more like a hearse,
In the hotel bedroom with flowering wallpaper
Which rings in wreathes above, I can ignore
The pressure of those names under my fingers
Heavy and black as I rustle the paper,
The wireless wail in the lounge margin.
Yet, supposing that a bomb should dive

Its nose right through this bed, with me upon it?
The thought is obscene. Still, there are many
To whom my death would only be a name,
One figure in a column. The essential is
That all the " I "'s should remain separate
Propped up under flowers, and no one suffer
For his neighbour. Then horror is postponed
For everyone until it settles on him
And drags him to that incommunicable grief
Which is all mystery or nothing.

I Think Continually of Those

I think continually of those who were truly great.
Who, from the womb, remembered the soul's history
Through corridors of light where the hours are suns,
Endless and singing. Whose lovely ambition
Was that their lips, still touched with fire,
Should tell of the spirit clothed from head to foot in song.
And who hoarded from the spring branches
The desires falling across their bodies like blossoms.

What is precious is never to forget
The delight of the blood drawn from ageless springs
Breaking through rocks in worlds before our earth;
Never to deny its pleasure in the simple morning light
Nor its grave evening demand for love;
Never to allow gradually the traffic to smother
With noise and fog the flowering of the spirit.

Near the snow, near the sun, in the highest fields
See how these names are fêted by the waving grass,
And by the streamers of white cloud,
And whispers of wind in the listening sky;
The names of those who in their lives fought for life,
Who wore at their hearts the fire's center.
Born of the sun they traveled a short while toward the sun,
And left the vivid air signed with their honor.

George Barker was born in 1913, and educated at Marlborough Public School, and at L.C.C. School, Chelsea, London. After teaching in Japan, he became one of the leaders of the post-Auden romantic movement. His first book, *Alanna Autumnal* (1933), published when Barker was twenty, was followed in rapid succession by *Poems* (1935), *Janus* (1935), and *Calamiterror* (1937). The best of the early poems, as well as several from *Lament and Triumph* (1940), were assembled in *Selected Poems* (1941), Barker's first representative American publication.

Barker's poetry is passionate, prolix, and often determinedly irrational. The pace is headlong, the pitch is high. Dudley Fitts, praising Barker's ingenuities, criticized his overquaint archness, his too surprising distortions, and " the violent hurling together of unpredictable images whose symbolic value seems often hopelessly private." In Barker, as in Dylan Thomas, there is great freedom of emotion matched by a freely flowing inventiveness. This emotional drive sometimes includes and sometimes ignores conventional standards of expression. The juxtaposition of the sublime and the banal, of surging syllables and pounding energy, are apparent in *Sacred and Secular Elegies* (1943) and *Love Poems* (1947). The heavy clusters of words, thick patches of sound used like impressionistic colors, are refined and clarified in the later work. The tone of the *Love Poems* is not only quieter but purer than anything Barker has written.

O Tender under Her Right Breast
(*Second Cycle of Love Poems: II*)

O tender under her right breast
    Sleep at the waterfall,
My daughter, my daughter, and be at rest
    As I at her left shall.

At night the pigeon in the eaves
    Leaves open its bright eye;
Nor will the Seven Sisters [1] cease
    To watch you where you lie.

The pine like a father over your bed
    Will bend down from above
To lay in duty at your head
    The candles of its love.

[1] *Seven Sisters:* a group of seven stars, also known as the Pleiades.

And in their mothering embrace,
  Sleep on the Rockies' bosom;
The Okanogan Valley shall grace
  Canada round your cradle.

The silver spoon and the one-eyed man,
  The rabbit's foot and the clover,[1]
Be at your bed from morning till
  As now, the day is over.

Shut the Seven Seas against Us

(*Third Cycle of Love Poems: II*)

Shut the Seven Seas against us,
Close the five continents,
Set sepulchred the North Star
In a forsaken tense;
Lay every Sun and System
For ever away in bed, —
Nevertheless that day shall come
That resurrects the dead.

When sleepless the wakes, weeping,
Mourn life on every leaf,
And the Moon covers her eye over
Rather than see our grief;
When in their dreams the liars and
The loveless regret life, —
The dove that stirs in every storm
Shall arrive bright with olive.

Step, Primavera, from your bed,
Dazzling with existence;
Put the Sun and the Moon and the Systems right;
Hang heaven on circumstance:
Lean from all windows like waterfalls,
Look, Love on us below: —
And so from their somnolence in sense
All things shall rise to you.

[1] *The silver spoon, etc.:* these are toys and playthings at the
child's cradle.

Dylan Thomas was born in Wales in 1914 and was educated at the Swansea Grammar School. He was a newspaper reporter for a year; after giving up hack journalism he earned his living at odd jobs, including reading poetry for the radio and writing film scripts. His vivid *Portrait of the Artist as a Young Dog* (1940) is largely autobiographical. At the age of twenty Thomas published his first volume, *18 Poems* (1934). Most of the poems in that volume and in *25 Poems* (1936), together with several from *The Map of Love* (1939), and eleven short stories were published in *The World I Breathe* (1939). *New Poems* appeared in 1943; *The Selected Writings of Dylan Thomas,* with an interpretive introduction by John L. Sweeney, in 1946.

At first glance Thomas' poems seem full of wild noises, with words, screams and shouts flung out in spectacular abandon. Upon re-reading, however, it is apparent that Thomas' poems, far from being disorganized, are curiously disciplined. The order imposed upon them does not stem from the strictures of traditional form but from a logic of emotion. Writing out of his own background and beliefs, Thomas plunges boldly into a new and dynamic language, a fierce vigor of speech remarkable even in a time of frantic experiment. Thomas is, as Stephen Spender wrote, " a poet obsessed with words, a linguistic genius, and with a mind filled with echoes of his Welsh Nonconformist religious upbringing and of childhood experiences which made a deep impression on him." " Fern Hill," for example, is full of gladness, a bright and joyful picture of summer on a Welsh farm; " The Hunchback in the Park " is a dark but poignant memory. Rhetoric is used too lavishly for immediate comprehension, but Thomas' identification with the elemental powers of nature is obvious: " the force that through the green fuse drives the flower drives my green age; that blasts the roots of trees is my destroyer." The feeling emerges, almost explodes from these poems; the emotion is communicated before the meaning is made clear. Thomas died suddenly November 9, 1953.

The Force That Through the Green Fuse Drives

The force that through the green fuse drives the flower
Drives my green age; that blasts the roots of trees
Is my destroyer.
And I am dumb to tell the crooked rose
My youth is bent by the same wintry fever.

The force that drives the water through the rocks
Drives my red blood; that dries the mouthing streams

Turns mine to wax.
And I am dumb to mouth unto my veins
How at the mountain spring the same mouth sucks.

The hand that whirls the water in the pool
Stirs the quicksand; that ropes the blowing wind
Hauls my shroud sail.
And I am dumb to tell the hanging man
How of my clay is made the hangman's lime.

The lips of time leech to the fountain head;
Love drips and gathers, but the fallen blood
Shall calm her sores.
And I am dumb to tell a weather's wind
How time has ticked a heaven round the stars.

And I am dumb to tell the lover's tomb
How at my sheet goes the same crooked worm.

The Hunchback in the Park

The hunchback in the park
A solitary mister
Propped between trees and water
From the opening of the garden lock
That let the trees and water enter
Until the Sunday sombre bell at dark,

Eating bread from a newspaper
Drinking water from the chained cup
That the children filled with gravel
In the fountain basin where I sailed my ship
Slept at night in a dog kennel
But nobody chained him up.

Like the park birds he came early
Like the water he sat down
And Mister they called hey Mister
The truant boys from the town
Running when he had heard them clearly
On out of sound

Past lake and rockery
Laughing when he shook his paper
Hunchbacked in mockery
Through the loud zoo of the willow groves
Dodging the park keeper
With his stick that picked up leaves.

And the old dog sleeper
Alone between nurses and swans
While the boys among willows
Made the tiger jump out of their eyes
To roar on the rockery stones
And the groves were blue with sailors

Made all day until bell time
A woman figure without fault
Straight as a young elm
Straight and tall from his crooked bones
That she might stand in the night
After the lock and chains

All night in the unmade park
After the railings and shrubberies
The birds the grass the trees the lake
Had followed the hunchback
And the wild boys innocent as strawberries
To his kennel in the dark.

Fern Hill

Now as I was young and easy under the apple boughs
About the lilting house and happy as the grass was green,
    The night above the dingle starry,
      Time let me hail and climb
    Golden in the heydays of his eyes,
And honored among wagons I was prince of the apple towns
And once below a time I lordly had the trees and leaves
      Trail with daisies and barley
    Down the rivers of the windfall light.

And as I was green and carefree, famous among the barns
About the happy yard and singing as the farm was home
    In the sun that is young once only,

Time let me play and be
Golden in the mercy of his means,
And green and golden I was huntsman and herdsman, the calves
Sang to my horn, the foxes on the hills barked clear and cold,
And the sabbath rang slowly
In the pebbles of the holy streams.

All the sun long it was running, it was lovely, the hay-
Fields high as the house, the tunes from the chimneys, it was air
And playing, lovely and watery
And fire green as grass.
And nightly under the simple stars
As I rode to sleep the owls were bearing the farm away,
All the moon long I heard, blessed among stables, the night-jars
Flying with the ricks, and horses
Flashing into the dark

And then to awake, and the farm, like a wanderer white
With the dew, come back, the cock on his shoulder: it was all
Shining, it was Adam and maiden,
The sky gathered again
And the sun grew round that very day.
So it must have been after the birth of the simple light
In the first, spinning place, the spellbound horses walking warm
Out of the whinnying green stable
On to the fields of praise.

And honored among foxes and pheasants by the gay house
Under the new-made clouds and happy as the heart was long
In the sun born over and over,
I ran my heedless ways,
My wishes raced through the house-high hay
And nothing I cared, at my sky blue trades, that time allows
In all his tuneful turning so few and such morning songs
Before the children green and golden
Follow him out of grace.

Nothing I cared, in the lamb white days, that time would take me
Up to the swallow-thronged loft by the shadow of my hand,

In the moon that is always rising,
   Nor that riding to sleep
I should hear him fly with the high fields
And wake to the farm forever fled from the childless land.
Oh as I was young and easy in the mercy of his means,
   Time held me green and dying
Though I sang in my chains like the sea.

NORMAN NICHOLSON

Norman Nicholson was born January 8, 1914, in the small mining town of Millom, Cumberland, one of the loveliest counties in England. Son of a well-known tradesman in the town, Nicholson actively took part in the everyday life of the people. He was connected with the music festivals, the church work, the cricket club, and the youth movement; he lectured for the Workers' Educational Association. "All this is very different from the life of the literary world," he writes, "with which I have dealings only by correspondence. My home is at the mouth of the Duddon — Wordsworth's favorite river. Thus we have almost on top of one another the sea, industry, and the finest scenery in England."

Nicholson catches some of that juxtaposition in his poetry. The Wordsworthian bucolic note is there, but it is sharpened by a critical observation. Nicholson's first book of poems, *Five Rivers* (1945), owes its title to the five little rivers which flow from the western mountains of the English Lake District into the Irish Sea. The volume is almost wholly lyrical in tone, lucid and personal. But it never depends on mere fluidity and the reiterations of the stereotypes dear to the nature-lover's handbook. *Five Rivers*, which won the first Royal Society of Literature Award, was preceded by *An Anthology of Religious Verse* (1942) and *Man and Literature* (1943). It was followed by *The Fire of the Lord* (1946), a novel concerned with the primitive feeling of awe and veneration for land, and *The Old Man of the Mountains* (1946), a play in which the prophet Elijah is placed in modern Cumberland.

Rockferns

On quarry walls the spleenwort [1] spreads
Its green zipfasteners and black threads,
And pinches tight its unfurled purses

---

[1] *Spleenwort:* a common fern.

In every crevice with the cresses,
As if a blast of dynamite
Had spattered it upon the slate
That where the bluestone spine was broken
Spores might penetrate and quicken.
For in the fractures of the rock
Roots dig further than a pick,
As, though the sinews may not feel it,
The worm probes deeper than the bullet.
When this pen is dropped, my hand
May thrust up in a buckler frond,[1]
And then my crushed and calcined bones
Prove better soil than arid stones.
Why need I fear the bursting bomb
Or whatsoever death shall come,
If brains and bowels be cast forth
Splintered to spleenwort on the earth?
And if a subtler part may cruise
Twice round the sun and Betelgeuse,[2]
My soul shall detonate on high
And plant itself in cracks of sky.

[1] *Buckler frond:* a shield-shaped leaf or shoot.
[2] *Betelgeuse:* a giant red star of the first magnitude.

INDEX

The names of authors are shown in SMALL CAPITALS. *Folios in roman numbers refer to the Introductory Appreciation of Poetry.*

O
P
Q
R   0
S   1